D0903229

The Rebellious Century

The Rebellious Century

1830–1930

Charles Tilly, Louise Tilly,
and Richard Tilly

Harvard University Press

Cambridge, Massachusetts, 1975

to Piera, Hector, Otto, and Naneth, esteemed parents

Preface

Give us a chance to confess, before the torture begins. We chose a tendentious, indefensible title for our work. Why should the period from 1830 to 1930 have any special claim to be called "rebellious"? Aren't most centuries filled with rebellion of one kind or another? What about the forty revolutionary years before 1830, the forty turbulent years after 1930?

Our motives mix cowardice, convenience, and calculation. Questions about the ways the emergence of an urban, industrial way of life affects the character of collective action got us started. We knew from the beginning that such questions should be asked, and answered, comparatively. Since each of us had some expertise in the modern history of a different country—Italy, Germany, and France—it seemed reasonable to start the comparisons there. We needed a period, or a set of periods, recent enough to provide fairly documentation, short enough to make that documentation manageable, comparable enough that we could treat the world conditions impinging on each country as similar, yet spanning a considerable amount of urbanization and industrialization, as well as violent conflict which might have been linked to the urbanization and industrialization. We feared to take on the French Revolution or the Nazi seizure of power.

Obviously no period could meet all our conditions. We compromised on one hundred years which took each of our areas from a largely agrarian economy through a substantial process of urban and industrial growth, which brought each of them major political crises, civil disorders, and shifts in the holders of power, for which the data concerning social change and conflict in each of them were relatively rich and continuous. Hence 1830 to 1930.

We compromise the time limits more than once. Our continuous data for Germany stop in 1913, cover only a few nineteenth-century decades in Italy, but run from 1830 all the way to 1960 for France. Our discussions sometimes wander up to the present, and occasionally reach back into the eighteenth century. Nevertheless, the century from 1830 to 1930 occupies most of our attention.

The period is arbitrary, yet it has some meaning. The book argues, and analyzes, a close interdependence among three heroic transformations which occurred in most western European countries during that very period: the emergence of an urban-industrial economy, the consolidation of a powerful national state, and a reorientation of collective action. In developing the analysis we rely especially on evidence concerning *violent* collective action, because it is on the whole more continuously visible and well-documented than nonviolent action. Yet we are not so concerned to discover the roots of violence itself as to trace and help explain the changing ways in which people act together for common ends.

William Gum helped us plan this book and bore with us cheerily through the many years of its creation. We have drawn extensively on unpublished work which Gerd Hohorst, A. Q. Lodhi, and David Snyder did under our direction. Priscilla Cheever, Judy Davidson, Freddi Greenberg, Leila Al-Imad, Virginia Perkins, and Sue Richardson provided essential research assistance, as Margaret Grillot, Pamela Hume, Debbie Polzin, Robert Schweitzer, and Diane Stephenson helped prepare the manuscript. Christopher Tilly, Kathryn Tilly, and Laura Tilly also did a number of research tasks. At the Press, Ann Louise McLaughlin edited the manuscript with cheer, skill, and dispatch. We are grateful to Otto Pflanze and Edward Shorter for critical readings of some chapters. The work would have been impossible without the generous financial support of the National Science Foundation, the Deutsche Forschungsgemeinschaft, and the Canada Council. Thanks to all who helped us create our book.

August 1974   C. T., L. T., R. T.

Contents

VI *Conclusions* 271

Appendixes

Tables

Figures

Illustrations

The Rebellious Century

CHAPTER I

A Time of Rebellion

The Problem

"Woe to the cities in whose midst lies tinder," wrote Friedrich Schiller in 1799. Despite his enthusiasm for Freedom in the abstract, ten years of revolution in France had dimmed Schiller's delight in the ways men actually seek their liberation:

> Woe to the cities in whose midst lies tinder!
> The people, breaking their chains,
> Take to self-help in terrible ways.
>
> Howling rebellion grabs the bell-ropes
> And sounds for Violence the bells consecrated to Peace.
>
> "Freedom and equality," we hear men cry.
> The peaceful burgher readies his defense.
> The streets and markets fill,
> And bands of cutthroats advance on every side.

The price of arousing the masses, it appears, was too great:

> It is dangerous to waken the lion.
> Deadly is the tiger's fang.

Yet the most terrible of terrors
Is man in his delusions.

Woe to them who loan the light
Of Heaven's torch to the eternally blind!
It gives them no vision.
It can only start fires,
Reduce to ashes the city and the country.

(Schiller, "Das Lied von der Glocke")

During the nearly two centuries since the beginning of the French Revolution, the fear, the disdain, and the imagery of fire and tinder have all remained part of the established view of popular rebellion. Westerners have fashioned a belief in rebellion as the sudden release of dark forces: anger, tension, sadness, frustration, fire. Just after the great series of takeovers of schools and workplaces by French students and workers in May 1968, Raymond Aron was writing:

It remains that the fire, even if lighted by little groups of revolutionaries, would not have spread if it had not reached inflammable material. Red flags and black flags still symbolize vague and boundless hopes. Students and workers will once again retain warm memories of these days of strike, holiday, parade, endless discussion, riot, as if the boredom of everyday life and the strangulation by technological and bureaucratic efficiency required a sudden release from time to time, as if Frenchmen only left their solitude in revolutionary (or pseudo-revolutionary) psychodrama. Participation—a vague word, but one with great power—expressed the hope for a communitarian life which our hierarchical and segmented society, with its juxtaposition of different sorts of privilege, only offers the French in fleeting moments of lyrical illusion (1968: 167).

There is more vision in Aron's rebellious students and workers than in Schiller's *Würgerbanden* of 1799. By 1968 the setting had changed, the slogans had changed, the specific actions had changed. Yet the sense of rebellion as a welling up of boundless impulse remained.

We begin with two constants and a variable. Constant one: European political life of the last few centuries has continually produced and absorbed movements of violent protest. Constant two: while collective violence was occurring, national leaders have ordinarily treated it as an irrational and dangerous expression of the times being out-of-joint. Variable: the predominant forms of collective violence have changed and varied greatly, despite the illusory continuity of words like "riot" and "rebellion." The constants are intriguing; they lead to marvelous speculations about the roots of human aggression and about the effects of social position on the way we read and misread the actions of others. But we have more business to do with the variable.

For good reason. The century from 1830 to 1930, with its many revolutions, wrought fundamental changes in the whole pattern of violent protest in Europe. It was also Europe's great period of transformation from agrarian to industrial society. One can hardly avoid making the connection. *Ça saute aux yeux,* the French would say: it hits you right in the eye. If the shift in the locus and character of collective violence occurred as European countries urbanized and industrialized, the two massive sets of changes must somehow have depended on each other. But how?

That simple question—how?—assembles in one puzzle a historical problem of the first order and a major point of uncertainty in the analysis of contemporary societies. By asking how, and how much, changes in the character of collective violence depended on the European process of urban-industrial growth, and vice versa, we ask what the explanations and prospects of collective violence are in the urbanizing and industrializing world of today. That is true even if there is no likelihood that China, Chile, or Mali will recapitulate the history of England, Russia, or the United States. For a great deal of the reasoning on the subject now available to us depends on notions about the consequences of large structural changes in societies which are drawn mainly from reflection on the western experience but which may be wrong even in terms of that experience.

Some of that reasoning is ambiguous, some of it contradictory, some of it wrongheaded, some of it just plain wrong. At the very least, a systematic reexamination of the changing conditions for violent protest in western countries will sharpen the argument and check some of our sloppier extrapolations from Germany or Spain to Indonesia or India. Most likely it can provide the materials for a revision of our understandings and expectations concerning contemporary collective violence throughout the world.

In the troubled world of the last few decades, theories of violence and protest have proliferated like honeysuckle vines. A thousand flowers have bloomed, and faded. Yet, if we brush our way past the leaves, bees, and hummingbirds, we find almost all the flowers springing from two old parent vines.

Breakdown Theories

The first vine is gnarled and twisted by now. No wonder. It is hundreds of years old, although it spread most vigorously during the nineteenth century. It is the idea that collective violence appears as a by-product of processes of breakdown in a society. Large structural rearrangements in societies—such as urbanization and industrialization—in this view tend to dissolve existing controls over antisocial behavior just as the very fact of rearrangement is subjecting many men to uncertainty and strain. The strain in turn heightens the impulse toward antisocial behavior. That behavior may take the form of personal disorganization or crime or protest. Then the society either succumbs to the threat, contains the antisocial behavior like a gall, or engages in a new phase of integration. In the last-named, the pressures for reintegration come both from within the anti-social group (for instance, through an extreme religious sect's gradual acquisition of vested interests) and from outside it (through a variety of sanctions imposed on deviant populations by the representatives of straight society). The end point of the process, in most versions of the theory, is not the status quo ante but a new equilibrium.

Within the discipline of sociology Emile Durkheim fashioned the breakdown theory into a standard interpretation of conflict. In a famous passage of *Suicide,* he argues that man is ordinarily governed by society's *conscience collective,* its collective awareness of rules and necessities. There is, however, a danger: "when society is disturbed by some painful crisis or by beneficent but abrupt transitions, it is momentarily incapable of exercising this influence" (1951: 252). Surges of suicide result from the weakening of societal constraint, and so do waves of conflict.

In developing this argument, Durkheim lays out an idea which became popular in the United States during the 1960s: that rising well-being often stimulates protest because once the old, limited expectations decay, aspirations rise much more rapidly than achievements possibly can. Observers of America applied the argument to angry blacks, to rioting students, to workers who refused to settle for wage hikes and job security.

The gap between aspirations and achievements, the argument goes, produces both dissatisfaction and unrestrained demands for more, ever more rewards: "At the very moment when traditional rules have lost their authority, the richer prize offered these appetites stimulates them and makes them more exigent and impatient of control. The state of de-regulation or anomy is thus further heightened by passions being less disciplined, precisely when they need more disciplining." Finally "the struggle grows more violent and painful, both from being less controlled and because competition is greater. All classes contend among themselves because no established classification any longer exists" (Durkheim 1951: 253).

The tone is familiar. There is the nostalgia for an ordered social life, the approval of moderation, the resentment and fear of pushy, strident, angry people. By and large the good, solid bourgeois of nineteenth-century Europe shared those feelings about their turbulent world. But it took Durkheim to dignify fear of rapid change and mass action into a sociological principle.

One of the best recent statements of the breakdown theory proceeds in the following way:

Within the economy itself, rapid industrialization—no matter how co-ordinated—bites unevenly into the established social and economic structures. And throughout the society, the differentiation occasioned by agricultural, industrial, and urban changes always proceeds in a see-saw relationship with integration: the two forces continuously breed lags and bottlenecks. The faster the tempo of modernization is, the more severe the discontinuities. This unevenness creates *anomie* in the classical sense, for it generates disharmony between life experiences and the normative framework which regulates them . . . *anomie* may be partially relieved by new integrative devices, like unions, associations, clubs, and government regulations. However, such innovations are often opposed by traditional vested interests because they compete with the older undifferentiated systems of solidarity. The result is a three-way tug-of-war among the forces of tradition, the forces of differentiation, and the new forces of integration. Under these conditions, virtually unlimited potentialities for group conflict are created.

Three classic responses to these discontinuities are anxiety, hostility, and fantasy. If and when these responses become collective, they crystallize into a variety of social movements—peaceful agitation, political violence, millennarianism, nationalism, revolution, underground subversion, etc. There is plausible—although not entirely convincing—evidence that the people most readily drawn into such movements are those suffering most severely under the displacements created by structural change . . . Other theoretical and empirical data suggest that social movements appeal most to those who have been dislodged from old social ties by differentiation without also being integrated into the new social order (Smelser 1966: 44).

Neil Smelser, the author of the passage, thinks of the master process as one of differentiation and integration. But the immediate origins of the collective behavior, in his interpretation, lie in the discontinuities and breakdowns of control the master process produces on its way. The theory has many special versions. The authors of the official report on the Los Angeles Watts riot of 1965, for instance, invoked its "uprooting" version, which says that long-distance migrants are more disorganized and disoriented than the rest of the population, and therefore more prone to riot as well as to crime (McCone Commission 1965: 3–4). There is also an "extremism" version of the theory, which says that political and religious extremists tend to come from the marginal populations of a changing society. We have little need to enumerate theories and theorists in this vein, because it has become part of our common-sense explanation of most varieties of disorder. It is well to remember, however, that the application of such theories by government officials in the nineteenth century may have had some important effects on collective violence itself (determining residential and voting laws, whom the police arrested first, and so on), so we'll certainly have to keep the theory in mind.

For all its popularity, the breakdown theory is not obviously valid. There is not much doubt that great transformations like industrialization sweep away traditional props of the social order. There is not much doubt that men often find the pervasiveness and the speed of the great transformations bewildering. What is doubtful is whether discontinuities regularly breed *anomie,* and whether anomie regularly breeds individual or collective disorder. The standard illustrations of this chain of effects— the disorganization of long-distance migrants, the incoherence of life in the slums, the recruitment of "extremist" parties from marginal populations, the criminality and madness of revolutionary crowds—have turned out to be dubious or downright false (see Cornelius 1971, Feagin 1973, Feagin and Hahn 1973, Nelson 1970, Oberschall 1973). So we have reasons for revaluation.

Solidarity Theories

We might call the major alternative to the theory of breakdown a *solidarity* theory. In this view the conditions that lead to violent protest are essentially the same as those that lead to other kinds of collective action in pursuit of common interests. Violence grows out of the struggle for power among well-defined groups. In the baldest, vulgar-Marxist version of the theory, changes in a society's organization of production realign the fundamental class divisions within the society, define new interests for each class, and (through an awakening awareness of those interests promoted by interaction with both class allies and class enemies) eventually produce new, expanding forms of class conflict.

A heroic rendition of this argument, in the same tradition as the paintings of Socialist Realism, portrays a huge, unitary Working Class, clean-cut and rippling with muscle, rising from misery to strike down all oppressors. A more cynical rendition appears in the word of Daniele Manin, the lawyer who led the revolution of 1848 in Venice: *il popolo è un cavallo che bisogna saper cavalcare;* the People are a horse you have to know how to ride (Bernardello 1970: 59). The crude versions of the solidarity argument have come in for a good deal of battering, especially on the grounds that the major units of collective action rarely correspond to the major divisions defined by the mode of production, and that in industrial societies class conflict has not steadily deepened.

Marx's own analysis was never as unsubtle as these caricatures, and Marxist thinking has developed since his time. From its very title, E. P. Thompson's *The Making of the English Working Class* offers an historical analysis of class as process and relationship. In a crucial passage Thompson says:

Thus working men formed a picture of the organization of society, out of their own experience and with the help of their hard-won and erratic education, which was above all a political picture. They learned to see their own lives as part of a general history of conflict between the loosely defined "industrious classes" on the one hand, and the unreformed House of Commons on the other. From 1830 onwards a more clearly-defined class consciousness, in the customary Marxist sense, was maturing, in which working people were aware of continuing both old and new battles on their own (1964: 712).

In his discussions of Luddism, Chartism, and the other major working-class protests of the early nineteenth century, Thompson is at great pains to demonstrate that precisely those groups of working men with the most highly developed sense of class divisions led the assault on their enemies.

The solidarity theory also has some non-Marxist proponents. They tend to think of violent protest as the early groping of a group gathering organizational strength. Clark Kerr has an hypothesis about the cycle of working-class protest:

The level of protest rises and then falls off again as the process of commitment advances. At first, the worker is so little connected with industrial life that he has neither a great desire nor sufficient means to protest. As his involvement in and experience with industrial life increase, his power to influence the industrial environment also increases, and his tendency to protest rises. Industrial life is now his life, and he wishes to mold it closer to his heart's desire. Later on, as machinery is established to meet his grievances and as the cost of the conflict begins to bulk larger, industrial protest may tend to fade away. The surrounding industrial environment comes either to be accepted or, at least, to be acknowledged as inevitable. What protest remains tends to be highly structural and formally expressed. Finally, in the overcommitted worker, organized protest tends to disappear (1960: 353).

In Kerr's analysis, industrial protest depends on a certain level of solidarity, organization, and consciousness; its violent forms give way to peaceful varieties of contention not because anomie declines but because violence becomes too costly and inefficient.

Solidarity theories have their own problems. They slip into circularity with extraordinary ease because it is so tempting to consider the development of protest both as the consequence of solidarity and as the very evidence of solidarity. They do not provide a ready means of accounting for the high proportion of today's collective violence which is incited and performed not by solidary rebels but by agents of government: police, militias, professional troops. Like breakdown theories, solidarity theories, ordinarily postulate so strict a separation of violence from normal politics as to make it puzzling that the two have so long coexisted.

Breakdown versus Solidarity

How could we resolve the differences between solidarity theories and breakdown theories of violent protest? Some compromises immediately come to mind. One is the idea that breakdown and solidarity are different phases of the same process, that each movement of protest develops from breakdown to solidarity or vice versa. A second is the suggestion that there are different varieties of violent protest, some growing out of breakdown, some growing out of solidarity. A third is the notion that "breakdown" and "solidarity" are two names for the same phenomenon as seen from very different angles: what the conservative experiences as breakdown the radical senses as the growth of new forms of solidarity. Given the broad and imprecise way we have stated the alternatives so far, we cannot rule out or confirm any of these possibilities.

Yet the more specific forms of the breakdown and solidarity theories do contradict each other. It cannot be true *both* that revolutionary crowds recruit their members mainly from the marginal, floating population of the city *and* that revolutionary crowds draw most heavily on groups strongly integrated into the collective life of the city, although it is possible that the activists are well-integrated, while the floating population supplies most of the bystanders. It cannot be true *both* that crime, mental illness, and rebellion spring from the same basic strains *and* that there is no connection among them, unless those strains are so pervasive as to have no predictive value. It cannot be true *both* that raw, swelling centers of new industry are ripest for protest *and* that settled industrial cities are most likely to produce movements of protest, although the truth could well be more complicated than either alternative. So we have some hope of appealing to real evidence.

What sort of evidence? We need information about at least three different things: (1) the timing and location of urbanization, industrialization, shifts in wealth, and other large structural changes; (2) the character, extent, and personnel of different varieties of political conflict in various periods and settings; and (3) the character, extent, and personnel of different varieties of sorts of disapproved behavior outside the political realm. The larger the range of units for which we are able to bring together these three kinds of information, the more directly we can confront the alternative theories relating conflict and disorder to structural change; if all we know is that for an entire country times of rapid change are also times of political conflict (or, for that matter, times of political peace), a large number of alternative interpretations are still open.

For western Europe since the French Revolution crude data on the pace of urbanization or industrialization for large geographic units like regions and big cities are not hard to come by. Census-taking and other attempts by European states to know what they were working with left a large residue of statistics. The real difficulties begin when we attempt to make the data comparable over long spans of time or between countries, when we press the data to make fine distinctions (for example, singling out the effects of changes in the sheer size of industrial firms as opposed to shifts in technology or organization of the labor force), and when we try to interpret the experience of individuals, households, neighborhoods, and other sorts of units poorly described by the bureaucrats. We usually can make a number of useful comparisons among periods, regions, and large segments of the population but have much greater trouble when it comes to finer comparisons.

How hard the job of collecting systematic information on political conflict will be depends on the range of conflict considered. Elections are relatively easy; they are often reported in censuslike formats; unfortunately, information on elections bears only indirectly on our main questions. Strike reporting begins to be extensive toward the end of the nineteenth century, and the pattern of strikes is more obviously relevant to the investigation of structural change and conflict; still, the usual strike is far too orderly to be a good representative of protest or violence and too marginal to politics to represent struggles for power accurately. Evidence on other major forms of conflict does not come ready-made; we first have to decide exactly what kind of event we are searching for and then dig the information from parliamentary proceedings, police records, local histories, and other widely dispersed sources. The work is almost always long, tedious, and risky.

As for disapproved behavior like crime, suicide, mental illness, or family conflict, the availability of systematic data depends largely on how much the government was involved in controlling the behavior. Abundant systematic statistics concerning crimes, for example, are commonly available from about the middle of the nineteenth century, although the data have the evident defect of reporting only those offenses which caught the eye of the police. Because each variety of "disorganized" behavior—crime, child neglect, alcoholism, insanity, and so forth—tended to produce its own reporting as new organizations grew up to define it and control it, the available information varies enormously in quality, uniformity, and continuity from one variety to the next. Nevertheless, enough data exist to make possible a wide range of comparisons among periods, places, and groups.

In short, the evidence necessary for checking different theories of "breakdown" and "solidarity" against the modern experience of west European countries exists; it will yield to people who are willing to do the hard work of accumulating it. At a minimum, we can examine broad questions about covariation: do crime and collective violence go together (as most breakdown arguments suggest)? Do strikes and collective violence tend to draw on the same groups of workers (as some versions of the solidarity argument insist)? In fact, it is possible to be a good deal more demanding than that for some periods, some kinds of structural change, some forms of conflict, and some varieties of disapproved behavior.

Traps to Avoid

To do the job properly we must avoid some tempting traps. The first temptation is to prejudge the direction of the long-term movement of political conflict and concentrate on the search for the new (and presumably more advanced) forms. That produces a teleological kind of history: every event is an anticipation or preparation of events that have not yet occurred, all actions are judged according to the standards of a later era than the one in which they happened, and Historic Tendencies are always being blocked or advanced.

The error is rife in historical studies of workers which assume that full class consciousness is the end state and anxiously gauge how far along the particular group in question has come: are they ready yet? Here we find the assumption that older forms of working-class action like machine-breaking or the food riot necessarily sprang from a blind and impulsive response to hardship—exactly the assumption which Thompson's work on the early history of the English working class contradicts. If the measure of class consciousness is, let us say, the adoption of a mass revolutionary movement instead of small-scale attempts to change working conditions, then the circularity of the argument linking political advance to class consciousness is complete.

Let us make clear what we are saying, and what we are *not* saying. So far as we are able to judge, large changes in working-class consciousness did occur in the course of European industrialization. This book treats some of them, although the treatment is less adequate than we would like; reliable evidence on class consciousness is rare. That is the point: we can't lightly assume that there is a close correspondence between states of class consciousness and forms of political action. Whether that correspondence exists is one of the chief historical questions calling for investigation.

Another temptation is to restrict the search for consequences of urbanization or industrialization to those areas, times, and populations which seem to form the leading edge of the change. Why study the countryside when the real expansion of factory production is going on in big cities?

In the case of western Europe, ignoring the countryside would be a blunder for at least two reasons. First, the rise of urban industry after 1750 produced a terrible contraction in rural industry, whose workers often responded with riot and rebellion. Second, the departure of 100,000 peasants for the city usually had a more unsettling effect on the villages they left behind than on the industrial towns they entered. The point is not just that indirect effects are sometimes more powerful than direct ones. The contraction of rural industry and the departure of the peasants from their home villages are every bit as much part of the process of industrialization as is the expansion of the big-city factory.

The third temptation is to ignore the places, times, and populations in which nothing happened. When conflict is at issue, why waste time writing the history of harmony? The simple answer: an explanation of protest, rebellion, or collective violence that cannot account for its absence is no explanation at all; an explanation based only on cases where something happened is quite likely to attribute importance to conditions which are actually quite common in cases where nothing happened. That is the characteristic defect of the many theories being bandied about today which treat rebellion as a consequence of frustrated rising expectations without specifying how often (or under what conditions) rising expectations are frustrated without rebellion.

Finally, there is the temptation to shift away from the task of examining the relationships between protest or collective violence and large-scale structural change to the task of explaining protest or collective violence in general. Most of us can distinguish easily between the logic of asking what difference attending a particular kind of school made to some group's chances for occupational success and the logic of framing a general explanation of the group's occupational success. Somehow it is harder to maintain that distinction in the study of political conflict and the large-scale structural change, probably because of the looming presence of theories which treat *all* political conflict as an outgrowth of big structural transformations. We mean to concentrate on the relationships rather than the general explanation, but at times the temptation to lean toward the general explanation will grow too strong to resist.

Our Approach

By now our prejudices and preferences should be clear. This book deals mainly with changes in the form, frequency, locus, and personnel of collective violence in three European countries over a substantial period of industrialization and urbanization. It repeatedly asks how industrialization, urbanization, and related changes affected the patterns of collective violence. It occasionally reverses the question: how did collective violence and its outcome affect the patterns of urbanization and industrialization? It attacks these questions most frequently through the comparison of different places, times, and kinds of people with respect to their involvement in collective violence, in other forms of conflict, in different varieties of widely disapproved behavior, and in large-scale structural change.

We have amassed a large part of the essential data on our own, but we have not labored in a vacuum. There are plenty of models to avoid, and some to imitate. Historians, political scientists, sociologists, and other students of political conflict have been working away at the accumulation of real evidence for some time. For the most part they have worked heads down, in isolation from each other. Only occasionally has a book like Crane Brinton's *The Anatomy of Revolution* or Barrington Moore's *Social Origins of Dictatorship and Democracy* forced them all to lift their eyes at once. Nevertheless, their ideas and methods overlap.

Students of collective violence have done two main kinds of analyses: clinical and epidemiological. *Clinical* studies follow the origins and histories of particular participants, disturbances, or series of disturbances. We have telling examinations of individual revolutionaries like Trotsky or Mao, searching histories of the Russian and Chinese revolutions, a few attempts to identify the common properties of all communist revolutions, and a few more efforts to trace the links among them. *Epidemiological* studies relate units—persons, cities, countries, and so on—

involved in collective violence to the larger set of units which could conceivably have been involved. That is a means of isolating the conditions governing involvement or noninvolvement. Some take the form of calculating rates of participation in riots for different segments of the urban population; others the comparison of many whole countries in terms of propensity to domestic violence; still others, the close comparison of cities experiencing rebellion. Combinations of clinical and epidemiological studies are possible but rare. Practically speaking, it is hard to find a mind or a method capable of dealing both with the richness of the individual case and with the common properties of many cases.

Comparative history offers a way. Since the basic question is how the great processes of industrialization and urbanization affect the character and magnitude of collective violence, we have a lot to learn from the comparison of the experience of several areas over considerable periods of urban-industrial growth. Such a comparison, if properly done, has the advantage of forcing us to attend to the context, the national variations, the peculiarities of the individual case, while still allowing uniformities to emerge.

Comparison at this scale has its risks and difficulties. Each of the authors is accustomed to a finer variety of comparison, within a single country and over a shorter span of time. Although we claim the right to cross national frontiers, Richard Tilly is most expert in German history, Louise Tilly most knowledgeable in Italian history, and Charles Tilly best informed about French history. We have exchanged ideas and materials for years, but each of us has adopted a somewhat different approach. The reader will see that readily as he makes his own comparison of our chapters on France, Italy, and Germany.

Even a single mind adopting a unitary plan would have difficulty treating the three countries in exactly the same way. The relatively late unification of Italy and Germany make them important cases for political analysis, but they also lead to a much greater dispersion and unevenness of the essential source materials than is the case for France. Although French scholars have not undertaken the sort of systematic quantitative description and analysis of collective violence reported in this book, they have done much more of the historical groundwork for it than German scholars have; Italians have been so busy debating a relatively small range of political questions with historical evidence that almost all the groundwork remains to be done. As a consequence, we have detailed data about France since the Revolution, a less full summary over a shorter span of time to offer for Germany, and a selective view of certain periods and incidents between 1830 and the rise of Fascism in Italy. The inequality of our three bodies of evidence leads us to concentrate much of our analysis on variations within each of the countries before pushing on to compare them in general.

Sources and Methods

Three features that our analyses of France, Germany, and Italy have in common are unusual, and may even be controversial: concentration on the systematic enumeration and study of samples of violent events; wide reliance on published sources, especially newspapers; use of quantitative comparisons over time and space to check alternative arguments linking collective violence to structural change.

First, we have given high priority to the selection of unbiased samples of all violent events—events in which more than some minimum number of persons took part in seizing or damaging persons or property—occurring in certain periods: several decades in Italy; 1830–1930 in Germany; 1830–1960 in France. This did not in any sense exclude the study of nonviolent strikes, demonstrations, or political crises. But it did mean gambling that aggregate variations in the larger violent events would give a clearer picture of the general drift of political conflict than would a treatment of a few crises or an attempt to summarize every form of conflict and protest, whether violent or not. The selection of samples of violent events made it possible to undertake systematic—epidemiological —comparisons of regions, periods, segments of the population, and even countries, without losing contact with the individual event.

The second unconventional feature of our work is a heavy reliance on published sources, including newspapers. Although in the case of Italy we relied on certain detailed political histories for enumerations of events to be studied, in Germany and France systematic scanning of daily newspapers for mentions of events meeting our criteria produced the basic samples. Once the samples of events were selected, we augmented and verified the newspaper accounts as much as possible with information from historical works, political yearbooks, contemporary reviews, pamphlets and commentaries, and documents in French, German, and Italian

violent ways of bargaining through the threat of force. Through a decree of 1763, the royal government has made its greatest effort so far to knock down barriers to the shipment of grain from town to town and province to province; "free trade" is the slogan, the prescription for France's economic ills.

Many provincial people see it differently. Confronted with a large and long-forecast food riot in April 1768, the Parlement of Rouen has reinstated many traditional controls—inventory of grains in private hands, requirement that all sales be made in the public market, strict control over the departure of grain from the community. It has declined to condemn the authorities of small Norman towns for actually setting the price of grain. (No one questioned their setting the price of bread.) And it has authorized the arrest of government commission agents sent out to buy wheat for Paris. The government's views of these "hindrances to trade" appear emphatically in a letter from the Controller General of Finances, l'Averdy, to the duc d'Harcourt, dated 27 May 1768:

I see, Sir, by the report that M. Bertin made to the King a few days ago concerning the news he had from you on the present circumstances of the province of Normandy, that you were worried about the provisioning of the province and believe that it is completely stripped of grain. It gives me the greatest pain to see the state to which the province has been reduced by a very ill-considered decree of the Parlement of Rouen; for I cannot help thinking that it is the hindrance to the food trade brought about by that decree which produced the shortage about which people are complaining today. I do not know, Sir, if you have accurate information about the amount of grain which has arrived in Rouen since the tenth of this month and about the grain which is still expected. I am sure that when you have informed yourself on that score you will support the measures taken by order of the King, which I made as prompt and effective as possible, and you will agree that it was impossible to do more than was done in those unhappy circumstances. If the merchants had not been discouraged and if they had thought it possible to take part in the free competition guaranteed to them by government decree, they would have made greater efforts and the rise in grain prices would have been negligible in the province (Hippeau 1864: II, 1, 478).

But the provincials persist. In a letter of remonstrance of October 1768, the Parlement goes so far as to intimate that the king is in cahoots with hoarders and racketeers. The idea of a Pact of Famine is spreading.

Behind this widespread belief in a conspiracy among merchants and royal officials to profit from the starvation of the provinces exists the usual refracted glimmer of truth. The king and his minions are bending every effort to pry resources from the grip of provincial particularism in order to devote them to their own national ends: the feeding of Paris, the maintenance of the army, the payment of a growing bureaucracy, the creation of a national market, the promotion of agriculture. The struggle pits the centralizers not only against the holders of grain but also against the hoarders of men, of land, of gold, and of loyalty.

The collective violence of the time expresses the titanic conflict. A substratum of old-fashioned violence still aligns members of one more or less communal group against another: the brawl among rival groups of artisans, the free-for-all setting two adjacent villages against each other, and so on. In the mid-eighteenth century, however, the characteristic forms of collective violence involve angry resistance to demands from the center. Food riots take first place, but revolts against conscription, tax rebellions, and forcible invasions of lands closed off from communal use by royal decree have essentially the same character. The century's largest series of disturbances before the Revolution of 1789 will be the garland of food riots draped around Paris in 1775, after Turgot's most vigorous efforts at freeing the grain trade. A very large part of the collective action of the Revolution itself will take quintessential eighteenth century forms.

We spring forward a century, to 1868. Napoleon III, no longer so lustrous as when he seized power sixteen years ago, governs France. By now, Frenchmen have virtually forgotten food riots and tax rebellions, although they were abundant only twenty years earlier. The gatherings which commonly turn violent are no longer casual congregations at markets or fairs; they are deliberate assemblies of men belonging to special-purpose associations. The International Workingmen's Association—later to be called the First International—is four years old and actively organizing in France. In June the Empire finally legalizes public meetings, although it still requires prior authorization for them. As settings for collective violence, demonstrations and strikes now prevail.

Now is the time of massive strikes, the first important wave of the Second Empire, strikes of a scale and sophistication never before seen in France. The workers of Lille and its vicinity have been striking, on and off, for two years. On the walls and urinals of Lille, this year's graffiti read:

VIVE LA RÉPUBLIQUE!
DES BALLES OU DU PAIN!
AUX ARMES, CITOYEN!
CI NOUS NE VOULONS PAS NOUS LAISSÉS MOURIR OU MANGÉ PAR LES
    ANGLAIS!
JE SUIS RÉPUBLICAIN PARCE QUE LE BONHEUR EST DANS LA RÉPUBLIQUE!

All of these are defined, naturally, as "seditious slogans" (Pierrard 1965: 490–491).

In this year of 1868 major strikes break out in the Nord, in Marseille, and through much of the industrial region of Lyon, Saint-Etienne, and Roanne. Many of them pass more or less peacefully, if not amicably. Some few produce violence—strikers stoning the house of a mine director, or scuffles between assembled strikers and the troops sent in to keep them in order. Although strikes have been legal, more or less, for four years, prefects are quick to aid the managers when workers show signs of turbulence and/or "socialism." However, the really bloody encounters of soldiers and workers—the so-called Massacres of la Ricamarie and Aubin in 1869, the struggles around the near-insurrectionary strikes of 1870, the Communes of 1871—have yet to come.

The deliberately organized demonstration is rapidly becoming the usual setting for collective violence. Toulouse, for example, has seen no disturbances of any note since its republicans' futile resistance to Louis Napoleon's 1851 coup d'état. But now the government is beginning to organize the militia (the *garde mobile*) in preparation for a possible war with Prussia. On the 9th of March there is a minor demonstration at the Prefecture: some singing, some stoning. The evening of the 10th:

a crowd of 1,500 to 2,000 persons sings the Marseillaise, and breaks the gas lamps. Then groups of young men go to the Prefecture, where the police station is broken into and sacked. They then run through the streets to shouts of Vive la République! Down with the Emperor! break street lights and windows of public buildings, and besiege the mayor at his house, on which they fly a red flag. The next day . . . many workers stay away from the job and new disturbances break out; many women take part, thinking that the militia will be garrisoned far away . . . youngsters take to the streets with a red flag (a towel drenched in an ox's blood at the slaughterhouse) and try to build a barricade of wagons. Another gang breaks gaslights around the Place des

Carmes. A third goes to the School of Law, breaks in, and smashes a bust of the Emperor. The authorities start preparing the military for action (Armengaud 1961: 420–421).

Many disturbances follow this script: a moderately disciplined demonstration shatters into rioting and vandalism. As Armengaud tells us, "It seems that the republicans were behind the first demonstrations, but they were overwhelmed by the exuberance of the young people and the calculated intervention of a few troublemakers" (ibid.). The well-organized mass demonstration, in which the usual violence takes the form of struggles between the demonstrators and the police sent to disperse or contain them, has not yet come into its own.

One more hundred-year bound brings us to 1968. General de Gaulle has survived ten years as president but his popularity seems frayed. Strikes still shake France's industrial life with fair frequency. In the early months of this year, however, student rebellions steal the headlines. A series of student strikes blend agitation against the American war in Vietnam with demands for greater student participation in the running of universities. PROFESSEURS VOUS ETES VIEUX goes one of the slogans.

In May the main action in Paris shifts from the new campus in the industrial suburb of Nanterre to the ancient one at the Sorbonne. After some vandalism and some threats of rough-and-tumble between militants of far left and far right, the rector asks police to surround, and then to disperse, a group of students meeting in the Sorbonne's courtyard to protest disciplinary action begun against some of the leaders at Nanterre. The clearing of the Sorbonne itself goes smoothly. But clashes between riot police and jeering students gathered just outside the old building begin six extraordinary weeks of demonstrations, street fighting, strikes, sit-downs of a new style in schools and factories, speeches, elections, repression: the Events of May.

This year's graffiti have a more fantastic touch than those of a century before:

LA CULTURE EST L'INVERSION DE LA VIE
LA LUCIDITÉ EST LA BLESSURE LA PLUS PROCHE DU SOLEIL
HAUT-PARLEUR = AMBIANCE PROGRAMMÉE = RÉPRESSION
QUAND LE DERNIER DES SOCIOLOGUES AURA ÉTÉ PENDU AVEC LES
    TRIPES DU DERNIER BUREAUCRATE, AURONS-NOUS ENCORE DES
    PROBLÈMES?
L'ANARCHIE, C'EST JE!

And *l'anarchie* sometimes seems to be the point of it all.

At one time it looks as though the disorders could bring down the regime. It could be the end of the Fifth Republic. The satiric *Canard enchaîné* runs a headline: MARIANNE PASSE L'EXAMEN EN SIXIEME. It turns out otherwise, at least in the short run. The elections at the end of June produce a Gaullist landslide. People are frightened. Nevertheless, the Events involve far more than a handful of fanatics. In May and June at least 20,000 Frenchmen take part in violent encounters with the police, perhaps 2,500 are wounded and 4,500 arrested during those encounters, and 5 men die as a more or less direct result of them. A far larger number of people—millions of them—join nonviolent strikes, sit-ins, and demonstrations. May and June produce the largest strike wave France has ever seen. Proportionate to the French population, it is one of the greatest national bursts of collective action ever to occur.

The violence itself does not distinguish the Events of May from a number of other disturbances since World War II: the insurrectionary strikes of 1947, for example, or the riots at General Eisenhower's installation as SHAEF commander in 1951 or the huge, bloody demonstrations during the Algerian war. For the great numbers of people involved, the destruction and casualties of May 1968 are slight. But the leadership of students, their reaching out to factory workers, the rejection of Communist patronage, the experiments with local control of schools and workplaces, the undercurrent of demands for communal autonomy within a complex society—all combine to give the Events a new and baffling character.

Veteran observer Raymond Aron finds the Events senseless and repellent, which is to say, baffling. Just after the fighting dies down, he rummages in his wordbag for the right label and chooses—"psychodrama."

The psychodrama brings into play the revolutionary propensity of the French people, the weakness of mediating institutions (accentuated by Gaullism, in which everything depends on General de Gaulle himself), the surge of irrational forces in a society which calls itself modern, probably the discontent of a number of Frenchmen in a phase of modernization lacking the morphine of inflation. There were enough frustrations, resentments, and griefs among Frenchmen for a great outburst to occur, given the right circumstances. Is it the end of a civilization? (1968: 44).

No revolution, but mass hysteria, says Aron. No hysteria, but mass revolution, reply the students. Both agree that something deep in French society is surfacing. They disagree whether it represents a change or a breakdown.

A little later Alain Touraine will claim it represents both, with the change in French society being the more fundamental:

The movement of May is a new form of the class struggle. More than any other collective action of the last decades, this movement revealed and thus constituted the fundamental social conflict of our society. That way of putting it is farther than it might seem from the proclamations of the participants themselves, for it means that we are dealing with a new social conflict, whose nature and participants are no longer the same as in the previous society, in truly capitalist society . . . The French students, like those of Berlin and Berkeley, began a struggle against the apparatus of integration, manipulation, and aggression. It is these words and not the word "exploitation" which best define the nature of the conflict (1968: 14).

And so—as in 1768 and 1868—the analysis of the violent events quickly becomes an analysis of the social order which produced them.

The Journey's Lessons

Our mythical journey is far from bootless. The two centuries we have paced off brought fundamental changes in the character of collective violence in France. That is the first and elementary lesson: collective violence has form—more than clumsy words like "riot" or "disturbance" convey. At any particular time and place people have a limited and well-defined repertoire of violent forms. The repertoire changes systematically with time and place, as the basic forms of organization for *non*violent action vary. That is the second (and less obvious) lesson: the predominant forms of violence depend on the basic structure of collective action. No tragic chasm separates violence from nonviolence, in 1968 or 1768.

The third lesson follows directly from the first two, although it may be harder to accept: in the French experience collective violence has been a cause, effect, and constituent element of the political process. If that is the case, it makes little sense to imagine violent protest as a geyser newly erupting through a weakened but level surface—as an expression of either "revolutionary propensities" or "accumulated tension." It then makes much sense, on the other hand, to suppose that if the nature of violent conflict changes significantly, other, much wider, changes in the political process must be going on. The rise of the food riot in the eighteenth century and the rise of the violent demonstration in the nineteenth century signified a far more general transformation of France's political structure. Perhaps the new features of the 1968 rebellion also signify more than an instant impulse.

If so, we are no longer making a choice among versions, simple or sophisticated, of "breakdown" and "solidarity" theories. Neither line of argument gives enough importance to ordinary political structure and routine political process. Some things are already clear. First, the way the rulers of France did their work strongly affected the character and frequency of collective violence. Second, local, regional, and national struggles for power (as opposed, say, to immediate responses to misery, sudden releases of accumulated tension, or spontaneous expressions of solidarity) accounted for a large part of the violent action in any period. Third, whatever effects structural changes outside the political sphere like urbanization and industrialization may have had on the pattern and extent of collective violence, those effects were largely indirect, mediated by the political structure. In order to trace the connections between the emergence of an urban-industrial society and the ebb and flow of different forms of violent conflict, we are going to have to do a lot of our searching in and around the everyday organization of political life.

The Centralization of Power

Part of the search takes us back to the broadest features of French political history. France has long stood out among nations for her centralizing verve. Although the so-called Absolutism of the seventeenth and eighteenth centuries went much farther in theory than in practice (the theory itself was a weapon fashioned in the long battle of the crown with provincial magnates), the center prevailed, its rivals succumbed. Tocqueville saw in the royal centralization of power, wealth, and population in Paris the roots of the Revolution and the origins of the subsequent fragility of democratic institutions in France. Much more recently, Herbert Luethy has commented that nonparliamentary institutions of modern French government represent:

the state apparatus of the absolute monarchy perfected and brought to its logical conclusion under the First Empire. When the crowned heads fell, the real
sovereignty was transferred to this apparatus. But it works in the background, unobtrusively, anonymously, remote from all publicity and almost
in secret; a monarch, a monarch whose only surviving driving principle is
routine. It is not so much a state within a state as the real state behind the
facade of the democratic state (1955: 19–20).

The French system has long subordinated local and regional authorities
to direct national control. The departmental prefect is an agent of the
central government. Even the mayor of a village is, to some extent, a national official. With the dissolution of the provincial National Guard units
and the reduction of the Parisian Guard to ceremonial functions in 1852,
the last legally armed forces not firmly under national control disappeared almost definitively—the deeply significant exceptions being the
revolutionary years of 1870 and 1871. (This is in striking contrast with
most English-speaking countries, in which a considerable variety of militias, national guards, and police forces continue to operate under local
and regional control.) At about the same time as he tamed the National
Guard, Louis Napoleon perfected an apparatus of spies, informers, and
informants already assembled by earlier regimes. Later innovations in
techniques of control—tanks, telephones, tear gas, automatic rifles—
simply increased the technical advantages of the government over its
challengers.

The administrative centralization promoted and fed on geographic
centralization in Paris and its protuberance, Versailles. Paris has towered
over all other French cities since there has been a France. The roads of
France, then the railroads of France, and then the airlines of France grew
up in the shape of a Parisocephalic octopus. Tocqueville entitled a pivotal
chapter of *The Old Regime and the French Revolution:* "How in France,
more than in any other European country, the provinces had come under
the thrall of the metropolis, which attracted to itself all that was most
vital in the nation." (A lexicon which permits "province" to mean every
part of a country but a single city would be fantastic almost anywhere
else.)

Marx, too, saw Parisian dominance as a major political fact: "If Paris,
as a result of political centralization, rules France, the workers, in moments of revolutionary earthquake, rule Paris" (1935: 39). Blanqui,

writing in the waning months of the Second Empire, elevated the political reality into a doctrine:

A year of Parisian dictatorship in 1848 would have spared France and would have spared history the quarter of a century now drawing to a close. If it takes ten years of it this time, let us not hesitate. After all, the government of Paris is the government of the nation by the nation, and therefore the only legitimate one. Paris is not just a municipality entrenched in its own interests. It represents the nation (1955: 166–167).

The sheer existence of such a doctrine illustrates the political centralization of France—and gives meaning to the old fear that monstrous Paris will devour all the nation.

The work of centralization went on for centuries. It did not stop with the Revolution and Empire but continued apace during the nineteenth century; the state drew larger and larger parts of men's lives under its direct control through public education, universal military training, manhood suffrage, and programs of public welfare. Eventually the state seized control over substantial parts of the economy: railroads, airlines, radio, television, mines, utilities, important parts of banking, and automobile manufacturing. The great moment for that expansion came at the end of World War II. If Louis XIV declared, *L'Etat, c'est moi,* his successors announced, *L'Etat, c'est tout.* Today much of the debate about governmental reform in France concerns ways of reversing, or at least arresting, a centuries-old process of centralization.

The Nationalization of Politics

In addition to a centralization of power, the France of the last two centuries has seen a nationalization of politics. The two processes depended on each other. Ordinary Frenchmen led fairly active political lives within their own communities and provinces long before the Revolution; they elected local officials, apportioned the local tax burden, wrangled over the expenses of the religious establishment. But they had only intermittent contact with national politics, through privileged intermediaries —and even then more as subjects than as participants. The political reforms of 1787 and of the early Revolution actually restricted formal participation in community politics (by substituting an elected council for the assembly of all heads of households and imposing property qualifications for voting and officeholding). On the other hand, the Revolution enormously increased the opportunities and incentives for ordinary people to participate in national politics through voting, holding office, joining clubs, adopting revolutionary styles, demonstrating, reading, arguing, volunteering.

The fashionable word for this drawing of people into intensive communication on a national scale is "mobilization" (see Nettl 1967). After the early Revolution, the next great surge of political mobilization in France did not come until the Revolution of 1848. Then universal manhood suffrage, election campaigns, proliferating political associations, a relatively free national press, and a great acceleration of the movement of political information via telegraph and railroad drew men much farther into national politics than they had ever gone before. Centralization promoted this process of nationalization by placing more and more of the important resources and decisions in the national capital or the national government.

The centralization and nationalization of French politics did not proceed smoothly and without hesitation. The French moved from regime to regime through revolutions and coups; 1789, 1799, 1830, 1848, 1851, 1870, and 1958 are only the largest markers. Today French leaders and parties still claim and contest the lines of descent from the eighteenth-century Revolution with a passion resembling that of the Russians or the Chinese more than that of the Dutch or the English (to name four regimes of revolutionary genesis). Although the Radicals acquired a special position as protectors of secular republicanism under the Third Republic, no party has ever been able to establish a monopoly of revolutionary legitimacy. Yet few parties have avoided claiming one. As recently as May 13, 1958, the insurgents who seized power in Algiers, and ultimately brought down the Fourth Republic, sang the Marseillaise and formed a Committee of Public Safety.

Still, 1958 is an exception in one crucial regard. It is the only occasion since 1799 in which the professional French military have taken an autonomous and fundamental part in the overthrow of a regime. Men who acquired their renown as soldiers have periodically come to power in France and have periodically appeared as threats to democratic continuity: Boulanger, Pétain, and De Gaulle are the celebrated examples; the two Napoleons are the Men on Horseback with whom they are most often compared. Louis Napoleon did use the army with grim effectiveness in

his 1851 coup. The question of civilian control over the military did almost
tear France apart during the Dreyfus Affair. Yet the army as such has
played only a small role in France's succession of revolutions and coups.
In that respect, France's instability is unlike that of Spain or Brazil.

Under the Third and Fourth Republics, the quick turnover of cabinets
combined with the memory of those coups and revolutions to give France
a worldwide reputation for political instability. That French fickleness,
Raymond Aron points out, had actually developed earlier:

Instability at the top is . . . less novel than the sociologists tend to think.
In Tocqueville's time, during the July Monarchy, people joked about the
same thing and told the story of the ambassador who didn't know, when
he left Paris, what ministry he would represent when he arrived at his post.
The presence of a king, of an emperor or of a Charles de Gaulle temporarily
removes the head of state from factional quarrels, but it does not do away
with the quarrels. The head of state presides over our disputes more than
he resolves them (1959: 40–41).

Although by now a number of younger nations have thrown down
serious challenges in this line of endeavor, France's reputation for governmental discontinuity was well-earned. Yet there are two important
qualifications. The first is that the personnel of government, especially
the state bureaucracy, persisted to a remarkable degree through changes
of regime. Despite the sudden shift from heavy property qualifications for
voting to manhood suffrage, a good half of the deputies elected in April
1848 had already served in prerevolutionary Chambers. At the level of
departmental councils the continuity was much greater. Administrative
personnel at all levels survived the change of regime with very little per-
turbation (see esp. Fasel 1968; Girard, Prost, Gossez, 1970; Tudesq
1964: II, 1065; Tudesq 1967: 85–102).

The second qualification is that "instability" does not equal "violence."
The French have had plenty of violent moments, but so have most other
peoples, regardless of whether they live under "stable" or "unstable"
governments. England, the United States, Canada, and Belgium have all
in their times experienced collective violence of the same general varieties as France's; their daily lives, over the long run, may have been even
more violent than France's.

Certainly the sheer amount of bloodshed does not account for France's
contentious reputation. Over the period from 1930 to 1960, for example,

about 100 Frenchmen died in political disturbances, mostly at the hands of the police. During the same period some 200,000 were killed in wars and 600,000 died in accidents. Obviously, political disturbances create fear and trembling disproportionate to their toll in human life. France's distinction does not lie in the amount of wounding and killing, but in the frequency with which violent protests have brought down governments and regimes.

That special political experience has produced a special set of political attitudes. As Philip Williams puts it:

The Frenchman's approach to the problem of political authority is . . . shaped by three crucial factors: a political struggle which has always been waged with sectarian bitterness and thoroughness, sparing no sector of the country's organized life: an experience of governments abusing their authority to maintain their position: and an immensely powerful administrative machine, which provides a standing temptation to such abuse. There is a latent totalitarianism in the French attitude to politics, which makes French democrats fear the power of government, and regard it as a source of potential dangers rather than of potential benefits (1958: 2; cf. Crozier 1964: 213–264; Tarrow 1969).

No doubt most men are ambivalent toward the state. Frenchmen, more than most.

France's political history is to some extent an explanation, and to some extent a result, of the changing character of her collective violence. The centralization of government, the nationalization of politics, the barriers to independent political action by the army, the revolutionary heritage, and the continuing vulnerability of regimes to challenge from the street give the country a greater resemblance to, say, Italy than to England. A France with a more independent military might well resemble Spain or Argentina.

Wealth

But only in some respects. The analogies of Italy, Spain, or Argentina lose some of their persuasiveness when it comes to matters of wealth, industrial structure, regional diversity, and urban population. The history of collective violence in France depends not only on the country's formal political structure but also on the great transformation of other features of the social structure.

Before the Revolution, France was one of the world's most prosperous, industrial, urban nations. France has a longer experience with comfortable levels of living than almost any other country in the world. With respect to income per capita, Holland and England no doubt pulled away as early as the seventeenth century. But the next-comers—Belgium, Germany, and the United States—did not pass her until fairly late in the nineteenth century.

All this is relative of course. If we were to cast about the world of the middle twentieth century for approximations of France's material condition at the beginning of the nineteenth century, we would have to seize on poor but civilized nations like Bulgaria, Yugoslavia, or Costa Rica. Even those analogies would touch on the grotesque; we would have to conjure up a Yugoslavia without railroads, without radios, without splashes of ultramodern industry. Our imaginary Yugoslavia would have a class of titled landlords still wresting their incomes from tenant farmers, and another class of merchants, bankers, industrialists, and officials just coming into their own. Even fewer of her people would be in big cities than is the case in contemporary Yugoslavia. Yet she would prevail in a world of nations poorer and less powerful than herself. That France has no counterpart in the western world today.

Over the long run since the Revolution, the wealth of France has accumulated slowly and surely. One informed guess at the long-run rate of growth of per capita income in France puts it at 1.25 percent per annum, about the same as England's (Cole and Dean 1965: 12). Figure 1 presents three of the best known national income series for France since 1810. They display a relatively steady growth throughout the nineteenth century. The twentieth century brought greater swings in income. According to these estimates, the most notable periods of decline were the depression of the 1870s, the two world wars, and the depression of the 1930s. World War II shows up as an economic disaster, even compared to the Depression it followed. The periods of most notable growth run from around 1855 to 1869, 1922 to 1930, and, incomparably, 1946 to 1960 and beyond. These dates correspond satisfactorily to what we know otherwise about the timing of industrial expansion. The curves register the steady increase of the older industries up to 1850, spurting growth (relying increasingly on steel, railroads, and other new industries)

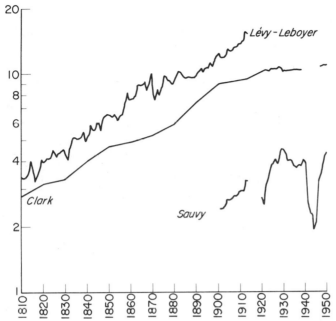

Sources: Maurice Lévy-Leboyer, "La croissance économique en France au XIXe siècle: résultats préliminaires," *Annales: Economies, Sociétés, Civilisations,* 23: 788–807 (1968). The statistic is an index number (1890 = 100) for "global product" of agriculture, industry, and construction, and excludes services, investment, government purchases, and net exports from among the items conventionally included in Gross National Product. (2) Colin Clark, *The Conditions of Economic Progress* (New York: St. Martins, 1957), pp. 123–229. The figures represent real income (including the imputed value of agricultural products produced and consumed outside the market) in billions of International Units. Up to 1913 the figures are annual averages for decades centered on the date shown. (3) Estimates of national income by Alfred Sauvy, 1901–1949, and, after 1949, extrapolation of Sauvy series at 1949, as reported in *Annuaire statistique de la France. Résumé rétrospectif, 1966,* table 14, p. 556. The units are billions of 1938 francs.

Figure 1. Estimates of Changes in French National Income, 1810–1960.

of the 1850s and 1860s, and the tremendous expansion both of modern industry and of services since that time.

The increase of national income which occurred meant more to the average Frenchman than it would have to the average Englishman or American because the population of France grew slowly. Fewer persons shared the spoils. (It may well be—and has often been argued—that a higher rate of population increase would have accelerated France's eco-

nomic growth.) France did not draw anything like the hordes of immi-
grants who sailed to Canada or Argentina. Her birthrate dropped pretty
steadily from the Revolution to World War II, generally faster than the
death rate. In whole regions of Burgundy, Normandy, and Languedoc
families began limiting births rather stringently by the time of the Revolution. As a result, France's natural increase was slow and uncertain. The
birthrate did tend to recover somewhat in prosperous days: the 1860s, the
1920s, and, sensationally, the 1950s. But war and depression actually produced substantial natural *decreases* in 1870–1871, 1914–1919, and 1936–
1945. Since World War II, on the other hand, with mortality still skid-
ding down and fertility up to *fin-de-siècle* levels, Frenchmen have multiplied at rates unrivaled in at least two centuries. After a century of aging
this made the French population young again. Both demographically and
industrially the postwar change of pace far exceeded what had happened
earlier.

Industrialization and Urbanization

The same is true for the structure of employment. Figure 2 shows what
a century and a half of industrialization did to the French labor force.
Some of the changes are factitious. The apparent decline of the total labor
force after 1954, for example, resulted almost entirely from the application of stricter definitions to the agricultural population. Nevertheless,
several facts are apparent:

1. Contrary to common notions of Revolutionary and post-Revolutionary France, as early as 1825 almost half the labor force was already
working outside of agriculture.

2. However, the absolute size of the agricultural population remained
virtually constant for a century after 1825, began to slide after the First
World War, and has only fallen off rapidly since the Second World War.

3. As a consequence, France had an exceptionally high proportion of
her labor force in agriculture, compared with other prosperous twentieth-
century nations, right into the 1950s.

4. The shares of manufacturing and services grew constantly except
around 1900 and during World War II. The pace of their growth, however, depended on the general level of economic activity; the greater the
prosperity, the faster the shift into manufacturing and services—and vice
versa.

5. The shares of manufacturing and services have remained roughly equal over the entire period. France has not so far experienced the shift from secondary to tertiary industries which is supposed to characterize advanced industrial economies.

The period under examination, then, saw France transformed from a fairly poor, predominantly agrarian, country to a prosperous industrial one, while a number of other countries traveled in the same general direction faster. Although by 1825 France already had long experience with traditional forms of manufacturing, the years following were the essential time of industrialization.

France also urbanized. Revolutionary Paris, with its half-million inhabitants, was one of the world's great cities. For centuries Paris had been reaching out to control the men, mores, and markets of northeastern France; by the end of the eighteenth century, a vast area was pouring migrants and food into the city. Marseille, Lyon, Bordeaux, and Rouen, each with close to a hundred thousand people, dominated their own much smaller hinterlands. The great majority of Frenchmen, nonetheless, lived in villages.

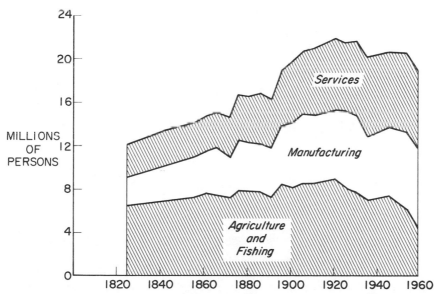

Source: J.–C. Toutain, *La population de la France de 1700 à 1959* (Paris: Institut de Science Economique Appliquée, 1963), pp. 135, 161.

Figure 2. The French Labor Force, 1825–1959.

For French statisticians, the word "urban" has traditionally singled out communes with at least 2,000 persons in the central settlement. By this criterion, about one-fifth of the French population lived in urban places in 1820, about three-fifths in 1960. As Figure 3 shows, the rural population has been declining both absolutely and relatively since around 1850. Big-city France has fed on that decline. Cities of 50,000 or more had 4 percent in 1821, 18 percent in 1901, and 25 percent in 1962. The pace of urban growth was relatively even. Over the long run it comes, like per capita income, to about 1.25 percent per year. The industrial expansion of the 1850s, the 1920s, and the 1950s accelerated the rate, the slower industrialization from 1870 to the First World War and during the Depression braked it, while the two wars and the loss of territory to Prussia in 1870 dented the curve, though not for long.

If the French population in agriculture reached its peak around the First World War, while the rural population began a steady decline around 1850, the two cannot have been the same. A good proportion—

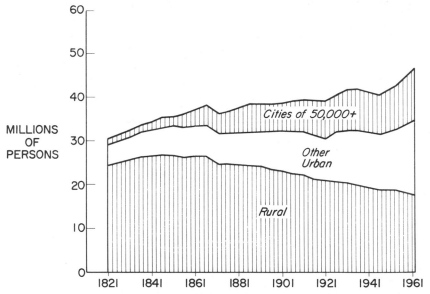

Sources: *Annuaire statistique de la France, Résumé rétrospectif, 1966,* table 3, p. 23; *Statistique de la France* (Paris: Imprimerie Royale, 1837), pp. 267–283. "Urban places" are communes with 2,000 or more persons in the central agglomeration. The figures for 1821 and 1836 are estimates from the ratio communes 2,000+/communes 10,000+ for 1851, as applied to the actual total in communes of 10,000 or more in 1821 and 1836.

Figure 3. French Urban, Rural, and Total Population, 1821–1962.

perhaps a third—of the so-called rural population of post-Revolutionary France was living from manufacturing, services, and other nonagricultural pursuits. The domestic textile industry (said in rural Mayenne, for example, to be the principal economic activity of the countryside before the Revolution) occupied far more people than its rivals, the wood-burning forges, woodworking, tanning, basketry, pottery. All these industries rapidly moved to the city during the nineteenth century, leaving a once-humming countryside more bucolic than it had been for centuries. Rural areas deindustrialized.

Apparently hundreds of thousands of rural artisans lingered on in small towns through the first half of the nineteenth century, living on half wages, seasonal work in the fields, and dwindling hope for a return of the "good old days." They and their descendants began to leave the land in growing numbers around 1850 as jobs in the new industrial centers became more plentiful, the railroads made travel to them easier, rural industry expired, and traditional rights to glean, cut, and hunt in common fields or forests disappeared before the advance of calculating, capital-intensive agriculture. So the "rural exodus," so often deplored by French lovers of rustic virtue, probably had three rather different, if overlapping, phases: (1) a draining of present and former workers in rural industry, peaking in the middle of the nineteenth century; (2) a tapping of agricultural laborers and "extra" children of farm families, especially during the period of relatively high natural increase up to 1890 or so; (3) the movement, especially after 1930, of families displaced by the closing down and consolidating of farms since 1890. The first movement had an air of desperation, the second offered a way out of poverty to several generations of ambitious young Frenchmen, and the third went on rather smoothly except for the worst years of the 1930s. The three kinds of movement were bound to have very different impacts on agrarian protest.

The growth of cities and the draining of rural population were no more evenly distributed across the map of France than was the development of industry on a large scale. Let us call "modern," for the sake of simplicity, those areas with high per-capita incomes, productive agriculture, large manufacturing establishments, high literacy, extensive means of communication, and so on. In these terms, the geographical distribution of modernity in France has followed a curvilinear path since the Revolution. Modernity was already somewhat concentrated in Paris and its hinterland,

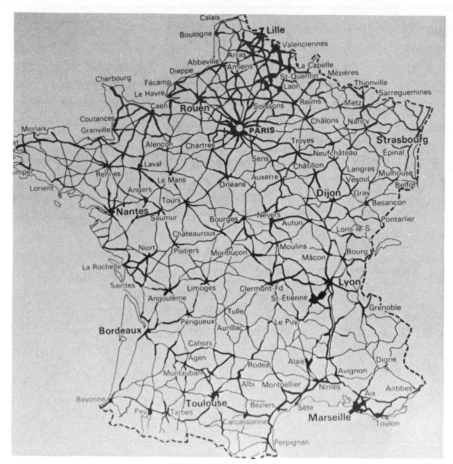

Source: Paul M. Bouju et al., *Atlas Historique de la France Contemporaine* (Paris: Colin, 1966), pp. 72, 73.

Figure 4. Road Traffic in France, 1856–1857.

and in much smaller regions immediately adjacent to a handful of other big cities. It became even more unequal during the nineteenth century as those regions (and, more generally, the northeastern quadrant of the country) urbanized and industrialized. Slowly after the First World War and rapidly after the Second World War the fruits of modernity—bitter and sweet alike—spread beyond those regions of initial importance, and a degree of equalization occurred.

One rather surprising feature of this process shows up in the changing distribution of agricultural yields (Bouju 1966: 56). From the beginning

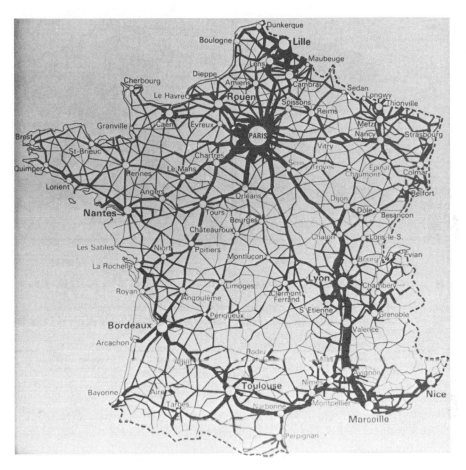

Road Traffic in France, 1955.

the hinterland of Paris has, under the stimulus of the metropolitan market, produced the highest yields per hectare. Regional disparities, especially the advantage of Paris, *increased* during the nineteenth century
(despite the spread throughout France of new agricultural practices),
only to give way to a much greater equalization during the twentieth.

The maps of road traffic in 1856–1857 and 1955 (Figure 4) identify
points in a very similar progression: inequality at the beginning, growing
inequality with the industrial urbanization of the north, eventual spread
of traffic to larger and larger portions of the country. The traffic maps

suggest the extent to which the twentieth-century spread of modernity occurred through the expansion and convergence of existing urban regions: Lyon and Marseille linking arms and reaching around to Nice; Toulouse and Bordeaux building their own metropolitan network; Paris extending its alliances in every direction.

The process touches everyday life. In an Angevin country town:

As the social networks in Chanzeaux have diminished in number, they have, mostly because of the revolution in transportation, greatly increased their geographic spread. Whenever the people of Chanzeaux are not working, they are on the move, usually in order to visit friends, relatives, acquaintances of far-reaching networks. Eight years ago if we wanted to talk to a farmer, we would be sure to find him at home on Sunday afternoon, and our visit was welcome since he seemed to have nothing else to do. Now people are rarely at home when they have leisure time. If they stay at home, it is because they expect visitors. The traffic on all the roads of the Maine-et-Loire, especially the back roads leading to hamlets and farms, is surprisingly heavy on Sunday nowadays. Sometimes farmers—and townspeople—go even farther away for the weekend. Faligand visits his cousins in Paris. Bourdelle visits a friend with whom he has kept up since army days in Lille. The Massonneaus drive down from Paris to visit the Guitieres. Only the ill stay at home—and they have visitors. It used to be that on Sunday afternoon the Chanzeans who wanted to get away from home would walk along the Hyrome River to stop and drink with friends at the little wineshops along the way. Today one can walk the length of the path and see only an occasional fisherman. The people of Chanzeaux have broader contacts and interests (Wylie 1966: 341).

It is not so much that Frenchmen move *more* than they used to. Despite enduring myths to the contrary, rural communities in most sections of France have been experiencing rapid turnovers of population for at least a century. The big change is that the circles in which they travel have spread and spread (see Tugault 1973). This extension of social relations began with Paris and its hinterland, followed the growth of industrial metropolises in the nineteenth century, and has in recent decades been knitting all of France together.

Not that the knit is smooth, regular, or harmonious. The French have shared a general experience of western peoples: a shift of the crucial lines of division of wealth, prestige, power, social access, and solidarity from local to national. Division remains; the principles of division change. Particular attachments to this village or that, this family or that, even this faith or that have lost much of their importance as promoters or inhibitors of collective action, however much sentimental value they may have retained. Position in national systems of occupation and wealth have come to matter a great deal more.

Through the long years we are considering, the urbanization and industrialization of France have transformed her class structure in four interdependent ways:

1. Control over liquid wealth, complex organizations, and the industrial apparatus has largely supplanted control over land as the central criterion of class position.

2. The numbers of persons working in large organizations under bureaucratic control (whether, through style of work and style of life, called "working class" or "middle class") has enormously and steadily expanded.

3. As the French have moved cityward, position and acceptability within a particular community have lost much of their importance as determinants of individual or group behavior; local notability, or notoriety, matters less and less as compared with position in the national occupational structure, membership in national associations, contacts, and experiences outside the community.

4. Largely as a result of changing little while other things were changing much, positions as local representatives or interpreters of national structures—priest, notary, government functionary—have lost much of their prestige and power; by contrast, positions presuming technical expertise—scientist, engineer, doctor—have gained in luster.

Familiar trends, all.

The hand of history has erased a France of peasants and artisans, of landowning local notables linked (not always happily) with urban officials and financiers. It has written in their place a France of farmers, bureaucrats, technicians, and industrial workers, dominated by professional organizers in a variety of specialties.

With some disgust Balzac read the writing on the wall in the 1840s:

The three orders have been replaced by what are nowadays called *classes*. We have lettered classes, industrial classes, upper classes, middle classes, etc. And these classes almost always have their own regents, as in the *collège*. People have changed big tyrants into petty ones, that's all. Each industry has its bourgeois Richelieu named Laffitte or Casimir Périer (Balzac 1947: 158).

Just a few years later, Karl Marx wrote of the same transformations from a rather different perspective:

French industry is more developed and the French bourgeoisie more revolutionary than that of the rest of the Continent. But was not the February Revolution leveled directly against the finance aristocracy? This fact proved that the industrial bourgeoisie did not rule France. The industrial bourgeoisie can rule only where modern industry shapes all property relations to suit itself, and industry can win this power only where it has conquered the world market, for national bounds are inadequate for its development (1958: I, 148).

The hand of history was, in short, busily producing a palimpsest.

Many traces of the old regime persisted into the twentieth century. That is what was special about France's version of a very general transformation of class structure in industrializing societies: small-town life, marginal family farming, the family firm, and the small shop all hung on tenaciously, only losing their grip under the battering of the Depression and the Second World War. Politics grew to a national scale far faster and far more decisively than did routine social life. The result was the disparity between the nationalization of politics and the segmentation of solidarity which Stanley Hoffmann (1963: 1–117) considers the foundation of the "stalemate society" of France under the Third Republic.

Organization for Collective Action

Hoffmann also argues that the poverty of French associational life contributed to the stalemate. On that score we are not so sure. Throughout the interdependent transformations of demographic, economic, political, and class structures we have been reviewing, Frenchmen turned increasingly to complex organizations, including associations in the narrow sense of the word, as the means of getting their work done. The trend is obvious in the worlds of industry and government. The history of voluntary association for political and economic ends is more elusive because successive governments from the Revolution to the beginning of the Third Republic set big barriers in the way of private association. They did it selectively, so that employers long had the organizational advantage in dealing with their workers. Nevertheless, even under the forbidding eye of the Minister of the Interior, French workers, peasants, bourgeois, and political activists persisted in forming clubs, secret societies, *compagnon-nages,* associations for mutual aid, rudimentary trade unions, and parties. As Henry Ehrmann says, "the legal obstacles were frequently ignored; many categories did not wait for the change in legislation to form groups and to constitute in fact the 'partial societies' condemned by Rousseau. But the necessity of achieving this by subterfuge was nevertheless bound to shape group practice and to spread doubts about the legitimacy of group activities" (1968: 171). The proof that associational life was far from extinguished lies in the energy with which the spies of the Interior Ministry eavesdropped and infiltrated during regimes of relatively strict control like the Restoration and the Second Empire, and the startling speed with which such associations proliferated—or came out into the open—in times of relative freedom like the spring of 1848.

It appears that the pace, scale, and complexity of formal organization increased rapidly as France urbanized and industrialized after 1840. The evidence is uncertain precisely because so much of the new organization took place in the shadows. Tocqueville did not detect it when writing *Democracy in America* in the 1830s; on the contrary, he considered the absence of associations a prime reason for the weakness of democratic institutions in France. Yet in his own time the Saint-Simonians, Fourier-ists, Blanquists, and other sects teetering between reform and revolution had gone into frenzies of organization.

As early as October 1831 a report from Paris' prefect of police, sum-marizing the reports of his spies, gives some of the flavor of organization in the capital:

The society of *Amis du Peuple* is vigorously continuing its organization of decuries. They reproduce, under another name, the *ventes* of the Carbonari . . . *The Société des Amis de l'Egalité* plans to blend into the *Amis du Peuple.* Both of them are counting heavily for new recruits on the return of the students; but generally speaking the young people coming back from the provinces appear little inclined to rejoin the popular societies (A.N. F^{1c}33).

At Lyon mutual aid societies began to flourish in the late 1820s and came angrily to light in the insurrections of 1830, 1832, and 1834. In general, Paris preceded the other big cities in the nurturing of association, the big cities preceded the towns, and the towns preceded the countryside.

It was not, however, a simple function of industrialization, at least not in any narrow sense of the word. The workers in the new, expanding, factory-based nineteenth-century industries—steel, railroads, cotton textiles—organized slowly (see Stearns 1965). The industries breeding extensive organization were older, more artisanal, smaller in scale, with the egregious exception of mining. Four main conditions promoted organization in industry and elsewhere: (1) the absence of hereditary memberships in community, family, and the like as bases for collective action; (2) a good-sized population in daily contact over a long period of time; (3) an accumulation of common lore, grievances, and political experience; (4) the visible presence of an antagonist. These conditions first obtained in traditional small-scale industries like typography and silk-weaving. Eventually they developed in factories and even among agricultural workers. Thus, over the nineteenth century the principal loci of working-class organization shifted from shops to factories, with a lag of several decades behind the shift of the labor force from one to the other.

Politics and industry set the standard for religion, sociability, and intellectual life; the Third Republic brought France into its golden age of association. Napoleon III had hastened the process (or at least conceded to it gracefully) by openly tolerating workers' associations throughout the 1860s, legalizing the strike in 1864, and considerably relaxing restrictions on public assembly in 1868. The real spate of organizing and joining came, however, after the French rid themselves of Napoleon III. Frenchmen have perpetuated a myth to the contrary. Confronted with the evidence of ubiquitous semi-secret lodges, sodalities, and religious associations in the South during the eighteenth and nineteenth centuries, Maurice Agulhon (1966) has postulated a *sociabilité méridionale* peculiar to the Midi; we have no good reason to limit that "sociability" to the South.

In our own time French rural communities are reputed to resist voluntary association. But when calm observers look carefully, this turns out not to be the case. In the small, and ostensibly backward, French villages he studied, Laurence Wylie (1966) found fire companies, multiple church-based associations, political parties, *classes* of all young men eligible for conscription in a given year, and other special-purpose organizations to be active participants in community life. Robert T. Anderson and Barbara Gallatin Anderson, studying a village sixteen kilometers from Paris, found voluntary associations proliferating from late in the nineteenth century: "The decades on either side of the turn of the century saw four voluntary associations introduced and sustained: a hunting society, an un-employment-funeral insurance (mutuality) society, a musical society, and a voluntary fire-fighting society. We are more concerned here with the last four decades of abrupt change when, under the impact of primary urban-industrial change, approximately forty associations were founded" (1965: 224–225). The Andersons go on to note how regularly the formal associations parallel and grow from older, existing groups in the community: the shop, the farm, the family, the church, and the community as a whole. In a sense the organization was already there; the association simply crystallized and formalized it.

In those times when the state blocked the formation of distinct special-interest associations (which means most of the time before 1901 plus most of the Second World War), the French tended to overload whatever existing, tolerated means of assembly and collective action they had at hand. During the Revolution church services were often the occasions for agitation, argument, and action. Under the Restoration and the July Monarchy, not only church services, but funerals and theatrical performances, became important contexts for demonstrations of political sympathies. About a year after the July Revolution, for example, the Parisian public attending the provocatively titled *Voyage de la liberté* (including medal-holders from the Revolution itself, who were deliberately seated together by the management) took the many veiled political allusions in the play as opportunities to manifest their opposition to the regime through cheers, applause, and commentary (A.N. F^{le}33, 20 July 1831). Often the crowd went further than that; the insurrection of 1832 began with the funeral of the popular General Lamarque. At the same time, Frenchmen were busily forming secret societies for mutual aid and political action. They seized whatever organizational means were at their disposal.

Two things are deceptive about French organizations: they often form as offshoots of organizations already in existence—the Catholic Church, the Communist Party, and so on; and, though coherent and active, many do not quite acquire formal, legal existence. Both conditions contribute to the illusion of underorganization in France. The state's long resistance to formally constituted voluntary associations of any kind, the consequent tendency to form such groups in the shadows, the consequent unwillingness of the state to collect and publish information on voluntary associations (even political parties) add to the illusion.

The long concentration of the French population in rural communities probably did slow the creation of autonomous voluntary associations. And Frenchmen probably are more loath to form community-wide associations, but more eager to form associations serving particular interests, than most other people. Duncan MacRae points out that, while on the whole joining was less common in the France of the 1950s than in the United States, France differed little from Britain and Germany in that respect. Then he goes on to suggest that "organizations that reinforced existing social divisions were more typical in France, while those that cut across other divisions and made decisions at the community level were more characteristic of the United States" (1967: 29–30). So the history we are reviewing is peculiarly a history of special-interest associations. From the later nineteenth century forward, craftsmen, students, teachers, winegrowers, farmers, big businessmen, veterans, professional women, and innumerable others devised new formal organizations to pursue their interests on a national scale.

The Changing Struggle for Power

This vast series of changes in French social structure reshaped the struggle for political power in three fundamental ways. First, position in the national structure of power came to matter far more than local for practically every purpose. Second, the struggle increasingly took the form of contention or coalition among formal organizations specialized in the pursuit of particular interests; communal groups virtually disappeared from politics. Third, new contenders for power emerged as the class structure and the organizational structure evolved. The rise of organizations speaking for segments of the industrial working class was the most important single movement. Other bids for power came from representatives of assorted groups of peasants, of youths, of schoolteachers, of Catholic employers, of government employees. Furthermore, as long-organized groups such as landholders and churchmen contended for power, they adopted the new associational style.

As in other western countries, the political parties which emerged to full activity in Third Republic France compounded diverse interests. The Radicals, the Socialists—and, for that matter, the Radical Socialists—long represented curious melanges of the French electorate. But, compared with her neighbors, France always had a remarkable susceptibility to party fragmentation, an exceptional openness to new parties representing new or old but separate political interests, a considerable tendency for parties to slim down to a single major interest. The Parti Ouvrier Français, the Parti Social Français, the Boulangists, the Christian Democrats, the Communists, the Poujadists represent different phases of this specialization.

Fragmentation was the normal condition of French parliaments, alliance among fragments the parliamentary game. Genuine threats to the parliamentary system came less from this kind of splintering than from the occasional appearance of an important political force acting outside the parliamentary arena: the Ligue des Patriotes, the Croix de Feu, Algerian nationalists, sometimes the Gaullists or the Communists. Inside or outside parliament, the twentieth-century political struggle pitted associations representing relatively narrow segments of the population against each other and aligned them with or against the regime. Interest-group politics emerged in France.

Our review of social change in France has pointed up spurts of industrialization, urbanization, and demographic transformation after 1850, after 1920 and—preeminently—after 1945; they contrast with crises and reversals at the times of the Franco-Prussian War, the two world wars, and the depression of the 1930s. These are but ripples in a fast-flowing stream. An urban-industrial class structure gradually emerged from a class structure based on land and locality. The new structure relied on control of capital and labor rather than on landed wealth. It separated owners and managers of large formal organizations (factories, governments, schools) from their employees. It emphasized position in the national labor market over local attachments, and gave exceptional rewards to technical expertise. Periods of urban-industrial growth accelerated this transformation of the class structure.

The centralization of politics through the growth of a massive and powerful state apparatus continued trends established centuries before, although the advent of Louis Napoleon after 1848 and the extension of controls over the economy in the 1940s speeded the process. The nationalization of politics through the shift of power and participation to an arena far larger than local went on more or less continuously, but the political mobilization of 1848, of the early Third Republic, of the Popular Front, and of the years just after World War II probably drew men into involvement in national politics faster than at other times. The shift of collective action—both political and nonpolitical—from communal to associational bases proceeded inexorably over the entire period, especially during those same periods of political mobilization. These changes transformed the struggle for power, and thus transformed the character of collective violence.

How? Most immediately by changing the collective actions characteristically producing violence. Group violence ordinarily grows out of collective actions which are not intrinsically violent—festivals, meetings, strikes, demonstrations, and so on. Without them the collective violence could hardly occur. People who do not take part in them can hardly get involved in the violence. The groups engaging in collective action with any regularity usually consist of populations perceiving and pursuing a common set of interests. And collective action on any considerable scale requires coordination, communication, and solidarity extending beyond the moment of action itself. The urbanization and industrialization and political rearrangement of France from the Revolution onward utterly transformed the composition of the groups capable of collective action, their internal organization, their interests, their occasions for collective action, the nature of their opponents, and the quality of collective action itself. The transformation of collective action transformed violence.

Again, how? It is easy to illustrate and hard to analyze. The classic French tax rebellion, for example, took two forms, singly or in combination: first, a group of taxpayers attacked the matériel of tax collection, typically by smashing tollgates and burning assessment records; second, many of the residents of a community greeted the tax collector by blocking his way, by beating him, or by running him out of town; if he brought an armed force the villagers fought them. A typical small version of the tax rebellion occurred at St. Germain (Haute-Vienne) in August 1830. Local tax collectors stopped a carter to check his load and collect their toll. A crowd of men, women, and children "armed with picks and with stones" surrounded them, shouted against the tax, and led away man and wagon from the helpless revenue men (A.N. BB[18] 1186, 14 August 1830). This elementary form of resistance sometimes compounded into widespread and grave rebellion, as in the years before the Fronde, during the early Revolution, and (for the last time) in 1849.

Although the sheer difficulty of paying when times were hard certainly had something to do with this common form of resistance to the state, it is important to see how regularly and directly it centered on the very legitimacy of the tax. Not long before the Revolution of 1830, the *procureur général* of the judicial district of Poitiers reported that "seditious posters" had been appearing in the city of Fontenay (Vendée); "the content of the posters is always to forbid the payment of taxes before the ministers who voted the budget are brought to trial" (A.N. BB[18]1181, 3 February 1830). The same sort of campaign was gathering strength in other parts of France at that time, and continued through the Revolution; often it operated secretly and without violence, but now and then it showed up in a public confrontation. The tax rebellion developed in the sixteenth century, flourished in the seventeenth, recurred in 1789, 1830, or 1848 as new revolutionary officials sought to reimpose the state's authority; it vanished after 1849. Its history traced the government's long struggle to secure both obedience and income.

Gabriel Ardant has identified the general conditions for waves of fiscal revolts in France: a sharp increase in the central government's demands for cash; a sharp decrease in the market for products of rural industry or agriculture (hence in the ability of villagers to convert their surplus into cash); or, more serious, both at once. He has also pointed their clustering in areas of "closed economy"—not necessarily poor, but little involved in production for the market, typically composed of self-sufficient farms. As he sums it up for the Massif Central:

The proportion of the population in agriculture remains relatively large. No doubt some industries have grown up in the Massif Central near the coalfields, but the coalfields themselves are less productive than those of the North and the East. Furthermore, the factories do not have the advantage of channels of communication comparable to the networks of rivers and canals in the North and the East. In any case, industries like agriculture are far from the important markets of the North, the East and the Parisian region. From all this comes a larger tendency than elsewhere to live in a closed economy. Thus we can explain that the regions of the Massif Central have been perpetual zones of fiscal rebellion, that movements like those of the Croquans have periodically reappeared in Limousin, Perigord and Quercy, that in 1848 and 1849 the resistance to taxation developed in these same provinces. In our own time the Poujadist movement started out from Haut-Quercy (now the department of Lot), and the first departments affected were the adjacent ones, the locales of fiscal sedition under the old regime (Ardant 1965: II, 784).

Tax revolts grouped together in time and space, primarily because the changes in national policy which incited them affected many localities sharing common characteristics at more or less the same time. The largest nineteenth-century bursts of tax revolts came in 1830, when the officials of the new monarchy sought to reimpose taxes on the provinces; in 1841, when the new Minister of Finances tried a special census as a step toward reorganizing the whole inequitable tax system; and in 1848 and 1849, when another revolutionary government tried to put its fiscal affairs in order.

The tax rebellion often succeeded in the short run. The tax man fled, the tollgates fell. Its success, its timing, its personnel, its very form, however, depended on the solidarity of small, local groups of taxpayers and on the vulnerability of a system of control which relied on agents dispatched from cities into treacherous hinterlands. While individual Frenchmen have shrewdly finagled and dissimulated to avoid taxes up to our own day, their capacity for collective resistance to the tax collector sank fast after the middle of the nineteenth century. When anti-tax movements revived with winegrowers after 1900, small distillers in the 1930s, or shopkeepers in the 1950s, the groups that joined the combat were no longer the taxpayers of a single commune, then of the next, but specialized regional and national associations responding to centralized direction. Marcelin Albert's Comité de Défense Viticole (in the first period), Henri Dorgères' Comités de Défense Paysanne (in the second), and Pierre Poujade's Union de Défense des Commerçants et Artisans (in the third) all adopted the defensive stance of earlier tax rebels, right down to their titles. All left violence aplenty in their wakes, but in these cases the defensive actions and the violence came after the deliberate, strenuous organization of protest groups through substantial sections of small-town France.

Changing Forms of Collective Action

Around the middle of the nineteenth century, both the scale and organizational complexity of the collective actions that normally produced violence—hence of violent action itself—increased rapidly and decisively. That happened for two related reasons: first, the scale and organizational complexity of the groups contending for power also increased rapidly and decisively, the expanding organization of industrial workers being the most notable; and second, communal groups dropped out of the struggle as the new associations, and new groups organized associationally, joined it. The organizational revolution reorganized violence.

There is something more, something the tax rebellion alone cannot reveal. Consider for a moment the point of view of the state. From that perspective the predominant forms of collective violence in France during the first half of the nineteenth century were *defensive:* tax rebellions fended off state employees; food riots beat back outside merchants; attacks on machines repelled technical innovations. The demonstrations, strikes, and rebellions which grew in importance over the century had a much larger *offensive* component; their participants reached for recognition, for a larger share, for greater power.

The crux of the contrast is the relation of the participants to organization at the national scale: the national market, the national culture, and, preeminently, the national state. In the earlier, defensive phase most of the participants were resisting the claims of national structures, especially the state. In the latter, offensive phase most of the participants were bidding for power over the operation of these national structures. In between the nation won out.

We can be more exact. Suppose by "violence" we mean damage or seizure of persons or objects. Suppose by "collective" we mean that a substantial number of people act together. (The minima may be arbitrary, later we will report what happens when we use as a threshold the participation of at least one group of fifty or more persons, plus at least one person or object damaged or seized over resistance.) In that case, "collective violence" will ordinarily grow out of some prior collective action which is not intrinsically violent: a meeting, a ceremony, a strike. A question about the causes of collective violence immediately breaks into two questions. Why do these forms of collective action occur? Why do they sometimes—but not always—end in violence?

The nationalization of politics and of economic life in France divided the major forms of collective action which commonly produced violence into three main categories.* They waxed and waned successively. The

---

* In an earlier version of this chapter (C. Tilly 1972a) as well as in other publications (C. Tilly 1969, for example), Charles Tilly has discussed "primitive," "reactionary," and "modern" forms of collective violence. We are inflicting a new terminology on our readers out of a conviction that these earlier discussions confuse the

first we will call *competitive* collective action. Competitive actions which once produced a good deal of violence include feuds, acts of rivalry between adjoining villages, recurrent ritual encounters of competing groups of artisans. Although each of these had a distinctive form, by the nineteenth century national observers tended to lump their violent forms together as *rixes:* brawls. The report of the Royal Gendarmerie for the Department of the Rhône in June 1830 expressed alarm that:

in the arrondissement of Villefranche the young men of its communes, having had some earlier conflicts, get together on holidays, Sundays, and days of fairs in groups of several communes, one against another, and fight tooth and nail; but if the Gendarmerie tries to intervene in those fights to restore good order, the combatants close ranks against the gendarmes, whom they often treat improperly, even making so bold as to attack them with stones, clubs, etc. (A.N. F^{7}6778).

Such battles are the most visible form of a general phenomenon: the constant contention among communal groups within small-scale, local political systems. They predominated, statistically at least, in France before statemakers such as Mazarin and Colbert began pressing the claims of the national state and the national economy over local commitments and resources.

That bitter struggle of the statemakers for control over the general population and its resources promoted defensive, backward-looking conflicts between different groups of local people, on the one hand, and agents of the nation, on the other. The vignette of 1768 with which this chapter began conveys part of their character. The word *reactive* describes them. The tax rebellion, the food riot, violent resistance to conscription, machine-breaking, and invasions of enclosed land rose and fell in their own rhythms. They often occurred in the course of transfers of power which our comfortable retrospect permits us to treat as progressive revolutions. Yet they had in common a tendency to involve communal groups jostled and outraged by the commotion of statemaking. This does not mean in the least that the actions of the groups involved were blind or incoherent. In October 1848 we find that the prefect of the Seine-Inférieure had first suspended exports of grains and potatoes because of a food shortage and then lifted the suspension:

---

forms of action leading to violence with the forms of violence as such. For an extended effort to work out the relations of the one to the other see C. Tilly 1974b.

Strong opposition arose at once. Groups gathered on the quay d'Ile about 10 A.M., near some ships which were loading. One of these ships, le *Blé*, was boarded by fifty workers, who started to unload the sacks of potatoes which were its cargo. They had hardly gotten fifty sacks onto the quay when they went to another ship, the English sloop *The Brothers,* which was completely loaded and preparing to sail from the outer corner of the quay. The workers climbed onto the ship themselves, towed the ship toward the bridge, and moored it in the basin, without any resistance from the crew. But the English captains raised their flags to protest against the visits their ships were receiving (*Le Siècle,* 21 October 1848).

The National Guard came to repossess the ships from the workers; after some scuffling they expelled the workers; then the ships sailed under armed guard. Only in the general pattern of such disturbances does their essential character emerge. They embodied resistance to the growth of a national market exercising priority over local needs and traditions. This was the pattern: the disturbances were clustered in areas torn between the needs of the local population and the demands of the national market; they followed a well-defined routine in which the actors assumed the places of the authorities but melted away when the authorities took the approved action, even if people remained hungry. Yet each incident, including the boarding of ships in Rouen, tended to display a kind of coherence and conscious intent which fits ill with the word usually applied: riot. From the point of view of the statemakers, such actions can only be ill-considered and disorderly; from the point of view of the participant, they are justice itself.

The state and the national market eventually triumphed. Their most difficult battles had been won by the time of our sketch of 1868; by 1968, they belonged to a fading historical memory. From the period of those eighteenth- and nineteenth-century victories by the state, *proactive* forms of collective action became the standard settings for collective violence. They are "proactive" rather than "reactive" because at least one group is making claims for rights, privileges, or resources not previously enjoyed. The deliberate attempt to seize control of the state is proactive. So are the majority of demonstrations and strikes. Daniel Guérin, a left-wing author, recollects a famous encounter between the far left and the far right. The setting is Paris, February 1934:

Toward 10 P.M., a column of marchers comes from the rue Royale, filling the whole width of the street, carrying tricolor flags. In the middle of the street gentlemen of mature and respectable appearance, with their ribbons of the Legion of Honor, shout the "Marseillaise." They don't look like rioters. Along the sidewalks, all around them, young workers in sweaters and caps sing the "Internationale." Neither of the two kinds of choristers seems inconvenienced by the presence of the other or bothered by the bizarre cacophony. Instead they give the impression of demonstrating together against the power and the police. Someone tells me they are veterans, some from the right, others from the extreme left. But most of the kids who are thundering the Red hymn aren't old enough to have been in the war.

The parade, not having been able to reach or cross the bridge, doesn't stay forever on the Place de la Concorde. And pretty soon the Place is taken over by scattered curiosity-seekers, come to see the damage left by the riot. But suddenly toward 11:30, the black curtain of demonstrators (which was still visible in the distance, on the bridge) rushes toward us in disorder. Under the influence, it seems, of a colonel of gendarmerie who, posing as History, roars "Follow me! Forward!," two columns of cops start to attack. One comes out of Cour-la-Reine toward the Champs-Elysées; the other passes between the horses of Marly where the demonstrators built a bit of barricade at the beginning of the evening, and tries to clean out the bushes of the Champs-Elysées in the direction of the Théâtre des Ambassadeurs. A crackle of gunfire breaks out. A mad panic comes over the bystanders. I have just enough time to put my bicycle on my shoulder, to run just like everyone else, as fast as my legs will carry me, to cross as best I can (given the weight of my machine) the half-barricade at the entrance to the Champs-Elysées, and at a full run try to make it to the avenue Gabriel. Bullets crash into the glass of the streetlights, which break into fragments. Next to me, people fall on their backs, all four limbs thrashing. Others crawl below the line of fire. A young man, a little farther along, complains about a burn on his ear; he touches it with his hand, which fills with blood (1970: 68).

On that February night thousands of individual experiences compounded into a grave conflict. Seventeen persons died and at least two thousand were wounded. As a more or less direct consequence, the Daladier government fell. Yet the events began with nonviolent, proactive demands for power.

This sort of collective action differs from the reactive varieties in important ways: in pivoting on attempts to control, rather than resist, different segments of the national structure; by involving relatively complex special-purpose associations rather than communal groups; through a great articulation of objectives, programs, and demands.

These characteristics imply further contrasts with reactive conflicts. One is a lesser dependency on natural congregations such as markets, church services, and festivals in favor of deliberate assemblies and shows of strength (since special-purpose associations rarely draw all their members from the same round of life but are often effective at calling together a diverse membership at crucial moments). Another is a tendency of the disturbances to be large and short. Communal groups, once committed to a conflict, rarely mobilize large numbers of men, rarely have leaders with the authority to negotiate quick compromise settlements, and rarely can call off the action rapidly and effectively; it may also be true (as it has often been argued) that communal groups have an exceptional capacity to hold out in the face of adversity. Associational groups, on the other hand, tend to become involved in violence as an outgrowth of brief, coordinated mass actions which are not intrinsically violent. Still another contrast between reactive and proactive movements is a prevalence of indignation about the loss of specific rights and privileges in the reactive cases, as compared with a greater emphasis in proactive cases on rights due as a consequence of general principles.

Two features of the shift from competitive to reactive to proactive forms of collective action as prime settings for violence stand out: the change in organization of the participants, and the change in locus of the conflict. First, the groups taking part in collective action become bigger, more complicated, more bureaucratized, more specifically committed to some public program or ideology, more open to new members prepared to support the group's special goals; earlier we called this a transfer from communal to associational bases for collective action. Second, the locus of the conflicts involved moved away from the purely local toward the national, even the international, scale; although by 1830 Frenchmen were making national revolutions and demonstrating in support of Poland, the bulk of violent conflict aligned local groups on essentially local issues; by the 1930s national issues and national antagonists took precedence. From a national perspective this change seemed to involve a "politicization" of conflict.

The trouble with that way of stating it is the fact that the competitive and reactive forms of collective action also grew out of well-developed struggles for power, out of political conflicts on a smaller scale. The tax rebellion, the food riot, the invasion of fields, and even the artisans' brawl pivoted on local questions of rights, duties, and power. For that reason, we would be better off speaking of a "na-

tionalization" of conflict, integrally related to the nationalization of
political life. In our own day we may have to speak of a further stage of
"internationalization."

It is wrong to picture competitive, reactive, and proactive collective
action as three distinct, exclusive stages. That image has two defects.
First, some communal groups gradually acquire associational characteristics, yet retain their capacity for collective action throughout the process:
a city's traditional elite joins a national pressure group; a religious
community becomes a corporation. During the transformation their characteristic *forms* of collective action, and thus of collective violence, also
change. Second, the proactive forms of collective action emerged early
in those sectors of French social life in which the national structures
emerged early: major cities, areas of advanced industry, the hinterland of
Paris, and so on. At the center of the centralized French system, men had
begun struggling for control of the state and the national market centuries before their brothers at the periphery stopped fighting the expansion
of the state and the market. The rapid nineteenth-century transition from
predominantly reactive to predominantly proactive forms of collective
action resembled the movement from one terrain to another rather than
the passage of a guarded frontier. We might visualize the statistical distribution of violence emerging from each of the major forms of collective
action as that shown in Figure 5.

In the absence of reasonable criteria for the "amount" of collective violence and of reasonable data for the period before the nineteenth century,
the exact shapes of the curves represent no more than informed specula-

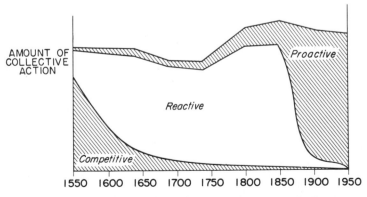

Figure 5. Hypothetical Evolution of Collective Action in France.

tion. The biggest speculation is that the volume of reactive violence swelled rapidly during the heroic statemaking of Louis XIII and Louis XIV. We know that popular rebellions of a reactive form abounded at that time, but too little work has been done on conflicts well before and well after the Fronde to verify the general timing. The graph rests on a firmer factual footing in stating that reactive conflicts rose to a nineteenth-century peak, instead of gradually diminishing. The real point of the diagram, however, is to portray the slow displacement of competitive by reactive forms of collective action as the French state extended its claims, and the rapid displacement of reactive by proactive collective action during the nineteenth-century nationalization of the struggle for power.

The Timing of Violence

After the Revolution the major periods of significant collective violence in France were:

1830–1832, beginning with the antecedents of the July Revolution and ending with a great miscellany of rebellions touching the whole range of French politics;

1846–1851, running from the last great round of food riots, through the February Revolution and the June Days of 1848, on past another farrago of tax rebellions, machine-breaking, and other conflicts, all the way to the angry but unavailing response to Louis Napoleon's 1851 coup;

1869–1871, starting with massive, violent strikes and ending with the repression of the Commune;

the trio 1891–1893, 1902–1906, and 1911–1913, in which major conflicts growing out of strikes occurred; in 1902–1906 struggles over the separation of church and state as well as widespread protests by wine-growers supplemented the continuing conflicts involving industrial workers;

1934–1937, with its great, rowdy demonstrations and strikes of all varieties;

1947–1948, encompassing a wide range of postwar struggles for power;

1958, the revolution—or coup, depending on your perspective—which brought De Gaulle to power.

The Chronology in the Appendix provides more details on the kind of events making up each of these clusters of collective violence.

The calendar of events just reeled off results from an intuitive combination of scale and importance. "Importance" depends on our judgment of what happened, or what could have happened, afterward. The year 1958 is a case in point—not actually a year of extraordinary killing and smashing, but one in which rebellions brought about the end of a regime. If we restrict our attention to scale alone, the relative weights of the different periods change somewhat. Figures 6, 7, and 8, portray the quantitative ebb and flow of collective violence in France between 1830 and 1960. The incidents represented include any event in which at least one group of fifty persons or more took direct part in an action during which some persons or objects were damaged or seized over resistance. The graphs record the incidents encountered in a day-by-day reading of two national newspapers throughout the entire period. (For details on the method, see the Appendix.) Because of the method and the sources our estimates are more reliable for the periods from 1830 to 1860 and from 1930 to 1960 than for the period from 1861 through 1929. Within each of those periods, nevertheless, we are fairly confident that the curves record the major fluctuations.

Figure 6 shows the number of violent incidents, smoothed into five-year moving averages for easier reading. Figures 7 and 8 present parallel information for our estimates of participants in such incidents and of arrests occurring in their course. Even with the smoothing, the graphs point up the wide contrast among adjacent blocks of years, the presence of some periods (especially those of extensive repression such as the 1850s) with almost no collective violence at all, and the rough correspondence of major bursts of collective violence with major crises of the French political system.

The peaks are interesting. The year 1848 produced more disturbances than any other single year. Yet the massive strikes and demonstrations just after 1900 and again in the 1930s produced sets of violent incidents as large as any comparable segments of the nineteenth century. The postwar period, though less turbulent in this respect than the 1930s, was far from calm. The enormous participation of 1968, after all, came in the years following the end of our curves. Collective violence did not fade away with modernization.

The major bursts of violent conflict accompanied the largest realignments of the French political system, and vice versa. Violence and politi-

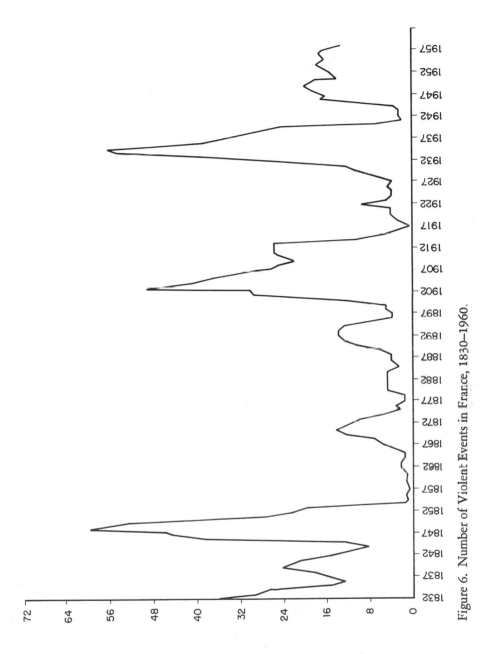

Figure 6. Number of Violent Events in France, 1830–1960.

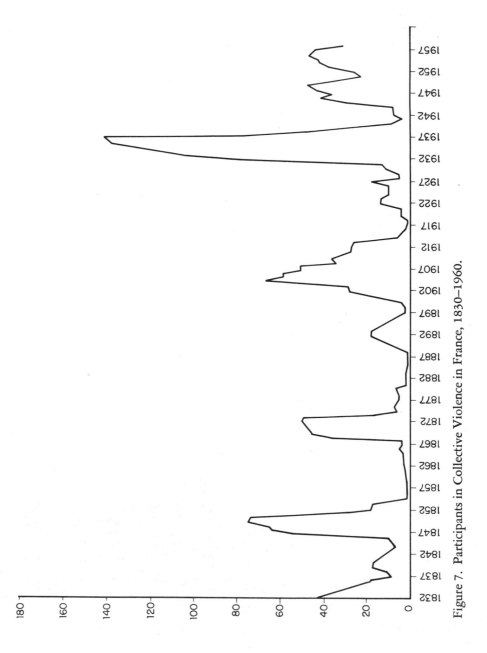

Figure 7. Participants in Collective Violence in France, 1830–1960.

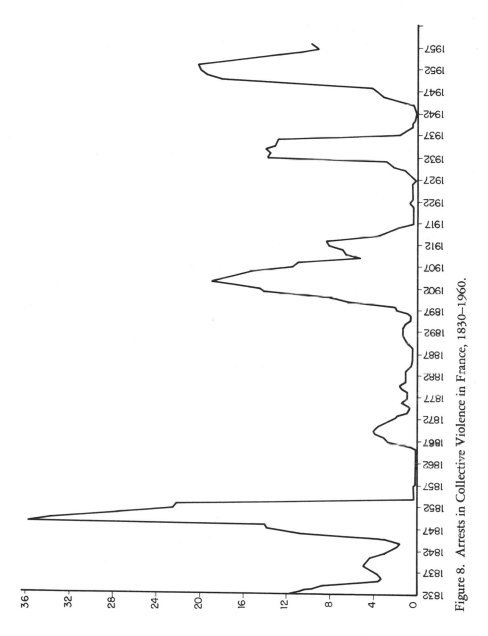

Figure 8. Arrests in Collective Violence in France, 1830–1960.

cal change depended on each other to an important extent. Although that general rule holds visibly for 1830, 1848, and the Popular Front period, our graphs pose two puzzles concerning the period between 1848 and the Popular Front. First, was the violence of 1870–1871 greater than our figures say? The curve of participants shows the substantial upswing one might expect, but the number of incidents and the volume of arrests are relatively low. Part of the answer lies in the fact that the bulk of the arrests growing out of the Paris Commune occurred after the fighting had stopped, and therefore did not enter into our statistics. At least 30,000 arrests disappeared that way. Also, the fact that the Communes of 1871— which sprang to life in Brest, Limoges, Toulouse, Narbonne, Marseille, St. Etienne, Lyon, and Le Creusot as well as in Paris—tended to produce day after day of violent encounters instead of the intense but more scattered conflicts of 1848 or 1934. As a consequence, we count the conflict of 1871 as a relatively small number of events involving many people. So the comparatively small amount of collective violence enumerated in that period is to some extent a function of our procedures.* Since we used the same procedures throughout the rest of the period from 1830 to 1960, however, we have little choice but to treat 1870–1871 as a doubtful case in the correlation between extent of violence and extent of political change.

Second puzzle: Was the realignment of 1900–1910 as great as our graphs suggest? In terms of incidents, participants, and arrests, the peak of 1904–1907 is one of France's three or four greatest since the end of the Napoleonic Wars. Yet historians do not customarily treat that period as a great transition. There we feel more confident than in the case of 1870–1871. Isn't that just the period in which the Church lost its favored political position and organized labor first gained power at a national

* As this book goes to press in the fall of 1974, we have almost finished a thorough review of our enumeration of violent events from 1861 to 1929. It reveals that, compared to the earlier and later periods, we consistently underenumerated the events of those sixty-nine years; the underenumeration appears to have been greater in the 1870s than in the other six decades. With that exception, the downward bias was fairly constant from one year to the next, and the year-to-year fluctuations were therefore recorded without too much distortion. We conclude tentatively that the crisis of 1870–1871 produced its expected peak of events and participants, but that the 1904–1907 surge of violence is greater than standard histories lead one to expect.

level? Haven't most historians underestimated the importance of those political shifts because the regime survived?

Let us note for later discussion some other significant features of the calendar of collective violence. (1) There was no particular tendency for violent protests to concentrate during or after the principal surges of urban expansion or industrial growth. Our curves offer no support for the idea that the pace of urbanization and industrialization itself determines the amount of protest. (2) The turbulence of 1846–1851 was the last in which reactive collective action played a large part. After that, the tax rebellion, the food riot, machine-breaking, and similar events virtually disappeared. (3) Periods of strong repression and central control—notably the early years of the Second Empire and the two World Wars—produced little or no collective violence.* (4) Despite all the fluctuations, France remained as violent in the twentieth century as she had been in the nineteenth; advanced industrialism did not bring domestic peace.

The transformations wrought by industrialization changed the contenders, the style of conflict, and the prizes to be gained in French politics. But the rhythm of collective violence itself depended very little on the timing of population movements, changes in the organization of work, or the introduction of technological innovations. It depended very much on shifts in the struggle for political power.

The curves of incidents, participants, and arrests resemble one another: there can be no participants without incidents, and the number of participants limits the number of arrests. The discrepancies among the three facets of collective violence are still interesting: the curves show a tendency for the number of people taking part in the average violent incident to rise over the long run and to expand in times of major crisis. Crises from which the existing government emerges victorious—1851 is a good example—tend to produce large ratios of arrests to participants. On the one side, we see the effects of mobilization; on the other, the effects of repression.

* Important qualification: the enumeration excludes acts of war with an external enemy. It thus distorts the actual level of violence in the territory of France during 1870, 1914–1918, and 1940–1944. The point is simply that violent conflict *among* Frenchmen declined in these periods.

Nineteenth-Century versus Twentieth-Century Patterns

We have much richer information concerning the first three decades (1830–1860) and the last three (1930–1960) than about the years between. Let us concentrate on them. The curve of incidents for the thirty-one years from 1830 to 1860 peaks in 1832, 1848, and 1851. The year 1832 brought a crisis; it eliminated the major enemies of the regime which had come to power in the Revolution of 1830, and consolidated the new regime's control over the country as a whole. There was an unsuccessful insurrection in Paris; its defeat practically completed the elimination of organized republicans and workers from the coalition which had made the 1830 revolution. There were also threatening guerrilla movements in the West, not to mention food riots and tax rebellions in several different parts of the kingdom (for details, see Rule and Tilly 1972).

Eighteen hundred and forty-eight brought a revolution with much wider participation than that of 1830. For the first time organized workers played a major part in the transfer of power; they remained involved in collective violence for the next two years. Nevertheless, many of the violent incidents of 1848 were tax rebellions, food riots, land occupations, and other classic reactive movements. They were related to the revolution—as any collective action then had to be—but they were not in any simple sense part of the effort to overthrow the previous regime. The so-called Forty-Five Centime Revolt of 1848–1849, for example, was one of the most widespread tax rebellions France ever produced. It arose as a form of resistance to the forty-five-centime surcharge the revolutionary regime placed on standard land taxes.

The violent conflicts of 1851, to take the third peak, occurred mainly in the course of the resistance to Louis Napoleon's coup d'état. The well-prepared coup came at the beginning of December; 76 of the 93 violent incidents we have enumerated for the entire year came in its immediate aftermath. In town after town the republicans and radicals, who had mobilized in 1848 and had felt a slow squeeze after that, declared their opposition to Louis Napoleon's suspension of the constitution, seized control of the local government, held out for a day or two, but succumbed to the government troops that swept across the country. Around 90,000 people took part in violent incidents during December 1851; over 25,000

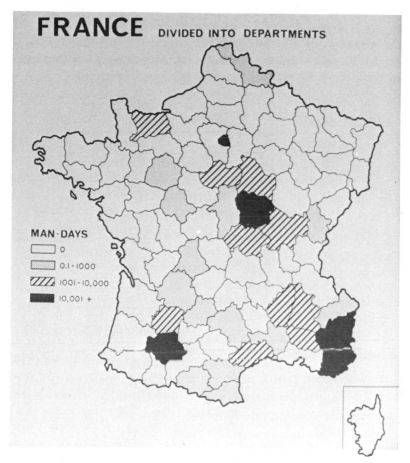

Figure 9. French Insurrection of 1851. Man-Days by Department.

were arrested for complicity, some in a general cleanup of the regime's enemies but most of them because of some form of involvement in the insurrection itself. Figure 9 is a map showing participation expressed in man-days (500 man-days could be 500 people for one day, 250 people for two days, or 125 people for four days). It is fundamentally the same as the map of arrests in C. Tilly 1972. As usual, Paris and the Seine stand out. But the largest totals come from the departments of the South and Southeast: Basses-Alpes, Gers, Var, Hérault, Nièvre, Drôme, Vaucluse. The map is broadly similar to the distribution of leftist strength at the beginning of the Third Republic. After the army and the courts put down the opposition, collective violence on any scale virtually disappeared from

France for more than a decade. What Howard Payne (1966) calls the "Police State of Louis Napoleon Bonaparte" locked itself into place.

World War II divides the second three-decade period in half. That violent interlude appears calm in the graph because acts of international war are not included. Most of the terror and counter-terror of Occupation and Resistance involved small groups of people, too few and too dispersed to meet our criteria. The great years for open, violent confrontation were 1934, a year of constant demonstrations and of street fights growing from the demonstrations, and 1947, a year of massive, often insurrectionary, strikes.

Between 1930 and 1960, the most turbulent series of years ran from 1934 to 1937, and from 1947 to 1952. In the first period two related struggles were going on: one over the place of labor and its representatives in the structure of power; the other between far-right nationalists and far-left internationalists. The arrival of the Popular Front gave the temporary advantage to the leaders of organized labor and to the internationalists. But World War II undid much of their success.

Organized labor played a fundamental role in the conflicts of 1947–1952, while the discredited far right was nowhere to be seen. Then the key points of contention were the relation of the Communists to the government and the relation of the French government to that of the United States. Between 1947 and 1952, however, the weight shifted as the French economy came back to health, France joined NATO, and the Communists settled into their role as a vigorous opposition party within the system. In 1947 the most important contexts for collective violence were demonstrations and direct actions against governmental economic controls and policies early in the year, and much more extensive strikes—including general strikes with occupations of railway stations, city halls, and factories—late in the year. By 1952, anticolonial demonstrations by North Africans and nationwide protests against the installation of U.S. General Ridgeway in France as NATO commander had become the chief settings for collective violence.

The geography of collective violence changed from the nineteenth to the twentieth century, as Figures 10 and 11 show. These maps indicate the estimated number of participants in collective violence per year in each department, expressed as a rate per 100,000 population. For France

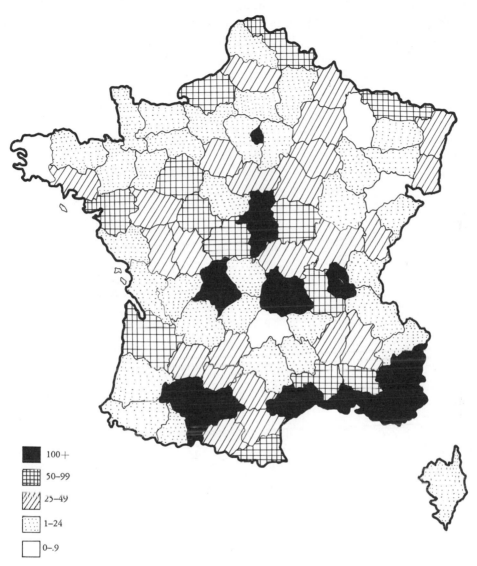

Figure 10. Participants in Collective Violence by Department, 1830–1860 (rate per year per 100,000 population).

as a whole the estimated participation rate was 79 from 1830 through 1860, and 105 from 1930 through 1960—a significant, but not enormous, increase.

The geographic pattern altered much more than the general level. During the three nineteenth-century decades collective violence spread

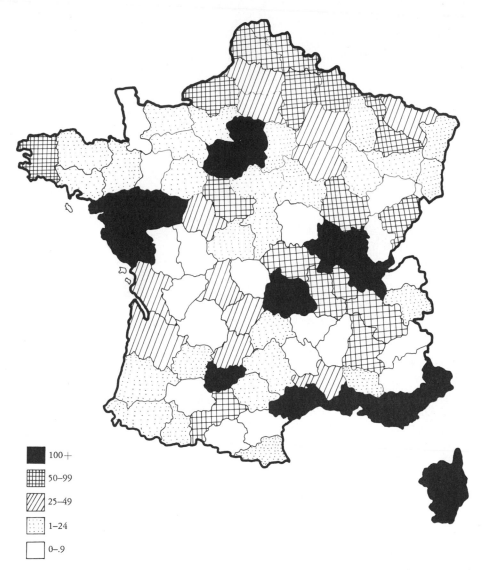

Figure 11. Participants in Collective Violence by Department, 1930–1960 (rate per year per 100,000 population).

across the entire country. The only departments which contributed no events to our sample for 1830–1860 were Cantal, Meuse, and Haute-Saône. Furthermore, predominantly rural departments were well represented among the high-violence areas: the Basses-Alpes had a rate of 316 participants per year per 100,000 population, the Gers 225, the Var 150.

The rural departments with very high levels of violence were essentially those which were turbulent from 1848 to 1851.

As expected, the departments containing France's major cities also had high rates of participation. The Seine (Paris) towered over all, with 816; Bouches-du-Rhône (Marseille) had 224, Rhône (Lyon) 297, Haute-Garonne (Toulouse) 240. Loire-Inférieure (Nantes) with 54 and Gironde (Bordeaux) with 67 were lower than a strict urban rank order would require. The southern half of France—especially the regions of Lyon, Toulouse, and Marseille—ranked higher than the north.

From this composite of many different kinds of conflict we discern two major kinds of high-violence area: major urban centers and their hinterlands; and peripheral rural areas being brought under the political and economic control of Paris, Lyon, and Marseille. A closer look would reveal demonstrations, strikes, and attempts to seize power concentrated in the first set, and food riots, tax rebellions, anti-conscription movements, and the like concentrated in the second.

From 1930 to 1960 the metropolitan centers dominated the map of collective violence much more than they had in the previous century. The regions of Paris, Nantes, Toulouse, Marseille, Lille, and Lyon account for the bulk of participants. This time, eighteen departments and the territory of Belfort have no violent events at all. Another dozen had only one or two small incidents.

At the other extreme, the Seine still leads with 411 participants per year per 100,000 population, but Loire-Inférieure (Nantes) is close behind with 406; Alpes-Maritimes (Nice; and not part of France before 1860) follows with 348, Bouches-du-Rhône (Marseille) with 216. Violent conflict has moved northward, although the southern regions still have more than their share. The industrial northeast is now better-represented. By contrast, the areas which experienced dramatic out-migration—the Massif Central and, especially, the mountains—went from relative turbulence in the nineteenth century to almost complete silence in the twentieth. By and large, the rural departments which were strongly involved in collective violence lay within the immediate vicinities of major cities.

The principal exceptions to that rule result from industrial conflicts in the cities of predominantly rural departments. For example, the Drôme's relatively high rate for 1930–1960 (72 participants per year per 100,000 population) is due to two major strikes: at Romans in December 1938, where shoe workers occupied their factory in the aftermath of a CGT-called general strike; and at Valence in December 1947, where strikers and demonstrators seized the railroad station in the course of a nation-wide strike movement spearheaded by the Communists. Likewise, the collective violence of Puy-de-Dôme resulted almost entirely from strike-related conflicts at Clermont-Ferrand.

The most dubious cases are Corsica (where the violence of the 1943 Liberation and the 1958 insurrection accompanies routine strike violence) and Vendée (where anti-tax movements shook la Roche-sur-Yon several times after World War II; la Roche-sur-Yon's attachment to Nantes's hinterland is debatable). Even in Vendée and Corsica, where the countryside had been quite turbulent in the nineteenth century, the major cities produced the collective violence of the twentieth century. In short, violence urbanized. It moved toward the large industrial concentrations. It gravitated toward the centers of power.

A breakdown of the magnitude of violent incidents by decade for 1830 to 1860 and 1930 to 1960 appears in Table 1. The table uses statistics similar to those commonly used in the reporting of strikes. It shows that the number of people involved in collective violence rose somewhat over the century of modernization: 850,000 in the first period, 1,300,000 in the second. The rate of violent incidents ran around 7 or 8 per decade per million population. (That is, 0.7 or 0.8 per million per year; strikes in contemporary France, Britain, and Italy are forty or fifty times as frequent as that.) The rate of participation ran between 3,000 and 17,700 per million population per decade. (To get annual rates comparable to our maps, divide by 100: the range is then from 30 to 177 participants per year per 100,000 population.)

The figures show a considerable rise in the mean number of participants and a drop in the mean days the average participant spent in a violent encounter. As a result, we find a fluctuation without trend in the total man-days spent in incidents. With due allowance for the repeaters who participated in encounter after encounter, the data make it appear possible that as many as one Frenchman out of a hundred took part in a collective action producing violence at some time during the average decade. If we considered only adults and only towns in which violent incidents actually

Table 1. The volume of collective violence in France, 1830–1860 and 1930–1960

Period	Number of incidents	Incidents per million population	Total participants	Participants per incident	Man-days per participant	Participants per million population
1830–1839	258	7.7	300,000	1,100	1.7	8,400
1840–1849	295	8.3	450,000	1,450	1.7	12,300
1850–1859	116	3.2	100,000	900	1.6	3,000
1930–1939	336	8.0	750,000	2,200	1.0	17,700
1940–1949	93	2.3	200,000	2,400	1.0	5,500
1950–1960	169	4.0	350,000	2,200	1.0	8,600

occurred the figure would be more like one in twenty. In either case, a small minority, but not a negligible one.

The figures show that from the nineteenth to the twentieth century, the typical violent event became shorter, and bigger. As a consequence, the number of man-days absorbed by the average event changed relatively little. To be sure, the decades varied considerably in the number of violent incidents, and therefore in the *total* man-days they brought into violent action. The ten years from 1840 through 1849 produced the greatest volume of incidents as measured by total man-days, but the 1930s produced a larger number of incidents. The total energy flowing into collective violence and the kinds of particles in which the energy was emitted varied somewhat independently of each other.

We are actually dealing with two interlocking processes, one determining the shape of the typical event, the other determining the frequency of events. The long, slow process of association, the move from communal to association bases for political action, lies behind the change in shape of the typical disturbance. In the 1830s the typical violent incident (whether invasion of fields, tax rebellion, or food riot) would bring men, women, and children from the same small area out in anger for a day, and then another, and then perhaps still another. By the 1930s the typical incident was the political party's one-day show of strength in a major city: a demonstration which often attracted determined counter-demonstrators, and frequently led to scuffles, or pitched battles, with the police. Associations came to be the important mobilizers of collective action, and thus the important participants in collective violence.

The other process affected the number of violent incidents at any particular time. It was (and is) a complex political process governing the occasions on which different contenders for power take collective action to assert their strength, defend their right, or vent their anger as well as the frequency with which such collective actions produce violence. The two questions are separate. A repressive government like that of Vichy holds down collective violence by making collective action of any sort difficult and costly. Whether repressive or not, a government faced with strikes, sit-ins, demonstrations, or other collective actions which, if illegal, are not intrinsically violent, has a considerable choice of tactics for dealing with them. Some tactics lead to killing and wounding.

Combat in front of the Ministry of Foreign Affairs, Paris, February 1848

Attack on the barricade of the Place du Petit Pont, Paris, June 1848

The omnibus strike of 1891

Peasant and police in Champagne, 1911

Demonstration of winegrowers of the Aube, 1911

A demonstrator seized by the police, about 1915

Leon Blum speaks during the general strike of 1936

On the other side, when new contenders for power are appearing or old ones are losing their places, the frequency of collective action rises; with it rises the possibility of violence. And as associations become more prominent in the struggle for power, the people who lead them gain a certain ability both to move their followers around and to calculate the probability that one action or another will lead to violence. They therefore acquire some of the same control over the frequency of violence that the state ordinarily possesses. So the number of violent incidents at a given point in time is a function of the intensity of the political struggle and the tactics of the contenders.

Economic Fluctuations, Disorder, and Collective Violence

A similar pair of interlocking processes—one organizational, the other broadly political—seems to have determined the evolution of strike activity in France (Shorter and Tilly, 1970, 1974). From the 1880s, when the first really comprehensive data on strikes became available, to the Second World War, the average number of strikers per strike rose irregularly from two hundred to around seven hundred. After remaining around five or six days for decades, on the other hand, the median duration fell precipitously to a single day sometime during or after the massive unionization of the Popular Front. Strikes also became big, but of short duration. The timing is different from that of the transformations of collective violence, but the processes are surely related. In both cases complex organizations, not only capable of mobilizing people for protest but also fairly effective in demobilizing them once the issue was decided, assumed a larger and larger role in the preparation of encounters between contenders and authorities.

The number of strikes at any given time and place, on the other hand, has fluctuated enormously in response to the intensity of grievances, the extent of labor organization, and the negotiating tactics of labor and management. Over the very long run, aggregate strike activity has risen enormously in France as the labor force has industrialized, but within the industrial labor force itself the rate has tended neither up nor down. Industrial conflict and collective violence have a lot in common. In both, the form of the individual conflict depends on the organizational structure of the contenders and changes with that structure; the frequency of con-

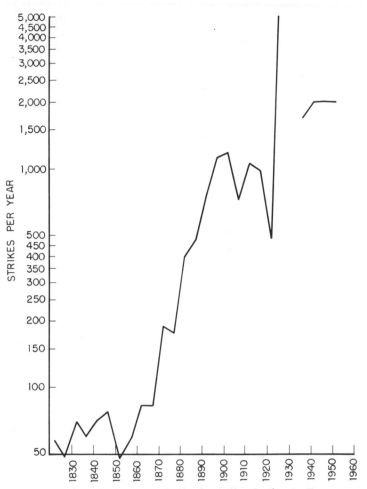

Source: Edward Shorter and Charles Tilly, *Strikes in France, 1830 to 1968* (New York: Cambridge University Press, 1974).

Figure 12. Average Number of Strikes in France, for Five-Year Intervals, 1830–1964.

flicts depends more directly on the give-and-take of the struggle for power.

There is also some similarity in timing between strike activity and collective violence. The evidence on strikes converges on the following periods as the outstanding times of acceleration in strike activity: 1833–1834, 1840, 1870–1872, 1880–1882, 1890–1893, 1899–1907, 1919–1920, 1936–1938, 1947–1949, and 1966–1968. Each of these periods had more

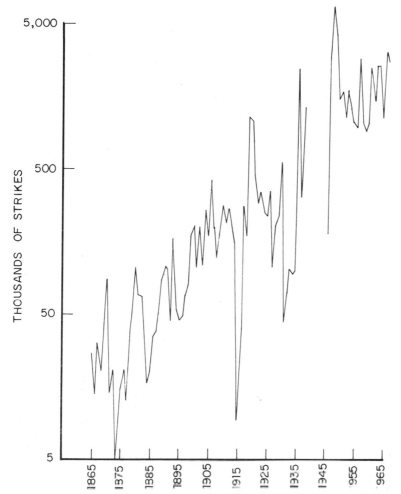

Source: Edward Shorter and Charles Tilly, *Strikes in France, 1830 to 1968* (New York: Cambridge University Press, 1974).

Figure 13. Number of Strikers per Year in France, 1865–1967.

strikers per year than the previous one. (However, 1936 set the all-time high for individual strikes: 16,907 by our count.) Figure 12 presents five-year averages of our best estimates for numbers of strikes between 1830 and 1964, and Figure 13 gives the number of participants in strikes for single years from 1865 to 1967.

Strikes were illegal in France until 1864 and poorly reported before 1885; accordingly, before those dates the figures are rougher than those which come after. Still, the graphs leave little doubt that strike activity accelerated almost continuously from the 1860s up to World War I, accelerated again in the 1930s, and remained high after World War II. We see an enormous increase in the total number of strikers (as well as the number of workers taking part in the average strike) after 1946. If the official totals for 1968 are ever released they will show that momentous year to have brought out more strikers than ever before—more than the 6.6 million strikers of 1948.

To some extent the schedule of strike activity fits the calendar of collective violence. At least that seems to be the case from the 1880s onward. Before that time our uncertain data suggest an alternation between collective violence and strike activity; afterward, they tend to go together. The correlations of year-to-year variation in strike activity and collective violence reported in Table 2 reveal a weak negative relationship from 1870 to 1890 and moderate to strong positive relationships in various periods between 1890 and 1960. More detailed analyses of the same data (Shorter and Tilly 1974) show that the general pattern olds up after allowances for trend, unionization, and economic fluctuations. The relationship appears to be valid.

Yet it is not true that either strikes or collective violence ebbed and flowed in immediate response to the pace of structural change. We might look back to the signs we have already inspected. The great periods of economic expansion in France came between 1855 and 1870, 1920 and 1930, 1945 and 1960. The first period started quietly and ended raucously. After a turbulent initial year, the second period produced little violent protest. The third saw insurrectionary years alternate with merely dis-

Table 2. Correlations of annual variations in collective violence and strike activity, 1870–1960

Period	Number of violent Incidents with		Participants in collective Violence with	
	Strikers per year	Strikes per year	Strikes per year	Strikers per year
1870–1890	—.15	—.20	—.32	—.30
1890–1913	.44	.63	.47	.65
1920–1938	.43	.32	.19	.05
1946–1960	.63	.29	.69	.24

orderly ones. The years of substantial downswing and depression were roughly 1870–1875, 1914–1920, 1931–1945 (with some small relief just before the war). The first period began with one of France's great revolutionary moments. The second, after the external disorder and internal order of World War I, ended with nationwide protests. The third might have been continuously turbulent if a brutal war had not diverted French attentions both inward and outward from the national political arena. One might argue a complex connection between economic *contraction* and protest, with the immediate proviso that war counteracts even that connection. But the interdependence between collective violence and the timing of economic growth is very weak, very complicated, or both.

During the period preceding 1860 there was some small correspondence between price swings and collective violence, resulting mainly from the rise of food riots in years of high prices. Figure 14 presents two composite price series for the years from 1825 to 1860. The score is about fiftyfifty: the high prices of 1838–1841 and 1846–1847 did correspond to the secondary bursts of protest in those years, and the lower prices of the middle 1830s and early 1840s did coincide with periods of relative peace, but neither 1830 or 1848 was an especially high-priced year; the great leap upward in prices of the 1850s may have distressed many people, but it did not lead them into collective violence. (A last scattering of food riots occurred in 1853 and 1854, but they were small and few by comparison with 1847 or 1839.) In short, this comparison produces little more evidence of any straightforward determination of protest by economic fluctuation.

Since the timing of mechanization, of new industrial employment, of technical innovation, and even of urban growth followed approximately the same calendar as that of overall economic expansion, the conclusion is a more general one. If there is a connection between the pace of structural change and the frequency of violent conflict, it is not a direct, mechanical one. Fast social change, does not, for all its bewilderments, incite disorder immediately or reliably. The relationship does not resemble that between the pushing of the button and the ringing of the doorbell. A better analogy might be the relation between the performance of an automobile and the stamping of the dies used in making its parts: indelible but indirect.

It could still be true that collective violence, as one type of "disorder,"

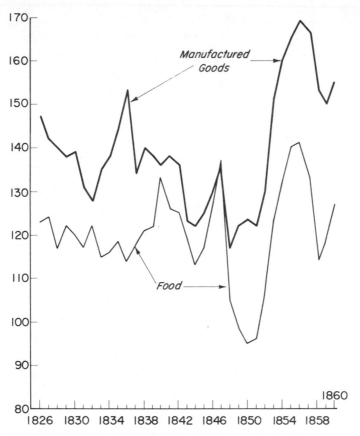

Figure 14. Wholesale Price Indexes, France 1825–1960.

appears with other signs of social disintegration and thus reflects a general weakening of social cohesion and control. Do the variations of conventional indexes of social disorganization in France correspond to those of violent conflict? We can at least examine fluctuations in reported suicide and crime.

Since Emile Durkheim wrote his famous *Suicide,* sociologists have usually been willing to accept the frequency of suicide as an indicator of the extent of social disintegration. France has long had an exceptionally high rate of suicide, a fact which seems to dovetail with her tendency to lapse into political chaos. But what of fluctuations in the reported rate (Figure 15)? During the nineteenth century the rate of suicide marched inexorably upward, almost heedless of political transformations; during the twentieth it has been relatively steady, except for the declines in suicide at the

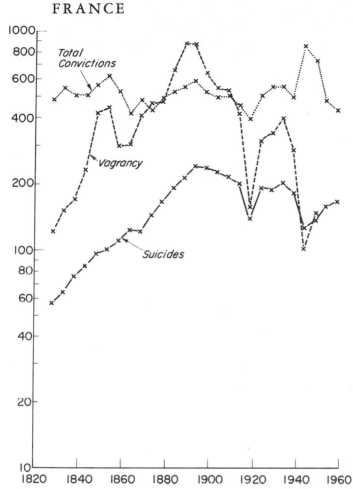

Sources: *Annuaire statistique de la France: Résumé rétrospectif, 1966,* tables 4, 5, pp. 114–127, tables 3 9, pp. 161–166. Émile Levasseur, *La population française* (Paris: Rousseau, 1889–1893), II, 126. Maurice Halbwachs, *Les causes du suicide* (Paris: Alcan, 1930), p. 92. "Total convictions" sums convictions in Cours d'assises, Tribunaux correctionnels, and (after 1952) Cours d'appel; the figure is an annual average rate per 100,000 population over the five-year interval centering on the date shown. "Vagrancy" presents arrests for *mendicité* and *vagabondage;* it is also an annual average rate per 100,000 population over the same five-year intervals. "Suicide" is reported cause of death, calculated as an annual average rate per 100,000 population over the same five-year intervals.

Figure 15. Criminal Convictions, Vagrancy, and Suicide in France, 1826–1960.

times of the two World Wars. The all-time peak came near 1890, about the time Durkheim began his study of the phenomenon. Since then, Frenchmen have destroyed themselves (or, at least, have been reported as destroying themselves, the incompleteness of suicide reporting being considerable) less often. At this level there is no detectable correspondence between suicide and collective violence.

Does crime come closer? Criminal statistics have some of the same weaknesses as suicide statistics. They ordinarily describe actions of the state—arrests, convictions, incarcerations, and so forth—rather than actions of its citizens. They therefore vary with the repressive powers and proclivities of the government. In the case at hand, the statistics include some of the direct responses of various French governments to political disturbances. At any rate, the figures for crime fit the temporal pattern of collective violence only a trifle better than do the figures for suicide.

Look at vagrancy, which one might expect to have some connection with the availability of insurrectionary masses. Arrests for vagrancy did rise dramatically before 1848 and again before 1870, as well as less emphatically in the early 1930s. They reached their greatest height, on the other hand, around 1890; that was not the century's vintage year for violence. They remained exceptionally low in the troubled years following World War II. If there is a connection there, it is mediated and attenuated by other factors.

The figures for total criminal convictions in France have maxima around 1833, 1852, 1894, 1912, 1934, 1942. They are at least in the vicinity of considerable clusters of violence. Their distribution might possibly justify the inference that repression tends to *follow* major upheavals, rather than that outbreaks of crime and collective violence come together. However, the violent years of the 1860s and 1870s were actually low points for criminal convictions. The turbulent period from 1944 to 1948 produced a significant decline in convictions. The record crime levels of World War II surely had more to do with the repressive policies of Vichy and the Nazis than with any tendency for disorder to run rampant through France.

If we narrow our attention to major crimes (those prosecuted by the Assize Courts) and separate property crimes from crimes against persons, something interesting appears. Figure 16 shows the rates of crimes against persons and property per 100,000 population in France as a whole for

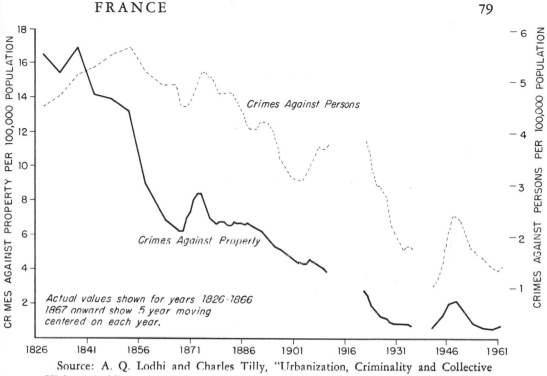

Actual values shown for years 1826-1866
1867 onward show .5 year moving
centered on each year.

Crimes Against Persons

Crimes Against Property

Source: A. Q. Lodhi and Charles Tilly, "Urbanization, Criminality and Collective Violence in Nineteenth-Century France," *American Journal of Sociology,* 79: 296–318.

Figure 16. Crimes against Persons and Property in France, 1826–1962.

census years from 1826 to 1962. The rate of major crimes against persons —murder, poisoning, infanticide, patricide—barely changed over the entire period. The rate of major crimes against property—theft, robbery, and willful destruction—plummeted down, down, down—from 160 per 100,000 in the 1820s to 10 in the 1930s. The only significant reversals were a climb to 174 in 1836, a sharp rise between 1866 and 1872 (resulting probably more from the loss of low-crime territories to the Germans than from a rise in French criminal propensities) and a minor increase after World War II.

There is no correspondence at all between these criminal trends and trends in collective violence. We are inclined to attribute the steady decline in property crime to the spread of policing, but that is debatable. In any case, it deals a hard blow to the notions that twentieth-century urban society is more "disorderly" than nineteenth-century agrarian society was, and that crime rises and falls as a function of the pace of social change.

Analyzing the geography of crime and of collective violence (at least in the nineteenth century) points the same direction. Statistical analyses of the eighty-six French departments from 1836 to 1851 reveal a strong association of the rate of property crime with the current urbanity of the department, a slight negative association with the extent of heavy industry, and little or no association with the rate of urban growth, the pace of migration, or the amount of collective violence (Lodhi and Tilly 1973). Crimes against persons display a strong regional pattern—for example, an extraordinarily high rate of homicide in Corsica and along the Mediterranean—but there is no significant association with industry, urban growth, and so on.

The geographic patterns of crime are fairly stable from year to year. The geography of collective violence, on the other hand, shifts markedly and rapidly, depending on the groups and issues currently in contention. The year 1841, for example, had thirty-six violent incidents, mainly tax rebellions and acts of resistance to the census. In that year there was a correlation of +.29 between the urbanity of a department and the number of participants in collective violence. (The correlations of urbanity with numbers wounded and arrested were much higher, +.89 and +.80; the higher correlations probably resulted from the greater concentration of the government's repressive force in urban areas.) When allowance is made for the effects of other variables, the association of collective violence with urbanity persists, while the independent effect of the current rate of urban growth appears to be nil and the effect of recent in-migration negative.

In 1851, the year of the massive rebellion against the coup d'état, the association of participation and urbanity disappears: +.02, and the coefficients for the number wounded and arrested weaken to +.82 and +.54. This time, however, allowing for other variables restores the importance of urban population. But it does so with a portrayal of the ideal setting for violence as a thinly populated, nonindustrial but relatively urban department currently losing population to out-migration. That is not, in fact, a bad description of the peripheral departments that were still fighting back in 1851.

Most of our over-time observations can be summed up in an elementary statistical way. Let us group the variables into two families: breakdown and hardship variables, and organization and power variables. The division is somewhat arbitrary, but it follows the distinction between "breakdown" and "solidarity" arguments with which we began. Within each category, let us examine the correlation coefficients between single-year values of each variable and the magnitudes of collective violence in the same years. Tables 3 and 4 lay out the results.

The correlations with time simply show whether collective violence tended to rise or fall significantly over the entire period from 1830 to 1960. They reveal no trend whatsoever for number of violent incidents and for arrests, but a weak tendency for the total number of participants in collective violence to rise over the long run. That much we could have guessed from earlier graphs and tables. The other items in the breakdown-hardship table—suicide, crime, prices, production, real wages, major crimes tried before the Assizes—generally show negligible relationships with collective violence. The only possible exceptions worth noting are the weak negative correlation of major crimes with each of the violence measures, and the weak-to-moderate positive correlations (+.27 and +.26) between arrests and current prices for food and manufactured goods. The first relation is the wrong direction for breakdown arguments. Since the corresponding correlations with number of incidents and

Table 3. Correlations of collective violence with "breakdown" and "hardship" variables

Variable	Period	Number of violent incidents	Participants in collective violence	Arrests in collective violence
Time	1830–1960	.00	.15	.02
Number of suicides	1830–1959	.00	.05	.02
Manufactured goods prices	1830–1954	.05	.09	.27
Food prices	1830–1954	.08	—.14	.26
Industrial production	1830–1960	.10	—.14	—.12
Real wages	1840–1954	.03	.13	.04
Major crimes	1865–1960	—.16	—.17	—.15

Table 4. Correlations of collective violence with "organization" and "power" variables.

Variable	Period	Number of violent incidents	Participants in collective violence	Arrests in collective violence
Days in jail	1886–1939	—.22	—.30	—.21
National budget	1830–1960	.07	.17	.25
National elections[a]	1830–1960	.17	.16	.23
Number of cabinet changes	1830–1960	.00	.06	—.07
Number of union members	1876–1938	.40	.41	.06

[a] Dummy variable in which election = 1, no election = 0.

number of participants are slightly negative or nonexistent, the two stray coefficients in the second case hardly seem to merit attention.

The relations to "power" and "organization" variables (Table 4) are stronger and more consistent, although not overwhelming. One could contest our inclusion of the number of person-days of detention in French jails during the year as a "power" variable; our reasoning is that its fluctuations represent changes in governmental repression more directly than changes in criminal activity. Its measured effect is not very strong. But it is, as expected, consistently negative: the greater the repression, the less the collective violence. (This result is not strictly comparable with the others, since we have data on jail-days only from 1886 to 1939.)

Years in which the governmental budget is large tend to be years of collective violence, at least as measured by participants and arrests. This is also true of election years, although the number of cabinet changes in a year shows no relation to the extent of collective violence. Finally, the number of union members (in years for which we have a good estimate) turns out to be a fairly good predictor of the number of violent incidents and of participants, if not of the number of arrests. In general, fluctuations in the organization-power variables are more closely connected with collective violence than are fluctuations in the breakdown-hardship variables.*

* In more complicated multivariate analyses we have examined the simultaneous effects of most of these variables and studied the impact of change in each of them

Conclusions

Where do these scraps of statistical evidence lead? Our conclusions must take the form of an argument—incompletely documented, but generally consistent with the evidence reviewed.

First, the conglomerate changes often thrown together in the bin labeled "modernization" had no uniform effects on the level, locus, form, or timing of political conflict in France. Some of the processes that observers usually have in mind when using that sweeping term did have well-defined effects. Rather than inciting protest through breakdown and hardship, "modernization" changed the prevailing forms of collective action. That in turn altered the character of collective violence.

Second, in the short run rapid urbanization and industrialization alike generally depressed the level of conflict. They destroyed various contenders' means and bases of collective action faster than they created new ones. Peasants who moved to cities, for example, ordinarily left settings in which they were sufficiently organized and sufficiently aware of common interests to throw up repeated resistance to taxers, drafters, and

---

from one year to the next. The hardship variables have no measurable effect, once the long-run trend is taken into account. When allowance is made for the influence of trend and of the other variables, the effect of jail-days and of national budget is negative, that of national elections positive. We get weak, inconsistent effects for two other variables: cabinet changes, and arrests in the collective violence of preceding years; for these results, see Snyder and Tilly 1972. Unionization does not appear in these multivariate analyses because the union membership series have breaks in them—a serious handicap for the particular sort of time-series analysis we have employed. When we simplify the forms of the variables and work with only the years for which data on unionization exist, the measured effects of unionization are consistently positive, but weak. For example, a fairly well-fitting equation for most of the years from 1886 to 1939 is: participants (square root transformation) $= 1589.4 - 46.880t + .364t^2 - .009$ (national budget) $+ .0003$ (union membership); (where t is time; $R^2 = .35$, $p = .002$). However, a slightly better-fitting equation for the same years runs: participants (sq. rt.) $= 2127 - 60.8t + .446t^2 - .007$ (budget) $- .03$ (jail-days) $+ .18$ (major crimes); ($R^2 = .41$, $p = .001$), which raises the intriguing possibility that there is, after all, a positive relationship between major crimes and collective violence. If the weight of our evidence favors the power-organization variables, it has not as yet crushed all the possible versions of hardship and breakdown.

grain-buyers. In the industrial city it generally took them and their children a full generation to form the new organization, and the new consciousness, essential to renewed collective action.

Third, urbanization and industrialization nevertheless directly stimulated political conflict when they diverted resources and control over resources from established groups which retained their internal organization: food rioters fighting to prevent the shipment of grain from their villages to cities and urban craftsmen fighting loss of control over their conditions of work are such cases. When these changes proceeded faster than the dissolution of existing organization (which appears to have been the case in the 1840s, for example), the effect was actually to raise the level of group conflict.

Fourth, the emergence of industrial capitalism, the development of a class structure organized around relations to a national market and the means of industrial production, the rise of bureaucracies and other formal organizations as the principal means of accomplishing collective ends combined to transform the identities and the interests of the major contenders for power, as well as the form of their concerted action. Since conflict, including violent conflict, grows out of collective action, the transformation of the contenders transformed the nature of contention in France.

If we restrict our attention to the public, collective forms of conflict which commonly lead to violence, we can see how much their frequency and outcome depends on the operation of the state. Nineteenth-century centralization and nationalization of politics, as the state crushed its local rivals, incited widespread protest and shifted the focus of violent conflict. State repression of collective action by contenders for power diminished the frequency of violent conflicts during the 1850s and the two World Wars, while the relaxation of that repression in the 1860s or later 1940s permitted the contention to reappear. Throughout the two centuries the state resisted the bids of new contenders for power in the names of those who already had established places in the structure of power; the tactics selected by the agents of the state (for example, in controlling hostile demonstrations) strongly determined the extent of violence. As a consequence, new contenders for power tended to pass through a cycle going from (1) quiet organization to (2) violent contention to (3) conquest of a position within the structure of power to (4) involvement in violence mainly through the proxies of police and soldiers. But enough new contenders came along and enough of them were rebuffed to keep the level of violence high. Today students, intellectuals, and technical workers seem to be hammering at the gates.

If our analysis is correct, the immediate stresses and strains of technological changes, population movements, and other such components of "modernization" play a rather small part in the promotion of collective action, and therefore of collective violence. Nor does material hardship as such—even the sudden increase of material hardship—seem to have had a primary role in France. The crucial exception is that when someone else appears to be creating or profiting by the new hardship and doing so through violations of his own duties and other people's rights, ordinary men often strike at the presumed profiteers in the name of justice. In general, justice—and conflicting conceptions of justice, at that—lies at the heart of violent conflict. Violent conflict remains close to politics, in origin as well as in impact. In that respect France resembles other European nations.

Nonetheless, France has a particular history, and that history affects her political conflicts. The foundation of all her modern regimes on one version or another of a revolutionary tradition has, paradoxically, justified the government's taking on of exceptional powers when it could declare *la patrie en danger*. That has probably produced greater fluctuations in repression, and sharper distinctions between "ins" and "outs" during times of repression, in France than in most other western countries. Likewise, the enormous centralization of power within the French system has probably defined more different kinds of struggles in France than elsewhere, as confrontations between the state and its enemies—and as struggles the state could not afford to lose. Before broadcasting conclusions from French political history throughout the world, we must treat these two features, the presence or absence of a revolutionary tradition and the degree of centralization of power, as major variables.

In the France of the last two centuries, political conflict shifted toward larger-scale, more highly organized forms of collective action. The changing relations of Frenchmen to a state which was increasing its hold over their everyday lives set one of the major rhythms: the change from competitive to reactive to proactive forms of collective action. At the same time, people's everyday organization for collective action changed slowly as France urbanized and industrialized; the reorganization of everyday life transformed the character of conflict; that long-run reshaping of solidarities, rather than the immediate production of stress and strain, constituted the most important impact of structural change on political conflict. In the shorter run, the state's tactics of repression and accommodation strongly affected the intensity, form, locus, and outcome of conflict. Throughout the two centuries the struggle to acquire or maintain established places in the structure of power, and thus gain control over the conditions of their own existence, brought different groups of Frenchmen into violent conflict with one another.

CHAPTER III

Italy

"Italy will win out," Carlo Pisacane wrote before Unification, "when the peasant voluntarily trades his hoe for a gun; at present, for him honor and country are words without meaning" (cited in Della Peruta 1954: 317). Then and now, critics of the Italian national effort have taken the widespread weakness of commitment to the national state as evidence of dormant political consciousness. There is something to that analysis, but it is not quite right. Italians have long maintained an intense political consciousness at a local level. Not apathy but *localism* distinguishes Italian political life over the century from 1830 to 1930.

Localism, first, in that effective social attachments tend to remain small in scale: the household, the local segments of the kin group, perhaps the local community as a whole, little more. Localism, second, in that major features of social life—agricultural practices, religious rituals, the language of everyday life—vary perceptibly from one community to the next. As two American sociologists sum up their twentieth-century observations of southern peasants:

Even with the advent of the radio, the peasant continues to identify himself with the village. Through bitter experience he has learned to trust, or distrust least, those who live within the sound of the local church bell (*campani-*

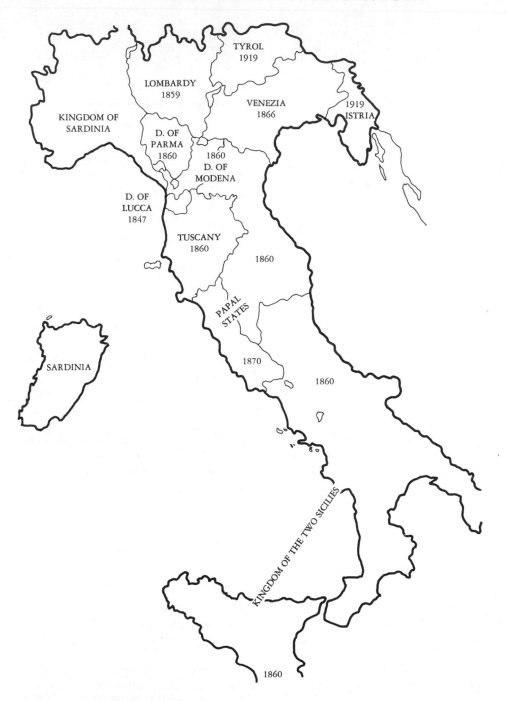

Figure 17. Italy before Unification.

lismo). Government is a meaningless and nebulous concept to the peasant. Rome is distant and epitomizes those who have lived off the labors of the farmer. The land owner, the police, the tax collector, even the priest have come to symbolize those who are out to milk the peasant (Moss and Capponnari 1960: 25).

The complement of this sort of localism, however, is the development of corporate kin groups and extensive systems of patron-client relations. Both frequently extend beyond the boundaries of any particular village; both have played an important part in the capacity of Italians to migrate long distances and yet maintain contact with their places of origin.

Localism, corporate kin groups, and extensive patronage systems all fit badly with political arrangements built on the assumption of informed individual participation. To be sure, all political realities everywhere fall short of that Lockean ideal. Among western countries, the political realities of Italy fall farther from the liberal ideal than do those, say, of England, Germany, the United States, or France.

What is more, with Unification the greater part of Italy, in all its diversity of tradition and practice, found itself rapidly subordinated to political forms fashioned in Piedmont, adapted to an important degree from French and English models: parliamentary democracy, centralized administrative structure, standardized local government. During a long period, the gap remained the wider because a powerful church opposed the very principles of the new national state and forbade its communicants to take part in the state's political life. As a consequence, we find haphazard and incomplete integration of Italians into national political life until the twentieth century. Equally important, we find an Italian state incapable of exerting its control effectively and uniformly throughout the territory nominally under its jurisdiction.

Many modern observers have remarked on the results of this peculiar confrontation of national institutions with local realities. In the south-central village he and his wife studied, Edward Banfield (1959) interpreted the entire complex as an ethos of "amoral familism," giving people little warrant to trust or aid anyone outside the immediate kin group, indeed encouraging them to fear and to exploit anyone outside that small circle. In their international survey of political attitudes, Verba and Almond (1964) find Italian respondents exceptionally "alienated" from national politics, unlikely to feel they have any significant influence, and disinclined to take pride in the country's political accomplishments. One of the sayings of the southern villagers studied by Guido Vincelli reveals peasant cynicism toward the state: "The state doesn't promote justice through law, it simply exploits" (1958: 253). In this community, unions were almost nonexistent, there was lack of interest in national politics, lack of respect for others' interests, "jealous guarding of one's own things" (182).

We are watching the interplay of two different systems: first, a national political structure which was first fragmented, then rapidly unified, then shaped on a liberal-democratic model and imposed (albeit often ineffectually) throughout the peninsula, finally converted into an authoritarian form; and, second, a set of local political arrangements which varied sharply from area to area, yet usually included a strong element of localism, extensive patron-client networks, important corporate kinship groups, and a variety of other barriers to the direct participation of individuals as independent individuals in national political life.

Let us not exaggerate Italy's uniqueness. Some inconsistency between national and local political arrangements is found in every national state. The tension and inconsistency just went farther in Italy than in most other parts of modern Europe. Nor are the local political arrangements described peculiarly Italian. They unite Italy with other parts of the Mediterranean rim (Pitt-Rivers 1963), and are, in fact, more prevalent in southern sections than in northern regions like Tuscany, Lombardy, and Piedmont. As a consequence, the gap between national institutions and local arrangements is (and was) generally much greater in the South than in the North.

Other frequently noted features of Italian political life also spring from the interaction of local and national systems of power. The slow oscillations of banditry—which long antedated the emergence of a national state—reflected the uncertain expansion and contraction of state power: expanding states outlawed men who had previously been making their own law, while faltering ones permitted local rivals to tax, appropriate property and coerce illegally. The fabled "corruption" of Italian political life commonly took two forms: local systems of control closely akin to banditry; and the extensive use of corporate kin groups and patron-client networks to accomplish political work which, in constitutional principle, should have been carried on by independent citizens, representative assemblies, bureaucrats, and public-minded public officials.

The famous parliamentary system of *trasformismo* consisted of the formation of shifting but workable governmental coalitions created from party fragments varying in degrees of liberalism. It came into being in response to the national-local problem. As Francesco De Sanctis said in 1877: "We have now reached the point where there are no solidly built parties in Italy except those based on either regional differences or the personal relation of client to patron; and these are the twin plagues of Italy" (quoted in Mack Smith 1969: 111).

Perhaps the exceptional importance of artists and adventurers—Manzoni, D'Azeglio, Garibaldi, Mazzini, Verdi, Mussolini, and others—in the national political life of Italy over our period also resulted in part from the tension of national and local systems. Where distinctly political activities of the type of parties, clubs, meetings, or electioneering are weak because of repression or ill-developed organization, artistic communications and ostensibly nonpolitical ceremonies tend to carry a political burden: joyful crowds greet the new Italian Bishop of Milan (who replaces an Austrian) in 1847; the audience of La Scala repeatedly cheers a chorus in *Norma* singing "Guerra! Guerra!" in 1859; in Austrian-controlled Milan the same year thousands turn out for the funeral of Dandolo; Manzoni's rewriting of *I promessi sposi* in Tuscan conveys a nationalistic message. And a fluctuating balance between national and local creates many opportunities and incentives for a *condottiere* (a dramatic leader) to form new alliances, gather a following, attempt a quick coup. In a sense, all the obvious peculiarities of Italian political life during the century following 1830 grew from the interaction of an unsteady process of national unification with a swarm of distinct, changing local social structures.

Unification

The manifest political facts of Unification are simple enough. The settlement of the Napoleonic Wars had reinforced Austria's hold—at least a foothold, perhaps a stranglehold—on the Italian peninsula. Austria directly dominated Istria, Venetia and Lombardy, and the Italian-speaking Tyrol, while Austrian princelings ruled the duchies of Parma, Modena, and Tuscany. Piedmont now had Italian territory running down to the sea at Genoa and over the sea to Sardinia. But (as the Kingdom of Sardinia), Piedmont remained a largely French-speaking regime, seated two-faced athwart the Alps. Farther south lay the Papal States, and the Bourbon Kingdom of the Two Sicilies, both likewise beholden to the Austrians. So Italian nationalists had a visible, powerful enemy: Austria.

In the 1830s and 1840s segments of a movement—sometimes literary, sometimes conspiratorial—for Italian regeneration, unification, and independence began to gain strength. During 1848 momentarily successful revolutions occurred in Palermo, Venice, Milan, and Rome. King Carlo Alberto of Piedmont took advantage of the Milanese revolution by declaring war on Austria and advancing into her territory of Lombardy. A few remnants of the political arrangements of 1848 actually survived the counterrevolutions and repression of the following year, notably in the retention of the liberal framework for government in Piedmont.

During the 1850s Cavour, the Prime Minister of Piedmont, carried on the work of shaping an efficient, centralized government in the kingdom. Meanwhile, Mazzini and his co-conspirators continued their attempt to incite rebellions elsewhere in the peninsula. In 1859–1860 Cavour's diplomacy brought Napoleon III's support for another war against Austria, the war annexed Lombardy to Piedmont, and its aftermath permitted plebiscites formally joining Tuscany and Emilia to the expanding kingdom. Then Garibaldi and his volunteers landed in Sicily. They marched northward to seize the rest of the Kingdom of Naples, only to be forced to yield the newly independent territory to Piedmont, while Piedmont herself grabbed some of the territory of the Papal States.

Thus, a Kingdom of Italy came into being in 1861. An alliance with Prussia permitted the new kingdom to add Venetia (although not without a good deal of military bungling) by intervening in the Austro-Prussian War of 1866. During this period the French had established themselves as the guarantors of the independence of Rome and of what remained of the papal territory. In 1867 the French repelled a halfhearted Italian effort (featuring one more invasion by Garibaldi) to annex Rome. But the diversion of French troops to the Franco-Prussian War and the decisive defeat of France by Prussia at Sedan gave Italy its chance to occupy Rome definitively.

At that point the Italian state had acquired its basic boundaries. The statemakers then turned to extending and consolidating their control at home and building a colonial empire—mostly in North Africa, and mostly without success. Movements of regional resistance to the center continued, anarchism had some moments of glory, and at some moments it looked as though Italy might turn to a federal system of the kind advocated by Cattaneo. Yet the subsequent political struggles of Italy were predominantly struggles for control over a national state which all parties assumed would continue to exist in one form or another. The Fascist seizure of power after World War I did nothing to alter that.

All these changes rested on a dangerous dualism of popular participation and elite control. Each of the major steps of unification relied on, and excited, temporary involvement of ordinary Italians in the national struggle. Yet each of the transfers of power saw a small elite seize the fruits of victory and spend much of its subsequent effort at fending off and demobilizing the majority of those who had made the victory possible. Mazzini spent most of the 1860s in exile, a hunted man with a death sentence waiting. After his last few attempts to mount movements of liberation during those same 1860s, Garibaldi found himself shunted off into beekeeping and symbolic protest. ("I dreamed of a very different Italy," he declared on his resignation from Parliament in 1880; two years later, he died.) The peasants of Sicily fell into stifled silence after helping to make the revolution of 1860. And the Fascists themselves secured their power through a massive *de*mobilization of the working class.

This repeated pattern of mobilization, manipulation, and demobilization satisfies the conservative historian of Italy; he can placidly agree, with Masnovo (1932: 89), that "by the way things were, the matters had to proceed slowly, by stages, and it was not in the power of men to hurry the pace." It enrages the radical; he can inveigh, with Del Carria (1966: I, 13), against the ruling bourgeoisie who "changed their political, social, and ideological character in order to keep on controlling, repressing, taming, and emasculating the subordinate classes, thus forestalling a radical reordering of the class structure." The pattern worked repeatedly because of the conjunction of three recurrent features of the Italian political scene: centralized instruments of government; small and relatively coherent elites in control of those centralized instruments of government; exceptionally fragmented popular movements.

Before unification, the governments of Italy ranged from the brisk administration of the Austrian territories to the Spanish traditionalism of Sicily. All of them made new beginnings at the close of the Napoleonic Wars. In the Kingdom of Sardinia (Savoy, Piedmont, Liguria, and Sardinia), the king reinstated the paternalism of the eighteenth century, staffing his government with nobles who had followed him into exile. A similar reaction occurred in the Papal States, with a clerical caste resuming control. The new Kingdom of the Two Sicilies, dominated by Naples, did extend the power of the crown over the largely independent barons of the South, but the extension went in the direction of absolutism rather than of constitutional government.

All of these regimes had to contend with secret revolutionary movements, especially with Carbonari drawn from the Masonic lodges, from the former allies of Napoleon, and from the liberal professions. The Carbonari actually forced the temporary granting of liberal constitutions in Naples (1820) and Piedmont (1821), as well as mounting other revolutionary attempts throughout the 1820s. But, with the continuing help of the Austrian army, all the regimes kept their oppositions at bay until the middle of the century. They did so by stringently limiting the possibilities of assembly and association, controlling the press, infiltrating, spying, imprisoning—in short, by the standard techniques of governmental repression.

Pope Leo XII, for example, sought to check the Carbonari of his territories through direct repression and through the promotion of a Catholic secret society, the Sanfedisti. At his death in 1829 the Carbonari did in fact manage a small insurrection. When they and their allies briefly succeeded in taking over most of the Papal States in 1831, through a revolution beginning in Modena, the new Pope (Pius VII) relied on the Austrians to restore him to temporal power. All popes of the period faced a continuing threat of revolution; they met it by organizing extensive systems of surveillance and control, and backing them up with Austrian guarantees. In this, they adopted the standard practice of Italian sovereigns.

Unification ended the multiplicity of governments. It did not end the vulnerability of government. The serious possibility of revolution opened up at least once in every decade from 1860 to the Fascist seizure of power in 1922. That possibility grew from the very manner of unification. The statemakers of Piedmont extended their French-style centralized adminis-

tration to all of Italy much more rapidly than they extended the administration's power to enforce decisions. In came a uniform system of
provincial prefects reporting directly to the capital, a uniform national system of taxation, a uniform judiciary, a unitary army, a set of local governments representing (at least in theory) the central administration in the
capital. Even the police underwent this rapid and radical centralization;
the multiple police forces of the years prior to 1859 reduced to two com-
plementary national forces, both enlargements of Piedmontese models:
the paramilitary carabinieri, with the mission of patrolling the countryside
and beating back rebellion; and the Guardia di Pubblica Sicurezza, with
responsibility for big-city policing.

The ordinary personnel of government also changed, not so abruptly as
its formal structure had. Before Unification each of the several Italian
governments had relied heavily on its property-holding elite for government service as well as for unofficial support. After unification two things
happened: a disproportionate tendency to staff the higher levels of government in all regions with men from the North, especially Piedmont;
and, more gradually, the emergence of a spoils system through which the
national elite traded control of office for the political support of local and
regional potentates. In the long run this produced a shift of governmental
personnel toward men from humbler origins, from rural areas, from the
South.

Italian Political Structure

The Italian states of the early nineteenth century had little more than
hand-picked consultative assemblies. The 1848 Statuto of Piedmont established a parliamentary system: suffrage severely restricted by property
qualifications, ministerial responsibility, considerable legislative power, a
royal veto. Note that it was even a classic "liberal" constitution; it reflected the French Constitution of 1830 rather than that of 1848. It had
three outstanding features: maintenance of Roman Catholicism as the
state religion; reservation of executive (and, to a considerable extent,
judicial) power to the king; and establishment of a bicameral legislature,
one composed of members named for life by the king, the other elected
through a suffrage stringently limited to taxpayers; the legislative power
was limited to the approval or disapproval of laws proposed by the king.
The property qualifications actually empowered about 80,000 men, out of

a total population of 4,200,000, to elect the lower house. Women had no representation at all. Though a considerable concession, the Statuto was far from mass democracy.

The Statuto became the kernel of the Italian constitution after 1861. The franchise broadened as tax payments rose. It grew in spurts as the Parliament gave in to pressure from groups which stood to gain from the inclusion of one portion or another of the electorate. The reform of 1882, for example, was the price of leftist support for the Depretis government of that year. By lowering the voting age from twenty-five to twenty-one, reducing the income tax requirement from 40 to 19 lire, and reducing the education required to two years, it raised the number of men eligible to vote from about 600,000 to 2,000,000. That extension, in turn, encouraged the nearly immediate creation of the first substantial workers' party: the Partito Operaio Italiano.

Figure 18, which charts the expansion of the electorate over the long run, shows the dramatic effects of the electoral laws of 1882 and 1912, both of which brought substantial new segments of the working class into the electoral process. The law of July 1894, maneuvered through by Prime Minister Crispi, actually *dis*franchised almost 30 percent of the existing electorate. It "called for an extraordinary review of the electoral lists, officially for the purpose of eliminating voters improperly registered via an inspection of school certificates or evidence of ability to read and write, but in fact for the purpose of striking at the socialist and democratic opposition" (Candeloro 1970: VI, 450). Over the long run, nevertheless, the pressure for expansion of the suffrage became irresistible.

Consequently, during the half-century following 1870, Italy moved unsteadily into its own version of a party system and of parliamentary government. Like the French parliamentary system, the Italian produced a plethora of parties, and a large bloc on the left, which eventually became more or less constant in size. This left bloc was based to an important degree on organized labor, and was frequently divided by questions of ideology, strategy, and international politics. A great deal of parliamentary maneuvering was directed toward excluding the left from power. There was a continuous shuffling of parties and fragments of parties to form governmental coalitions pivoting on the center-right until 1900, then on the center-left. Before World War I, Italy went through long periods in which the provincial prefects had major responsibility (and

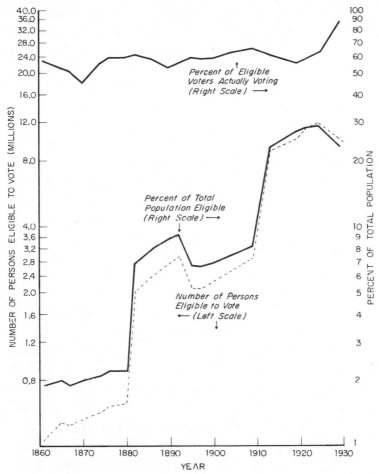

Source: Istituto Centrale di Statistica, *Sommario di statistiche storiche italiane* (Rome: ISTAT, 1958), p. 105.

Figure 18. Eligible and Actual Voters in Italian Parliamentary Elections, 1861–1929.

substantial means) for delivering votes favorable to the governmental coalition.

Italy differed from France in the slower expansion of the electorate, the greater importance of strictly regional blocs in the Italian parliament, the somewhat greater involvement of Italian peasants and rural workers in the most leftward parties, and the greater political presence of the Catholic Church in Italy, especially after 1918.

Further, Italy began to experience consolidation of state power within constant boundaries only after 1870. The regional heterogeneity of Italy complicated the task of exerting centralized control and a shortage of competent bureaucrats slowed the adoption of routine methods of extraction and control. Thus, despite the appearance of centralized administrative rationality, at the local level, the Italian system depended on working compromises between the elites of each region—especially the landed elites—and the operators of the central government. The compromises essentially exchanged guarantees of public order, tax payments, and electoral support for assurances of access to jobs, use of governmental resources, and exemption from the more onerous national laws.

These limits to centralization produced a pattern of governmental repression both before and after Unification which was arbitrary, variable, and often both bloody and ineffectual. In their territories the Austrians set an example of control through military force and severe punishment for political offenses. In Milan, in 1851, two men were condemned to death for having distributed Mazzinian tracts. At least 960 persons in Lombardy died as a direct result of Austrian political repression between August 1848 and August 1849 (Colajanni 1962: 309). The consequence was to deflect opposition toward indirect actions like the "smokers' strike," undertaken in Milan in 1848 to deprive the government of its revenues from the sale of tobacco. (Even that sort of boycott had its risks, as Eugenio Messa and Davide Bellone of Milan discovered; in April 1851 they were sentenced to fifty blows of a staff each for having "kept others from smoking.") A similar pattern of repression prevailed elsewhere in Italy, notably in the Papal States and Naples.

Unification made the pattern somewhat more uniform, and subject to the instances of various holders of power at the national level. Yet it persisted. Close surveillance and periodic suppression of the left edges of the press continued. In the 1870s the Italian section of the International was dissolved and many of its leaders arrested. In the 1880s it was the turn of the Partito Operaio; and in the 1890s of the Sicilian Fasci and of the Socialist Party.

With regard to Italy, all such generalizations require one fundamental qualification: political change varied greatly from region to region. Before unification, the separate governments of Italy each encompassed a good deal of variation in terrain, agrarian structure, industrial activity, and cultural traditions; after political unification, Italy's heterogeneity continued. Over the period surveyed, the North was more directly involved in the national political process than the South. The provinces acted, to some extent, as political units, with Sicilians, Calabrese, Neapolitans, and Piedmontese contesting for power. And in the long run the region—especially in the form of the Problem of the South—itself became a major political issue.

The Economic Divisions of Italy

In 1821 Francesco Gandini, Controller of the Royal Postal Service of Lombardy, published a guidebook, *Viaggi in Italia* (the edition cited is the second, 1833), which gives a traveler's view of the peninsula in the early nineteenth century. Gandini is a great enthusiast: he praises the natural wealth of Italy, particularly in agriculture: "Italy is an ample garden, where one finds in abundance all that can make human life comfortable and delightful; that is, grains, vegetables, grapes, oil, wool, silk, linen, hemp, honey, wax, wood for fuel or construction, all kinds of fruits, cedars, lemons, oranges, spices and olives" (I, 12).

Italy's mineral endowment evokes less extravagant prose: "many stone quarries, iron mines; in the Apennines alabaster, jasper, agate, chalcedony, crystals, and other precious stones . . . marble . . . copper, a little gold and silver, . . . tufa . . . alum" (I, 13). Not too impressive an inventory for an industrial base; mineral fuels are not even mentioned. When he comes to manufacturers and commerce, however, Gandini's exaggeration returns: "Italy, master of all nations, already great when the other European nations were still dormant in the shadows, contains within her breast all the elements with which to lead in the sciences, arts, traffic, navigation. There is no branch of human industry which is not diligently cultivated and promoted" (I, 17). The branches of industry turn out to be mainly luxury crafts: silk and fine cotton and wool, gold and silver ware, gloves, leather, artificial flowers, precision instruments, and optical products. The exports of Italy are mainly agricultural and luxury products, while its imports are products of mass consumption: "woolens, canvas cloth, cotton fabric, trinkets" (I, 18).

As he leads the traveler through Italy, Gandini refines his descriptions.

There are important regional variations. He points out that irrigation is used "to perfection" in Lombardy, producing the "pleasing sight . . . of constantly smiling vegetation" (III, 17). In the Veneto, grain production —wheat, rice, corn—exceeds local needs (III, 33). In the Duchy of Modena "there are indications of iron and copper mines, but no flourishing ones" (IV, 122).

Unproductive and unprosperous areas turn up as Gandini moves south. The Tuscan Maremma is depopulated, desolate, unhealthy (V, 5); around Rome: "The soil is generally very fertile, but agriculture is not pursued there with sufficient vigor" (VI, 13). Although the Kingdom of Naples is generally prosperous, real problems are visible: "Beggary and thievery are in style in several provinces of this kingdom, especially in the part contiguous with the Papal States" (VII, 7).

Basilicata is desolate: "Earthquakes are frequent here. Agriculture is neglected. The best lands are almost desert" (VII, 203). In the plain of Calabria "the heat is unbearable . . . the stagnant waters contribute to the unhealthiness of the air, and cause fevers which make this plain uninhabitable" (VII, 206). As for Sicily, its former powerful political position has disappeared, but its natural attributes remain: "beautiful sky, mild climate, surprisingly fertile soil." But all this is in a setting of "destroyed cities, depopulated villages" (VIII, 21).

Gandini's Italy was a politically fragmented peninsula with well-conducted agriculture in the North, backward and desolate areas in the South. Despite skilled craftsmen, industry did not go beyond luxury crafts, and the mineral resources of the peninsula showed no prospect of being able to support modern industry.

Yet the impoverished Italy of the early nineteenth century had more than once been the apex of wealth, intellectual activity, and political power in Europe and the Mediterranean. Arthur Young, on his famous French and Italian journey of 1789, committed to his journal the rather smug reflections of an Englishman on Sicily:

that island, the most celebrated of all antiquity for fruitfulness and cultivation, on whose exuberance its neighbours depended for their bread—and whose practice the greatest nations considered as the most worthy of imitations; at a period too when we were in the woods, condemned for barbarity, and hardly considered as worth the trouble of conquering. What has effected so enormous a change? Two words explain it: we are become free and Sicily enslaved (Young 1915: 277).

In bewailing the paucity of the peninsula's natural endowments, the standard account of Italy's modern economic development ignores the past. Sicily long served as the granary of the Mediterranean. For a long portion of the Renaissance northern Italy was the principal industrial region of Europe; city-states like Genoa, Venice, and Florence were fabled for their culture. Only in the age of national states did Italy lose its prosperity. As Carlo Cipolla tells us:

At the beginning of the seventeenth century, Italy, or more exactly Northern and Central Italy, was still one of the most advanced of the industrial areas of Western Europe with an exceptionally high standard of living. By the end of this century, Italy had become an economically backward and depressed area; its industrial structure had almost collapsed, its population was too high for its resources, its economy had become primarily agricultural. The great change came mainly between 1600 and 1670. In these seven black decades the industrial structure of Italy collapsed (1952: 178).

The industrial collapse left Italy with a stock of skilled craftsmen and a population concentrated in and around old cities filled with reminders of past political, economic, and aesthetic supremacy. The drift of textile production away from the cities toward the cheaper, more pliant labor of the countryside did not compensate for Italy's loss. By the beginning of the eighteenth century, as Cipolla concludes, Italy had begun her long career as "a country at once depressed and overpopulated."

In spite of the glorious past, the European industrial expansion of the eighteenth and nineteenth centuries left Italy far behind such areas as Holland, England, France, and even Prussia. The country as a whole did not begin to close the gap in prosperity between itself and the great industrial powers until after World War II.

Yet comparison of Italy with other nation-states is misleading. It disguises the great contrast between the enduring economic stagnation south of Rome and the industrial growth plus extensive commercialization of agriculture to the north. Milan and Turin, which served as foci of wide networks of domestic industry and cash-crop agriculture in the eighteenth century, developed into major centers of factory production at the end of the nineteenth. In one way or another, the entire band of Italy from Florence north to the Alps shared in the building of nineteenth-century industrial capitalism.

The political fragmentation of the peninsula before 1860 makes it hard to trace this earlier development. Although some of the political subdivisions (like those controlled by Austria) mounted extensive systems of social reporting, each principality kept records on its own terms. Some (like the Papal States) seem not to have kept them at all.

Table 5 brings together some available fragments of information concerning the relative "modernity" of different sections of Italy before Unification. It shows Piedmont and Lombardy-Venetia with far more extensive railroads, a much denser road system, substantially higher rates of literacy, a greater proliferation of "improving" agricultural journals, and most likely a considerably more active foreign trade than the rest of Italy. In these regards the areas of central Italy (including the Papal States) consistently fell behind the northern areas, but still outstripped Naples and Sicily. Sicily and Sardinia differed from the mainland even more drastically: no railroads, few roads of any kind, few literate people, little trade, much poverty. Roughly speaking, modernity declined as a function of distance from Milan.

Do not read too much into the term "modern." Before the end of the century a large part of northern Italy's industrial development took the form of cottage industry and related forms of dispersed, small-scale production. Industry without factories expanded widely in eighteenth-century Europe, and continued into the nineteenth century; northern Italy shared in the continental movement. Lombardy led the growth in textiles:

The development of the textile industries in this region did not, in fact, create the typical industrial city, and did not transform the peasant all at once into a salaried worker. The description which Giuseppe Sacchi gave in 1847 of weavers in the cotton industry indicated the persistence of the dual agrarian and industrial activity of the weaver, who (being unable to do anything in the fields) worked assiduously at his loom in the winter and in the spring took up his hoe and sickle and went with other peasants to manure the fields. Thus the development of that industry, concluded Sacchi, gave them "all the benefits possible, avoiding all the economic and moral consequences which, alas, so greatly disturb other populations" (Romano 1965: 159).

This extension of rural industry greatly increased the production of goods in Italy, as elsewhere in pre-factory Europe, but in the short run it did not produce industrial cities. Hence an important degree of industrialization without notable urbanization.

Mill towns developed mainly in the North. Although Italy had no cen-

Table 5. Some indicators of modernity in Italy, 1848–1862

Item	Piedmont	Sardinia	Lombardy-Veneto	Tuscany	Modena-Parma	Papal States	Naples	Sicily
Km. of railroads in 1848	8	0	112	160	—	0	85	0
Km. of railroads in 1859	938	0	522	257	—	101	99	0
Km. of roads per km. of area, 1862	1	0.10	1+[a]	0.75?		0.10	0.10	0.05
Percentage literate in 1861[b]	45.8	10.3	46.3	26.0	22.4	16.6	13.7	11.4
Number of agricultural journals published, 1856	87		85	48	5	30	56	
Ducats per capita foreign trade, 1858	40		—	32	—	9	7	

[a] 1862 road figures refer to Lombardy alone.
[b] Geographical areas for literacy are Piedmont without Liguria, Sardinia, Lombardy, Tuscany, Emilia-Romagna, Marches-Umbria, Naples, and Sicily.

ter rivaling Manchester or Birmingham, it did contain regions of moderate to large textile mills. Piedmont's Biella region had 79 woolen mills with some 5,300 workers in 1844; it had expanded to 94 mills and 6,500 workers in 1864 (Quazza 1961: 53). The woolen production of Biella ran to a value of 10,000,000 lire in 1840 and 15,000,000 in 1859, placing the area ahead of the entire production of the only important southern industrial region, that of Naples.

In cotton, the industrial plants of Piedmont, Lombardy, and Naples stood in a ratio of approximately 3:3:2. (Per capita, that translates into something like 5:4:2.) The less-developed metal and machine industries were likewise concentrated in Lombardy and Piedmont, with a secondary center in Naples. If we were to add a little silk-production in Venetia and around Florence, as well as the small but crucial sulphur mines of Sicily, we would have the essential map of industrial Italy during the first half of the nineteenth century.

At the other extreme from the industrial areas of the North stood Capitanata, Basilicata, Latium, and most of Sicily—almost devoid of industry. A Basilicata Chamber of Commerce report of the 1860s read:

But in our region there is no industry to relieve the poverty among rural folk: shops are rare and run by the labor of one man, chief and worker at the same time, and dependent on his own labor, to wrest a slim return, hardly sufficient for himself and his miserable family . . . the products are primitive and rough . . . neither steam nor water power substitute for muscles; thus to extract olive oil or grind wheat the press and the millstone of our forefathers are used (Milone 1950: 258).

In Latium of the late 1860s, the unsuccessful struggle to establish sugar beet production and operate a refinery illustrates the weakness of even those industries that were directly based on agriculture (De Felice 1965: 119).

After unification, the organization of production in Italy changed more rapidly than the numbers of people involved. Within each sector, the shift toward specialized, capital-intensive, large-scale organization came about quite slowly. Tremelloni (1961: 194) sums up the rhythm of industrial transformation in Italy during the century after 1861 as comprising four unequal phases: 1861–1894, establishment of preconditions; 1894–1913, first intensive development of modern industry; 1914–1945, fluctuation with intermittent development; 1946–1961, active industrialization. This summary corresponds quite closely to the major divisions both in the growth of Italian national income and in the transformation of economic organization.

As Figure 19 indicates, the Italian national income rose only slightly until the 1890s; that is especially true of income per capita. There followed a rapid surge up to 1908–1910; after World War I a new phase, whose character Tremelloni's summary tends to obscure, occurred; two more substantial pushes were separated by the three or four depression years of the early 1930s. The years after 1945 brought Italy far faster and greater economic expansion than anything that had gone before. The periods of exceptionally rapid growth, then, were 1898–1913, 1921–1929, 1934–1939, and after 1945.

During the nineteenth century the food industries, then textiles (both organized on a very small scale, although undergoing some concentration) made the largest contributions to national income. Only during the expansion of 1898–1913 did the machine industries, as typified by the

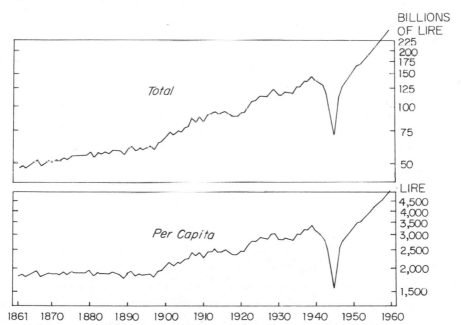

Source: drawn from Benedetto Barberi, "Aspetti dinamici e strutturali di sviluppo economico dell'Italia," in *L'Economia italiana dal 1861 al 1961* (Milan: Giuffrè, 1961), p. 655.

Figure 19. Italian National Income, 1861–1960.

automobile manufacturers of Turin, take over the lead. Producers' goods finally came to prominence in Italian manufacturing later still—during the 1930s and 1940s. This shift brought about a slow, irregular net movement of the work force into larger establishments; in manufacturing, the mean employees per firm went from eleven in 1903 down to nine in 1911, back up to thirteen in 1951, while machine horsepower per employee rose from 0.4 to 0.5 to 3.1. At the end of the period, much of Italy's industry—especially outside of the manufacturing North—still operated on a very small scale.

Cities and Urbanization

The peculiarities of the southern agrarian structure help account for a statistical oddity: by conventional criteria, the South's nineteenth-century population was far more "urban" than that of the North. The usual correlation between urbanity and prosperity fails. In the South, the regions of latifundi (large estates) featured agrotowns, populated largely by day laborers and by peasants who rented the small holdings into which the estates were divided and traveled daily from town to the distant fields. Further, major cities such as Naples and Palermo continued to collect the surplus population forced off the land, until overseas migration became a feasible alternative late in the nineteenth century. Finally, throughout Italy cities surviving from an earlier urban age continued to hold their contingents of lawyers, officials, monks, and absentee landlords.

Our estimates of the percentage of population in cities in 1848 and 1862, by region, appear in Figure 20.* The figures make it fairly clear that the modest urban increase of the time was occurring in the North. Yet they make it even clearer that Piedmont, Lombardy, and Venetia had less concentrated populations than the rest of Italy. Sicily had the most concentrated population of all. Nor was it some peculiarity in the distribution of small towns which produced this difference. Table 6 gives the populations of the ten cities in Italy which had at least 100,000 inhabitants at some time between 1848 and 1871. The substantial increases during this period were occurring in the industrial cities north of Rome, yet

* Because of the absence of uniform data from before unification, we have adopted the expedient of summing by region the population in provincial capitals which had 15,000 inhabitants or more in 1901. The net result undoubtedly overestimates the relative urbanity of regions with many centers which crossed the 15,000 line between 1862 and 1901. Principal source: Raseri 1907.

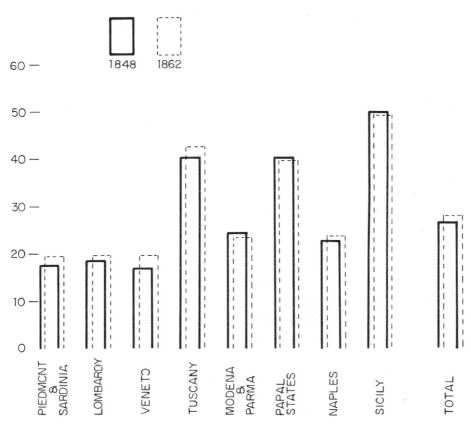

Figure 20. Estimated Percentage of the Population in Cities of 15,000 or More for Major Regions of Italy, 1848 and 1862.

Naples was by far the largest city throughout the period. In the beginning, Palermo was second and Rome only slightly behind third-place Milan. Obviously urbanity and modernity were independent of each other. The first temptation is to preserve our prejudices by conveniently modifying the definition of "urban," perhaps by including industrial activity or insisting on a bourgeois style of life. In the present case, we would learn more by recognizing that before recent years the Italian patterns of industrial activity, cosmopolitan life, and urban concentration were far more independent of each other than anyone accustomed to northwestern Europe and North America of the twentieth century would ordinarily expect.

Over time, the urbanization of Italy followed the general pace of industrialization, but not at all closely. The vagaries of Italian census-taking

Table 6. Populations of Italy's ten largest cities, 1848–1871 (in thousands)

City	1848	1861	1871	Percentage of increase
Genoa	145	151	162	12
Turin	144	205	213	48
Milan	187	242	262	40
Venice	106	119	129	22
Florence	133	143	163	23
Bologna	73	109	116	59
Rome	179	184	244	36
Naples	418	449	448	7
Palermo	217	194	219	1
Messina	98	103	112	14

and the highly concentrated rural settlement pattern of much of the South make it hard to trace the movement into smaller cities. Until about 1930 the population of the big cities—those of 50,000 or more—tended to increase by 10 to 15 percent each decade. From 1901 to 1911 and from 1921 to 1931 the figure ran around 20 percent. As a result, the percentage of the population living in cities of 50,000 or more was as follows: 1861, 17.2; 1871, 17.7; 1881, 18.8; 1901, 20.7; 1911, 22.8; 1921, 23.5; 1931, 26.3; 1936; 24.0; 1951, 30.1; 1961, 34.2.

The above-average periods of big-city growth were 1901–1911, 1921–1931, and 1936–1961. These periods bracket the major periods of industrial expansion. Italy entered the modern era with an exceptionally urban population, added to it at a relatively modest pace, and still ended up with a population exceptionally urban for its degree of industrial activity.

The structure and productivity of agriculture also varied sharply from region to region. In Table 7, we have schematized the salient features of the agrarian economy in Italy's major sections. The classification is too crude to capture the subtle variation in land tenure, fragmentation of holdings, crops, and techniques. Yet it identifies a general difference between North and South: sharecropping and small-holding on medium-sized farms prevailed toward the North; in the South, there was a much greater frequency of latifundia farmed by virtually landless laborers, surrounded by tiny holdings, and devoted mainly to wheat or stock-raising.

Despite appearances, the contrast was not between commercialized,

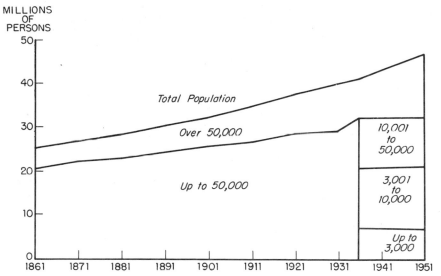

Source: Associazione per lo Sviluppo dell'Industria nel Mezzogiorno, *Un secolo di statistiche italiane, nord e sud* (Rome: SVIMEZ, 1961), pp. 13, 21–22, 1039.

Figure 21. Distribution of the Italian Population by Size of Place, 1861–1951.

capitalist agriculture in the North and pre-capitalist subsistence agriculture in the South. The most highly developed capital-intensive farming for the market did appear up North, in the Po Valley; what is more, the cash-crop farming of the Po supported Italy's largest concentration of truly landless agriculture labor. But most of the latifundia (for all their technical inefficiency) were also capitalistic enterprises grinding their profits out of a peculiarly vulnerable force of agricultural workers. The later collapse of agricultural exports sometimes obscures the fact that in the early nineteenth century the peasant producers of the South supported a whole superstructure of merchants and landowners devoted to the trade in grain. "There was in the Sicilian agrarian economy," De Marco explains, "an element of quasi-capitalism, although it continued to exploit the peasant in traditional ways" (1957: 257). Anton Blok (1974) calls the system *rent-capitalism*.

Italians have sometimes said that Christ stopped at Eboli, just below Naples; Carlo Levi used the saying as the title of a famous novel about the misery of the South: *Cristo si è fermato a Eboli*. From the retrospect of the twentieth century, the South's miserable conditions—masses of impoverished day laborers, rack-renting, stagnant agriculture—appear to

Table 7. A summary of Italian agrarian structure by region, around 1860

Region[a]	Usual size of farms	Prevalent landholding system	Principal agricultural products
Piedmont	Medium	Sharecropping and small property	Grapes, wheat, corn
Sardinia	Small	Small property common pastures and fields	Stock, dairy products
Lombardy-Veneto	Medium	Sharecropping and small property	Grapes, corn, wheat, silk
Papal States	Medium	Sharecropping and small property	Grapes, wheat
Latium	Large	Rent in cash and kind from latifundia	Wheat
Naples	Large	Rent in cash and kind from latifundia	Wheat, stock
Sicily	Large	Rent "a gabella" from latifundia	Wheat
Tuscany	Medium	Sharecropping and small property	Grapes, olives, silk, wheat

[a] No data available for Modena-Parma.

be the region's fate. Actually, the partial penetration of capitalism into the southern countryside during the nineteenth century played a major part in creating those conditions.

Different sections of the southern kingdom were evolving in substantially different directions during the nineteenth century. In Apulia (the heel of the Italian boot) large wheat farms worked by landless gang labor were becoming important; they developed in the company of smaller plots leased directly to cultivators under conditions providing incentives for agricultural improvement. In Campania, Basilicata, Abruzzi-Molise, and Calabria (the shank and toe of the boot) large holdings were disappearing. They declined, not in favor of owner-cultivators, but of rentiers and property managers who drew their incomes from short-term leases and sharecropping contracts. In Sicily both large estates and medium-sized farms were leased or sharecropped in small plots with unstable tenure. There, the estate managers (*gabellotti*) were growing increasingly powerful, in alliance with the quasi-government of mafia. As a consequence of this consolidation of ownership as well as of relatively rapid natural increase, the number of landless laborers in the deep South's agriculture was growing fast.

However, by the end of the nineteenth century, the latifundi were of less importance in the deep South. This was a consequence partly of the agricultural depression after 1880, when absentee landlords sometimes sold unproductive lands to small holders. The parliamentary inquiry of 1911 concluded that large properties were few in Campania, Basilicata, Calabria, Abruzzi, and Molise (Rossi-Dorria 1958: 52–53). In 1930 peasant owned and operated land amounted to 58.7 percent in southern Italy; in the North the percentage was 63. Central Italy (except for Latium, which followed the southern pattern) was the exception: there, sharecropping (*mezzadria*) was the method of operation of over half of the farms in Tuscany, the Marches, Umbria (Milone 1955: 510).

At the end of the First World War, peasant farm ownership was still rare in Italy as a whole. One analysis of Italian agriculture sees a process of "deproletarianization"—the reduction of numbers of landless workers (which went along with acquisition of small property or workers' leaving the agricultural sector)—starting in the early 1920s (Acerbo 1961: 152). By 1936, according to this review, only 28.4 percent of those working in agriculture were day workers. (Milone's figure, based on the same census, is even lower: 19.8 percent; 1955: 510). This can be compared to over 50 percent landless in 1871. This reduction was largely the result of the abandonment of southern lands with low productivity to small owners.

In the Po Valley the growth of capitalist farming accelerated in the late nineteenth and early twentieth centuries. Those who worked the land were *braccianti*. As Procacci (1964) points out, these braccianti were not landless peasants with ambitions to buy land, but landless wage-earners with no hope for change. Although not large, even by Italian standards, Po Valley holdings were highly productive because of intensive cultivation and fertility. (Large farms, in fact, predominated in mountainous areas of low productivity. Milone 1955: 511).

The other Italian region of capitalist farming, Apulia, differs from the rest of the South and from the Po Valley as well. There, large farms were, and are extensively cultivated (Milone 1955: 511; Franklin 1969: 130). In 1936 almost half of its agricultural workers were landless laborers— the highest proportion in Italy (Milone 1955: 798).

The flow of migrants within Italy and out of the country depended to an important degree on these regional variations in agrarian structure. For the period of mass emigration, around 1900, John S. MacDonald argues that emigration, labor militancy, and acceptance of the status quo were alternative responses to agrarian hardship in the various regions of Italy. The alternative people took depended mainly on two factors: the pattern of landholding, and the extent of local involvement in the market. Where there was little marketing of agricultural products, as in Sardinia, passive acceptance prevailed. Where marketing was extensive, the choice was between militancy and emigration. The Center and Apulia chose militancy, according to his analysis, because the concentration of land ownership created sharp, visible class differences. The greater mixture of tenures in the deep South and the Alpine regions promoted emigration.

MacDonald's analysis echoes the observations of Francesco Coletti, who commented on the "embittering effect of the contrast between the poverty of the laborer and the profit of the landowner in Lower Lombardy and Lower Venetia." He saw militancy and emigration as closely competing alternatives: "Emigration, by the test of experience, showed itself to be a more pleasurable substitute for the strike" (Coletti, 1911: 113, 115). The Coletti-MacDonald analysis, though it makes good sense for the early twentieth century, misses a considerable change in the regional patterns of migration. Southern migration became dominant only after 1900; before then, the heaviest migration came from the North.

If only transatlantic migration were considered, we would have to award the honors to the South from the very beginning. But from 1876 through 1930 almost half of Italy's emigrants went elsewhere in Europe and the Mediterranean basin, and nine-tenths of them came from the North and Central regions (Pasigli 1969: 11–12). Of the total emigration from 1876 through 1930 over half came from north of Rome. It was in the period between 1900 and World War I that the enormous transatlantic migration from southern Italy surpassed the continuing flow of northern migrants to other parts of Europe.

In this period there was also considerable internal migration consisting primarily of two elements: agricultural workers following the harvest; and rural-urban migration within regions, especially in the northern industrial zone. This internal migration and the heavy international migration resulted in a net shift of population to cities and to the North and an eventual depopulation of densely settled sections of the South.

General Characteristics of the Population

Throughout the nineteenth and twentieth centuries the urban, industrial, and agricultural patterns of Italy moved slowly toward those of northwestern Europe. "Slowly" is a crucial word. The basic distributions of population and activities changed far more sluggishly in Italy than in France, Germany, or England; its population increased more slowly than that of most other European countries.*

In Italy, crude birth rates ran from 35 to 40 until the 1890s, when they began to decline. Crude death rates hung around 30 until their decline began in the 1870s. The downward movements of birth and death rates (with the exception of mortality peaks in the two World Wars and short-run recoveries of fertility immediately afterward) continued to the 1960s. They were sufficiently parallel to produce a fairly constant rate of natural increase: about 10 per 1,000.

The Italian population grew slowly—at the rate of 1 percent per year—because from 1880 onward, emigration subtracted a substantial number. In the peak period of emigration, 1901–1913, some 2 percent was leaving the country annually; the net loss to emigration (after allowance for those who returned) was probably about 1 percent. The long-run effect of emigration, war, and declines in fertility and mortality was to age the Italian population and produce a shortage of younger men, which affected the labor force. Figure 22 shows surprisingly constant numbers in agriculture, in manufacturing, and in services (the bulk of our "other") in the aggregate labor force from 1861 through 1921. Thereafter, the figures show only a slight decline in agriculture and modest rises in manufacturing and services.

A regional comparison of persons active in industry and agriculture between 1881 and 1936 reveals considerable change not apparent in the aggregate figures (Giusti 1951: 199–203). The base figures from the

* From 1800 to 1850 some average annual percentage rates of growth were: Russia, 0.71; Germany, 0.84; Italy, 0.66; France, 0.47; Great Britain, 1.30. From 1850 to 1900, Russia, 1.14; Germany, 0.95; Italy, 0.53; France, 0.25; Great Britain, 1.14 (Wrigley 1969: 185).

1881 census obviously included workers in rural industry and craftsmen in the category of the industrial workers, so that category is inflated. There was also inconsistency among the censuses as to how unqualified workers were assigned to agriculture or industry. Nevertheless, the regional changes described in this comparison describe the regional effects of industrialization in Italy. The changes between 1881 and 1936 are most dramatic at the geographic extremes. In Piedmont, Liguria, and Lombardy there was a great and steady increase of industrial workers, a corresponding decrease in agricultural workers. In the deep South—Calabria, Basilicata, and Apulia —there was a sharp drop in numbers employed in industry (a drop which continued after 1901, when the definitional problem disappears). After 1881 a deindustrialization of the southern countryside resulted because of the entry of manufactured goods from the North and from abroad.

Aggregate change is visible in the population *supported* by the slow-moving labor force. Between 1861 and 1951 the percentage of the total population in the labor force declined from 58 to 41. This increase in the dependent population resulted to some extent from rising school attendance, swelling numbers of old people, and (more indirectly) the loss of young men to emigration and war. But its main cause was the progressive withdrawal of women from the labor force (Livi Bacci 1965: 70–84). Women comprised 36 percent of the labor force in 1871, 29 percent in 1921, 25 percent in 1951. Some of that decline results from increasing reluctance of the census-takers to count women working at home as in the labor force. But the rise of wage-labor in agriculture and the eventual predominance of men in factories undoubtedly produced a genuine shrinking of the female labor force.* The general picture remains: a working population rather slow to change in shape and exceedingly slow to change in size, until well into the twentieth century.

Shifts in Class Structure

We have already identified some important changes in the Italian class structure. One was the post-Unification growth of landless labor in capitalist farming areas. Another is the rural-urban migration of former northern peasants into the growing cities where they found employment

---

* In the early period of Italian industrialization, women and children were frequent recruits. In the census of 1861, 54.2 percent of the persons listed as employed in industry were women (Giusti 1951: 183).

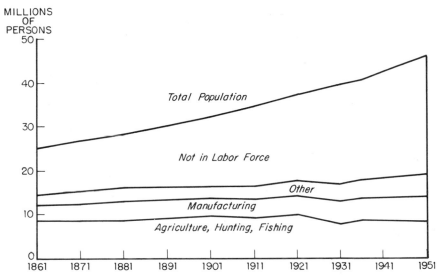

MILLIONS
OF
PERSONS

Figure 22. Labor Force Distribution of the Italian Population, 1861–1951.

Source: Associazione per lo Sviluppo dell'Industria nel Mezzogiorno, *Un secolo di statistiche italiane, nord e sud* (Rome: SVIMEZ, 1961), pp. 49–51.

as construction workers, as service workers in restaurants, hotels, and homes, or as unskilled day labor. In Milan, for example, peasants and unskilled workers predominated among its migrants until the early 1890s, when the city's growth as a center of railroads, commerce, and heavy machine industry attracted more skilled migrants. Persons calling themselves unskilled workers or peasants made up 36 percent of the in-migrants in 1885, but only 8 percent in 1910. Over the same period, the proportions of skilled and white-collar workers increased notably. In the rural-urban migration of the 1880s, individuals often came alone, leaving part of the family behind to continue running the farm. Those most easily employed in textile mills or service positions were often young women whose economic contribution in the rural setting was relatively low. Consequently, young female migration into cities was at least equal to male migration, and sometimes larger (Coletti 1911: 115). Other consequences of migration from the countryside were the aging of the rural population, the eventual availability of land in southern areas from which migration was especially heavy, and the depopulation of the Alpine region.

Higher up the social scale, the middle class was growing and thriving. The unification of Italy, the initial free-trade policy of the new kingdom, and a series of temporarily favorable circumstances in world agricultural markets (such as the disappearance of United States competition during its Civil War and the devastation of French vineyards by phylloxera) all led to a thriving period for merchant-agriculturalists in the 1860s and 1870s. In the South these men were able to buy confiscated church lands which were sold by the new kingdom; they allied with other landlords and officials to exclude peasants from such sales, and were quite successful at buying out indebted peasants who had managed to capture some of the church lands for themselves. The result was that by 1880 the South's rural bourgeoisie often rivaled the old nobility in landholdings. The once-sharp distinction between nobles and bourgeois faded as a consolidated land-lord class appeared. Tomasi di Lampedusa's great novel, *The Leopard,* portrays that very process in the grudging accommodation between the Prince of Salina, the chief of an ancient Sicilian family, and Don Calogero Sedára, the notary and mayor of Salina's country seat, whose lovely daughter marries Salina's nephew and heir. The aristocratic author hardly considers the relationship to have been mutually advantageous.

The increase in the bourgeois share of land was not accomplished so much at the expense of the nobility, however, as at the cost of crushing the aspirations of peasants. The peasants, besides losing out in the sale of church lands, also suffered from the intermediate layer of estate management: the gabellotti. These managers were free to coerce the peasants and extract their own share of the returns from the land, just so long as they delivered the necessary rents to the (normally absentee) landlord and kept things quiet on the estate. In return, the landlords provided the middlemen with protection from the authorities. This was precisely the situation that gave rise to mafia in Sicily: the building of exploitative local counter-governments by estate managers and their armed bands under the protection of great landlords (Romano 1963; Blok 1974).

In the North, during the 1870s and 1880s, an enlarged commercial and industrial bourgeoisie emerged, based mainly on the expanding textile industry. Many of the new families had strong links with the then-prospering agricultural sector. New families joined long-established ones (such as the Sellas of the Biella woolen industry) who already had members on the national political scene. Another group of bourgeois investors and businessmen, farther removed from agriculture, gained power in the 1880s and 1890s, with industrial growth in the machine and metal industries, development of electric power, and the invention of the automobile. Imaginative and daring entrepreneurs, they were also more open to change in traditional class relations. After 1901, these northern industrialists supported Giolitti's promotion of industrial development and accepted some of the claims of organized labor for bargaining rights and better wages (Romano 1965: 197).

Although any generalization about class structure bogs down instantly in local and regional qualifications, we can risk a provisional summary of the largest trends: (1) the slow fading of a highly heterogeneous peasantry; (2) the dwindling of the large landlords; (3) the expansion and long survival of a class of rentiers half-engaged in the urban professions and in politics while drawing their revenues from rural land; (4) the creation of a large, fragmented rural proletariat in several different sections of Italy; (5) the fairly rapid creation of an urban proletariat in the industrial cities of the North after 1890; (6) the earlier but slower creation of a national bourgeoisie linking industry, finance, commerce, administration, and the professions. Every one of these calls for important region-by-region qualifications.

Organization for Collective Action

The rough sketch just completed leaves out a set of transformations which is absolutely crucial to the analysis: the mobilization and struggle for power of different segments of the Italian population. There we must search for the most important connections among the changes in Italian social structure, the growth of the Italian variety of national state, and the shifting patterns of collective violence in the diverse regions of Italy.

The explorer of collective action in Italy has to clear away a dense growth of mythology to arrive at his objective. The debate about what *could* have happened during the nineteenth century and the related debate about the contribution of what *did* happen to the twentieth-century development of Fascism leads to a kind of writing about non-elites half hypothesis and half polemic. Accordingly, we have little systematic description of the development of certain forms of organization among Italians—surprisingly little documentation of the changing forms of labor organization, little comparative analysis of strike activity, few fragments of information on political associations outside the national elite, and so on down a discouraging list of negatives. Yet for our purposes it is essential to put together a general view of changes in the pattern of collective action, and to do it as much as possible without drawing our evidence from the violent conflicts we are attempting to explain.

The task is easier where the elite is concerned. In Italy, a national political elite existed long before the national state did. It was mainly united by nationalism of a relatively modern variety, with Austria's role similar to that of a twentieth-century colonial power. Italian nationalism permitted men of such diverse political sentiments as Garibaldi, Mazzini, Gioberti, Manzoni, Balbo, and Cavour to claim a common cause—a cause common until Unification. As early as the 1820s the shadowy, conspiratorial Carbonari were bringing together with intellectuals and professionals men who had held military and administrative posts under the French occupation. The Sublimi Maestri Perfetti (also devoted to a program first nationalist and then democratic, and drawn mainly from the bourgeoisie) also expanded their numbers and organization in the years just after the Restoration.

Both movements absorbed many smaller groups, anti-Napoleonic in the time of French occupation, into programs which often blended a Napoleonic mythology with an anti-Austrian rhetoric. Nationalism provided a unifying theme. Writing in the 1830s, Stendhal (himself expelled from Milan for "carbonarism" in 1821) made a young Carbonaro one of the two chief characters of his "Vanina Vanini." In this story, he captures the sense of a conspiracy of Italian monarchs with the crowns of Europe against the Italian people.

The activity of underground organizations—and the reaction of Italian states to their preparations for subversion and revolution—led directly to the formation of colonies of patriotic exiles, plotting and bickering and manning a nationalist press based in the other capitals of Europe. Mazzini created Young Italy at Marseilles in the 1830s; the Princess of Belgiojoso founded the anti-Austrian *Gazzetta Italiana* in Paris during the 1840s. But they also appear to have gathered a following among the craftsmen and shopkeepers of the Italian cities, to have linked with the followers of such early industrial prophets as Saint-Simon, and thus to have played an important part in laying the groundwork for the nineteenth-century Italian variants of socialism.

The political coalitions among Italian nationalists were always uneasy, and with Unification they fell apart. From the 1860s an important part of national politics consisted of the defense of the Piedmontese system of control against dissident members of the coalition: individually against a Garibaldi, a Mazzini, or a Cattaneo, collectively against the republicans. The defense relied on two strategies: first, the drawing of the landed elite of each region (which meant, of course, a somewhat different kind of elite in each region) into the national political coalition; and, second, forming alliances with the mercantile bourgeoisie of the North.

Leaders from the Italian labor movement did not achieve much national importance until the 1880s. But from that point one branch or another of organized labor provided the many new entrants into the national political arena.* By the end of World War I the major political struggles often involved socialist and labor leaders. Within five years after that, virtually every segment of the Italian political elite had been either demobilized or absorbed into the Fascist network.

The timing of organization for collective action by the bulk of the Italian population was no simple response to the organization of the national political elite. In the 1840s signs of mobilization appeared among the craft workers of Milan, Naples, Turin, Bologna, and other industrial cities: mutual aid societies, primitive unions, demonstrations, strikes. During the revolutions of 1848 Italy experienced some expansion of working-class collective action; workers' newspapers, for example, flourished for the first time. Working-class organization receded for a decade or so after 1848, and the 1850s were nearly devoid of strike activity. Some new efforts at organization and propaganda appeared among the craftsmen of Turin and Genoa. We shall see later that ordinary people in several different parts of Italy participated in the conflicts surrounding the first stages of national unification in 1859 and 1860; but their mobilization was temporary and not based on durable working-class organization.

The big, long strike in the wool textile region of Biella in 1864 marked the real beginning of large-scale industrial conflict in the mills of northern Italy. Not until the 1870s did substantial working-class or-

* Remember the lifeline of Mussolini. He made his beginning in Italian politics as secretary of Trent's Chamber of Labor, and came to national prominence as editor of *Avanti!*, the socialist party newspaper. (This does not mean that Mussolini or most of his party colleagues rose from personal origins as manual workers; on the contrary, they more commonly began as journalists, professionals, officials, or intellectuals.)

ganizations appear in the large industrial centers; at that time they frequently took the name of *Fasci operai*. (In the 1870s the term had none of the implications of authoritarian nationalism which the Fascists later gave it; the words conveyed a sense of "workers' solidarity.") Despite periodic repression by the government, the Fasci began to form national organizations, to hold national conventions, to establish relations with socialists outside of Italy.

The 1870s gave other signs of working-class mobilization. Up to the death of Bakunin (in Bern, 1876), the anarchist movement fed on the Fasci and flourished as nowhere else in western Europe. Independent of the anarchists, but with the considerable involvement of Fasci, mutual-aid societies, and other workers' organizations, strike activity accelerated. After a handful of strikes in the 1850s and 132 in the 1860s, the *Annuario statistico* enumerates 520 strikes in the 1870s and 866 in the 1880s. Again this was a regional phenomenon: almost all the large-scale organization and strike activity took place north of Rome. With that important qualification, the 1870s saw the "takeoff" of working-class organization at the regional and national levels.

Organization was still more durable, intensive, and widespread in the older, smaller-scale industries. With the exception of the Biella mills, textile factories never organized extensively in Italy, considering the large numbers employed. The metal-working industries were rather late in organizing; even in 1907 the proportion unionized was about 40 percent in trades like typography or hatmaking, as opposed to 20 percent in metals.

In the 1880s, most notably with the formation of the Partito Operaio, representatives of organized labor entered directly into national politics. The first working-class party deputies were elected to Parliament in 1882. Thenceforward the presence of overlapping (but far from identical) socialist and working-class movements in Italy affected national struggles for power. After 1900 syndicalism—in somewhat the form eventually advocated by Sorel—was gaining ascendancy within the Italian labor movement. Often enough, the anarchists' version of syndicalism prevailed: destroy the state now and let each group of workers rule itself.

The idea and the practice of the strike as a political weapon (as a means of applying direct pressure on the government and the national structure of power) spread rapidly. In 1904 Italian workers brought off the first more or less successful general strike held anywhere in the world; it began at the initiative of Milan's Chamber of Labor, in direct response to the killing of workers and peasants during a number of separate incidents in the South and in Sardinia. From that time and into the Fascist period, a large part of the energy of the Italian labor movement went into political struggles rather than actions against individual employers.

The timing of mobilization of agricultural workers differed from that of the industrial population. Some groups, such as the day laborers of the Po Valley, developed a capacity for collective action early and maintained it through most of the period we are considering. This was not generally the case of the areas of true peasantry, including important parts of Calabria, Sardinia, or the Alps. There mobilization came mainly as a defense against encroachments from outside and rarely lasted long. The strike was the tactic of landless laborers. As early as 1831 harvest workers of the Roman Campagna struck against their poor food rations and low wages. They went so far as to organize a march on Rome to present a petition to the Pope—only to be stopped by the papal police.

Because many Italian laborers became pure proletarians and yet remained in agriculture, the propensity of Italian agricultural workers to strike was high. Agriculture accounted for a significant minority of Italian strikes from before Unification. Strikes did not, however, become common occurrences until the 1880s. From 1880 to 1900, agricultural workers produced about a sixth of the strikes and a tenth of the strikers in Italy. But the strikers and their organizations were highly concentrated: the Veneto, Emilia, Romagna, Tuscany, Umbria, the Marches, Lombardy, Apulia, and Sicily—or rather sections of each of them. Other parts of Italy in which the rural population was just as poor and the pressure on the land just as great responded with mass emigration rather than labor militancy.

The union and the strike were not the only manifestations of mobilization among agricultural workers. Consumer cooperatives proliferated widely in the 1870s. Occasional messianic movements sprang up in the countryside, the most sensational being the sect led in Tuscany by Davide Lazzareti during the 1870s, which began by calling for "a republic and the Kingdom of God" and ended in a fatal clash with the carabinieri. In the 1880s the rural areas began to produce their own Fasci for mutual aid and political action. In 1893, the Sicilian Fasci organized takeovers of land, protests against taxation, and interventions in local elections—all of which sooner or later brought them into serious conflict with the authorities.

Throughout most of this period, the Catholic Church played an exceedingly conservative role. Shortly after his loss of the Church's temporal domain, the Pope forbade the faithful to take part in national politics. The full prohibition lasted until 1904, and lingered on as a shadow until 1919. (Actually, the electoral turnout from 1882, when suffrage was expanded, on demonstrates that millions of nominal Catholics went to the polls anyway.) But the hostility of the Church to the secular state (to say nothing of socialism, anarchism, the labor movement, and untold other modern evils) kept clericals and clerics from active, public participation in politics and facilitated the merger of anticlericalism with support for parliamentary democracy. For this reason, even the vague and tentative approval of labor organization in Pope Leo XIII's *Rerum Novarum* of 1891 seemed a dramatic break with the past.

Despite *Rerum Novarum,* priests who indulged in secular politics or involved themselves with the labor movement ran a serious risk of condemnation, transfer, harassment, or unfrocking well into the twentieth century. What was to become Christian Democracy in Italy did not get a serious start until the end of World War I. Then the Popolari (led by Don Luigi Sturzo, a Sicilian priest) became one of the major parties; even they received uncertain support and attempts at control from the Pope. As a body, the Church applied pressure on the Italian government from time to time. (In matters of moral concern that pressure could be quite effective, as illustrated by the fact that the legalization of divorce, first proposed in the Italian parliament in 1870, was not effected until 1970.) For the half-century after Unification, the Catholic Church reacted negatively to the Italian State, hampering national political participation by its loyal followers.

Long-Run Shifts in Violent Conflict

Was pre-Fascist Italy a violent country? Some parts of Italy maintained the vendetta into the twentieth century; the country won its unity by the sword; rebellions and insurrectionary strikes were common between 1830 and 1930; the Fascists strong-armed their way to power in many towns. Yet the question remains: Did Italians have a greater propensity to violent conflict than other people? No one can answer without applying precise and comparable definitions of "violence" to a number of countries over considerable spans of time, and without replicating for Italy the sort of tedious enumeration we have undertaken for France and Germany. We have made only the first moves in that direction (see Appendix D).

Our study makes it fairly clear that the overall level of collective violence in Italy since 1830 falls within the European range rather than approximating, say, the enormous frequencies of death, damage, and destruction reported for India in recent decades. Beyond that rather obvious conclusion it is hard to be confident. Our general impression is that the Italian levels of participation in collective violence from 1830 to 1930 resembled those of France and Spain, but were a little higher than those of England and Germany.

Nevertheless, we know that in Italy, as elsewhere, most political action occurred peaceably. There, too, collective violence appeared as a by-product of struggles for power which ordinarily went on without the bashing of heads or the smashing of windows. Furthermore, in Italy as elsewhere very little collective violence seems to have come about in direct response to breakdowns or deprivations created by rapid structural change. In Italy also, mobilized, organized groups bore the brunt of violent encounters—encounters usually involving representatives of the state, at that—while the marginal, depressed, demoralized, disorganized, or criminal segments of the population rarely joined the action.

Yet Italy had her own history. The outlines of her political transformations impressed themselves on the shape of collective violence; the several stages of unification, the acquisition and loss of power by different segments of the working class, the rise of the Fascists were the events governing the largest fluctuations in violent conflict. The regionalism of Italy's social and political life also was present in her collective violence: Much of the North was involved in what we earlier called "proactive" forms of violent conflict, while some parts of the South were still producing "reactive" conflicts. Compared with France and Germany, Italy's agrarian population played an exceptional part in collective violence throughout the century after 1830; the fact has to do with the forms of organization for collective action which grew up in the Italian countryside and not just with the numerical preponderance of the peasantry.

Over the century as a whole, banditry, mafia, the use of strong-arm mobs, and other forms of action at the margins of legality frequently assumed a scale and a political significance rare in the rest of Europe. Finally, the period ended with the Fascists' repressive system. This repression, for all of its blundering, proved capable of holding down autonomous collective action, and thus of restricting collective violence to the acts of repression themselves. All these features distinguished Italian collective violence from most European experience.

Italian collective violence came in bursts closely related to major struggles for power at the national level. Although apparently "nonpolitical" events such as food riots, tax rebellions, violent strikes, or collective seizures of land occurred every year, even they concentrated around the major political crises. In the 1830s and 1840s the pivotal crises were attempts at revolution in the various states of Italy, most of them led by secret societies such as the Carbonari, the Filadelfi, or Young Italy. There had been one such chain of rebellions in Naples, Palermo, Turin, and elsewhere in 1820–1821; another similar cluster came in 1828–1831; it had repercussions for another two years. The years 1843 and 1848–1849 brought a longer and larger series, first centering on Mazzinian plots but later running the full range from food riots to street-fighting to temporarily successful bourgeois revolutions in Sicily, Naples, Lombardy, Venice, Tuscany, and the Papal States.

In the fluid situation of new regimes promising change throughout Italy, two factors led to continued disorder. First was the effort, especially in the South and in Sicily, of peasants and workers to make their claims (whether for bread and work in the cities or for distribution of land in the countryside) heard. Second, the efforts of the revolutionary regimes to reimpose order (in the form of taxation, criminal justice, conscription, and so on) in the surrounding countryside met with determined, sometimes violent, resistance. While the workers and peasants turned against revolutionary regimes which did not address their problems, the middle and upper classes, horrified at continued violence and fearful of worker-peasant "communism," also began to see a strong restoration as the only guarantee of law and order. The revolutionary coalitions throughout Italy collapsed. But it was less the schisms within the coalitions than the advance of the Bourbon, French, and Austrian armies which cut short the constitutional and republican experiments.

After the abortive revolutions of 1848, the string of plots and coups continued *diminuendo* up to Piedmont's conquest of Lombardy in the 1859 war with Austria, and her later annexation of Tuscany, Modena, and Parma. In May 1860, Garibaldi and the Red Shirts landed in Sicily and began their armed march northward. Their invasion culminated, somewhat against the intentions of Garibaldi, in the annexation of the Two Sicilies to Piedmont in October 1860. As the great consolidation proceeded, four other kinds of violent confrontation occurred throughout Italy: (1) the forcefully repressed demonstration of sympathy for the national revolution in one of the territories (the Papal States) as yet unliberated; (2) vigorous resistance, vigorously repressed, to the efforts of the new regime to collect taxes, install officials, and carry on the routines of government; the mainland South saw repeated conflicts of this kind after Piedmont annexed them; (3) seizures of land, attacks on landlords, and related settling of scores at moments of interregnum or governmental weakness, especially in Sicily; (4) guerrilla and other attacks on the new regime by supporters of the old regime and/or enemies of the particular newcomers to power, in Massa, Apulia, Naples, and elsewhere. Conflicts of these varieties occurred through the 1860s, with the new kingdom's land reforms gaining increasing prominence as the focus of discontent.

The annexation of Venetia in the Piedmontese war with Austria (1866) had nothing like these wide repercussions. Garibaldi's 1867 invasion of the Papal States (turned back by the French army) followed the classic model of conspiracy and coup, complete with tacit, ambivalent Piedmontese backing. But the other conflicts of the 1860s drew in a much wider range of the Italian population than had been the case before. The demonstrations, strikes, attacks on mills, invasions of municipal buildings incited by the imposition of a national *macinato*—the infamous milling tax—in 1868 and 1869 involved more Italians than any previous cluster of collective violence. The multiple republican insurrections of 1870 took on a scale previously unprecedented except in 1848.

Though far from calm, the 1870s were somewhat less turbulent than the 1860s. Protests against the macinato continued, agricultural strikes in Lombardy led to violent clashes, food riots broke out through much of central Italy during the crisis of 1874, the followers of Davide Lazzaretti mounted their insurrection in Tuscany, and several different bands of anarchists raised unsuccessful rebellions. Events of the same general kind continued into the 1880s at a moderate tempo, with groups of workers—especially agricultural workers—playing a larger and larger role.

During the 1890s the scale and intensity of violent conflicts rose sharply. Agricultural strikes, tax protests, organized land seizures, and (in 1897 and 1898) food riots continued to occur throughout much of the countryside. The new fact was the clustering of disturbances, first, in 1893 and 1894, around the activities of the Sicilian Fasci, which were eventually put down brutally; and second, in 1898, around a series of actions by workers and peasants related to the subsistence crisis of that year. Strikes in industry and agriculture, including several general strikes, dominated the collective violence of the following decade. The same was true of the period before World War I, except that concerted urban demonstrations somewhat independent of strike activity provided an increasingly important setting for collective violence.

In most western countries, collective violence at home declines in wartime, because of tighter governmental control over any collective action, because of the absorption of young men into the armed forces, and perhaps because of the temporary integration of dissident groups into the national effort. But Italy's respite during World War I was exceptionally short. It ran from the violence accompanying the prowar demonstrations and antiwar strikes of May 1915 to the Fatti di Agosto of Turin in August 1917, during which a general strike in protest against high prices and bread shortages involved some 80,000 workers in five days of street fighting and led to hundreds of casualties.

In terms of sheer numbers, however, 1917 fell far short of 1919, 1920, and 1921. Those three years may well have produced the highest level of involvement in collective violence of any trio in Italy's modern history. We find food riots in the Center and South, land occupations from Rome southward, strikes, insurrectionary communes, factory takeovers by workers' councils, and assaults on newspaper offices, labor headquarters, working-class organizations, and, finally, individuals by strong-arm *squadre* (squads). In this enormous panoply of conflicts, the struggle between Fascists and socialists became dominant after 1920.

In 1922, however, the socialists clearly lost strength. The Fascists acquired increasing freedom to smash, intimidate, and even wield governmental powers. During that year different groups of Fascists broke strikes, destroyed socialist headquarters, occupied Fiume, forcibly took over town councils, and continued to beat up leftists. The culmination was October's March on Rome; a threatening gathering of Fascist forces in and around the capital which ended with Mussolini's being called to form a government.

Mussolini became prime minister within the legal forms; he spent another three years consolidating his control of the government both by squeezing and reshaping the existing forms of rule and by permitting his squadre to continue their work of vengeance and intimidation. (In some senses of the word "revolution," the continuity of the legal forms means that no revolution occurred when the Fascists took power, but for much of 1922 the counter-government of the Fascists was strong enough for us to call the situation divided sovereignty, civil war, or even revolution.) From 1923 through 1925 Italian collective violence was that of hunters against their prey rather than of warriors in combat. Antifascist demonstrations were few, clandestine—and severely repressed. After 1925 Italy saw very little collective violence of any kind until the regime's collapse in World War II. Up until then, the opposition was demobilized, deported, destroyed, or absorbed; repression worked.

The Italian experience from 1830 to 1930 falls into three rough stages, each more violent than the previous: before unification, with relatively localized and small-scaled collective violence; from about 1860 to 1890, with fairly frequent violent conflict, sometimes on a large geographic scale; and from 1890 to the Fascist consolidation of power, with large swings from year to year and with degrees of participation never before reached. If our chronology extended beyond 1930, we would have to define at least a fourth and a fifth stage: collective violence dropping off to very low levels from 1926 to the end of World War II, then returning to frequent disturbances and widespread participation.

The distinction among "competitive," "reactive," and "proactive" forms of collective action leading to violence applies less neatly to Italy than to France. Individual conflicts fall into the categories well enough; the Italian *rissa* resembled the French *rixe* in its typical pitting of communal groups against each other; the tax rebellion has a similar form in both countries; and the conditions under which strikes turned violent had much in common. But in Italy the competitive forms of action thrived (at least in the guise of the vendetta in parts of Sicily and Sardinia) into the twentieth century, the reactive forms held on in some parts of the

South long after they had disappeared from the North, and in most regions there was a greater mixture and fluctuation among the types of
action than was the case in France.

All of these resulted from the relative weakness and inconstancy of
central control in Italy. Before Mussolini, the Italian state was often
incapable of mounting effective repression; it wiped out the Sicilian Fasci
and put down the protests of 1898, but could not prevent the explosion of
food riots and land occupations in the aftermath of World War I. Its
control varied greatly from region to region and even time to time; it
encountered virtual counter-governments in more distant corners of the
realm. The result kept a number of kinds of political action, each operating within a somewhat different political system, going at the same time.

In an indirect way, Cavour himself recognized that the Piedmontese food
riots of 1853 actually posed a question of political principle:

Consumers worry and become irritated when they see grain rise in price after
a good harvest. The cry against "hoarders" . . . the extremist parties, and
especially the clerical party, try to draw an advantage from this unfortunate
circumstance to arouse the ignorant mass against the government and especially against me, since I have a special claim to their antipathy. I am determined not to yield one bit to these complaints and to maintain intact the
principles of commercial liberty which I have made prevail in Parliament
(1884: 321).

He could not quite see, classic liberal that he was, that the "ignorant
mass" also operated from principle. Most of the creators of the Italian
national state believed as a matter of political principle that neither control of commerce nor "feudal" constraints on property nor public charity
could do anything but stem the flow of the greatest good to the greatest
number. As a result, food riots, attacks on landlords, land occupations,
and other agrarian conflicts acquired their reputation as misguided and
impulsive responses to immediate hardships, as "unpolitical" events. A
good look at the calendar of Italian collective violence makes that conclusion hard to accept.

The chronology also challenges any simple view of collective violence
as a function of the pace of industrialization and urbanization. Some might
argue that the high levels of violent conflict after 1890 resulted from the
quickening pace of structural change in Italy, and point to the heavy in-

volvement of organized workers in that conflict as confirmation of the argument. But the wide fluctuations in collective violence before 1890 could hardly result from the very slow and fairly steady economic and demographic transformation of Italy during those years. The enforced quietus of the later 1920s came amidst rapid urbanization and industrial growth. There are even grounds for arguing a *negative* relation between collective violence and pace of change. Whatever the exact relation, it is subtle and mediated by the political process.

We are not saying, by any means, that Italian collective violence had nothing to do with economic and demographic change. The tax rebellions and land seizures of the 1860s had to do with money, land, consumption, and work. Economic and demographic transformations produced the agricultural proletarians and mill workers who fought with the authorities in the 1890s. Postwar inflation and unemployment became critical issues in the conflicts of 1919 to 1921. The general timing of collective violence in Italy does not challenge the significance of these matters for political conflict; it challenges the more special but widely held idea that rapid structural change itself tends to generate protest, conflict, and violence.

Unification and Local Conflict, 1848–1859

Until the revolutions of 1848, the decade of the 1840s was mainly a time of nationalist plots and insurrections radiating from Mazzini and his collaborators. Nevertheless, there were typically reactive food riots in Lombardy and other areas of North and Central Italy in 1846 and 1847. In February 1847 a crowd angered by the high price of bread and potatoes attacked Swiss merchants who were buying grain in Varese for export. In other towns between Como and Milan, bands of peasants attacked convoys of grain wagons and granaries. Soldiers sent to keep order allowed themselves to be disarmed and locked into their barracks. The Austrians temporarily forbade export of wheat or corn and, when disorders continued, sent Croatian troops to occupy the troubled areas (DeMarco 1950: 13; Della Peruta 1952: 534).

On a more consciously political level, many of the Italian states had experienced, by early 1848, growing mobilization of the middle class around constitutional demands and schemes to liberalize their regimes. In Piedmont and Tuscany, newspapers and discussion groups were appearing. Pius IX had started to modify authoritarian papal rule, but in the Two Sicilies, King Ferdinand II was unmoved.

It was in Palermo that a group of bourgeois and noble leaders got the revolutionary movement going on January 12, 1848. They placed themselves at the head of armed popular bands which skirmished with police and troops, built barricades, and eventually proclaimed a provisional governing committee. Although armed peasants joined the fight the next day, it was not until January 14 that the original leaders succeeded in forming, with others of their own class, four more committees. The special assignments of these committees were the quintessential concerns of bourgeois revolutionaries faced with the delicate task of restoring order after a change in regime: provisioning, public security, finances, information. The earlier committee continued in charge of military operations (Candeloro 1966: III, 125). During the next few weeks Bourbon officials and troops were chased from their posts throughout Sicily; in rural areas peasants destroyed grist tax offices and land records.

On the mainland, the populace of the city of Naples was traditionally loyal to the Bourbons. Consequently, the Neapolitan middle-class men who wished to emulate the Sicilian revolt moved into the countryside, starting with the region of Cilento. There armed bands began the attack on local record offices and hated Bourbon officials. Troops sent into the area were successfully hunting down the bands, when the situation was transformed by the decree promising a constitution, issued by Ferdinand II on January 29, 1848, followed by the constitution itself.

This dramatic turn of events was followed by similar constitutional decrees in Piedmont, Tuscany, and Rome. So far, only in Sicily had the changes been prompted by insurrection. Elsewhere, constitutional compromises had been worked out by the monarchs and political moderates, under popular pressure to be sure. In the next months the question was whether the interest of the urban poor and of the peasants could be served by the narrowly based new governments, obsessed with a "fear of communism" and concerned above all with restoring and maintaining order.

In Lombardy and Venetia the Austrian government had started the year 1848 by arresting suspected conspirators, repressing student demonstrations, issuing a decree instituting summary justice, and reinforcing its troops in Italy. For these areas, the wave of revolution starting from Paris in February rather than Italian events were the model for revolt. In

Venice and Milan rebellion came with the news of Metternich's resignation in Vienna. Demonstrations in Venice on March 17 demanded the release from prison of the patriot Daniele Manin. Once freed, Manin planned and carried out a successful seizure of power.

In Milan, despite the presence of Radetzky and a large Austrian garrison, a popular demonstration on March 17 was transformed into the beginnings of insurrection. The acting governor of Lombardy was captured and forced to sign decrees establishing a civic guard and ordering the police to turn their stored arms over to the city. The street fighting that followed drove the Austrian troops from the center of the city, then forced them to withdraw into the heavily fortified area at the border of the Veneto, the Quadrilateral. The main cities of Lombardy and the Veneto also rose and drove out Austrian troops and officials. Peasants and workers participated in many of these battles. In Piedmont the newly constitutional regime of King Carlo Alberto transformed the movement into a war of national liberation against Austria by invading Lombardy.

Each of these revolutions initiated a lesser series of conflicts. In the South, urban and rural disturbances pushed the government from the left, until King Ferdinand finally fled. Urban disturbances included demonstrations of the unemployed (February 1848, Naples), a strike of printers (April 1848, Naples), and a series of machine-breaking expeditions in textile mills, especially in Campania. In Piedmont, the Veneto, and Tuscany a series of strikes and agitations disturbed the cities, but in both the North and the South, the popular movement was most serious in the countryside.

In the rural areas of the South (in the Sila of Calabria and in Basilicata, for example) communal lands were occupied, private woods burned, and animals stolen or killed. Tax and land records were destroyed. Men who protested or criticized such actions were beaten or killed. Rural property owners and urban bourgeois alike feared the primitive radicalism expressed in these events, and the revolutionary government was hard-pressed to restore order (DeMarco 1950: 19–20; Genoino 1948: 253–258; Soldani 1973). Carlo Poerio (an anti-Bourbon but politically moderate activist imprisoned after the restoration of Ferdinand) wrote in July 1848: "The robbery and extortions of the armed bands have disgusted most proprietors and honest citizens. In the Cilento the wretches have formed an antisocial, bestial sect which is concerned only with sacking and robbing the countryside" (quoted in DeMarco 1950: 31). In Sicily, in the South, and in Tuscany the violent claims of urban workers and peasants challenged government and led to a growing sentiment that an efficient government of order could only come with a restored monarchy.

In Lombardy the failure of the new government to listen to the claims of the peasantry was only partially the cause of their defection from the revolution. Also important was the fact that, in its overriding political goal to continue the fight against the Austrians, the Lombard government had to keep collecting taxes (especially consumption taxes) and conscripting young men. The moderates in power wanted to control the revolutionary movement closely, so they tried to limit popular initiative and participation. Two trends coincided: the moderates, from fear of radical initiatives, worked to prevent peasant autonomous action; at the same time they alienated peasant support by continuing unpopular policies.

In the Alpine province of Sondrio there were peasant agitations for the return of ex-communal lands to common use. In Brescia and Como provinces there was refusal to pay taxes. In Brianza there was a dispute over rents and contracts of the peasants farming the land owned by the orphan asylum of Milan. The urban middle-class revolutionaries came to be identified as the rich—the *signori*—and they lost early peasant cooperation and support. When Radetzky and his Austrian troops marched back into Lombardy in July 1848, they were greeted with cheers of "Viva Radetzky!" "Morte agli signori!"

In the North, Carlo Alberto and the Piedmontese army definitively lost the war in the battle of Novara, March 1849. The counterattack of Bourbon and Austrian troops toppled the already tottering revolutionary regimes in Tuscany, Naples, Rome, and finally Venice. Everywhere the monarchs returned to power. Carlo Alberto abdicated in favor of his son; despite Piedmont's defeat in the field, its liberal constitution was the only one to survive the revolutionary period.

The pattern of collective violence in the 1850s greatly resembled that of the decade preceding 1848. The year 1851 saw a "bakers' mutiny" against the lowering of wages in Palermo, which resulted in the arrest and deportation of a hundred workers. In December 1852 another Mazzinian conspiracy for insurrection in Mantua and Belfiore was followed two months later by *I Barabba,* an unsuccessful insurrection in Milan. The year

1853 brought food riots in Lombardy, Piedmont, and the Papal States as well as an abortive invasion by Mazzinian republicans, this time in Carrara. In 1855, 1856, and 1857 the chief events were attempts to raise rebellion in Belfiore, Corleone, Genoa, Livorno, and Sapri. All were signally futile.

Not until the Piedmontese-Austrian War of 1859 did any transfers of power actually take place. Then, under the patronage of the Piedmontese, "peaceful revolutions" (sometimes, as in Avenza-Carra, April 1859, supported by popular demonstrations) brought plebiscites attaching Parma, Modena, Tuscany, and the ex-Papal legation of Bologna to Piedmont. Meanwhile, the Pope put down nationalist demonstrations in the rest of his territories, and the Piedmontese crushed scattered resistance to their own takeover.

In April 1860 an uprising in Palermo touched off marauding bands throughout much of the Sicilian countryside; peasants refused to pay taxes, attacked mills, chased governmental officials away, and demanded land. The following month Garibaldi and his Red Shirts landed in Sicily; peasant attacks on officials and bourgeois continued in the wake of his conquest. About the same time, an attempt of the bourgeois of Apulia to mount an anti-Bourbon rebellion led to a popular revolt *against* the bourgeoise and *for* the Bourbons. In July, Garibaldi crossed over into the mainland South, to the accompaniment of liberal coups and some peasant protest. To prevent his continuing north to Rome and triggering foreign intervention, the Piedmontese army invaded the Papal States through the Marches and Umbria and joined forces with Garibaldi at Naples. Relatively few land occupations occurred, compared to Sicily in the same year, or the same area in 1848, but reactionary protest gathered force: at the plebiscite for annexation to Piedmont in November, armed peasants in Basilicata demonstrated against annexation.

Thus, 1859 was marked by transfer of power in the North and Center, but 1860 and the transfer of power in the South produced the great bulk of collective violence in Italy between the revolutions of 1848 and the establishment of the Kingdom of Italy in 1861. For that reason, we shall break our close analysis of the period into two parts: the decade from 1850 through 1859, and the turbulent year of 1860. For the ten-year period, we recorded eighty disturbances.

A very crude classification of locus and participants permits us to break

Table 8. Types of groups in collective violence by region, 1850–1859

Region	Urban population	Rural population	Political activists	Bandits	Soldiers	Total
Piedmont	12	3	1	1	0	17
Sardinia	3	1	0	0	0	4
Lombardy-Veneto	5	2	1	0	0	8
Papal States	8	2	1	8	0	19
Modena-Parma	5	1	1	0	0	7
Tuscany	3	0	1	0	0	4
Naples	4	6	1	0	1	12
Sicily	3	0	5	1	0	9
Total	43	15	11	10	1	80

down the eighty disturbances from 1850 to 1859 by political subdivision in Table 8. The heading "bandits" is misleading for two reasons: first, bandits struck much more often in the 1850s than the table indicates; these are only the rare cases in which they numbered fifty or more; and, second, the eight cases of banditry in the Papal States are repeated attacks by the giant band of *Il Passatore* in 1850. Nevertheless, because of the political protection bandits often enjoyed, because of the alliances they sometimes formed with local landlords, and because of the reputations they occasionally acquired as redressers of wrongdoing, it would be even more misleading if no bandits appeared in a sketch of the collective violence of the 1850s. The single case of "soldiers" as participants came in July 1859 in Naples when six hundred guards mutinied and were subdued, with fifty killed, by loyal troops.

The table deliberately excludes the military actions of the 1859 war between Piedmont and Austria (even the colorful warmaking of Garibaldi and his freebooters). If included, these events would significantly augment the numbers for Piedmont, Lombardy, and Veneto. But they would not fundamentally change our conclusions concerning the distributions of the major types of collective violence.

Proportionate to their populations, Sardinia, Modena-Parma, the Papal States, and Piedmont had relatively frequent violent events, while Sicily, Tuscany, Naples, and Lombardy-Veneto had less than their share. The differences are not enormous; given the crudity of the count, they might have no significance at all. The concentration of urban conflicts in Piedmont and the cluster of attempts to stir up nationalist insurrections in Sicily probably have somewhat more importance, for they correspond to major political problems faced by the two regimes: an uneasy urban population in Piedmont; ineffective control of the hinterland in Sicily.

The "urban" conflicts consist of those occurring in cities in which the participants (aside from troops or police sent to put down the movement) were not identified as supporters of some defined political program, but as a mob, a crowd, *il popolo,* or something similar. Most consisted of groups of people who gathered to protest some governmental action or inaction—a new tax, a political arrest, failure to stop the cholera epidemic of 1855, and so on—and began to fight with the troops or police sent to disperse them. About a third of the urban disturbances, however, were food riots; in them the participants ordinarily began the action by seizing commodities or by attacking the property of persons presumed to be withholding food from ordinary people.

The distribution of the fourteen food riots is interesting. Most occurred between the sparse harvest of 1853 and the better harvest of 1854, when the Crimean War cut off grain imports from the Near East. Despite the fact that the shortage extended throughout Italy, the riots occurred only from Rome northward. The reason: public provisioning policy. By the 1850s the states of the North, especially Piedmont, had adopted policies of free trade in grain, the Papal States had bumbled their way to a set of compromises between favoritism to grain merchants and paternalism toward the masses, and the Two Sicilies had maintained thoroughgoing controls over prices and distribution.

"Free trade" for domestic producers, merchants, and exporters did not preclude protective tariffs on imports. After the first protests against rising bread prices, in Genoa and its suburbs (August 1853), Cavour's government reduced the tariff on incoming grain and cut railroad rates for grain shipments—though not soon enough to prevent an attack on the house of Cavour as *il affamatore del popolo,* the starver of the people (Omodeo n.d.: I, 257–266).

The attempt to let the market do its own work unhindered not only failed to feed the hungry but also offended the popular belief that the government had an obligation to assure and control the supply of food. In the South such an obligation was built into government policy. As the bemused American minister in Naples reported in 1860: "The tobacco of this country is poor but it must be sold cheap, as it seems to be regarded

with bread as one of the necessities of life whose price is somehow connected with the safety of dynasties . . . Bread is here the staff of life,
and when the coarse food rises above a certain price sufferings which
lead to disaffection are consequent" (Marraro 1952: II, 488). The government met high food prices directly by forbidding exports, suspending
taxes on food, and buying up wheat to sell to the poor at a controlled
price. These were precisely the kinds of measures the food rioters of the
North were demanding. Many people in the South were hungry, but they
did not demonstrate, smash, and grab.

The importance of public policy comes out in an interesting way: when,
in 1860, the Two Sicilies did liberalize the grain trade, they finally experienced food riots on their home ground. The new king, Francesco II,
did away with some of the controls over grain, although he and his government continued the prohibition on exports. During the moderate price
rises of early 1860 there were angry protests including shouting women
attacking bakeries and ovens in Naples, Terra di Lavoro, Campania, and
Apulia. A good spring harvest stopped that round of food riots, but similar protests occurred in late July at the collapse of the monarchy. What
is more, the themes of cheap food and government obligation to feed the
poor reverberated through the reactionary movements which followed the
annexation of Naples and Sicily to the new national kingdom.

Nor was the outbreak of collective violence in the southern kingdom
in 1860 merely a result of weakened repressive capacity. The Two Sicilies
did experience 21 of the 80 conflicts we have enumerated from 1850
through 1859, including 7 of the 43 urban conflicts—none of them food
riots. Moreover, they contributed 6 of the 15 "rural" events. (We included in this category all conflicts in which the principal participants
were peasants, even if they occurred in big towns, plus all other conflicts
occurring in predominantly agricultural areas.) The category includes an
encounter in which countrymen from the Val d'Aosta presented themselves
at the gates of Aosta in December 1853 to protest the imposition of a
property tax, and skirmished with the police and national guards of the
city. It includes a single rural food riot in Lombardy (Arona 1853), a
number of conflicts centered on taxation of commodities, and three ex-
emplars of an event which became very common in years of political
crisis: the land occupation.

As it occurred in southern Italy during the 1840s, 1850s, and 1860s, the land occupation ordinarily laid a claim for the division and distribution of lands formerly held in common, as a compensation for lost common rights. The law was often on the side of the squatters, even when the lawmakers were not. When the Bourbons returned to power in the South after the defeat of Napoleon, they had accepted the French-inspired liberalization of landholding. Theoretically, common land, once distributed, was inalienable for ten years. Practically, however, lack of credit meant that small-holders found it hard to exploit their land and often soon lost it. Cassese (1954) has described the process for the Val di Diano. There the distribution of land was very slow, surrounded by disagreements and litigation. When portions of land could not be retained by the peasants, they were returned to the commune, which in turn rented them out to the large landholders, several of whom were on the communal council. The rent from these lands, they argued, was an important part of the income of the commune, and the exploitation of the land by large landowners provided work for the poor.

This classic but circular argument was not accepted by the kingdom's central commission on land distribution; after 1849, the commune was ordered again to distribute land according to the law. In the Diano there were no land occupations, even in 1848. The big landlords had the collaboration of the authorities and won without too much of a fight. An agricultural league which set out to better conditions for the peasants of Diano via a program of mutual aid, better wages for day-laborers, and better leases for tenants found itself suppressed by the government.

In the Sila area of Calabria, by contrast, there were a series of land occupations in 1850–1853. The area had the same dreary history of dodging the law, avoiding distribution of land to the landless, and usurpation by the big landlords of land earmarked for distribution. In 1848 this part of Calabria had been especially shaken by land occupations, wood-burning, and the "kidnaping" of animals (Valente 1951). The land occupations between 1850 and 1853 were, by comparison, quiet and orderly. And after 1853, they ended, probably because the peasants had finally elicited a commitment from the land commissioner, the Intendant, and the central government to distribute the land as the law required (Basile 1958). Once again, an action which appears at first to grow from ignorance, greed, and despair turns out on closer examination to embody a rather precise, coherent sense of law, justice, and obligation.

The other major category of violent events of the 1850s were led by avowed political activists. We find eleven in our compilation. All play variations on a theme: a small group of conspirators strike an initial blow, send out a call for insurrection in the name of nation and liberty, get no more than a momentary response, flee, and are apprehended, tried, and executed. In Milan (February 1853) the conspirators who attacked the Austrian guard appear to have been a group of artisans in league with, or infiltrated by, Mazzinian activists; at any rate, of the approximately thirty executed for taking part, all eighteen for whom we have occupational information were artisans (Pollini 1953: 234–235). Again artisans predominated among those arrested for participating in the Genoan insurrection of 1857, although the search for Mazzinians which followed reached into the ranks of the bourgeoisie (Comandini 1918: III, 718, 720, 759–760).

Urban working-class activists figured in all the northern insurrections; their genteel collaborators remained discreetly in the background. If the best-documented series, the Sicilian insurrections of November 1856, are a reasonable sign, the regional elite played a larger and more direct part in the equally unsuccessful attempts to foment revolutions in the Two Sicilies. In 1856, the Baron Bentivegna anticipated an island-wide uprising, coordinated by middle-class plotters, planned for January 1857. His group from Corleone managed to capture Mezzoluao and free prisoners held there but not to bring the Palermo committee into the revolution. After Bentivegna's flight, another group at Cefalù got word of the rebellion, raised the tricolor, opened the prison, and renewed the fight, though not for long. And so went all the insurrections until 1859, when there were armies to support them.

Transfers of Power, 1859 and 1860

The 1859 annexations went off with conspicuously little popular participation—planned that way by Piedmontese who had seen the risks of too strong a popular movement in 1848. Most of the presumably spontaneous demonstrations in favor of national unity in the North responded to signals and subsidies from Turin. The most massive involvement was on the part of the French army, which incurred about 20,000 casualties in fighting the Austrians. Military engagements aside, 1859 was actually a year of little collective violence.

Not so 1860. That year featured both the Garibaldian invasion and a great scatter of rural and urban conflicts, for and against the new regime, throughout the South. We have excluded the movements of Garibaldi and his Red Shirts from our enumeration, because they fall on the margin between military action and popular movement. Even so, we find 105 disturbances meeting our criteria in the year 1860 alone, as compared with a total of 80 for the previous ten years. What is more, they are enormously concentrated in the Two Sicilies. As Table 9 indicates, 61 of them occurred in the territory of Naples, 35 more in Sicily, and only 9 throughout all the rest of Italy. More than half the southern disturbances were rural —land occupations, tax rebellions, and attacks on landowners. The 24 conflicts involving "political activists" in the territory of Naples consisted entirely of efforts by partisans of the Bourbons (especially soldiers, former officials, and priests) to raise popular movements of resistance to Garibaldi and Piedmont. The 22 urban movements in the South covered a wider political range, but almost all had a direct connection with the great transfer of power.

Sicily shook with insurrection for a month before Garibaldi's landing. The unsuccessful Gancia uprising in Palermo, on April 4, was the most visible and best organized. It inspired violent demonstrations in Marsala, Messina, and Catania and was followed by the disarming and expulsion of Bourbon troops at Trapani. Demonstrations, often repressed with violence, continued up to the invasion.

The first wave of rural protest came in the form of attacks on the property, personnel, and symbols of the Bourbon government. The typical scenario was for a *banda insurezzionale* to descend on a settlement, drive off or kill the tax collector, divert the mill stream, or steal the tax money —all obviously related to the much-resisted macinato. Some peasants surely took part, but the political focus of the attacks and the roving nature of the bands differ greatly from the later patterns and imply different participants. Both outlaws and political activists probably played a larger role in these bands than did peasants or bourgeois (cf. Falzone 1960: 499; Romano 1952: 172).

The period just before and after the arrival of Garibaldi abounded in raids, demonstrations, and battles directed against officials and supporters of the Bourbons. But the whole pattern of collective violence shifted significantly as the Garibaldini began to establish their control

Table 9. Violent events of 1860 by region and participants

Region	Urban population	Rural population	Political activists	Bandits	Soldiers	Total
Piedmont	1	—	—	—	—	1
Sardinia	—	—	—	—	—	0
Lombardy-Veneto	2	—	—	—	—	2
Papal States	4	1	—	—	—	5
Modena-Parma	—	—	—	—	—	1
Tuscany	1	—	—	—	—	1
Naples[a]	15	22	24	—	—	61
Sicily[b]	7	28	—	—	—	35
Total	30	51	24	0	0	105

[a] The urban riots in Naples in May–July had political ends—they were anti-Bourbon—but the general population took part. The events involving "political activists" were the beginning of the Bourbon reaction; some of the participants were rural workers, but the leaders were ex-soldiers, former officials, and priests, with a particular message: restore the Bourbons.

[b] In Sicily (and the South in general) division between urban and rural is tenuous since the agricultural population lived in towns. We have restricted the term urban to major centers such as Messina, Trapani, and Palermo.

over Sicily. Although Garibaldi quickly issued decrees abolishing the macinato and promising land distribution, he also quickly established a de facto alliance with the island's bourgeoisie and with its militia, which was largely bourgeois in origin (Mack Smith 1950: 204–205, 214). The bourgeois shifted their allegiances rather rapidly as a way of maintaining order and property in the face of serious threats from the radicals and the poor; the shift aligned the enemies of many peasants and workers with the very government from which the peasants and workers had hoped for redress of their grievances. The numerous land occupations and attacks on proprietors rapidly took on the coloration of opposition to Garibaldi and the national revolution. The rising level of conflict finally induced the Garibaldini, as one of them wrote regretfully, "to play the carabinieri against our allies of yesterday" (ibid.: 211).

On the mainland there was no significant rural movement against the Bourbons. There were, on the other hand, repeated attempts to raise insurrections against the bourgeois allies of Garibaldi. In other respects, the patterns of disturbance in the two parts of the Two Sicilies resembled each other: antigovernment demonstrations turning to violence in Naples, Salerno, and Avellino before the invasion by Garibaldi; urban food riots; attacks on supporters of the old regime at the time of Garibaldi's take-over; land occupations. Land occupations were less frequent on the main-land and more concentrated geographically, especially in Matera and adjacent areas of Basilicata. But where they occurred, as in Sicily, they in-volved much the same veering of the poor away from hopeful attachment to the new regime toward nostalgia for the old.

In Matera itself, the conflict over division of the domain lands had been going on for years. At the end of July a series of tumultuous assemblies against the usurpers of the communal domain began. "Nitrate smugglers, tanners, and stone-cutters aroused the people of the countryside," accord-ing to one observer (Racioppi 1867: 150), "and the artisans and plebs of the city joined the chorus." An old liberal of 1848 became mayor; he promised expropriation and division of usurped common lands. At one meeting, members of the gendarmerie encouraged peasants to take action against the gentlemen if they wanted redistribution of land. Another ad-viser, a radical lawyer, suggested the peasants get themselves a surveyor to pace out the land to be divided (Pedio 1960: 205). A certain Franceso Gattini, a supporter of the liberalizing changes emanating from Naples, was the chief target of complaints. He was accused of usurping land earmarked for distribution to the poor. He and other landlords (including the bishop) took legal action to break up their estates and redistribute some of the land. Their initiative did not calm the situation. On August 8 a turbulent mob at the gates of the town prevented the farm workers from going to the fields. A general riot ensued, Gattini was found and killed, and another landowner died as well. Other proprietors fled, and the crowd—joined by the gendarmes—sacked the city, attacking homes and municipal offices to shouts of "Long live the King!" and "Down with the Constitution!" (Racioppi 1867: 150–152). The rioters then took possession of land in the name of the commune. Although these and similar events have often been described as the work of desperate and ignorant peasants with no sense of politics, these poor men were clearly responding to the realignment of power and seeking to enforce what they regarded as their legal rights.

As in Matera, throughout most of the mainland the bourgeoisie quickly became the mainstays of the new regime, while the workless and landless found themselves just as quickly detached from the revolutionary coalition. Racioppi, the patriot who had responsibility for provincial and municipal administration in the Basilicata revolutionary committee, described a gratifying parade of three thousand men of the revolutionary army through Vietra, a suburb of Potenza:

There were in those columns representatives of all the social classes of the province; in lesser numbers . . . the men of the countryside with strange weapons, and rigged out with agricultural implements; in larger numbers, bold in look, paying attention to their officers, the artisans and workers, priests and brothers . . . but in the conspicuous majority were noted the wealthy class of society . . . the representatives of the possessors, those of intelligence and of the liberal professions . . . There were from the richest and most notable families of the province and from the farthest borders of it, the flower of youth—much more, the flower of the country (1867: 62).

This was the country where disaffected groups squeezed out by the rapid consolidation of the governmental coalition rioted against the plebiscite on unification, fled into the hills to avoid the draft, attacked the new national guard, and declared their support for the deposed Bourbon king.

The contrast between the experiences of the North, of Sicily, and of the mainland South at unification tells something about the political roots of collective violence. The movements of 1848 in the North had depended on a considerable mobilization of the urban working class, if not of the peasantry, and had been correspondingly difficult for the elite to keep under control. In 1859 Cavour and his collaborators in and out of the National Society deliberately minimized that mobilization and easily neutralized or absorbed those who worked with them in the annexed territories. The long death throes of the Bourbons encouraged a wide mobilization of diverse groups with contradictory grievances and programs which could move in the same direction only so long as the task at hand was to overthrow the existing government. As the consolidation of the new structure of power began, those who were to lose were already mobilized for action. Consequently, the levels of violent conflict were much higher *after* the nominal transfer of power than before. Where the working out of a new political modus vivendi and the demobilization of the malcontents took longest, the collective violence hung on for months, even years.

Naples in 1849, as seen by Daumier

Popular demonstration for Garibaldi in Milan, 1862

Streetcars as barricades in Milan, 1898

Troops camped in front of Milan's cathedral during the Fatti di Maggio, 1898

Peasants of Terranova, Sicily, occupy land

The snail's pace of industrialization and urbanization through most of Italy in the 1850s makes it unfit as a test case for the effects of sweeping structural change. Except negatively. The pattern of conflict does not correspond to such economic expansion as was occurring, which was essentially limited to the city of Naples and the industrial and commercial cities of Piedmont, Lombardy, and Tuscany. The apparent responses to misery, such as land occupations and food riots, not only failed to match the distribution of poverty but also rested on a subtle and coherent relation between the action of the authorities in each region and the conceptions of justice of the bulk of the population.

The big facts which governed the form, frequency, and locus of collective violence in those years were the transfers of power, shifts in political structure, and changes in public policy. The grievances and demands were real, and often economic in character. The economic structure of each region shaped the groups contending for power. But the process which produced collective violence was essentially political.

Early Industrialization and Industrial Conflict, 1880–1900

The final decades of the nineteenth century provide an opportunity to deal directly with the political impact of economic modernization. The sharp contrasts in both time and space within the Italy of that period allow us to single out the populations affected most deeply by industrial expansion and urban growth, and then to ask what was distinctive about their political experience. Earlier we used a broad national income criterion to characterize most of the 1880s and 1890s as times of slow growth, with a real acceleration coming in the last years of the century. At the scale of a century, the characterization works. But when we examine Gerschenkron's estimates of growth rates for the distinct phases he detects from 1881 through 1913, we must qualify (1962: 72). Arranged by periods, the average percentage of yearly growth is as follows:

1881–1888	4.6
1888–1896	0.3
1896–1908	6.7
1908–1913	2.4
1881–1913	3.8

The 1880s brought eight years of rapid growth, which ended in a depression, extending well into the 1890s, and then followed by a period of even more rapid growth. The growth was heavily concentrated in the modern urban industry of the North. The South as a whole had probably deindustrialized since Unification and its agriculture was changing slowly. Regions and times can therefore be compared quite effectively.

Important political questions were also met in the 1880s and 1890s. These years brought socialists and representatives of organized labor into the national political arena as participants, encompassed a series of expensive and disastrous colonial adventures, and repeatedly exposed the weaknesses of a parliamentary system based heavily on secret pacts and payoffs.

For the labor movement, there were several landmarks: the expansion of the suffrage in 1882, which made possible the election of the first avowed socialists to Parliament; the immediate formation of the Partito Operaio; the first steps toward laws regulating employment and working conditions; the establishment of a socialist party in 1890; the founding of Chambers of Labor (first in Milan, then elsewhere in the North), bringing together the organized segments of the work force at the municipal, regional, and eventually national levels; the first experiments with governmental arbitration of labor disputes.

The combination of pressure from a strengthening left, corruption in government, and costly but ineffective military operations overseas brought Italian national politics into a state of crisis in the 1890s. To this we should add the emergence of a growing group of industrialist-investors in modern industry, who in the 1890s saw their economic interests hurt by the Crispian program of colonial war and tariff protection for agriculture. These men, mostly northerners, hoped to influence government policy in an anticolonialist sense and improve the climate for the growth of industry.

The principal conflicts of the 1880s occurred in agriculture, especially in the capitalist farming area of the Po Valley. Agricultural strikes, political demonstrations, and industrial conflicts continued into the 1890s as backgrounds for collective violence; the first high point was the struggle growing out of the organization (first among urban workers, then in agriculture) of Fasci in Sicily from 1891 onward. By 1893 the Sicilian Fasci were making concerted demands for tax reductions, land distribution, and political representation throughout the island—and facing the determined repression which finally destroyed them the following year. In 1897 and, especially, 1898, another high point: widespread food riots interlaced with tax protests, demonstrations, violent strikes, and street-fighting, most notably in the great Milanese upheaval of May 1898. And in 1900, at Monza, an anarchist assassinated King Umberto.

The great bulk of the disturbances from 1880 to 1900 cluster in 1893–1894 and in 1898.* Nevertheless, a series of Po Valley agricultural strikes and related demonstrations, often accompanied by violence, came in geographically discrete waves throughout the 1880s. They were roughly related to organizing efforts by middle-class reformers and to government repressive action—especially arrests of strikers and activists—which stopped the movement in a region at least temporarily. In 1882 the Cremona and Parma regions were the scene of strikes; in 1883 it was the turn of Verona's hinterland. The Polesine, organized in mutual-aid societies after 1880 and politically activated after the electoral reform of 1882, struck in 1884.

The same year, in the Mantovano, peasants joined two large associations: the Mutual Aid Society of Peasants of the Province of Mantua, and the General Association of Italian Workers. Both organizations were sponsored and aided by reformers who hoped to educate the braccianti, improve their health, and better their economic position, which was among the most miserable in Italy. There was a spurt of activity, the founding of many branches of the associations, as the authorities and farm owners looked on in dismay. Slogans were shouted and graffiti appeared on the walls: "To arms, peasants!" "The union makes us strong" (Castagnoli 1954: 413). A strike was scheduled for April 1, 1885, unless wages were increased. The growers' association refused to deal with the braccianti; the police harassed them; even the priests preached against the associations, because heaven was reserved for the poor.

The authorities found an excuse to crack down on the Mantovano movement in late March, when vandals cut the vines of a farm in Rèvere. The entire leadership of the movement (some 168 persons) was ar-

* In our closer look at 1880–1900 we have again begun with Comandini's chronology, and expanded from there. In this section, we have relied heavily on two unpublished reports by David Snyder, prepared at The University of Michigan under our direction: "Non fanno sempre l'amore: Collective violence in Italy, 1880–1900" (1969), and "Industrialization and Industrial Conflict in Italy, 1878–1903" (1970).

rested; the police tried to confiscate all membership cards. Nevertheless, when the unsatisfactory wage levels were confirmed by employers on April 2, the strike started and spread widely throughout the Mantovano and adjacent provinces of Milan and Cremona. This so-called "La Boje" rebellion was actually less a rebellion than an organized, sometimes turbulent, strike. Eventually it was ended by thousands of arrests. Most of the arrested were never brought to trial, and the original arrestees were acquitted, since they had simply organized the braccianti and had been jailed before the strike even started. Organization in the Mantovano tended to be cooperativist and less militant for some years thereafter.

The last years of the 1880s were also the years of the spread of the cooperative movement and of socialism into Emilia. Again the message was carried by a reformer from outside, Camillo Prampolini. Again the result was strikes and demonstrations. The largest strike, mostly nonviolent, was in Reggio Emilia in 1886—a strike of masons, construction day laborers, and rice workers. The rice fields of the Vercellese zone of the Po Valley also struck in 1886, after being organized by Partito Operaio activists into Resistance Leagues.

Del Carria (1966: 221–224) observes that the leaders of the Partito Operaio and the anarchists were, in the 1880s, much readier to lead the peasant and worker leagues into confrontation with the authorities than was the later socialist party leadership. However, part of the frequent violence arising from strikes and demonstrations in this period resulted from the unwillingness of the authorities to recognize the legitimacy of any organization and their quickness to send troops to break up strikes.

In 1888 and 1889 the upper Lombardy region (cotton textile mills) and the Comasco (where silk was produced, from cocoon to cloth), were the scenes of strikes and violence. Again, Partito Operaio organizers from Milan were on hand; again troops were sent. Rice workers continued to strike under Partito Operaio leadership and be put down in the same years, this time the rice workers of the Romagna. A song of the period goes, "We'll pay a fig to the padrone—with a pitchfork and a scythe!" (Del Carria 1966: I, 222). The final bloody moment came in 1890, when at Conselice (Ravenna), rice workers and unemployed braccianti demonstrating at the municipal building were fired upon by soldiers and carabinieri, leaving three dead, some twenty seriously wounded.

The Partito Operaio and the anarchist movement lost many of their leaders through arrests and prison terms; a considerable number of these men emigrated after their release. Meanwhile, silk and rice workers and other agricultural workers abandoned the countryside for the city. The late 1880s were years of the highest in-migration into Milan before the twentieth century; large contingents of men calling themselves *contadini* (peasants) registered every year at the city's record office.

A relatively quiet period ensued in the North, as the organizing efforts of the Partito Operaio ceased. Meanwhile, a new socialist organization, the Lega Socialista Milanese, was founded in 1889. Its chief theorist was Filippo Turati. For the most part it recruited middle-class intellectuals committed to Marxist but legalitarian politics. In 1891 remnants of the Partito Operaio, especially those reformers who had roused the Po Valley in the 1880s, merged with the Milanese group to form the Italian Socialist Party.

At just this time, February 1892, a delegation of workers from Milan went to Sicily on the occasion of the National Exposition in Palermo. They visited Palermo to deliver an inscribed flag, in a spirit of solidarity among workers. But they found no workers' organization meeting their standards of independence and strength, so the banner was left undelivered in the city hall (Romano 1959: 15–17). The relatively new movement of the Fasci dei Lavoratori was being founded almost contemporaneously, however. The Palermo Fascio received the banner, inscribed "From the workers of Milan to those of Palermo," in a ceremony some months later.

The first Sicilian organization with the title Fascio was that of Messina, founded in March 1889. Its chairman was promptly arrested, convicted, and not released until March 1892, when the group resumed activity. In the meantime, a less exclusively working-class Fascio was founded in Catania, May 1, 1891, with middle-class sponsors. The main impetus of the movement which spread through the cities of the island in 1892, however, grew out of the Palermo Fascio. The Fasci were quickly accepted in urban settings by artisans. In some cases they were not too different from the old corporations and guilds, though in other cases they resembled the nascent unions and resistance leagues of the North. Native Sicilian bourgeois reformers and working-class activists carried the form of organization to rural areas at the end of 1892, more widely in 1893.

Then, in January 1893, troops attacked some hundreds of peasants who had begun to hoe the fields of formerly communal land which they had occupied at Caltavuturo. Eleven were killed on the spot and others mortally wounded. Although there was no Fascio in Caltavuturo, there was a group in the community with a vague aim of establishing a producer cooperative (Colajanni 1895: 134). The massacre gave much impetus to urban socialists and "Fascianti" in their mission to the peasants. The Fasci looked like a form of organization well-suited to carry the grievances of workers, peasants, and miners into the political arena. Their goals: reduction of municipal consumption taxes (the highly urbanized character of life in Sicily meant that agricultural workers who lived in large communities were liable for communal taxes); better wages; more favorable contracts for sharecroppers and tenant farmers. From May 1893 throughout the summer, strikes and demonstrations were held in the agricultural areas around Palermo, Corleone, Caltanisetta. Colajanni lists ninety-one communities in which some kind of demonstration or violence occurred.

As economically oriented strikes and demonstrations were repressed, the action became more violent than the original Fasci protests. Colajanni, an influential deputy as well as historian of the Fasci, described an example of the interaction of protest and repression. At Racalmuto he was met by a demonstration. The leaders waved a red flag, but all was peaceful, right down to the absence of subversive slogans. Nevertheless, the carabinieri tried to break up the demonstration, threatening with drawn pistols to shoot, as the crowd hesitated before dispersing. Colajanni persuaded the police to disarm and talked the crowd into going home without further provocations. Forty persons were arrested the next day.

From October through December 1893 and into the first days of 1894, in dozens of Sicilian rural areas communal and tax offices were attacked, records and buildings sacked and burned. The Fasci leaders tried to pull back their members and others involved. (According to Colajanni 1895, Romano 1959, Del Carria 1966, and others, the most highly organized areas had less violence.) The December crowds seem to have been less often organized workers demonstrating than temporarily thrown-together groups with fairly specific targets—especially tax and government offices —for their protests. By this time troops and police were quickly on the scene. By the end of 1893 some ninety-two had been killed and hundreds injured.

The organization of peasants into Fasci can often be detected as ante-

cedent to some of these seeming angry mob scenes. In Giardinella, in November, a Fascio was founded. Its peasant leaders went to the mayor with
a list of grievances—municipal taxes, the country police, a conflict over
water rights with a local proprietor. The complaints were referred to the
prefect, who turned them down out of hand. After Sunday Mass on December 10, a procession formed, marching to the municipal offices, shouting slogans. The Fascio leaders urged the mayor to make some concilia-
tory gesture. He steadfastly refused; to make matters worse, his wife
hurled a bucket of water on the already angry crowd. Part of the crowd
furiously attacked the municipal offices, burning furniture and records,
others carried the Italian flag around the countryside, shouting "Viva il
Re, Viva la Regina!" Assorted troops and police rushed to the scene,
opened fire and killed eight persons, then retreated in fear. In the resulting chaos a hated local official and his wife were murdered (Del Carria,
1966: 290–291).

A familiar story, the Sicilian rural riot—there were similar events in
1848, 1860, 1865, and 1876. Yet what brought angry people into the
streets in 1893 was a political mobilization of a reformist bent, the Fascio.
The events of Giardinella had started with a petition of grievances, then
moved to an organized demonstration, both organized by the Fascio. The
circumstances of rejection and repression, plus Fascio leadership that
could not control its members, changed the affair into the traditional
form. Its origin lay in the mobilization of the community into associations
for political action.

In August 1893, as Fasci activity was sweeping Sicily, a series of large-
scale street demonstrations and riots were taking place elsewhere in Italy.
They occurred as reaction to an event in Aigues Mortes, France, near
Marseilles. A group of Italian workers, regarded as scabs and strikebreakers, had been set upon by French workers, beaten up, and several killed.
Nationalist, anti-French, pro-Triple Alliance demonstrations, all rather
formal and restrained, were held in various cities around Italy. Working-
class demonstrators increased in number the next day, and French con-
sulates were attacked; in Naples and Rome the demonstrators changed
their targets: foreigners in general, the rich, "exploiters" were attacked.
In Milan socialists tried to lead demonstrators against an ideological enemy: international capitalism. In Genoa, Naples, and Rome there were
fewer visible leaders, less focused targets, a good deal of angry violence.

In Naples the fighting lasted four days and ended in an anti-police riot (a child had been killed by a policeman), with trams overturned, huge processions, street fights, a thousand arrests, and imposition of martial law.

In early 1894 there were echoes of the Fasci troubles in Lunigiana (Massa-Carrara) and Apulia, after martial law had been declared in Sicily. As early as January 6 and 7, there were demonstrations in Lunigiana against the extraordinary decrees for Sicily. There were rumors of a planned insurrection by anarchists; and modern historians of the region (Bernieri 1961: 156–162; Mori 1958: 192–198), although they disagree on many points, agree in being unable to uncover any evidence of a plot. Socialist organizations were practically nonexistent in Lunigiana, but anarchism had taken firm root. Several anarchists had been conducting local lecture series just before the troubles started (Del Carria 1966: 249).

From whatever source their consciousness came, the marble quarry workers and their fellows, who struck and demonstrated again on January 13, 1894, had a notion of revolutionary mission. They attacked police barracks and headquarters, made off with weapons, then burned tax-collection stations. Large bands of workers tried to march into cities (Carrara on the 14th, Massa on the 16th), but were stopped by the military. Some were driven into the hills, with consequent killing and bloodshed. General Nicholas Heusch arrived on January 17, with exceptional powers of administration and justice; hundreds were arrested and tried by military tribunals.

The final burst of violence of the 1890s came in 1898. Part of the background lies in the poor grain harvest of 1897; unusually high bread prices were driven higher in 1898 by reduced imports from the United States, preparing for the Spanish-American War. In some areas and cities, to be sure, high bread prices were protested at peaceful meetings or at unruly ones. Elsewhere, violence came discontinuously with price protests, and over different issues. High prices are only part of the complex picture of 1898.

An overall picture of that year's hundreds of disturbances can best be drawn by focusing on three major kinds of events. The first are disturbances growing out of local struggles and rancors, but resented more keenly in times of economic distress. Typical of this category were protests about municipal taxes, objections to hated officials, demands for jobs, arguments about how charity should be distributed; such disturbances occurred mainly in January and February, in Sicily and the South. Second are violent demonstrations and protest over food prices, which occurred in clusters, some in Sicily, others in and around Ancona, Bari, Naples, and Florence, especially in February and March. In Ancona and Naples, at least, anarchists probably promoted, and certainly tried to seize the leadership of, these food-focused disturbances (Del Carria 1966: 301–303, 308; Santarelli 1954). The third large group of violent disturbances were those of more organized workers and peasants whose goals were both economic (better wages) and organizational (the right to form unions, strike, demonstrate). This group clustered in the northern industrial area and the Po Valley. In timing, they occurred mostly after mid-April. They posed the most serious political threat, representing, as they did, more organized, differentiated, and conscious groups.

The conflicts of 1898 passed through three phases, from diffuse and local to focused and political. This temporal phasing reflected a geographic progression; disturbances started in the South, moved to Central Italy, and finally to the North. The participants changed, too. The residents of the Sicilian towns who opened the year of protest were an undifferentiated group of workers. Specifically identified workers (the porters of Ancona, for example), or political activists formed the core of the northern crowds.

To illustrate differences in the three kinds of political violence in 1898, let us look at some examples. On February 18, 1898, at Troina, in the province of Catania, Sicily, a crowd of three hundred men, women, and children, carrying banners, some armed with hatchets, sticks, revolvers, appeared at the town hall to ask aid for the unemployed. They were ordered to disperse by police and carabinieri. As a group of soldiers marched up, rocks started to fly, and shots rang out; two peasants were killed on the spot and another twenty were wounded, three or four of whom later died. The deputy from the area explained that there had been a dispute over how to disburse a recent voluntary contribution of proprietors and wealthy citizens. The demonstration was blamed on misery; there was no socialist, or other "subversive" party organization in Troina, and the village had been quiet in the Fasci period (*La Lombardia,* 19, 20, 22 February 1898).

On January 17, 1898, in Ancona, a medium-sized port city in the

Marches, hundreds of men, women, and children demonstrated before the communal buildings, calling for reduced bread prices and an end to the city tax on flour. Skirmishes between people and police started, and continued through the next day. The *facchini* (porters) of the docks led the demonstrations and later street fighting, throwing stones and shouting "Viva la anarchia!" and "Viva la rivoluzione sociale!" Courthouses, newspaper offices, and, finally, the jail, were attacked. At the jail, the attackers freed several imprisoned demonstrators. Troops arrived, but someone cut telegraph wires to impede communication, and others stretched wires across the streets to trip the horses of the cavalry. Fighting continued on the 19th, with the day ending in an attack on the suburban house of a grain merchant accused of being a speculator. On the 20th martial law was declared and mass arrests were made. The city flour entry tax was reduced. In Ancona, unlike Sicily, active socialist and anarchist propaganda and public protest meetings had preceded the violence. The socialist Bocconi, and the anarchist Malatesta were on hand at the first demonstrations, along with other anarchists, actively trying to direct the street action (Del Carria 1966: 301–303; Santarelli 1954).

On May 6, Milan was the scene of a fateful demonstration.* A group of Milanese gathered outside a police station in the industrial section of the city to demand the release of several men who had been arrested while distributing socialist manifestos. Filippo Turati, the prominent socialist deputy, as well as various factory owners hastened to negotiate with the authorities for the release of the prisoners. The municipal council, meeting in extraordinary session, immediately rescinded the local tax on grain and flour. But the official response to the demonstration itself was harsh. Troops were sent to the station house, and their gunfire eventually dispersed the demonstrators. One policeman was killed because he failed to move out of the line of fire. So were several workers. A group of their fellows started to take one of the critically wounded men to the hospital of the Fatebenefratelli; when he died en route, they continued to the Piazza del Duomo with his corpse. Police patrols prevented the regrouping of demonstrators in any numbers downtown, and finally a rainstorm sent home the hangers-on.

The next day a strike spread in the industrial neighborhoods. Demon-

* The following description is taken with little alteration from L. Tilly 1972a: 124–125.

strating workers again skirmished with troops, who were by then stationed at the city gates. Many of the industrial workers lived in the suburban area, outside the old walls; that is where the factories were located and where the first day's demonstration had taken place. May 7 saw attempts by some of these workers to march to the center of the city, down the big avenues leading to the cathedral square from the gates, picking up other workers to support their protest and strike. In view of the readiness of the military and the police for confrontation, both the socialist party leadership and the officials of the Chamber of Labor did what they could to calm the situation. In the morning there were fights between workers and soldiers—mostly in the northern half of the city, through which demonstrators were attempting to move toward the center. Barricades were built, defended, and destroyed. Although there were frequent reports of sniping, apparently the weapons of the battling demonstrators were stones and roof tiles to throw at antagonists, boards and iron bars to break up streetcars, and heavy furniture and metal grilles to form the barricades. By afternoon violence had spread throughout the city. Another series of barricades was thrown up from the Ticinese Gate on the south toward the cathedral square. A state of siege was declared. The military established its superiority; and spent the next two days (employing heavy artillery and enjoying blanket orders to shoot) rooting out real and imagined troublemakers, with only sporadic resistance from workers.

Behind the events of Milan lay a tradition of street protest with wide participation by various occupational groups, as well as a period of intense organizational activity centering on the more modern industrial workers but reaching into most occupational categories.

Nearly everywhere the disturbances of 1898 began with an organized strike or demonstration. Contagion or imitation probably accounts partially for the phased temporal distribution and the geographic clustering of disturbances. To be imitated, however, a disturbance had to fit into a self-defined mode suitable to another city or area. Thus, the January Sicilian outbursts were looked at as curiously provincial, backward, and uncomfortably close to anarchy by *La Lombardia,* a Milanese newspaper (reports of 3 and 4 January 1898 on events in Siculiana and Cinisi, Sicily). Social backwardness is stressed in the reports that almost all property in Siculiana was concentrated in the hands of one Barone Agnello, who was also mayor. The village of Siculiana is described as unchanged physically from medieval times; obviously there was nothing in its riot for progressive Milan to imitate.

As to the Ancona pattern, a socialist newspaper of Voghera compared organized, deliberate Milanese politics to Anconese anarchy: "In Milan, a united, determined mass of workers strove politically within the commune to convert its goverment, and from that base distributed a communally produced inexpensive bread, which is one of the first steps toward socialism; at Ancona, instead, rock-throwing, ill-considered shouts, and . . . many arrests" (*L'Uomo chi ride*, 20 January 1898, cited by Santarelli 1954: 268).

Milan's Fatti di Maggio were superficially similar to disturbances in both southern and central Italy: there was much rock-throwing and destruction of property. Nevertheless, the Fatti grew out of a more clearly labeled political struggle. They began with a strike protesting the repression of demonstration in Pavia, followed by a mass demonstration; the initially articulated goals were enlarged suffrage and political rights: the right to demonstrate, the right to organize, the right to participate in the political process. In order to secure economic gains by their own efforts through building associations, workers needed the elementary political rights of petition and assembly.

At this point, whether or not the government responded by repression made all the difference. In many places, taxes were lowered, prisoners freed, charity distributed in hopes of cooling angry citizens. Sometimes this worked; sometimes it worked only temporarily. Colajanni, Romano, and Del Carria concur in arguing that the reason for less widespread involvement of Sicily in 1898 than in 1893–1894 was some willingness, or even haste, on the part of municipal governments to make concessions because of the memory of 1893–1894. We would point out that working-class organization in Sicily had still not recovered from the post-fasci restrictions. There are also suggestions that the alternative of emigration was already operating: a contemporary newspaper account reported a sudden spurt in emigration in 1898 from Sicily to America (*Corriere della Sera*, cited by Del Carria 1966: 305).

The geographical extent of the incidents and their seriousness hastened military intervention on the part of the national government, and once the initial phase in Sicily had passed, martial law was quickly declared

as troubles started in an area, arrests made, and military tribunals insti-
tuted to try those arrested. Because of the phase pattern and the clustering of disturbances in 1898, moreover, the government succeeded in
moving troops from one troubled area to another as they flared up con-
secutively, rather than simultaneously. As soon as martial law was declared in a city or province, arbitrary arrests of socialists, republicans,
anarchists, and other antiregime activists followed. Labor organizations
(unions, cooperatives, and Chambers of Labor) and opposition newspapers and journals were closed down. Although the government was
most concerned with ending subversive propaganda and forestalling possible conspiracies, it succeeded in prohibiting nearly any kind of association, and collective activity was choked off effectively. From roughly the
middle of May collective violence also almost disappeared from Italy,
and for the rest of the year, even strikes were few and relatively timid.

The available data on strikes provide another way of examining the
conflicts of the late nineteenth century. Although most varieties of strike
activity were technically illegal until 1901, the Italian government compiled rather full and uniform reports of strikes from 1878 through
1903. David Snyder, a member of our research group, has coded each of
the 6,242 strikes reported over that period, and analyzed their distribution over time, region, industry, and type of conflict (Snyder 1970). As
one might expect, given the expansion of labor organization and the
decreasing willingness or ability of the government to repress strikes, the
level of strike activity rose enormously over the twenty-five-year span
(see Figure 23). From 25 or 30 recorded strikes and four or five thousand
strikers per year in the late 1870s, the averages became more like 1,000
strikes and two hundred thousand strikers at the beginning of the twentieth century. The curve of strike activity describes a rapid rise from 1878
to 1885, a leveling off from 1885 to 1895, and an even more rapid increase
from 1896 on. It corresponds in a crude way to the timing of industrial
growth.* One might also try to force a parallel between the evolution of
strike activity and the flow of collective violence over the period, but the

---

* However, a set of time-series analyses Snyder (1970) conducted for Italy as a whole
over the period from 1878 to 1924 show no significant relationship between the *pace*
of industrial (or, for that matter, urban) growth and strike activity, once the trend
is allowed for. Instead, they point to a causal sequence going from industrial expansion
to more extensive labor organization to heightened strike activity.

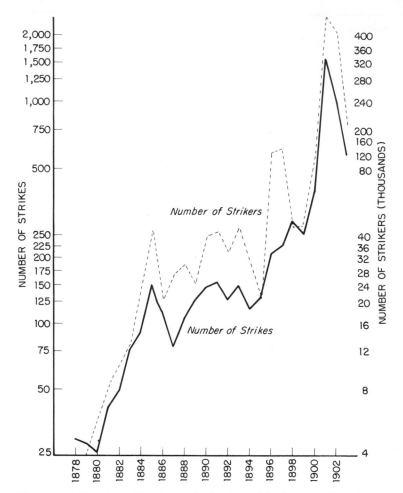

Figure 23. Number of Strikes and Number of Strikers per Year in Italy, 1878–1903.

parallel would be weak. There is some overlap, since a certain number of strikes generated collective violence, even before the turbulent general strikes of the 1900s. Out of all the strikes enumerated in the government reports from 1894 (when detailed descriptions of each strike began) to 1903, 11 percent were reported to have produced some damage to persons or property.*

* Most of these cases would not qualify as disturbances by our criteria, however since the number of people taking direct part in the destructive encounter was so often fewer than fifty.

Table 10. Strike activity by industry, 1878–1903

Industry	Number of workers, 1901 (thousands)	Man-days in strikes, 1878–1903 (thousands)	Man-days per worker	Percentage of strikes reported as violent, 1894–1903
Mining	92	1,462	15.95	8
Metal-mechanical	429	689	1.61	9
Public administration	176	242	1.37	5
Construction	701	2,109	3.01	12
Chemicals	23	382	16.53	8
Lumber, etc.	411	109	0.27	8
Paper	20	69	3.45	7
Printing	39	72	1.87	6
Textiles	773	2,720	3.52	7
Leather	47	197	4.21	14
Laundry, personal service, garment-making	1,114	459	0.41	15
Food	314	477	1.52	13
Transportation and communication	424	541	1.28	13
Agriculture	9,611	3,663	0.38	19
Commerce, etc.	1,332	193	0.14	13
Total	16,174	13,507	0.84	11

Violent strikes came with special frequency in agriculture. Nevertheless, the extent of strike activity is only one of several factors affecting the frequency of labor-related collective violence. The form of organization of the workers, the reaction of the employers, and the regulatory or repressive activity of the government strongly affect the likelihood of violence. Combats and property destruction frequently resulted from the agrarian conflicts of this period because the owners and the state challenged the very right of the workers to organize and strike. The bloody repression of the Sicilian Fasci provided the *reductio ad tragicam.*

Agriculture constituted by far the largest segment of the Italian labor force. Unlike the situation elsewhere in Europe, it also contributed the largest share of strikers. Our table of strike activity by industry (Table 10) shows that a solid quarter of all the man-days in strikes from 1878 to 1903 came from agriculture. The bulk of agricultural strikes was so great that the peaks of aggregate strike activity—1885, 1890–1893, 1896–1897, 1900–1902—are essentially those of the agrarian sector.

When we make allowance for the number of workers in each industry by calculating man-days in strikes per individual in the labor force, the picture naturally looks different. By this measure of strike propensity, mining and chemicals appear far more strike-prone than other industries; construction, paper, textiles, and leather stand together well above the average; and agriculture remains near the bottom. Among other factors the differentials reflect the extent of labor organization within each industry.

That underlying factor comes to the surface in the regional distribution of propensity to strike. With allowances for size of labor force, Liguria, Lombardy, Emilia, and Sicily were the regions of high strike activity during the closing decades of the nineteenth century. In agriculture, Lombardy, Veneto, Emilia, and Sicily had strike propensities significantly above the national average (see Figures 24 and 25). Outside of those few areas, agricultural strikes were virtually unknown. In both agriculture and industry—more dramatically in the former—we are observing the effects of extensive labor organization on strike activity. The cities which early formed Chambers of Labor were the foci of industrial conflict. The rural recruiting grounds of the Partito Operaio were also the areas of big strikes by braccianti. Strikes and organization went together, and the causation was reciprocal.

The General Patterns of 1880–1900

There lies the common ground between the collective violence and the strike activity of the period. It was not so much the tendency of strikes themselves to generate violence (although that happened from time to time) or the expression of the same rage in two different ways (although many historians have read strikes and riots as related indices of the temper of workers) as the fact that it took a good deal of mobilization to carry on substantial strikes, more or less the same kind of mobilization which was likely to bring workers into conflict with owners and authorities outside the context of the strike. The fundamental political change of the 1880s and 1890s was the mobilization of Italian labor, both agri-

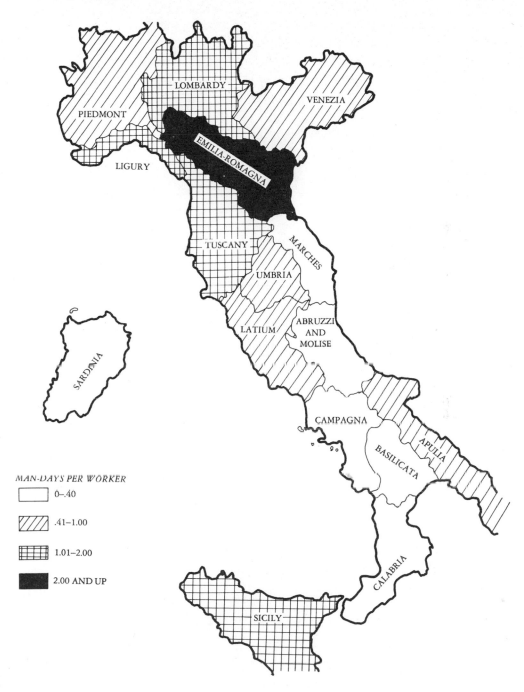

Figure 24. Strike Propensity by Province in Italy, 1878–1903.

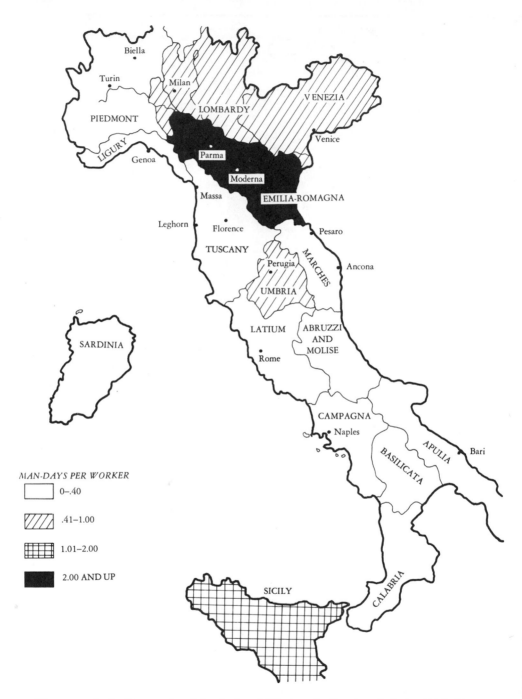

Figure 25. Strike Propensity of Agricultural Workers by Province in Italy, 1878–1903.

cultural and industrial. That was the change which shaped the collective violence of the time.

What about the connections between large-scale structural change and the incidence of upheaval? To begin with industrialization and urbanization, there is a lack of congruence between trends of structural change and the high point of urban disturbances in 1898. By all accounts, the periods of greatest overall industrial growth were in the 1880s, before 1888 or so, and then after 1898. Industrial strikes in the 1880s were distinctly few, and the level of violence in industrial areas was even lower. In the 1880s the regional incidence of disturbances was significant only in the agricultural areas of the Po Valley.

What about urbanization, the concentration of population in cities? We do not have the complete picture here (there was no national census between 1881 and 1901) but we do know that the city of Milan underwent its highest net in-migration and consequent urban growth in absolute numbers and rates in 1887, 1888, and 1889. After that there was a drop to rates lower than the early 1880s, until 1896 and 1897, when net in-migration returned to the range of 1886 figures. It was not until 1899 and 1900 that high in-migration resumed into Milan, parallel to the resumption of industrial growth. If either the rate of industrial growth or of urban growth were crucial variables to the incidence of collective violence in the cities of Italy, there should have been high rates of urban violence in the 1880s. There were not.

What about structural change in agricultural zones, especially in the Po Valley, where growth of capitalist agriculture and an increase in numbers of landless labor, braccianti, was occurring? The process of concentration of property, increased capital investment in agriculture (through irrigation and canal-building, the break-up of small farms, and use of day labor) had been going on for years—from before 1860 in some regions. Did things speed up or get worse in the 1880s? Did the number of braccianti reach a critical mass whose explosion was inevitable?

A complete answer to these questions would have to consider very small regions as the unit of investigation; there are enough clues in the literature to sketch out a partial answer. Structural change of the type described above was most rapid in the years *before* 1880. Po Valley agriculture shared in the general European agricultural prosperity before about 1880, and expanded with it. The effects of the worldwide agricultural depression were slower to affect Italy than the rest of Europe, and 1874 to 1879 were years of continued development and prosperity for the proprietors of the Mantovan, for example. After that, profit margins were cut, and change slowed down; proprietors as well as braccianti were upon difficult years (Castagnoli 1954: 410).

The landless laborers of the Mantovano had increasingly emigrated in the 1860s and 1870s, especially to Brazil. A contemporary newspaper reported that, whereas 354 people emigrated from the province of Mantua in 1867, in 1876 there were 2,725. The sight of their fellow countrymen fleeing their homes was the reported impetus to several Mantuan middle-class democrats to found their General Association of City and Country Workers in 1877 (ibid: 409). If Coletti and MacDonald are right, emigration slowed down with organizational activity in the early 1880s; it resumed, this time city-bound, in the late 1880s when the strikes had been broken.

Although the dating of large-scale structural change did not coincide with moments of political violence, what about the commonly attributed cause of misery? The end of agricultural prosperity came to the Po Valley around 1880; when grain prices collapsed, the depression followed. Low pay and job shortages may have been important background factors, and even requirements for violence, but they do not explain *why* strikes and violence occurred first in one area, then another, or *why* migration ebbed and waned in opposite rhythms from those of militancy. There was a long period of misery for Po Valley farm workers in the 1880s, and into the 1890s, but they only revolted *some* times.

The early 1890s were years of industrial depression, starting about 1888 in the North. In Sicily, there was from the late 1880s on a far-reaching depression of the artisanal crafts resulting from the loss of markets to international competitors and northern industry. In a general way, there was a good deal of economic malaise in the industrial North and in Sicily after 1888. Yet this depression does not in any way predict or specify where and when violence will take place.

What does? The coincidence of recent organization and activation of workers and peasants with disturbance fits again and again. It fits in the Po Valley in the 1880s, where the penetration of Partito Operaio organizers and reformers who went to the aid of the braccianti preceded each wave of strikes or violence. It works in Sicily, where the Fasci, the first class-based organization in the island's history, triggered the events of 1893–1894. It works for 1897–1898, when socialist and labor organizations sprang up like weeds, once government controls were relaxed. In Milan fifty-one new workers' leagues were founded in 1896 and 1897, joining the twenty or so that had come into being over the thirty preceding years. By 1898, almost all workers were touched to some degree by organized working-class activity (Società Umanitaria 1909; viii). In Prato, among the textile workers, union organization and worker political activity were high. The price of bread was not terribly elevated. Yet in 1898 there were disturbances in Prato (Pinzani 1963: 131).

But why should the activity of reformist groups making moderate economic and political demands lead to violence? Here the role of government, of the climate of the political life of the nation, matters. We pointed out earlier how the political spirit of the late 1880s and of the 1890s was one of the polarization and disenchantment for many middle-class people, and of a drive for enfranchisement on the part of the working class. Middle-class intellectuals and northern businessmen lacked sympathy for government policies like colonial adventurism and favoritism for agriculture; they were dismayed and disgusted by corruption in high places. These men, who had the franchise and full rights of political participation, in the 1880s and 1890s came to support the political and social demands of workers and peasants. Their activity in favor of the lower classes ranged from journalism and propaganda to organizing and mobilizing people themselves.

The ruling coalition was under pressure from within and without the political arena. In the Crispi–Di Rudini years, there was a repressive climate—physical repression via military and police presence, and social repression through controls on associations and the press. So each organizing thrust produced a concomitant build-up of repression, pressure which often led to violence, despite the fact that the political and social demands were being pressed in essentially nonviolent ways. This off-and-on pattern of repression explains the phaselike pattern of political disturbances.

Once leaders were arrested and organizations dissolved, any capacity for group action was dramatically reduced in a region or city. It took years to rebuild. Sometimes, as in Sicily and the Po Valley, emigration followed repression. In the case of Sicily, anyway, militant activism never resumed in our period. Repression worked.

After the 1898 martial law decrees, the trials of leftist leaders and propagandists, and the closing down of associations, there was a falling off of group activity throughout Italy. Since even the number of eligible voters had been reduced by the manipulation of eligibility lists, political action became more individualistic. So the far-left parliamentary group indulged in parliamentary obstructionism and outrage, and the anarchists tried bombs and assassinations. Organizations reappeared in 1899, but only after 1900 did a realigned political coalition legalize the right to strike, and spark the resumption of vigorous group activity.

The Background of Fascism

In order to make sense of the turbulent years of Fascist mobilization after World War I, it is necessary to recall the prewar situation: the expanding organization of labor, swelling labor-management conflict, important new political alignments, and eventually, bitter struggles over Italy's role in the war itself. We can outline the political changes this way:

(1) Giovanni Giolitti, first as Minister of the Interior under Zanardelli, then as Prime Minister himself and the dominant political figure of the prewar period, constructed a new political coalition which supported his policies from about 1901 to 1910. The chief members of this coalition were northern industrialists and northern industrial workers, and the chief policy change which ensued was liberalization of government policy toward the unions. Giolitti's program was anti-imperialistic, based on tariff protection for industry, high salaries for industrial workers, free unions, increased centralization of government (to ensure continued domination of the North over the South), and suffrage limited by literacy (another anti-southern feature). The program elicited a minimum of acquiescence by the socialist party, causing the communist Gramsci to write (years later) in an accusatory tone that the socialists "became the instrument of Giolittian policy" (1952: 22).

(2) Catholics reentered national politics, first in the election of 1904, with papal permission to vote when such votes could help defeat a socialist. Conservative Catholic candidates, labeled as such, presented themselves in 1909, and in 1913 the "Gentiloni compact" was concluded between Giolitti and Count Ottorino Gentiloni, leader of the Catholic Union. Liberal candidates who accepted in writing the platform of the

Catholic Union could count on Catholic votes. The Catholic presence was basically conservative, pressing on the Giolitti coalition from the right.

(3) Industrial and agrarian employers organized to strengthen their economic position vis-à-vis the burgeoning unions and also to translate their political goals into action. In 1906 the Piedmontese Industrial League was established in Turin. It was the first of the really large employers' associations (Abrate 1967). Shortly after, in 1907, an Interregional Agrarian Foundation came into being in Bologna. In 1908 the Agrarian Employers' Association of Parma started to gain a reputation for effectiveness against strikers by sponsoring armed squads (*squadre*). The industrial employers founded their national association, the Confederation of Industry (Confindustria) in 1910, and the farm owners, the Confederation of Agriculture in 1911. Both these organizations became very effective agents for making the conservative voice of employers heard on the national political scene.

(4) On the side of labor, there was first a growth in federated unions, of the industrial variety, which disagreed in philosophy and method with the older Chambers of Labor. After the strike wave of 1902 subsided, the Chambers of Labor went into a declining period, as organizations withdrew or disappeared. Reformist groups sponsored a national federation, which they ended up dominating; the General Confederation of Labor (C.G.L.), founded in 1906, represented 700 local unions and leagues, 250,00 members.

Both the socialist party and the labor movement split into reformist and revolutionary sections. After 1912 the revolutionary socialists were in the majority in the party, but the C.G.L. remained reformist. Outside the party revolutionary ideology directed the action of the syndicalists, who captured control of some unions and Chambers of Labor after 1904. The railroad unions were an early syndicalist stronghold, but syndicalist strength was concentrated in the Po Valley agricultural areas, especially Ferrara and Parma in 1907–1908. Syndicalist bases tended to be geographical, not occupational; syndicalism was strong also in the old anarchist areas— Ancona, Massa-Carrara, Rome. Avowed anarchists served as members of the directorate of the syndicalist federation, the USI.

Collective violence in the prewar era can be divided into two periods; in the first, up to about 1908, the interplay of the political developments just described with economic and political strikes was the main dimension in which violence occurred. In the second period, after 1910, a mutation in Giolittian policy prompted a change in the setting of collective violence, away from strikes and toward the political demonstration or explicit revolutionary attempt.

The general strike of 1904, the large sympathy strikes of 1906 and 1907, and the tumultuous agricultural strikes of 1908 were characteristic of the first period. After 1908 the level of strike activity remained low until the end of World War I. After 1910 protests of any scale clustered on the political axis of opposition to the Libyan War, antimilitarism, and antinationalism. There were urban antiwar demonstrations in 1911. In June 1914, Red Week followed the killing of two people by police when the police prevented the crowd leaving an antimilitarist demonstration from marching into downtown Ancona; there was a popular insurrection in Ancona, as strikes and takeovers of municipal governments occurred in the Marches and throughout Italy.

Immediately before World War I, Italian politics were as deeply riven by disagreement over basic questions as if the Giolittian compromises had never occurred. Polarization over questions of working-class political and economic rights was extreme; nationalists were at loggerheads with the internationalist position of working-class groups; tactical disagreements continued among socialists and unionists. The country was brought into the war by ministerial and royal effort. The government ignored both liberal and socialist opposition to war and underestimated Italy's lack of material preparation as well.

The First World War provided little respite in Italy from political disagreement and collective violence. Before the brief national unity which the defeat at Caporetto inspired, there were, in 1916 and 1917, a high and increasing rate of desertions from the army, flight from induction by many recruits, hundreds of demonstrations, and many strikes (see De Felice 1963).

The most serious episode was a general insurrection in Turin in August 1917; in many ways it forecast similar violence in the immediate postwar period. Turin's industrial plant had expanded greatly to meet the demands of war production. Tremendous profits were made in the metal and machine industry, yet workers and middle class alike were suffering from lack of consumer goods in general and high food prices in particular.

A severe and seemingly inexplicable shortage of bread brought tempers to the breaking point. On August 21, 1917, women and young people began stopping trolleys, then attacked the neighborhood police headquarters. Rioters were shot. At the factory gates, workers refused to enter, shouting "We want bread!" Municipal authorities hastened to promise them bread to be borrowed from military supplies. The shouts changed to calls for peace: "Down with the war!" Strikers marched to the Chamber of Labor and around the factory district, urging others to join in the strike. The next day matters worsened; the strike continued, barricades were built, gunfire exchanged. The industrial suburbs of the city were "captured" and held by bands of workers. The strike and fighting continued from August 21 to 26; casualties were heavy—fifty workers and perhaps ten soldiers. The socialist leadership of Turin and the nation called for an end to the strike and a return to work. The small-scale mutinies, strikes, and demonstrations, as well as the Turin Fatti di Agosto, were all rejected by the socialists. Yet the party, with its internationalist antimilitarist positions had formed the opinions of those who opposed the war in more vigorous ways. And the militant antiwar movement was concentrated in northern industrial areas long organized and mobilized by socialists and unions.

Postwar Collective Action

The postwar period provided the immediate setting for the rise of Fascism. The war had been accompanied by a great concentration of economic activity in supplying war material. There was an accompanying expansion in iron, steel, and machine production. With the end of the war and the cancellation of weapons contracts, this sector, highly concentrated geographically in the industrial North, was bound to decline, with subsequent unemployment. The borrowing of the state for its war debt had initiated an inflationary spiral, and consumers needed government price controls, especially on food, in order to survive.

Finally, there was the demobilization of the armed forces. The army returned half of its three million recruits to civilian life in 1919, another million in 1920. Economic demands by workers and peasants had been put aside or played down in the war years. Now, not only new needs arising from demobilization but postponed claims led to calls for government intervention: demobilized troops for employment, peasants and agricultural workers for land, ailing industries for subsidies, consumers for price controls, industrial workers for higher wages. The goverment, which had during the war reduced its level of responsiveness to citizen pressure and even to Parliament, had again to face its constituents both on the electoral front and in the streets.

A massive political mobilization ensued; people organized to press their economic and political demands for change or favoritism in the public and private sectors. Socialist Party membership and parliamentary representation underwent a huge increase. From 50,000 members before the war, membership climbed to 200,000; 156 socialist deputies were elected in 1919, as compared to 50 in 1913. Thousands of communes elected socialist governments in 1920. In January 1919 Italy's second mass party was founded: the Popular Party, a Christian Democratic party. Led by the Sicilian priest, Don Luigi Sturzo, the Popolari had a Wilsonian, anti-imperialist, international policy, a populist domestic program, calling for increased small property holdings by means of the breakup of large estates. Many Catholic agricultural leagues came onto the scene, especially around Cremona. Nevertheless, there was quite a range of political position among the Popolari, some of whom were exceedingly conservative and Catholic. They elected 100 deputies in 1919.

Apart from political parties, the postwar mobilization of the masses was most dramatically visible in the explosion of union membership. The C.G.L., now led by a more radical group than in the prewar period, expanded from 321,000 members at the beginning of the war to 2,200,000 at the end of 1920. This included almost a million farm workers. There was also a growth in the number of agricultural cooperatives, and increase in their acquisition of land. In May 1918 the nationalist trade unionists, mostly syndicalists, established a new federation, the Italian Union of Labor, which also grew in 1919–1920.

A third kind of association which proliferated after 1918 was the veterans' group. The Associazione Nazionale Combattenti, composed of veterans with moderate political goals, focused mainly on land for the peasants and a constituent assembly to define the future constitution of Italy. (Their demands were heeded to the extent that the government established a semi-autonomous, goverment-funded corporation, the Opera Nazionale Combattenti, which bought up land for redistribution to veterans.) A more aggressive and activist veterans' group, the Associazione degli Arditi d'Italia, had a vague program of promoting the grandeur and glory of the fatherland, and a disquieting inclination toward violence.

The Fascists, in their early form, were another postwar activist group. Their members included many veterans, some ex-socialists, and ex-revolutionary syndicalists. Their leader, Benito Mussolini, formerly a revolutionary socialist, then an interventionist, was, in 1919, still a little of both. The first meeting of the Fascists, in Milan, March 21, 1919, resulted in a resolution to wage internal war against the enemies of Italy. Two days later a national organization was founded, with the name Fasci Italiani di Combattimento; the name suggested its affinity to other veterans' groups. The Fascist program vigorously opposed any imperialism of other nations which might be harmful to Italy, called for the integration of all Italian "national" territories into the nation, and pledged to sabotage all neutralist politicians of whatever party. To this was added a popularly oriented domestic social and political program: universal suffrage, referenda on continuing questions, a constituent assembly, a republic with communal and regional autonomy, elimination of the Senate and all noble titles, an end to conscription, reduction of state intervention, expropriative taxes, an end to speculation and monopoly profits, an eight-hour day, worker participation in factory management, land to the peasants!

Although there was a flurry of founding branch Fasci, mostly in the North, the movement did not grow as quickly as Mussolini had predicted. He and the rest of the leadership were ambivalent from the start about the program. It was published only piecemeal in his newspaper, *Popolo d'Italia,* and often modified before it actually was printed.

Nevertheless, right from the beginning the Fascists participated in demonstrations and fights against what they considered unpatriotic, internationalist socialism. On April 15, 1919, they took part along with *arditi,* futurists, students, and other veterans, in a counter-demonstration in Milan which physically attacked an anarchist/socialist march protesting repression. The affair culminated in the sacking and arson of the headquarters of the socialist newspaper, *Avanti!* (An ominous target: Mussolini had once been *Avanti!*'s editor.)

Later that year, at the time of the general strike in July, the Fascists and other veterans' groups offered their strong-arm services to help the Nitti government combat alleged socialist and anarchist threats to order.

The government, in an ambiguous way, warned the groups that autonomous action was unacceptable, but that it would accept their cooperation in maintaining order (Vivarelli 1967: 453). As it worked out, the strike was peaceful; its extent was not especially great, and workers even seemed to show "apathy," as Nitti wrote (Salvatorelli and Mira 1964: 90). What happened in 1919, however—the acceptance of Fascist illegal methods in service to the state, or as an alternative to the state in keeping the peace—was to become a familiar pattern in 1921 and 1922.

Based on their previous high level of organization and long activism, one would expect the unions to act most quickly and most vigorously. This they did. Huge strikes of metal-workers in the North, of farm workers in the Po Valley provinces of Novara and Pavia, plus smaller strikes in Como, Trieste, Rome, and Parma started the 1919–1920 strike wave. Their first goal was the eight-hour day. They then sought to bring wages in line with inflated living costs (perhaps five times the prewar level). Of the 1,663 strikes in the 1919 statistics, more than half were concentrated in April, May, and June. Over the entire year, furthermore, a much higher rate of success prevailed than had been common in prewar strikes: out of 755 strikes for higher wages, 610 were successful (Vivarelli 1967: 410–411).

Contemporaneously with the strikes came the land occupation movement, growing not out of the earlier farm worker league experience but harking back to an old peasant tactic. The traditional aspect had more to do with the form of the incidents—land occupations—and their geographical incidence—starting in Latium and moving south (Apulia, Calabria) and to Sicily, than with the organization and carrying out of the occupations. All observers agree that the socialist party had little to do with the movement, partly because it had little organization in the South and partly because of ideological disagreement over the notion of distributing land in small parcels to peasants. This does not mean that organization was absent, however; in Latium local units of the Federterra (Federazione Laziale Lavoratori della Terra), ad hoc veterans' groups, and even Catholic leagues led the movement.

In Latium, most of the land occupations probably do not meet our criteria for collective violence; they were carried out without resistance from the landowners (notorious absentees mostly) or public forces. In Sicily resistance was present, and in two incidents in the province of Caltanisetta, nine peasants were killed. In both Sicily and Calabria (disturbances there occurred at the end of 1919, after the sowing of the winter wheat) there is evidence that leagues and cooperatives participated in the occupations. The socialist deputy Mancini wrote about Calabria, "Here also we have land occupation, revolt against the old agrarian contracts, peasant strikes, violent acts. Workers' leagues are springing up here and there" (quoted in Del Carria 1966: II, 80; see also Caracciolo 1952; Vivarelli 1967: 418–425).

There was another wave of land occupations, especially in Latium, in the second half of 1920. These occupations more often qualify as collective violence because both the public authorities and the landlords, who now had their own association, resisted. Noteworthy also was the November 1920 takeover of farms in Soresina (Cremona province) by Catholic radical peasants who claimed that the landowners should receive a much smaller share of the profit from their farms, commensurate only with the actual time they put into directing them (Del Carria 1966: 84–85).

The food protest of early summer 1919 was initiated less by new or old formal organizations, than by exasperated consumers. Nevertheless, incidents were often sparked by the workers of a plant or several plants acting together and the form of protest was sometimes a strike, sometimes a demonstration, and sometimes the sacking of bakeries, butcher shops, or groceries. The first strike-demonstration-riot (there were elements of all three) was in La Spezia, June 11, 1919; nearby Genoa followed suit within two days. From there, the movement spread to the Romagna and the Marches. In July, Florence was swept by three days of disturbances in which seven hundred were arrested and three killed; disturbances occurred also in Piedmont, Lombardy, and several large southern cities. Generally, however, the greatest number of protests over food prices took place in central and northern Italy.

To illustrate the mixture of form, of spontaneity and organization, and of tactics, let us look more closely at Florence, 3 to 6 July 1919. On the 3rd, the protest started as a "spontaneous" strike. Spontaneous in the sense of not being formally called by an organization; obviously the word was spread from plant to plant by some means. Thousands of workers went to the Chamber of Labor. The Chamber's secretary, in turn, went to the Prefect to ask for measures to calm the crowd. Meanwhile, the strikers moved into the shops of the city; they requisitioned clothing and shoes which they proceeded to sell at lower-than-usual prices. Requisitioned merchandise not sold on the spot was sent to the Chamber of Labor or cooperative or union headquarters.

The next day the Chamber found itself setting prices and rounding up trucks to bring food and other products into the city. Only one violent skirmish between police and workers occurred. Also on July 4 various groups of the left—socialist sections, unions, an anarchist group, the Chamber of Labor, acting in concert—reduced by 50 percent the prices of all previously price-controlled products. By the 5th, buying and selling was resuming, at the new low prices, but the strike continued. The police became more active and started to make mass arrests. Although the Chamber of Labor called for the end of the strike, it continued through July 6, on which day street fighting between police and strikers brought about deaths and injuries, and more arrests. The strike ended the next day (Del Carria 1966: II, 65–67).

Although the Florence protests retained some elements of the traditional market riot (such as selling commodities at drastically reduced prices), it was more similar to modern protest because it took the form of a strike, with organizational intervention and direction, if not origin. Elsewhere also, socialists as members of communal governments, or as pressure groups, called for enforced price controls, requisitions if needed to guarantee adequate supplies of food and other commodities, and sometimes formed squads of vigilantes to enforce the controlled prices.

In the Marches and Romagna, some of the labels connected with socialist action had a distinctly Bolshevik sound: provisioning "soviets" were the committees which established prices and organized requisitions, "red guards" enforced the action. The socialists continued to act within the political system, and they, along with most Chambers of Labor, condemned the sack of shops and granaries. The anarchists and some syndicalists, on the other hand, tried, in the old revolutionary strongholds of Ligury, the Marches, and Romagna, to lead the food riots with the notion of transforming them into insurrection (Vivarelli 1967: 412–418, 440–442).

Although the food protest came to an end in 1919, and the land occupations dwindled, the strike movement continued into 1920. That year brought out the largest number of industrial strikers in Italian history. Some 1,300,000 strikers took part in the same number of strikes (1,818) as in 1907, the highest previous year. This meant a huge jump in the size of strikes, from 170.9 strikers per strike in 1907 to 727.8 in 1920. There was a 15 percent increase in average strike size even as compared to 1919. The main component of this spectacular increase lay in a new tactic, the factory occupation or sit-down strike, and in the month-long occupation of factories in the fall of 1920.

In the Turin area the idea of the factory council had been developed by a group of young socialists associated with the journal *Ordine nuovo*. (Some were later the core of the Communist Party.) The councils were to be elected units within the factory organized by industrial instead of craft unions. The FIOM, the metalworkers' union, gave them some support in their April 1920 attempt to force management recognition of the councils.

In March, the Confindustria owners' group had already determined that it would not accept the factory councils; it forced a strike and lockout by fining and disciplining members of the internal commission, a unit within the craft union hierarchy which they had hitherto accepted, in one of the FIAT plants. The metal and machine works of Turin were occupied by police, royal guards, and carabinieri.

The union called an industrywide strike which lasted ten days before the Chamber of Labor joined in support and called a general strike, to be enforced throughout Piedmont. Public services, commerce, and businesses were shut down for two weeks. In the countryside, thousands of braccianti joined the strike. Violence developed in Turin, with fighting between cavalry and strikers, the Chamber of Labor surrounded by the police. Although enormous, the strike failed.

A new round of protest started with a union-sponsored slowdown on August 30, 1920, at the Alfa Romeo plant in Milan. The management responded with a lockout. Following a tactic planned in advance by the FIOM, workers on the earlier shift refused to leave the factory. In Milan, factory after factory was occupied by its own workers. The next day, the metal and machine industry declared a general lockout. The sitdown strikes spread to the Turin area.

The FIOM had tried to keep the issue of the prospective strike limited to wages, but once the strikes started, the tactics began to affect the content of the struggle. So, when employers offered wage concessions, the whole question of negotiations was passed on to the C.G.L. and the socialist party. Since the factory occupation, originally a strike over wages, had been transformed into a political, potentially revolutionary, strike, the party and unions fell into debate and recrimination about strategy.

Giolitti, again Prime Minister, resolved to wait out the strike. He refused to attack the workers, as some employers demanded. (Wryly he pointed out that an attack on workers would also be an attack on *their* plants.) But he defended the cities against a breakout from the plants, where the workers were by then armed. He was again hoping that inertia would dampen the situation until the moment when a settlement could be negotiated. Since the socialist party and the C.G.L had agreed on a division of responsibility between themselves for strikes with economic ends and those with political ends, a high-level debate about strategy evolved.

Despite the self-arming and military planning of the factory occupiers, and despite the more than half-million strikers involved, there were only small and isolated incidents of violence. At the Miani-Silvestri plant in Naples, workers were prevented by force from entering the plant by police. And at Foce, in Liguria, on September 2, three workers were shot when they tried to enter a plant surrounded by royal guards (Spriano 1964: 65, 73). The movement finally simply lost impetus. Giolitti was able to negotiate a settlement which was ostensibly favorable to the workers but in fact was never implemented.

In late 1920, in Emilia, the agrarian sector saw its last great pre-Fascist strike. Here mezzadri and braccianti worked together in the Federterra leagues to try to force change in their contractual and wage conditions. Although it aroused much bitterness, the strike was generally peaceful except for two bloody police–worker encounters which resulted in ten dead. It ended in October 1920, its economic goals achieved by agreement with the Confagricoltura. But, like the FIOM settlement after the factory occupation, the new pact disappeared in the almost immediate landowner-Fascist counteroffensive (Del Carria 1966: II, 85–88).

The most violent and overtly revolutionary incident of the troubled year 1920 was the mutiny-insurrection of Ancona, in June. It started as a protest over the Italian occupation of Albania. A peaceful demonstration, sponsored by the Chamber of Labor and the Socialist Party, on June 22 protested the government's militaristic policy. On June 25, plans for a joint military-civilian insurrection were made by soldiers from a unit about to be sent on board ship for Albania and by anarchists within the Chamber of Labor. The plot got off to a premature start when the troops mutinied before dawn the next day, captured their officers, and let some workers into the military base. Working-class groups in the Chamber of Labor were in the usual disagreement about how to proceed: although they finally agreed to strike (as the socialists proposed), an insurrection (the anarchist proposal) had already started. Street fighting ensued, with workers armed by the mutinous troops, who in some cases joined the defenders of the barricades, for two days. The weight of arms was on the side of the authorities, however; the insurrection was put down by the evening of June 27, 1920 (ibid.: 93–97).

The first phase of postwar collective action, that dominated by socialist and working-class militancy, ended in 1920. Though the strikes, land occupations, and food protest had caused much confusion and fear of upheaval, and doubtless a large amount of lost profits and wages (no one seems to have worked out a numerical estimate of this figure), it is interesting to note that violence was not inherent in much of the movement, and occurred only sporadically. The popular mobilization frightened agricultural landowners and industrialists, small shopkeepers, and even a good many workers who did not see great benefits gained to them. Even those who had felt the revolution at their fingertips felt a psychological letdown, Tasca tells us; union and socialist membership started to melt away at the end of 1920 (1963: 122–123).

The wave of left-inspired strikes, food protest, and land occupations had not resulted in general repression as in the 1890s or even the selective repression of prewar Giolittian politics. Although the police and military were sometimes called out against strikers or demonstrators, there were no rapid declarations of martial law, arrests of leaders, military trials, and suppression of organizations.

Liberal governments tried to defuse irritations and prevent violence by concessions. Strict government controls on the price of bread and subsidies to keep flour costs down continued until mid-1921; some of the land occupations were retrospectively legitimized in September 1919, and again in 1920. No vigorous action was taken against the factory occupations. Some of the absence of government moves against illegal working-class activity resulted as much from government weakness as from any civil-libertarian scruples. Yet Giolitti at least seemed to have acted deliberately, in the belief that the challenge from the left was not a serious one and would end quickly from disagreements within the movement.

Many people in Italy were convinced otherwise. They believed that the threat of the left was real, and illegal, that their welfare and property were threatened. They were willing to ally with the equally illegal and subversive Fascists to eliminate the socialist–working class challenge. The Fascist mobilization of nationalist patriots and veterans, armed and organized in paramilitary units, provided an ally for industrialists and landowners who wanted to tame the left. The Fascists linked patriotic and antisocialist sentiment in an attack on socialist and Catholic working-class groups. Nationalism and patriotism were not merely ideological rallying points for the Fascists; they were also powerful weapons against the internationally oriented working-class organizations.

The Fascists en Route to Power

The second wave of postwar collective action was predominantly Fascist-initiated. It began in the fall of 1920, in the Po Valley areas which had been the scene of powerful strike movements earlier in the same year. After a Fascist attempt to protest socialist electoral success in Bologna was fought back in a riotous council meeting and street fighting by socialists in Bologna, 21 November 1920 (the Palazzo Acurso incident), there was a sudden increase in Fascist support in Emilia. Ivanoe Bonomi described the change:

The agrarian classes began to move, meet, organize themselves. In the townships of the Po Valley, young veteran officers called together their friends and relatives who were landowners and told them that it was necessary to defend themselves against those who had been against the war . . . ., those who were causing violence and disorders, against those who would establish the dictatorship of the proletariat and repeat the Russian Revolution in Italy.
   A battle air fluttered through the country . . . The grafitti on the walls . . . were no longer only communist ones. Added to the numerous "Long live Lenin!" "Long live the dictatorship of the proletariat!" were counterposed other mottos which exalted the nation (*patria*) and victory (quoted in Salvatorelli and Mira 1964: 171).

Although Fascist violence started in the countryside, the squadre of Fascists who were willing tools for the attack on the unionized braccianti were closely linked to urban bases. Milan and Ferrara played the role of home base for many of the Fascists; once the countryside was intimidated, they turned against the stronger urban socialists.

The hundreds of violent encounters in which Fascist units were involved from late 1920 on were at first concentrated in the Po Valley. Black Shirt "punitive expeditions" were directed against voluntary associations (peasant leagues, Chambers of Labor, cooperatives, mutual-aid societies) and also against socialist communal governments. Truckloads of Fascists would arrive in a community, attack the headquarters of the workers' organizations, beat up anybody foolish enough to stay around, throw files and furniture into the street, sprinkle with gasoline, and burn them. (Where the Popolari had organized their peasant leagues, they too were attacked.) Then the Fascists would seek out union, league, or cooperative officers, socialist communal officials, and bully or beat them into resigning, "banishing" them from the region (Alatri 1956: 94–103; Salvatorelli and Mira 1964: 178–180.

In the first half of 1921, Fascists were reported to have destroyed 17 newspapers or printing plants, 59 Case del Popolo, 110 Chambers of Labor, 83 Peasant Leagues, 151 Socialist circles, and 151 cultural circles (Tasca 1963: 178). Figure 26 shows the distribution of these Fascist "destructions," first catalogued by Chiurco in the official Fascist history. The list of incidents gives equal value to each incident, and there is no definition of what a "destruction" entailed, so the incidents cover a disparate range of units. However, the magnitude of the number of events in each location is at least proportionately accurate, and the geographical distribution correct as far as the data go. The map shows incidents which occurred from some unknown starting date, up to September 1, 1921, without periodizing them. Therefore, we have a mixture of the earlier agrarian attacks along with the first urban ones. Nevertheless, the map illustrates the point we wish to make. Fascism destroyed working-class economic and political associations and fought its own way into power in the very areas where the socialist and labor movements had been most active and, seemingly, most successful. This is illustrated by the case of the South, in which the only area with appreciable incidents was Apulia, the only southern area with active working-class organization (see also Szymanski 1973).

As socialist organizations crumbled, Fascist membership grew: from 190 fasci in mid-October 1920, to more than 800 at the year's end, a thousand in February 1921, 1,500 in May, and 2,200 in November 1921

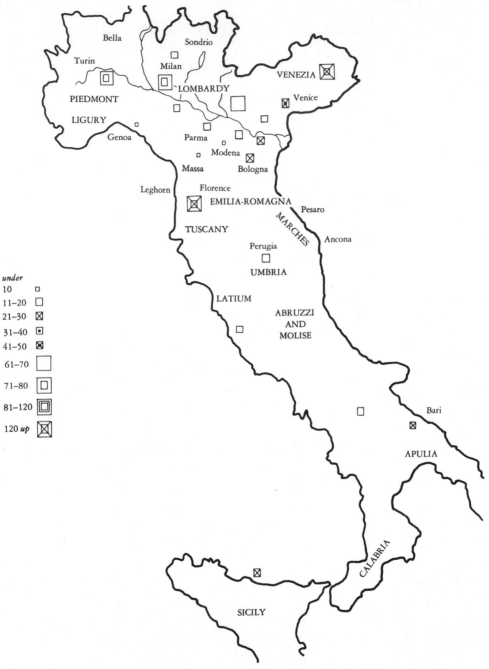

Source: Angelo Tasca. *Nascità e avvento del Fascismo: L'Italia dal 1918 al 1922* (Florence: La Nuova Italia, 1963) p. 178.

Figure 26. Incidents of Fascist Violence against Property of Working Class Institutions, up to September 1921.

(Salvatorelli and Mira 1964: 180). By the end of the first six months of 1921, the Fascists had forcibly ousted working-class organizations and socialist governments from Venezia Giulia, all the Po Valley (except Cremona, Parma, and the Romagna), and a large part of Tuscany, Umbria, and Apulia. In Piedmont, parts of Alessandria and Novara provinces were occupied, but Turin still held out despite the arson of its large Casa del Popolo. Except for the Po Valley areas of Pavia and Mantua, Lombardy was still outside Fascist hegemony (Tasca 1963: 177–178).

The spectacular Fascist successes were partly the result of military orientation and organization. The larger urban fasci sent contingents to smaller towns, rural areas, or other cities not yet organized. There was also relatively little organized resistance to the Fascist squadre. The one incident always mentioned is the Sarzana "massacre" (so-called by the Fascists) in July 1921. This started with military resistance by the eleven carabinieri in town to Fascist demands, threats, and perhaps sniping. Once the Fascists were in retreat, however, angered citizens and peasants from the surrounding countryside rushed to attack and harass them (ibid.: 226–228).

There was also a left-wing paramilitary organization, the Arditi del Popolo, which modeled its fighting units after the Fascist squadri. Units were established by various elements of the far left in Rome, Bari, Parma, and a few other cities, and at the time of the general strike of August 1922 and of the March on Rome in October of the same year they managed successfully to resist Fascist attacks on their institutions and cities (Del Carria 1966: 188–225).

The Sarzana incident also illustrates, negatively, another contributor to Fascist successes: complicity in all levels of government. Local officials simply looked the other way when Fascist squadri drove into town. There were reports of truckloads of carabinieri, also singing Fascist songs, driving behind the trucks of Black Shirts (Salvatorelli and Mira 1964: 179). The police and the military actually supplied weapons to Fascist squads. There is still much question about how far up in the bureaucracy this kind of helpful sympathy went, and whether it reached into the cabinets and judiciary. There certainly was a degree of philo-fascism, even among ministers and judges, but whether and how they implemented it is still a matter of debate.

In Parliament, men across the whole political gamut, excluding only some republicans and most socialists, refused to be alarmed by Fascism. The liberal Giolitti welcomed Fascist candidates to his national list in the 1921 elections. The Popolaro De Gasperi, as late as April 1921, limited his criticism of Fascism to a condemnation of the punitive raids while uncritically accepting the Fascist claim that they represented merely a "reaction to communist internationalism which denied liberty and nation" (De Felice 1969: 143). Organized farm workers thought otherwise. Consider the farm workers' league of Marzano, near Pavia, whose report on a Fascist attack poignantly concluded: "In striking at us, Fascism was not striking at the 'harmful madness of bolshevism,' but at the marvelous structure which, with thirty years of constant work and sacrifice, the workers of the Pavese had built for their own liberation and for a new world of right and justice" (Alatri 1956: 100–101).

As the Fascist squads carried on their vicious campaign in 1921, national politics confirmed the disarray of both the left and the liberals. In January 1921, at the Socialist Congress of Leghorn, the Communists seceded, leaving the party divided between a large majority which supported the maximalist, revolutionary position, and a small reformist group, following Turati. In May of the same year elections were called when Giolitti failed to get parliamentary support for needed taxes.

The 1921 elections show, in a rough way, the results of Fascist extra-parliamentary activity on the political situation. These elections mark the end of the postwar growth in electoral strength of northern socialists. The socialists were still the largest parliamentary group. They had received the highest percentage of votes of any party, as Table 11 shows, but their deputy count was reduced by separate communist slates. In the northernmost tier of provinces, Fascist attacks on the left had not reduced the combined communist-socialist vote, except for Piedmont; still, this vote had not increased.

In the central tier of provinces, Emilia, Tuscany, Umbria, and the Marches, the vote percentages of the combined left parties were much lower than they had been in 1919. This center zone had absorbed most of the Fascist violence to date. That was especially true of Emilia, which includes the southern Po Valley area. In Emilia, besides a big drop in the percentage of votes going to the far left (and an increase in vote percentage to the Blocco Nazionale, which included the Fascists, as compared to liberal votes in 1919), there was an absolute drop in the number of votes cast by 8 percent. There was also a decrease in the number of votes cast in the Marches.

We are probably observing here a forced demobilization arising from Fascist violence against left organizations (cf. Lyttelton 1973: 67). From Rome south, on the other hand, socialist-communist percentages of the vote were as high or higher than in 1919. There had been little intervention up to this time of Fascists against the left in the South. The Fascist campaign had been exceedingly successful in the Po Valley area, especially in "bleaching" Emilia Rossa (Red Emilia), least successful in the Veneto and the North in general, while their lack of activity in the South meant continued left electoral strength.

Another political development which points up the ambivalent political position of Fascism at this time was the so-called Pacification Pact of August 1921. Drawn up at the urging of Bonomi (who had succeeded Giolitti), this was an agreement to call off violence on the part of socialists and Fascists. Bonomi, most liberals, and most socialists all hoped that the Fascists could be drawn into the parliamentary system. Disagreement from the squadre and their militant leaders forced Mussolini to back away from the agreement. There was no change in the parliamentary intransigence of the Fascists, and little reduction of the level of violence.

The end of 1921 saw the Fascist Congress in Rome. There the Pacification Pact was officially denounced by Mussolini. At the same Congress, the hierarchical paramilitary movement of Fascism was transformed into a so-called political party. The paramilitary cast remained: the squad leaders and members proved hard to handle within the party context. The party defined itself (following the conception of the movement as a force acting in place of the state) as a rival to the state, outside traditional politics. Mussolini wrote (*Popolo d'Italia,* 4 November 1921, quoted in Salvatorelli and Mira 1964: 203) that the squads would be continued, "considering that the state appears unable to contain and smash the antinational forces."

Fascist violence continued in 1922. Although still concentrated in the North, it now ventured more often into older urban working-class strong-

Table 11. Comparison of elections of 1919 and 1921 (percentages)

Region	Number of votes (thousands)	"Constitutional lists"	"National Bloc"	"Left Bloc"	"Liberal Bloc"	Republican Party	Popular Party	Socialist Party	Communist Party
Piedmont									
1919	1,131	27	—	4	—	—	19	50	—
1921	1,169	—	15	—	22	—	22	29	12
Ligury									
1919	404	32	—	16	—	—	20	32	—
1921	423	—	31	—	13	—	24	23	9
Lombardy									
1919	1,457	19	—	5	—	—	30	46	—
1921	1,511	—	25	—	3	—	26	42	4
Veneto									
1919	1,036	21	—	10	—	—	36	33	—
1921	1,143	—	24	—	5	2	36	32	1
Emilia									
1919	956	12	—	10	—	—	18	60	—
1921	879	—	33	—	2	8	19	33	5
Tuscany									
1919	894	28	—	8	—	—	20	44	—
1921	915	—	33	—	2	5	19	31	10
Umbria									
1919	228	25	—	11	—	—	17	47	—
1921	360	—	28	—	8	9	30	20	5
Marches									
1919	367	31	—	8	—	—	27	34	—
1921	360	—	28	—	8	9	30	20	5

Lazio									
1919	393	37	—	12	—	—	26	25	—
1921	402	—	42	—	1	6	22	25	4
Abruzzi									
1919	381	69	—	12	—	—	3	16	—
1921	392	—	—	—	76	—	7	15	2
Campania-Molise									
1919	1,157	70	—	8	—	—	17	5	—
1921	1,197	—	—	—	77	—	14	8	1
Apulia									
1919	647	61	—	10	—	—	11	18	—
1921	675	—	52	—	16	1	10	18	3
Basilicata									
1919	165	93	—	2	—	—	—	5	—
1921	168	—	—	—	85	2	4	9	—
Calabria									
1919	451	55	—	20	—	—	18	7	—
1921	467	—	—	—	70	—	19	10	1
Sicily									
1919	1,211	58	—	23	—	—	12	7	—
1921	1,253	—	—	—	79	—	13	7	1
Sardinia									
1919	238	55	—	24	—	—	12	9	—
1921	246	—	47	—	29	—	11	13	—
All Italy									
1919	11,115	37	—	10	—	—	21	32	—
1921	11,447	—	22	—	26	2	21	25	4

SOURCE: Derived from Ugo Giusti, *Dai Plebisciti alla Costituente* (Rome, 1945), pp. 72, 82.

holds. There were large threatening processions and meetings of armed Fascists in the spring, attacks on socialist May Day demonstrations in North Italian cities, and finally an attack on Bologna and its unsympathetic prefect, Cesare Mori. A director of public security was sent from Rome on June 1, 1922, to restore order in Bologna; he bargained to exchange the withdrawal of the terrorizing squadre in return for Mori's transfer. In June and July, Fascist attacks on city halls multiplied. As the Fascists joined with the left and the Popolari in July to vote no confidence in the Facta government, Mussolini explained in Parliament that they could not both uphold the goverment and "act in the countryside as they had to act now" (quoted in Salvatorelli and Mira 1964: 222).

In the interministry hiatus in July 1922, an ad hoc group of unions, the Alleanza del Lavoro, called a general strike for August 1; they hoped to make a meaningful protest against Fascism. Although expressly announced as "legalitarian," the effect of the protest strike was to preclude a left ministry, bring back Facta, and unleash a new wave of Fascist violence. Somehow having got advance notice of the date of the strike, the Fascist executive board issued an ultimatum to the strikers and to the state. They gave the state forty-eight hours "to exert its authority . . . on those who are attacking the existence of the nation. Once this time is up, Fascism will claim full freedom of action and will substitute itself to the State which will once again have shown its impotence" (Tasca 1963: 323). The Alleanza had to call off the strike, but chose to do so twelve hours after the Fascist deadline.

Figure 27 illustrates the geography of the Fascist attacks at the time of the Alleanza general strike. The largest number of attacks radiated out from the Emilia-Romagna base already securely held by Fascists. These attacks, which continued until August 8, extended Fascist control to the regions around Genoa, Leghorn, and Ancona, all old anarchist areas. The city hall of Milan was occupied, and the socialist municipal administration expelled. The plant and offices of *Avanti!* were again attacked and burned. A sniper shot at a Fascist in the Via Canonica brought a wholesale attack (seconded by the police) on this "subversive neighborhood." (The Via Canonica's radical reputation went back at least to its barricade during the Fatti di Maggio, 1898.) The city of Parma was the scene of four days of militant resistance by working-class neighborhoods

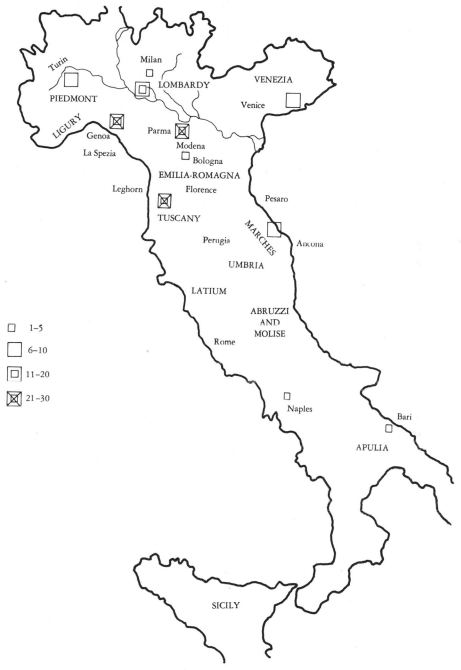

Source: Angelo Tasca, *Nascità e avvento del Fascismo: L'Italia dal 1918 al 1922* (Florence: La Nuova Italia, 1963), pp. 325–328.

Figure 27. Fascist Attacks on Left-Wing Institutions and Socialist Local Government, August 1922.

led by the Arditi del Popolo against the inevitable Fascist attack. The Fascists had to admit failure, but the military authorities who occupied the city dislodged the militants. The Fascist attack on Bari also failed.

The road to power was opening to the Fascists. The second Facta government was even weaker than the first: Facta had "ceded" Milan, Genoa, and Leghorn to the Fascists in the general strike, with the understanding that they would keep clear of Rome (Tasca 1963: 400). The entire Po Valley, much of North and Central Italy were in Fascist hands. Only Turin and Parma in the North, and the passive South were "free." The Milanese newspaper, *Il Corriere della Sera,* started a press campaign for a new goverment, including Fascist ministers (Sturzo n.d.: 109). Mussolini shrewdly held back, hoping for the prime ministership. A group of Milanese senators and representatives of the Confindustria asked Salandra to support Mussolini for prime minister. With his threat of a march on Rome by Fascist legions, Mussolini bullied the King into inviting him to form a cabinet.

Although the March on Rome did not materialize as a military attack on the city, it was preceded by violence in other cities. Fascist violence followed it in Rome, and the whole business of the transfer of power took place in a situation which could be called constitutional only in the loosest sense of the word. Salandra, disenchanted later, wrote that it was "the first time in Italy since the establishment of the constitutional monarchy, that the transfer of political power came about by an act of force, before which the King, and later Parliament had to surrender unconditionally" (quoted in Salvatorelli and Mira 1964: 238).

While the King was being persuaded, by threats and personal worries, not to sign the martial law declaration which Facta had drawn up, Black Shirts were occupying prefectural palaces, postal and telegraph offices, and police stations, around the country. Most often, this took place without resistance from the authorities. Sometimes (in Bologna, Verona, Cremona, and Genoa, for example) the Fascists had to fight their way in (Lyttelton 1973: 89–90).

Mussolini's coalition government was formally constituted on October 31, 1922. It contained all parties of center and right. The Black Shirts completed their March on Rome the same day in an impressive parade through the city. Groups of them then launched a series of violent attacks on newspapers, "dangerous" neighborhoods, and organizations. The later Fascist Congress of Naples was held in a mood of celebration; Black Shirts left it to move in on the South.

Black Shirt squad violence now went officially hand-in-hand with the government. Although there seem to have been fewer incidents after October 1922, violent action did not disappear. Opposition newspapers and individuals with intransigent leftist views were favorite targets. In the South, the Fascists found it necessary to battle the nationalists, who had been their allies. In Turin, on December 18, there was a final assault on socialist and union buildings and individuals connected with the left, atrocious murders, and many arrests of socialists and communists.

In January and February 1923 the violent incidents continued, but the public violence tapered off as Fascist intimidation worked, other organizations disappeared for good, and official repression took over. By January 1925 Mussolini with impunity could publicly accept responsibility for the murder of Matteotti. Parties were outlawed soon afterward, political opponents silenced or imprisoned, and the independent press crushed.

So far, in speaking of the participants in collective violence, we have been able to give them economic or social class labels—peasants, landless agricultural workers, artisans, industrial workers. But in trying to describe the Fascists, the major participants in collective violence in 1921–1922, simple labels are impossible. The actual class basis of early Fascist membership has yet to be spelled out. Table 12, derived from the count made at the Fascist Congress of 1921, at which the movement was transformed into a party, shows the range of occupations of a group of party members.

Tasca, the former *Ordine Nuovo* militant, is very reluctant to admit any voluntary working-class membership in the Fascist party: he explains that the agricultural workers were mostly ex-members of socialist or syndicalist leagues, forced into Fascist organizations by the attacks of squadre. He claims that the industrial workers were recruited from members of destroyed organizations. The Fascists had "inherited" 138 cooperatives and 614 unions, with 64,000 members, two-thirds of them in Emilia, Tuscany, and the Veneto (1963: 247).

The general view of contemporaries and historians was that Fascist activists were mostly middle-class, many of them former soldiers. Nevertheless there are quite a few cases of former socialist and syndicalist *leaders* taking part in the early Fascist movement. Some disillusioned rank-and-file socialist or union members also joined, attracted by Fascist na-

Table 12. Occupations of a group of Fascist Party members, 1921

Occupation	Number	Percent
Landowners	18,084	12.0
Shopowners	13,878	9.2
Manufacturers	4,269	2.8
Learned professions	9,981	6.6
State employees	7,209	4.8
White collar workers	14,998	10.0
Teachers	1,680	1.1
Students	19,763	13.2
Agricultural workers	36,847	24.5
Industrial workers	23,418	15.6
Total	150,127[a]	99.8

SOURCE: Angelo Tasca, *Nascita e avvento del Fascismo. L'Italia dal 1918 al 1922* (Florence, 1963), p. 247.

[a] Tasca gives the total as 151,644, which leaves 1,517 unaccounted for. We have calculated our percentages of the actual total of the breakdown figures he gives. The total membership of the Fascist Party at the time was 320,000.

tionalism and its initial social programs. The Fascists also recruited formerly nonunionized, unemployed, and unskilled workers (Lyttelton 1973: 68–70).

How can we understand the recruitment of workers into Fascism? We have Tasca's testimony that both the socialist party and the labor movement were losing members even before the Fascist counter-attack (1963: 122–123). The energy and level of mobilization of the left declined considerably at the end of 1920. At about that time Mussolini, always sensitive to shifts in the political climate, wrote, "in the last three months the psychology of the mass of Italian workers has been profoundly modified" (quoted in Tasca 1963: 521). The Fascist position came to represent a basic realignment of politics along non-class lines, of nation versus anti-nation, along with the demobilization of men organized by class. The Fascists not only rejected alliances with the organized working class, they succeeded also in labeling it the enemy of the nation, of the people.

Contemporaries recognized this fundamental feature of Fascism. Bonomi, for example, wrote that "All the peculiar characteristics of Fascism, its original anti-bourgeois spirit, its proletarian inclinations, its plans for political and economic renovation, were submerged and for-

gotten in the predominantly anti-Bolshevik character of its predilections"
(quoted in De Felice 1969: 142). All working-class institutions were
labeled as dangerous and Bolshevik. They were attacked by Fascist squadre
in the name of patriotism. This aggression worked, partly because the
failure of socialist and working-class militancy in 1919 and 1920—or perhaps its success in making limited gains for some workers who then had
no further reason to pursue the revolution—released workers for recruitment to other organizations, or for just plain apathy. After the class-based
organizations were destroyed, nationalist, patriotic Fascism built its own
system of worker organization. Always the pragmatist, Mussolini explained in a March 1923 speech that Fascist unions had not been part
of the original program, but "Fascism practices unionism by a physio-
logical necessity of its development" (quoted in ibid.: 288).

The Fascists were successful in "monopolizing" patriotism, the Popolaro-
turned-Fascist Cesare degli Occhi remarked (quoted in De Felice 1966:
123). Malatesta, the aging anarchist, accused the left of allowing the
middle class to claim patriotism, and thence the state, as uniquely their
own: "It was the error of the proletariat, the revolutionaries, the socialists,
and the anarchists to permit the conservatives and lowly tools of the
bourgeoisie to monopolize in a way the shout 'Long live Italy,' and they
thus succeeded in making the simple-minded believe that the others hated
the country in which they lived" (quoted in ibid.: 232).

The tactic of using nationalism as a weapon against the left was successful in northern Italy; Bonomi, again, suggested that this tactic was
not as useful to the Fascists south of Rome. He wrote as an observer of
the spread of Fascism in the Po Valley:

The Fasci were at first few and scattered, but grew by recruiting new members, especially from among landowners. Almost every little town of the Po
plain had its Fascio. The movement reached the Appenines, crossed them,
spread through Tuscany and Umbria, but was stopped at Rome, where the
competition of the nationalists blocked the way, so that only a few were able
to spread in the South (Salvatorelli and Mira 1963: 141–142).

We have suggested that the concentration of Fascist violence in the
North was due to the concentration there of its chief target: the organized
working class. Bonomi's explanation gives the picture another dimension.
The weapon which the Fascists used effectively in the North was already
monopolized, south of Rome, by the nationalists.

The final element that went into Fascist appeal and eventual Fascist success was their insistence that they were defending law-and-order, and their ability to act as a stand-in for the state in order to guarantee it. From the view of the left, this was "terrorism . . . gone from the private to the public sector; it no longer was content with concessions made to it by the state; it wished to become the state" (Gramsci 1955: 351, comment written at the end of 1920). To the Po Valley landowners, the Fascists were welcome allies in crushing their troublesome workers who were trying to bring the Revolution to Italy. In the process, the Fascists established an organized alternative to the state in the vital matter of preserving order. Finally, all were forced to pay allegiance to Fascism, for it merged with the state. After the nation had been used as the rallying cry to demobilize the working class, the idea of nation was used to repress participation of *all* free groups in politics. Political organization, economic association, and even social groups became the tools of Fascism. Collective action flowed only in narrowly defined channels, and collective violence all but disappeared from Italy.

CHAPTER IV

Germany

The German Varieties of Violence

Germany, like France, Italy, and most other countries, has a violent history. Names and clichés such as German militarism, Bismarck's "blood and iron," Hitler, and the Gestapo spring to mind. Violence directed by Germany's rulers against its internal and external foes has been an important force—and hence an important theme—in the country's history. Our main concern here, however, is with a species of collective violence less often identified with—and *in*—German history: the popular actions (riots, revolts, rebellions, and revolutions) mounted by large groups of Germans against the state. It is unconventional to report German history from the point of view of such events, but it makes sense to do so, not least of all because that may permit a revision of certain now outdated stereotypes, for example, the "docile Germans."

The history of collective violence in Germany over the long period from roughly 1815 to 1930 may be divided into three phases: Phase one, increasingly turbulent and culminating in the revolutions of 1848–1849, in which local, informally organized groups employ largely traditional forms of violent protest (mass trespassings or machine-breaking, for example) directed above all against the pressures of commercialization in a rapidly changing, but only slowly growing, economy. Phase two, with relatively modest levels of protest, increasingly involving offensive and/or forward-looking protest forms, operating in urban contexts against the background of a rapidly growing economy and increasingly formally organized social relationships. Phase three, 1918–1933, in which large-scale national organizations carry and focus massive protest actions against one another and against the state, all the while against the background of extreme economic instability and uncertainty about the state's claim to political authority.

Some concrete examples of protest can best introduce this periodization. We begin with a report from a Saxon village, Kieselbach, in September 1842.

Thanks to the long-continuing drought this year grain dealers have been coming here from all over, buying up local reserves of grain for export. The costs of these arrangements are of course borne largely by the poor local artisan, who is thus unable to buy the grain he needs. Traveling through Kieselbach recently, I had the opportunity to witness a revolt against these developments. Grain dealers had just loaded their wagons and the poor inhabitants of the village were assembled around the village foreman, loudly and bitterly complaining and beseeching him to intervene. The foreman saw no way out. He strode at the head of the protesters to the place where the wagons stood and, with heavy blows of his ax, split the grain bins of the wagons in two; at the same time the crowd subjected the grain buyers to the harshest imaginable verbal abuse, until at last the police rescued them from a threatening, excited mob (*Frankfurter Journal,* October 3, 1842).

We have here a typical German protest scenario of the first half of the nineteenth century: a local group of village poor defending with traditionally informal means traditional rights and resources against the impersonal forces of a spreading commercialization. The growth of a national market and the dependence of increasing numbers of persons upon the market for satisfaction of consumption needs characterized the first half of the nineteenth century; but since overall consumption levels and new employment opportunities grew very slowly for most people, they tended to see commercialization as a threatening intrusion to be resisted wherever possible.

We hurtle forward, across the deep divide of 1848–1849 and into the century's second half. Industrialization of production speeds on, the labor force organizes, and urban populations—especially in the great cities—

swell disproportionately. By 1910 mass political organizations like the
Socialist Workers' Party (hereafter SPD) are a major force in Germany's
big-city life, particularly in Berlin—by 1910 a city of more than two million people and the Reich's capital. In 1910 the party organizes mass
demonstrations demanding reform of the Prussian three-class electoral
laws. In Berlin the police ban street demonstrations—in the name of traffic needs!

In March:

Berlin's [Socialist] Party leadership called on party members to attend an
electoral law demonstration in Treptow Park set for March 6th. The park
was a favorite spot for workers' meetings and well known to Berlin and
Treptow police. On March 5th the park had already been ringed and occupied by police. But to their surprise, only a handful of strollers appeared
[on the 6th]—and not the hundred thousand they expected. Berlin's [SPD]
organization had functioned perfectly. Its 2,500 District Chiefs had redi-
rected the "Electoral Stroll" without the police catching the slightest wind of
it. By word of mouth, the message had traveled around: "everybody meets
at the Reichstag" . . . The lone policeman making his rounds along the
Königplatz was no doubt perplexed: 150,000 Berliners gathered there. Orderly and disciplined, without controls and interference from the police, they
carried through their protest demonstration. After more than two hours they
dispersed—just as the first police arrived, charging up on foam-bedecked
horses (Lange 1967: 451–452).

Massive, disciplined, and nonviolent acts of protest were becoming,
by 1910, hallmarks of the German socialist movement. In this very same
period, however, Berlin saw great violence. In September 1910, 141
workers of Kupfer, a coal company in Berlin's Moabit district, struck for
higher wages. The management, backed by the influential Stinnes *Kon-
zern,* reacted fiercely, and the struggle escalated.

Strikebreakers were brought in under heavy police protection. At night the
strikers tore the cobblestones out of the street in front of the coalyard, to
hinder delivery, and forced houseowners to repudiate all rental agreements
made with the police on behalf of strikebreakers . . . The Berlin [SPD]
Party leadership remained neutral toward the strike. Nevertheless, solidarity
grew spontaneously, and in several days Moabit's 141 strikers had grown to
a mass of 20,000 to 30,000 protesters . . . During the noon hour on September 24, a strikebreaker fired into the crowd. The police protected him
and moved against the workers—who responded with a hail of bottles, pots,
and stones . . . On September 26 and 27, the struggle was intensified

through clashes between police and Loewe workers. AEG [German General Electric] workers also joined in. On the 27th, owner Stinnes' complaints occasioned police president von Jagow to order the use of firearms . . . "The district filled with gun-fire . . . When quiet arrived that evening, two workers lay dead in the streets and hundreds of men and women were wounded" (Lange 1967: 448–449).

The workers lost this strike. The SPD disassociated itself from it. Fourteen "ringleaders" received sentences totaling sixty-seven months' imprisonment. This violence probably contributed to the growth of working-class solidarity in Moabit, as Annamarie Lange or Helmut Bleiber have argued. But the episode is interesting in other regards: there is the systematic employment of strikebreakers and police protection, the solidarity of a big-city working-class district, and the reluctance of large-scale labor organizations (Berlin was the national headquarters) to act on a local bread-and-butter issue and on behalf of a marginal group of workers. The contrast to the "Treptow Electoral Stroll" is striking and illuminating (for this episode see also Bleiber 1955).

Collective violence in the Weimar years (1919–1933) shows interesting contrasts and also some sequels to the previous period. Here is a report from Hamburg, August 2, 1929:

In Hamburg 15,000 workers attended the Communist Party's indoor peace rallies. But that was not all. Under Party leadership they formed numerous marching columns to demonstrate. They stayed on the streets far into the night . . . At different points in the city the police fired into the ranks of the marchers. Numerous workers were wounded. But not even these shots of the police could restrain the workers from publicly showing the bourgeoisie their opposition to imperialist wars. The threatened workers defended themselves with rocks. In Hammerbrook they disarmed five police officers. (Laboor 1961: 320).

Discounting the ideology, this example reveals once again the typically big-city context of collective violence, but now a clearly associational framework involving formal, national organizations, national political issues, large numbers of persons, and quite fierce resistance to repressive measures.

This brief look at Germany's violence and "street politics" begins our story. Processes of large-scale change loom large in the background as conditioning factors: the commercialization of socioeconomic relations, the industrialization of production and rising living standards, the urban-

ization of a growing population, the nationalization of economic and political life and the accompanying growth of large-scale organizations that
replace local informal ties. Perhaps these processes explain the shifts in
quantity of violence observed; their influence on the quality and character of violent protest should already be visible. However, the causal connections between Germany's collective violence and these processes,
though close, is by no means obvious, and we are only beginning to understand them.

The Political Framework

The degree of initial decentralization in Germany and her subsequent
unification were important structural features. The treaties which concluded the Napoleonic Wars in 1814–1815 reduced the number of sov-
ereign German states from the more than three hundred members of the
old Holy Roman Empire to thirty-eight, including Austria. One of those
treaties also created the German Bund, a confederation whose purpose
was "preservation of the independence and sovereignty of the individual
German states." As such, it served as a brake on centralization. Prince
Metternich, the conservative Austrian chancellor, used it to prop up
various ruling dynasties and to check the spread of democratic ideas and
reform—if necessary, as in 1830, by military intervention.

Unification, therefore, had to travel by another route: economic union
and force of arms. Prussia, the largest German state, led the way. A law
of 1818 eliminated internal tariff barriers in Prussia and established a low,
external tariff wall. She then offered her neighbors favorable terms of entry to this large, internal market, and one after another they accepted. With
the Zollverein's founding in 1833, the most important German states—
with the exception of Austria—were economically united, though fiscal
and monetary integration lagged somewhat.

Economic union bound important German states closer to Prussia
(Saxony, for example), and represented a threat to Austria's hegemony
in German affairs. Austria's Slavic possessions and high-tariff orientation
prevented her from closer association with the low-duty Zollverein. This
was a major reason why the Zollverein, though economically invaluable
to all members, could not lead to German unification (Boehme 1966: esp.
211–212).

War and revolution proved more effective unifiers. In 1830–1831 the inability of rulers in smaller states like Hesse-Cassel, Braunschweig, and even Saxony to withstand dissidents' challenges to their authority without Prussian and Austrian military help increased the prestige and power of those states within Germany. The suppression of revolutionary movements in 1848–1849 had similar, though more pronounced, consequences: once again, Prussian and Austrian troops held the balance of power. The Austro-Prussian war against Denmark in 1864 brought Schleswig-Holstein into the Bund, and at the same time supplied an object of contention which led to the civil war of 1866. Prussia's decisive victory over Austria and her allies in that war is well known. The North German Confederation built on that triumph and created essentially the same electoral and political machinery which would be confirmed in the Imperial (or Reich) constitution after the German defeat of France in 1870–1871. In contrast to the Bund, the North German Confederation—and after 1871 the Reich —provided for a national executive branch in control of foreign policy, the army and navy, monetary standards, weights and measures, and so on. The policies of this executive were jointly determined by a national parliament (the Reichstag), elected by all adult males and the Bundesrat (or Federal Council), consisting of the representatives of the remaining twenty-five German states.

Prussia dominated the Reich's government of course. Prussia's king was Germany's emperor; the Prussian minister president was chancellor of the Reich government; and, significantly, control over the armed forces was to remain until 1918 in the hands of the Emperor. But Prussia had to make significant concessions in 1871 to German states like Bavaria and Württemberg, and consequently controlled only a large plurality, not a majority, of votes in the important Bundesrat. As Table 13 suggests, centralization of power under the Reich was not insignificant, but substantial centrifugal tendencies nevertheless remained. It took defeat in World War I and the Revolutions of 1918–1919 to establish a unified state approximating, say, the British model, and Germany remained at all times far less centralized than France.

Germany's political unification slowed in the nineteenth century and remained relatively incomplete before 1914 because it clashed with the conservative, antidemocratic aims of the country's rulers. Metternich's role up to 1848 has already been mentioned. His influence was one reason why most of the German states which introduced representative assem-

Table 13. Annual average consumption expenditures of German Reich, Länder, and Gemeinden as percentage of total public consumption, 1875–1913.

	1875–1879	1890–1894	1910–1913
Reich	46	44	36
Länder	34	29	28
Gemeinden	20	27	36
Total in billion marks	1.2	1.9	4.5

SOURCE: Walter Hoffman et al., *Das Wachstum der deutschen Wirtschaft seit der Mitte des 19. Jahrhunderts* (Berlin, 1965).

blies after 1815 gave them only limited powers. The Prussian Landtage, for example, were provincial bodies which discussed only local administrative matters. In any case, they were far from being popular bodies before 1848. In Prussia only the propertied could vote, and it is doubtful whether as many as one-fifth of all adult males possessed the privilege (Conze 1962: 238). Because of the class voting system, landed aristocrats controlled more than half of the seats in most of Prussia's Landtage. Other German states had similar or even more restrictive systems. Zorn's estimates for elections to the Bavarian lower chamber during this pre-1848 period suggest that around 1.2 percent of adult men might hold office and around 6 percent vote (Zorn 1962: 128–129).

Middle-class demands for a widening of this suffrage and the enlargement of parliamentary prerogatives played a major role in the revolutions of 1848–1849. Those revolutions did in fact accelerate the development of parliamentary democracy. Prussia's 1849 constitution created a national house of lords and national house of representatives. The latter possessed nominal control over the annual budget. Prussia's new legislative organs, however, meant much less than similar bodies elsewhere (including those of most other German states, where parliamentary powers and their popular bases expanded after 1848). The three-class electoral system powerfully restricted the suffrage. It allocated the total number of electoral votes equally to three groups, corresponding to the top, middle, and lower third of income-tax revenues distributed by size of payment. Thus, the small number of high-income recipients who accounted for the "upper third" of income-tax revenues controlled one-third of all electoral votes.

This institution well symbolized Germany's political backwardness. Increasingly after 1871 liberal and socialist politicians alike trained their fire on this system—which contrasted sharply to the universal manhood suffrage laws governing Reichstag elections. The system held until 1918, however. It provided, after all, a most effective bulwark against the Worker's Social Democratic Party. In 1908, for example, the Conservative Party attracted 14 percent of the total votes and won 152 seats in the Prussian lower chamber (out of a total of 435); Social-Democrat candidates received 24 percent of the vote and held one seat! (Ritter 1967: 123). Critics demanded application of Reichstag electoral rules to Prussian lower house elections. The previously mentioned Socialist demonstrations of 1910 had this aim. In 1908 Reichschancellor (*and* Prussian Minister-President) von Bülow admitted that some liberalization was desirable, but he quickly qualified:

His Majesty's government is as firmly convinced as ever that the application of Reichstag electoral law to Prussia would not be in the best interests of the state, and therefore must reject any such application. Nor can His Majesty's government consider at this time the substitution of voting by secret ballot for the present system of public balloting. No reform of Prussian electoral law can be permitted to weaken the influence of the broad strata of the middle class upon the election results or to ignore the need for an equitable system of weighting votes. We are therefore now examining whether this goal can be attained with the help of the income-tax criteria alone, or whether, and to what extent, additional criteria such as age, property, education, etc. can be reasonably introduced (Hüber 1957–1969: IV, 377).

The adoption of universal manhood suffrage at the Reich level of government in 1871 produced unforeseen results. Most important, it enabled the Workers' Social Democratic Party to grow into the numerically strongest national party. This threat to Germany's ruling elites only became clear in the course of the 1870s, but it explains two developments: the "extraordinary" laws against the Social Democratic Party introduced in 1878 and maintained in force until 1890; and the slow and limited transfer of powers (including fiscal powers) from the German states (mainly Prussia) to the Reich government.

As Table 14 shows, the official ban on the SPD's activities failed to stop its growth. But it is important to recognize that this quantitative growth by no means meant an increasingly potent socialist threat to the Wilhelminian political system. Despite the SPD's size (more than one million members by 1914) and militant rhetoric, it opposed challenges to the state which threatened violence. Was this lack of militancy, particularly clear from around the turn of the century, the product of rapidly rising living standards or of the power of the state? Of the growing weight of the trade unions? Of unrealistic doctrine? Does Peter Nettl's notion of the SPD as an "inheritance party"—that is, the political organization which is to take control "come the revolution"—make sense?

A look ahead to the Weimar political arrangements throws interesting light on what the question of representation could and could not mean. The Weimar Republic realized universal suffrage and considerable centralization of political power. It also placed, temporarily at least, the SPD in the center of the parliamentary stage (the Republic's first prime minister was Scheidemann, a Social Democrat). Nevertheless, we may speak of the "reduced authority of the state" as compared with pre-1914 years, if we define "authority" to mean the popular consensus, the willingness of major contending groups to accept and work within the framework of the existing political system. Naturally, the military defeat in 1918, the harsh peace in 1919, especially the inflation in 1923 (in which that crucial element of political sovereignty, the ability to guarantee monetary order, was thrown into doubt), and the mass unemployment of 1929–1933 dealt the Weimar state heavy blows, shocks which would have hurt the prestige of any government. Under the historical German conditions, such blows proved fatal. There was a significant discrepancy in the Weimar government system between the formal power enjoyed by parliament (the Reichstag) and its practical impotence. This discrepancy built on the

Table 14. Reichstag election results, 1871–1912 (percentages)

Year	Eligible voters voting	Voting for Social Democratic Party
1871	50.7	3.2
1877	60.3	9.1
1884	60.3	9.7
1898	67.7	27.2
1912	84.5	34.8

SOURCE: Gerhard Ritter, *Historisches Lesebuch 2, 1871–1914* (Frankfurt am Main, 1967), pp. 366–367.

historical importance of military and civil bureaucracy in German politics and the related supremacy of interest group organizations as "lawmakers" —particularly where economic interests were involved. Karl Bracher's study of Weimar is an elaboration of this message:

The Reichstag proved itself unable, even in the calmest and most stable of times, to satisfactorily fulfill its two most significant functions: (1) the shaping and control of policy in foreign affairs; (2) the resolution of social and political antagonisms and the integration of their sources in a system of democratic compromise in domestic affairs. It thus proved unable to develop into a lasting and adaptable tradition [in Germany] (1955: 45–46).

This failure itself encouraged popular skepticism, at best indifference, with regard to the state's legitimacy and authority.

Summing up these developments in terms of our three-phase schema we have the following: Phase one is a period of aristocratic-bureaucratic resistance to democratic institutions and to a bourgeois share in power, accompanied by a partial consolidation of central administrative power and a large role assigned to the military as an internal watchdog. Phase two is a period of alternating aristocratic and bourgeois experimentation with, and resistance to, further extensions of democracy and also of centralization of administrative-political power on a still wider scale—with more systematic use of the military as a weapon of foreign policy. Phase three witnesses the mass extension of parliamentary democracy and full centralization of administrative power, whose importance was weakened by the collapse of the state's prestige due to World War I and its aftermath.

Industrialization and Living Standards

Taking industrialization to mean roughly economic change, and falling back on Rostow's "stages" we can distinguish among (1) the preconditions period, 1800–1840, during which the social economic and political resistance to economic modernization is gradually beaten down; (2) the takeoff period, during which explosive growth takes place, dominated by a few modernizing sectors, roughly 1840–1873; (3) the drive to maturity, 1875–1918, during which growth impulses, modern technology, and so on spread throughout the rest of the economy; and (4) stagnation and extreme instability, 1918–1933 (the Rostowian era of "mass consumption" does not emerge in Germany at this time).

Weavers' Rising, by Kathe Köllwitz

Soldiers at the barricades in Berlin, March 1848

Parade in Leipzig, 1863

Children jeer the military patrol during the miners' strike of 1889 in Rhine-Westphalia

Red Army troops in Lohberg, 1918

Muster of the Red Army, 1918

This periodization can be expanded into the chronology of industrialization found in the appendix at the end of this chapter. One important qualification, however, is necessary at this point. Economic progress foreshadowing the industrial growth of the nineteenth century may be traced back (at the very latest) to the first half of the eighteenth century, concentrated though it was in a relatively small number of regions (such as Saxony, Lower Silesia, the Mark in Westphalia, the Duchy of Berg, and the Lower Rhine district of the Rhineland), and limited though it was to labor-intensive industry and a related increase in population and agricultural production. Some historians have referred to this complex of changes as "proto-industrialization" (see R. Tilly and C. Tilly 1971), but whatever label one prefers, its importance lies in showing that German growth did not begin with the political-institutional changes initiated between 1800 and 1815 and its identification of the origins of the problem of rural poverty in Germany which became so acute in the 1830s and 1840s.

Referring back to the three-phase schema of collective violence we must point out three corresponding facts. First, German, and especially Prussian, agriculture responded well to the challenges of industrialization, registering substantial productivity increases in the 1820s and 1830s. Though much of this was swallowed up by capital formation in agriculture itself, there may have well been some substantial release of a surplus for other sectors even before the 1850s. This suggests that the stagnation in overall living standards reported for the period in the literature was more distributional than technological in origin. Second, growth in productivity was interrupted in the 1840s. This may explain in part why the German takeoff of the 1840s concentrated on producer's goods, like railroads, and why it was so dependent on the state's help at first. In any case the resultant disproportion between strong industrial investment activity, on the one hand, and slowly changing agricultural capacity and sluggish living standards, on the other, seems particularly significant as a factor explaining some of the great violence of the 1840s; and the congruence between these two sectors thereafter is another factor explaining to some extent the relative calm of Germany between 1850 and 1913. The congruence referred to here may be clearly seen in the rising living standards and shrinking workweek, which dates from the 1860s. Is it possible that the growth in Germany's organizational life, also associated with the 1860s, derived from higher incomes and more free time, and does that growth help to explain the moderate levels of violence in this period? Third, the economic instability of the 1919–1933 period has obvious implications for Weimar's great and notorious turbulence. The chaos of 1918–1919, the reconstruction difficulties of 1919–1922, the inflation of 1923, and, finally, the deepening depression of 1929–1933 generated enormous masses of hungry and insecure persons and, *ceteris paribus,* rendered them more responsive to the radical mobilization appeals directed at them by left-wing and, increasingly, right-wing political organizations. The coincidence in timing between collective violence and economic difficulties in Weimar seems very clear. Moreover, even the relatively prosperous years between 1924 and 1928 were plagued by the problem of unemployment—which by official definitions rarely dipped below 10 percent of the total nonagricultural labor force—so that here too economic discontent, and hence protest potential, could breed further.

Commercialization

The pace and extent of economic change through industrialization had significant social and political consequences. However, the institutional, distributional, or qualitative context in which that industrialization took place is of crucial importance in understanding its influence on social protest and protest movements. Industrialization in Germany meant the thoroughgoing commercialization of social relationships. Markets for the collective services of labor, land, and capital increasingly replaced the rule of tradition and levy from above as resource allocators; even the final consumption needs of households became by 1914 largely dependent on the market mechanism. Security from poverty and from social descent thus became less a matter of knowing and abiding by local traditions, more a matter of one's capital accumulation—human and nonhuman.

Historians have generally associated this commercialization with the Stein-Hardenberg Reforms of Prussia's heroic 1806–1813 era (see R. Tilly 1969). Three main complexes are discernible: (1) the land reforms which abolished many feudal and most manorial rights and privileges, established individual property rights in land, and strongly benefited the aristocratic landlords and already well-to-do peasants (who were also the main beneficiaries of the related distribution of the commons); (2) the abolition of restrictions on occupational choice, on personal freedom and mobility (which destroyed what remained of the guilds and helped create a labor market); and (3) reforms subordinating the old agrarian aristocracy and even the monarchy itself to the "rules of money capital," for example, the law of 1807 which threw open the ownership of landed estates (and associated privileges) to bourgeois wealth, or the law of 1820 which set a statutory limit on the national debt. The question of how strongly one should weigh these state-sponsored measures as agents of change in relation to market forces already in evidence before 1806—forces which the Prussian reforms from 1806 on may well have hindered—remains unsettled; in the long run, however, their effect insured that land use, labor income, and capital deployment became more dependent upon the test of the market. Commercialization sharpened social competition and increased the penalties of failure for those without capital. This negative aspect of commercialization dominated up to around 1850, because economic growth up to that point was too limited to reward commercialization on a mass scale.

One point worth stressing about this commercialization and the institutional measures related to it turns on the extent to which the landed aristocracy, particularly in Prussia, was able to protect itself from the test of the market (or, rather, to strengthen its market position) through a number of legal and political devices and channels, which softened the transition from "feudalism" to "capitalism." In Prussia, for example, especially east of the Elbe, the aristocratic landowners (the Junkers) increased their holdings at the expense of the smaller peasants, and became capitalist agriculturalists. V. I. Lenin, who knew something about agrarian social dynamics, called this the "Prussian way" to agricultural capitalism: "Prussian manorial property was not smashed, but preserved and became in fact the basis of the Junker agricultural estates, which although fundamentally capitalistic, nevertheless maintained a politically dependent rural population, as, for example, the Master-Servant Law shows" (1954: 879–881). This made the Junker more formidable, more attractive partners for the bourgeoisie in times of trouble (as in 1848–1849). According to Barrington Moore, it is why the latter "threw itself into the arms of the landed aristocracy and the royal bureaucracy, exchanging the right to rule for the right to make money" (1966: 437).

The commercialization of work relationships—signalled by the emergence of a dependent wage labor class—may well have been the most momentous of all of the structural changes unfolding in nineteenth-century Germany. It lay behind the development of the socialist labor party, whose importance for German politics has already been discussed. Its origins cannot be exactly pinpointed, but with the disintegration of effective guild control and with mechanization of production in major branches of the economy from the late eighteenth century on, its effects assumed large-scale proportions. We may usefully distinguish, once more, three periods. In the first, lasting to around 1850, many occupational groups, especially artisans, fight the loss of control over the terms of their employment, occasionally with nonviolent strikes, occasionally with violence. In the late 1840s, 1848 in particular, there is some attempt to build supralocal and even supraoccupational organizations of workers, but they showed serious centrifugal tendencies and weaknesses, even before the reaction which concluded the revolutions of 1848–1849 crushed them (cf. Balser 1962; Dowe 1970; Noyes 1966; Pelger 1968).

The second period, from roughly 1850 to 1914, opens with a period of repression of working-class organizations, moves through a phase of political liberalization in the 1860s—including toleration of trade unions and, interestingly, a substantial wave of strike activity—witnesses a new phase of repression following the Paris Commune and lasting into the 1880s (with the antisocialist laws applied with great rigor to trade unions, 1878–1882, and thereafter relaxed somewhat, thus permitting renewed craft union growth). From 1890 to 1914 direct repression of working-class organizations diminished and the trade union movement spread into many parts of the economy. By 1914 there were more than 2.5 million union members in Germany. This period is also marked, significantly, by a rising crescendo of strike activity.

The third period, from 1914 to the 1930s, witnesses the rise and fall of trade unions. War mobilization needs lead to the full acceptance by government and employers of the trade unions as partners determining wage-employment conditions (with a law of 1916 marking the first official acceptance of unions as preferred bargaining partners). The Weimar Republic's political arrangements built on this law and expressly provided for collective bargaining involving unions (see Hartwich 1967). This machinery remained in operation throughout Weimar, though it did *not* eliminate great strike activity nor guarantee an end to collective violence stemming from labor disputes. With Hitler's assumption of power in 1933 this machinery, as well as the labor movement itself, was swept from the political scene.

In understanding the great eruption of violence after 1918 it may be useful to point to a late manifestation of commercialization which had politicizing effects. The threatened proletarianization of white-collar workers and civil servants (up to World War I still relatively privileged groups in German society) was powerfully aggravated by the destruction of petty bourgeoisie savings associated with the postwar inflation and currency reforms, 1923–1924. There seems to be a close link between these groups and the growth of right-wing political organizations which gave their discontent political focus—including considerable violence.

Urbanization and Nationalization of Social Relationships

The commercialization of socioeconomic relationships promoted the mobility of the population, above all, in an urban direction; it contributed at the same time to the creation of a national network of relationships which tended to have priority over local ones.

The data on urbanization are almost too obvious to cite. Figure 28 is a statistician's view of Germany's urbanization between 1816 and 1930. By 1900 more than half of the German population lived in municipalities having 2,000 inhabitants or more (this is the standard German lower limit to "urban" populations). By 1910 this proportion was 60 percent, and nearly one-fifth of all Germans lived in cities with at least 100,000 inhabitants. As late as 1852 the corresponding percentages had been 33 and 3. In absolute numbers to be sure Germany's rural population continued to grow over these years: between 1852 and 1910 from 24 to not quite 26 million. Which helpfully reminds us that urbanization is not identical with the physical movement of persons out of rural, agricultural areas into cities. If urban populations reproduce faster than rural ones, we will witness the relative growth in numbers of urban dwellers that is called "urbanization." And much of the migration absorbed by German cities during the century could be, and was, of urban origin. By the turn of the century the lateral movement of workers from city to city—as in the United States—may have quantitatively become the most important urban movement of all. Nevertheless, growth of the most important urban areas *was* essentially through immigration. In the process of becom-

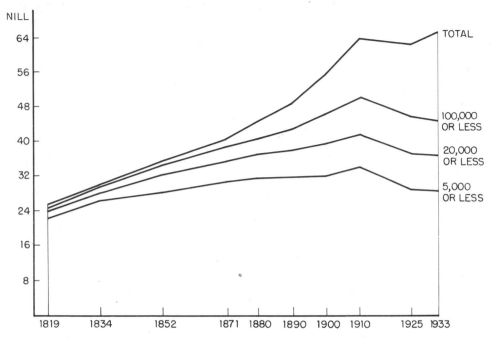

Figure 28. Population in Germany by Size of Community.

ing a *Millionenstadt* between 1820 and 1880, for example, the capital city of Berlin owed nearly 80 percent of its growth to net immigration (Markow 1889: 212–218). In short, urbanization and migration were closely related (see Köllmann 1959; Obermann 1972).

At the same time the nationalization of relationships was going on. The autonomy of local, rural, and even city life was being progressively reduced—a natural result of the interregional exchange and specialization accompanying commercialization. This meant that centers of power were shifting from local to national bases, and that whoever or whichever groups wanted to retain control over their lives would increasingly have to fashion national organizations to do so, not least of all, to influence the national state, itself the combined product of commercialization and nationalization of social life whose emergence has already been noted.

We may observe, for example, that the Rhenish bourgeoisie began to challenge Prussian economic policy in the 1830s and especially in the 1840s, but if we look closely we are struck by the fact that the challenge is to national institutions and policies, not simply their local manifestations. We will discover that by the 1830s, major Rhenish industrial and commercial interests were becoming interregional and even international in scope, that these trading interests called for the development of inter-regional-international transportation and financial systems, and, finally, that the implementation of such systems required a mobilization and coordina-tion of resources on a national scale (Hansen 1919–1942: I). Similarly, we may detect a significant difference between the local, unorganized character of popular, working-class politics during the first half of the nineteenth century (with the first really important worker associations originating during the Revolution of 1848) and the growth of national parties and national unions from the 1860s on (Engelsing 1968; Noyes 1966).

Population Change

Demographic change should be added to the politically relevant ele-ments of social change already discussed, not because of its quantitative impact per se but because the social tensions associated with those other changes mentioned were powerfully reinforced by population growth.

The quantitative changes themselves were considerable. The population of the several German states (including Alsace-Lorraine) grew from around 25 million in 1817 to roughly 67 million in 1913. These figures, moreover, understate the rate of natural increase, because during the same period the German states lost an estimated 4 million persons through net emigration. By the standards of this century's developing countries, such growth was modest; by other standards it was significant. For ex-ample, while French population grew by about 40 percent, 1815–1914, German numbers were increasing by around 160 percent. Substantially larger numbers were increasing by around 160 percent. Substantially larger numbers of people were living longer in Germany; the social framework had to adjust to that fact.

The problem, however, was not the increase in numbers alone but that the increase was concentrated in the lower members of the social body. The growth of the proletariat, to begin with, was largely a matter of earlier and more frequent marriage for those whose existence—thanks initially to the growth of rural industry, thanks later to the liberal agrarian reforms and the potato—no longer depended on access to the standard family plot of cultivable land alone. The falling and/or stagnating living standards associated with proletarianization up to around 1850 must similarly be attributed in large measure to the relative growth in the numbers of the poor (through earlier and more frequent marriage and higher fertility) which drew average living levels down, and not to the mass transplantation and immiseration of individual families within the course of a single generation. In this sense we can appreciate the rather Malthusian discussion by German historians of the period up to 1850. Wolfgang Köllmann, for example, has developed the concept of "labor force potential" (based on the proportion of the population in "productive" categories) and shown that the growth of this potential badly outstripped employment opportunities (defined as the number of occupied persons) during the first half of the nineteenth century—despite emigration and even in the more progressive regions. This, then, amounts to a new explanation of social distress in Vormärz Germany:

The population growth of the first half of the century was too great to be economically absorbed, not even in such areas as Westphalia or Württemberg, where emigration was reducing the labor surplus. The evidence of growing mass misery, culminating in the great hunger crisis of 1846–48, was grounded in these demographic conditions (Köllmann 1968: 225–226).

It is interesting in this connection to speculate whether the markedly reduced fertility for Germany from about the 1880s and the rupture of a previously visible link between real income increases and fertility at around that point reflected a "mature" stage of proletarianization, one in which commodity consumption and/or savings was replacing or beginning to supplement reproduction as the principal material achievement of working-class existence. Such a change may well signal mass acceptance of capitalism's "rules" with consequences for collective protest potential.

The Rhythms of Collective Violence

Figure 29 reports on the quantity of collective violence in Germany from 1815 to 1913. Naturally any measure of collective violence is sensitive to the definition and data source used. Our index—relying mainly on newspaper reports and excluding small-scale events involving fewer than twenty persons—only claims to be the best representation of collective disorders currently available; it does not purport to be flawless. The figure shows what a general reading of German political history would lead us to expect: marked growth in violence, 1830–1833; a great increase in the late 1840s, culminating in the Revolutions of 1848–1849; relative

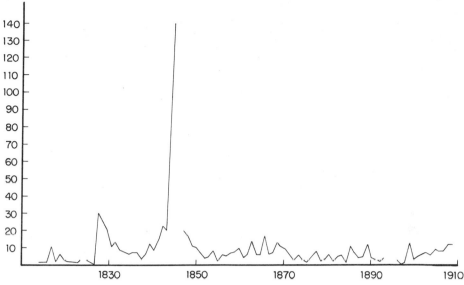

Source: *A.A.Z.*, 1816–1871; *Kölnische Zeitung*, 1871–1913.

Figure 29. Frequency of Violent Events in Germany, 1816–1913.

steadiness of violence (though with interesting and possibly significant fluctuations) until World War I. Our documentation of violence during the Weimar period is less complete and our inventory less reliable, but, as Table 17 reflects, there can be no doubt about the enormous increase after 1917.

Two additional features should be noted. First, the two major concentrations of violence in 1830 and 1848 follow closely upon increased turbulence in neighboring France. As contemporary German political discussions and also the French symbolism employed by mobs—the Tricolor and "Marseillaise," for example—showed, the connection was more than chronological. The study of international links and diffusion may thus throw light on the causes of collective violence. Second, collective violence is almost always present in some degree, even if the analytic task implied by these figures is the explanation of the large increases of the pre-1850 and 1919–1933 periods (*or* the quiescence of the 1850–1913 period).

Significant regional differences should also be observed. For example, both the concentration of violence in Central Germany before 1848 and in the eastern and western parts of Prussia thereafter demand explanation (see Table 15). The map (Figures 30 and 31) reveals still finer differ-

Table 15. Regional and temporal distribution of violent events

Region	Period						
	1816–1847	1848–1849	1816–1849	1850–1913	1850–1881	1882–1913	1816–1913
East Prussia	2	1	3	9	7	2	12
West Prussia	8	3	11	13	10	3	24
Brandenburg	17	19	36	51	28	23	87
Pomerania	7	4	11	11	6	5	22
Posen	11	12	23	16	13	3	39
Silesia	24	8	32	33	16	17	65
Saxony (region)	16	5	21	12	2	10	33
Saxony (Kingdom)	17	6	23	13	9	4	36
Westphalia	19	11	30	58	22	36	88
Rhineland	28	17	45	67	20	47	122
Hesse-Nassau[a]	28	5	33	9	5	4	42
Hohenzollern-Sigmaringen	0	1	1	0	0	0	1
North German states[b]	34	9	43	31	21	10	74
Hesse[c]	30	21	51	30	21	9	81
Bavaria	23	27	50	42	31	11	92
Wurttemberg	7	7	14	7	5	2	21
Baden	20	20	40	12	9	3	52
Middle German states[d]	14	10	24	6	6	0	30
Hanse cities[e]	14	5	19	20	14	0	39
Total[f]	319	191	510	442	235	207	952
	(323)	(197)	(520)	(450)	(236)	(214)	(970)

[a] The Regierungsbezirke Kassel and Wiesbaden.
[b] Hannover, Schleswig-Holstein, Mecklenburg, Mecklenburg-Schwerin.
[c] Frankfurt am Main, Starkenburg, Oberhessen, Rheinhessen.
[d] Weimar, Meiningen, Altenburg, Sondershausen, Eisenach, Coburg-Gotha, Dessau, Reuss.
[e] Bremen, Lübeck, Hamburg-Altona.
[f] Totals in parentheses include events which could not be "located" regionally.

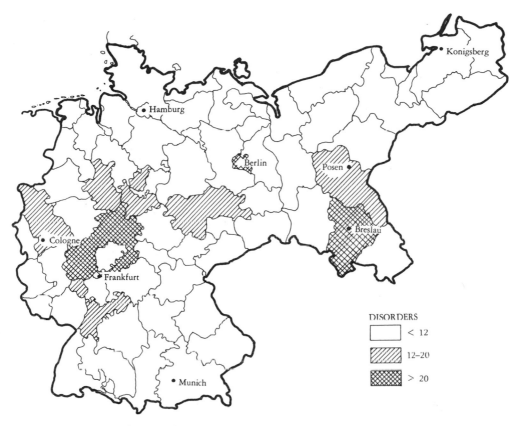

DISORDERS

	< 12
///	12-20
###	> 20

Figure 30. Distribution of Violent Events in Germany, 1816–1848.

ences. It shows the Hessian states and the districts of Breslau, Arnsberg, and Berlin as especially sensitive areas. The analysis which follows should bear on those differences, as well as on the movements of the national aggregates of Figure 29.

Table 16 depicts the size of events up to 1913 (as measured by the number of estimated participants).* It calls for several comments. It underscores the importance of the late 1840s as a watershed in the history of German collective violence. The size of violent crowds increases up to 1848 and then declines. Second, the tendency for the average duration

* Because our estimates of crowd size derive in part from the reported size of repressive forces, it is not entirely clear whether our numbers are a better measure of popular behavior or of state policy. If the political impact of collective disorder is being investigated, data on the state's relation (for example, the size of the counterforces) are preferable.

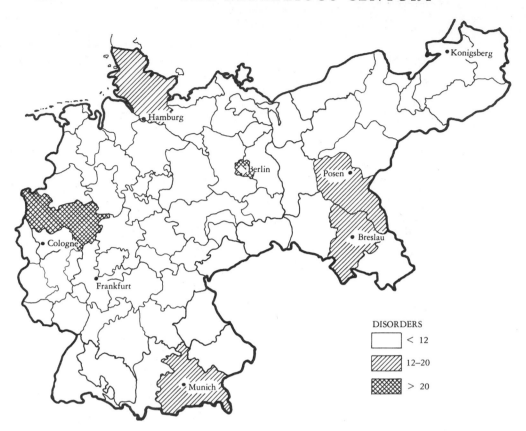

Figure 31. Distribution of Violent Events in Germany, 1850–1913.

of disorders to sink is clear and may be attributed in large part to the improved efficiency of the state's repressive forces. Third, the decline in average crowd size is striking because it takes place despite the rising population densities produced by Germany's urbanization and despite, or perhaps because of, the growing importance of formal organization. In

Table 16. Estimated man-days and duration of collective violence in Germany, 1816–1913

Period	Number of disorders	Average duration (days)	Average size	Man-days per year
1816–1847	323	1.5	3,200	48,450
1848–1849	197	1.2	3,000	354,600
1850–1881	236	1.1	1,120	9,086
1882–1913	214	1.0	670	4,481

Table 17. Comparative indicators of disorders in Germany, 1900–1913 and 1919–1932

Period	Number of convicted rioters[a]	Number of major disorders[b]	Average number of participants[c]
1900–1913	3,870	23	847
1919–1932	6,084	135	17,800

[a]*Statistik des Deutschen Reiches,* Criminal Statistics.
[b] All disorders reported in *Chronik der deutschen Arbeiterbewegung,* vols. I and II.
[c] Estimated for 1900–1913 from reports in *Kölnische Zeitschrift;* for 1919–1932 on the basis of data for 44 disorders.

terms of violence per capita, the decline from 1848 to World War I is pronounced.

As noted above, however, collective violence remained very much a part of the German scene throughout the entire period observed. Moreover, if we look beyond 1913 to the years following 1917, we observe not only a steep increase in violence reminiscent of the 1830s and 1840s but an enormous increase in scale. Table 17 compares 1900–1913 with 1919–1932 to put this point across.

Checking Some Obvious Hypotheses

Can this historical picture of Germany's collective violence be explained by reference to some simple, obvious, but powerful economic factor? The temptation to invoke "economic forces" in explaining political history has always been great. Figure 32 yields to that temptation. Its message is clear: until about the middle of the nineteenth century periods of great violence were immediately preceded by years of high food prices. Supplementary data on the trade cycle such as the bankruptcy rate also show that bad harvests were an important brake upon the economy.

Does this mean that a Malthusian-type argument applies? The answer is a qualified no. Years of high food prices recur beyond 1850 and continue to influence the economy until the 1860s, whereas collective violence no longer appears to react to that stimulus. Even 1848 and 1849, the years of greatest turmoil, were years of relatively low food prices, after all. Moreover, we need to distinguish between the direct popular reaction of consumers to high food prices (as reflected in food riots) and the indirect influences (operating through a diminished demand for industrial consumption goods and creating unemployment, distress, and so on). Making

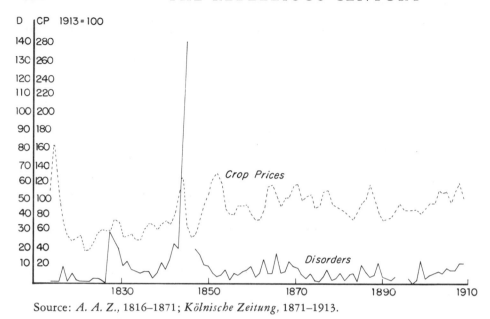

Source: *A. A. Z.*, 1816–1871; *Kölnische Zeitung*, 1871–1913.

Figure 32. Number of Violent Events and Agricultural Crop Prices in Germany, 1816–1913.

that distinction, we discover that many of the disorders of 1830–1833 and most of those of 1846–1847 were food riots.* That is, the influence of high food prices upon collective violence operated largely through consumers' attitudes and the food riot; and this form of protest became only insignificant in the second half of the nineteenth century.

Generalizing further, we may reject any kind of clear and simple relation between collective violence and economic fluctuations. For example, although the depression years of the 1919–1932 period were also years of much social protest, the years of the "Great Depression" of 1873–1896 were not. Whatever the importance of "long waves" of economic activity (Kondratieff or otherwise) for German *economic* history, their recent reintroduction into German political history (Rosenberg 1965; Wehler 1969) does not fit the history of collective violence very well.

The great transition in the overall quantity of collective violence around mid-century demands a more satisfying explanation than food

* About one-fifth of the disorders of 1830 and more than two-thirds of those in 1846–1847 were related to food prices. The riots, however, did not concentrate in places where food prices were highest or rising fastest.

prices and the trade cycle can produce. Perhaps the history of urbanization can provide it. Urbanization indicates, after all, the kind of population growth, mobility, and increase in the importance of nonagriculutral activities which have been associated with industrialization and "modernization." Moreover, there is a very substantial literature attributing increased crime, violence, and political radicalism, as well as other presumed symptoms of social breakdown, to the rapid and large-scale transplantation of population from rural agricultural into urban-industrial settings. What does the record show?

The collective violence recorded in our sample was an urban phenomenon: between 1816 and 1847, cities registered about 55 percent of all disorders, though in 1840 they contained no more than 15 percent of the total population; between 1850 and 1913 close to 75 percent of Germany's disorders were "urban," though as late as 1880 only 40 percent of the population lived in cities. Yet the force of this observation is weakened by another: that the newspapers upon which our sample relies tended to report urban events more completely than rural ones.

In any case, these observations refer to urbanity rather than urbanization, that is, the rate of population shift into cities. Urbanization itself doesn't seem to relate closely to collective violence in a statistical sense. Table 18 presents some relevant data.

The conclusion reached by analysis of cross-sectional data are somewhat different to be sure. Highly urbanized and rapidly urbanizing regions do appear rather more turbulent than slowly urbanizing ones, but if we relate the numbers of convicted rioters to population by region—for ex-

Table 18. Urbanization and disorder frequency in Germany,[a] 1816–1913

Indicator	1816–1847	1850–1881	1882–1913
Number of disorders	175	201	194
Percentage growth of urban population	99	200	149
Percentage point increase of urban population	4	14	21

[a] Defined as Prussia, Bavaria, and Saxony, 1816–1847; as these states plus Kassel, Wiesbaden, and Schleswig-Holstein, 1850–1913.

ample, in Prussia, 1882–1913—the urban areas emerge as the relatively peaceful ones. Moreover, the fastest growing cities were definitely not the most turbulent.

Though the difference in frequency of violence from one place and time to another are surely not randomly distributed, urbanization does not look like a structural process which can explain them. There are grounds for using these results to introduce a very different hypothesis: that rapid urbanization and industrialization *reduced* the level of collective violence, because they moved masses of the potentially violent from familiar contexts and thus destroyed their means of collective action. The large numbers of Brandenburgians and Silesians who crowded into the great city of Berlin during the first half of the nineteenth century, or the endless stream of industrial recruits arriving in the *Ruhrgebiet* after 1850, arrived mainly without the large-scale, organizational ties which might have permitted effective protest.

If this line of reasoning were correct, we might well expect a statistical study to show, first, regions gaining population through immigration to contain much less collective violence than other regions; and second, migrants to be strongly under-represented among identified participants in collective violence. Unfortunately, that handy statistical investigation does not exist. Available, if scattered, evidence, however, supports both points. Regions of high turbulence between 1816 and 1850, like Silesia, the Hessian states, the Palatinate, Baden, or eastern Westphalia, were major exporters of people. Among major gainers only Berlin was particularly turbulent—a major exception to be sure. Participants in collective violence were invariably local inhabitants of long standing, though not necessarily well-off ones. For example, Kuczynski and Hoppe's study of Berliners killed during the "March Days" of 1848 shows that "Berlin-born" accounted for almost two-thirds of the dead, though a much smaller proportion of the total population (less than half). And most accounts of the March Revolution insist upon the relatively large role played by local artisans, shopkeepers, and other established members of the petite bourgeoisie. Evidence for other instances of collective violence confirms this impression; few sources contradict it (R. Tilly 1971).

These observations do not pretend to offer a new theory of collective violence. Their purpose is simply to discredit the notion of collective violence as some kind of mechanical by-product of "large-scale" structural change involving industrialization, urbanization, and the like. The results of exploring that notion encourage us to look elsewhere for a satisfactory explanation. In particular, we need to examine more closely the *political* bases of collective violence. This means two things: examining the state's control apparatus; and taking a close look at the quality and character of collective violence.

The Political Bases of Violence and Repression

One of the most important direct determinants of the volume of collective violence in Germany—particularly the transitions around mid-century—was *political*. It lay in the ability and willingness of the holders of power to open nonviolent channels for the settlement of popular group grievances, and/or to mobilize repressive force against popular challenges. We have already pointed out how slowly those nonviolent channels were opening in Germany in the nineteenth century. This was partly a matter of hindrances to more parliamentary democracy and to the assocational forms essential to that system of government. It was a matter of permitting organizations such as workers' associations or trade unions to exist. When such organizations and associations became possible—as in the 1840s and again in the 1860s—an upsurge in collective activity including collective violence resulted. The huge increase in strike activity and jump in violence in 1869 offer an interesting example of that connection (cf. Steglich 1960 and Figure 29). If the state controlled over powerful repressive machinery, however, violence could be kept in check.

Improving the control system of the state meant raising the cost of collective violence to authors of the latter. It also implied the solution of the state's fiscal problems. That meant in turn that contending members of the polity had to arrive at some general consensus, and the lack of consensus among the powerholders (simplified: bourgeoisie, aristocracy, and bureacracy) and accompanying internal administrative weakness of the 1816–1848 period may be contrasted with the growing consensus and administrative strength of the post-1849 period. Friedrich Engels fixed the political turning point even more precisely: "1847 is that point in Prussia. At precisely the same moment in which the weak-kneed Prussian bourgeois classes find themselves virtually forced by circumstances to change the system of government, the King's money problems are forcing him to set that process of change in motion himself—by summoning the

Prussian Estates-General" in MELS 1954: 145). 1847, we recall, was a year of great violence, so that Engels' observation is particularly relevant. What applies to Prussia, moreover, applies, with minor qualifications, to her weaker German neighbors.

Two related aspects of this transition are important: the weakness and inelasticity of the state's repressive forces before the late 1840s and their increasing strength thereafter; and the sheer quantity of violence in 1848–1849 and its resultant impact upon all those having something worth losing.

Prussia was a poorly policed country before 1848.* Rural areas—which as late as 1848 contained about 75 percent of the country's population—were policed by some 1,500–1,600 *Landgendarmen*. The supposedly well-off Rhine province, for example, maintained a force of around 230 men —implying roughly 11,000 rural inhabitants and 140 square kilometers for each gendarme. Cities were slightly better off. In 1848 Berlin, the capital, maintained a police force barely 200 men strong, or one per 2,000 inhabitants. Most other Prussian cities were worse off than Berlin. An effective civil guard, moreover, scarcely existed anywhere.

A mixture of political and fiscal motives had produced this situation. The landowning aristocracy initially supported the drastic reduction of the Landgendarmerie carried out in 1820. Thereafter they opposed its strengthening lest it challenge the feudal police powers they retained, mainly east of the Elbe, on their estates. In addition, the traditionally large role assumed by the military in governing Prussia placed a further brake on the development of civil "contact and control" instruments. The crown's general interest in economy measures after 1820 strengthened this resistance (cf. R. Tilly 1966). The cities for their part refused to bear the burden of maintaining an adequate police force, partly because their ability to raise revenues was limited by the central government. The municipal civil guard in most cities was totally inadequate both because citizens found it a burden and because the monarchy feared to support it.

How could "poor policing" and weak "secondary control" instruments affect popular feeling toward the state? It meant on the one hand that government contacts with most of the population were irregular and in-

* The best discussion of this question is to our knowledge in Reinhart Kosselleck 1967: esp. 460–463, 542–553, 565–571. A dissertation on the development of policing and crowd control is still needed, however.

frequent. It meant that local authorities either had to ignore totally or handle arbitrarily the minor challenges to the public order. Contemporary witnesses of collective violence frequently cited arbitrary, unjust, and occasionally brutal, police behavior as a cause of popular resentment and disorder. This applied especially to the aristocracy's poorly paid feudal police, as in Silesia, but was well known in the larger cities like Berlin as well (Bleiber 1966: 100–102; Dronke 1846: 298–300; Valentin 1946: I, 58–61).

On the other hand, the state responded to major challenges to its authority by mobilizing the army. From 1815 to 1848 internal policing was one of the principal functions of the Prussian army—though not one military leaders or soldiers relished.* Prussia's military strength—the average number of men under arms, 1816–1852, was 142,000—was adequate to meet these domestic demands (Von Reden 1856: II, 521).

Mobilizing military force, however, caused popular resentment and could easily escalate and politicize otherwise administratively tractable situations. In April 1821 events in Eupen (on the Rhenish-Belgian border) well illustrated these difficulties. The local Landrat reported the destruction of wool-shearing machinery by hundreds of local workers and requested his superiors in Aachen "to order your force of Gendarmen to Eupen immediately, since no armed police are stationed here and the civil guard is totally unreliable." On the following day he was calling for the mobilization of the border guards and forest police as well. Still one day later, however, he showed misgivings and pleaded against sending the military since that would be likely to incite Eupen's citizens—not least of all because troops would be quartered and provisioned locally (S.A. Koblenz: 402, no. 671).

Local officials in Prussian cities became highly familiar with the negative effects of military presence by mid-century—in Cologne, 1844–1846, and Berlin in 1847 and 1848, for example—and rural areas fared no better. Reinhart Kosselleck has nicely summarized the entire issue: "It was the wide gap between impotent Gendarmerie and rigid army which made the transition from lax police controls to harsh military force appear

---

* On this see Kuczynski 1960, ch. 3 (covering the suppression of the Silesian Weavers' Revolt of 1844). Even as late as 1910, military leaders displayed misgivings about being used as internal policemen. See Bleiber 1955.

so abrupt; this was one of the factors sharpening the sense of alienation between population and state in *Vormärz*" (1967: 462).

If the situation in Prussia was bad, in most other German states it was catastrophic. Smaller states such as Nassau, Hesse-Darmstadt, or Hesse-Homburg experienced even greater financial difficulties. Poor administration and policing were the results. It is no surprise that collective violence in these states, 1830–1832, frequently turned on just such issues. An interesting report on turbulence in southern Germany during these years, prepared in 1832 for Prussian officials (possibly by a professional informer), commented on the relative calm of Prussia and attributed the difference to financial-administrative causes. Governments in these regions not only avoided heavy spending because of the taxes and democratic concessions that they would necessitate, but, because of their small size, relative administration costs were higher (and/or the quality of administration lower) (S.A. Koblenz: 403, no. 2454). A similar report issued from Munich in 1844. Commenting upon possible explanations for the beer price riots which had ensued there, it emphasized "the exaggerated thrift of the Bavarian government as one of the main causes of national discontent . . . Thanks to this incredible system of thrift, we observe scientific and social welfare institutions of all kinds in decay, roads in disrepair, important waterways unusable, the entire civil service and military disaffected. A court investigation into the 'May Riots' revealed that local troops . . . were held on such short rations last winter that they literally starved to death" (Chroust 1951: 59–60). The connection with violence was revealed clearly in 1848. One of the principal targets of rural collective violence in that year was Standesherrschaft—the rule of petty princes— and one of the principal achievements of the violence of 1848–1849 was its virtual elimination.*

As the number and size of disturbances grew in the 1840s the Prussian government bolstered its repressive forces. Substantial improvement, however, came first in 1848–1849. Between 1844 and 1855 the annual expenditures of the Interior Ministry grew from 2.8 to 4.7 million talers, mostly

---

* According to G. Franz (1959: 178–180), the peasant cry heard in the principate of Hohenlohe in 1848: "Down with the Hohenlohes! Long live Württemberg!" symbolizes agrarian visions in 1848. However, since this cry was a way of dignifying the pursuit of direct pecuniary interests, it should not be interpreted as a kind of petty peasant nationalism.

for police needs. By 1855 the 1500-odd Landgendarmen and border guards of 1840 had swollen to close to 2,500 men. The cities were especially strengthened. Berlin's police force grew from the 200–250 of 1848 to a corps of more than 1,200 men. By 1855 the central government's budget provided for a force of more than 4,000 men and local municipal governments began to supplement this financing with increased spending of their own (Von Reden 1856: II, 326–327, 429–430). Moreover, these figures may underestimate the political impact of police reform after 1848 because of organizational changes, especially the development of a well-equipped political police division with close links to other German states (Haalck 1959–1960). The diminished role of the military in quelling disorders in the second half of the century (shown in Table 19) is one significant product of these changes. The general decline in the quantity of collective violence during that time may have derived in large part from the same source.

Political consensus among the ruling classes and the resultant fiscal elasticity, then, must be considered among the factors explaining the changing character of Prussian and German security forces. Paradoxically, one reason for that "consensus" was the enormous amount of violence in 1848 and 1849 which had signaled, initially, the absence of consensus. The sheer amount recorded by our sample for one year, 1848, was reported in Table 15, and 1849 and even 1850 were far above the long-run German average.

One more feature of the 1848 conflict deserves notice. Turbulence was spread through time and across space much more than is commonly supposed. Historians commonly write of the *Märzrevolution,* but significantly more violence took place in the second quarter of 1848 (April 1 through June 30) than in the first: 52 events compared with 43. Even the last quarter registered about as much violence as the third: 22 to 23. During all of 1848, the *Augsburger Allgemeine Zeitung* reported 116 separate disorders as occurring on 98 different days.

Violence was also widely distributed geographically, as Table 15 shows. In our sample, ninety different places reported collective violence in 1848. There were probably few Germans who were not directly or indirectly affected in some significant sense. Had the 600,000 man-days of violence recorded in our estimates been evenly distributed, they would have involved more than one German adult out of every fifty. A list of revolutionaries sought by the Prussian police in 1851 (for their part in the 1848–1850 "troubles") reveals a broad geographical and occupational spread of involvement: 279 persons, with ten of Prussia's twenty-six districts reporting at least ten fugitives, representing nearly a hundred different occupations, and of which close to one-third clearly had middle-to-upper-class connections—merchants, estate owners, army officers, lawyers, and so on (see "Nachweisung der politischen Fluchtlingen . . .," S.A. Koblenz, 403, no. 2458).

Considering only those newspaper reports in which a specific number of deaths are noted, we count more than 2,200. Add the much larger number of wounded and the property damage, and one begins to sense what an impression those months must have produced on the average German with property, education, or political or bureaucratic rank. A substantial number of Germans—property owners and otherwise—fought during 1848 on the side of the repressive forces, the former especially in the widely used civil guard units. This experience was quite likely to have placed them firmly in the law-and-order camp, even if pre-1848 developments had not. The *Vormärz* Prussian government worked busily toward this end by insisting on Simon-pure bourgeois civil guard units. In Westphalia in 1847, for example, district presidents recommended the use of existent security guards or volunteer fire defense units to combat attacks on property, but warned that: "a watchful eye will have to be kept over the selection of personnel for said security units, to insure, for obvious reasons, that members of the lower classes—who have especially suffered from the recent scarcity—be excluded as completely as possible" (S.A. Münster OP. no. 1178, II).

In many parts of Germany during 1848–1849 concern for control of the security forces was evident. For in such troubled times the power struggle between classes spilled over from the workshop, public assemblies, or streets into the very organization of coercive instruments themselves, especially the local militias (cf. Obermann 1970; R. Weber 1970).

The role of repressive forces during these years calls attention to a very important point: that putting down revolutions and less serious challenges to the state not only maintained the status quo but also contributed to the centralization of power in Germany. Unrest from 1830 to 1833 and, much more so, the Revolutions of 1848–1849 created a power vacuum into which the Prussian (and a lesser extent the Austrian and

Bavarian) military moved. Smaller states like Braunschweig, Hesse-Homburg, Hesse-Darmstadt, and even Saxony were unable to maintain order without outside assistance. The big challenges to the old order in 1848–1849—in Posen, Saxony, Baden, and the Palatinate—were crushed mainly by Prussian troops.* Prussia's position within the German Bund was strengthened and clarified as a result. The troubles of 1830–1833 and 1848–1850 forced the pace of power centralization, a process already being driven forward, gradually and irresistibly, by economic forces (Boehme 1966). There is irony here, interestingly, because the democratic movement in 1848 had strong nationalist, pan-German tendencies to which, in the short run, Prussian repressive forces were opposed.

In the short run the extension of Prussian military influence generated increased conflict. The revolutionaries in Saxony, Baden, and the Palatinate, 1848–1849, no doubt gained strength from the fact that their enemies were *Prussians* as well as antidemocrats. And the subsequent occupation of these turbulent areas produced continued violent protest well into the 1850s. Furthermore, Prussian hegemony remained partial and incomplete until its successful wars against Austria in 1866 and France in 1870–1871. (The reforms begun in 1858 first began to create a military machine adequate to those tasks.) Nevertheless, we can recognize the centralization of power as a visible characteristic of collective violence as early as 1830 and very clearly after 1848.

What has to be stressed in a study of social protest, however, is not so much the financial backing or physical capacity of the state's repressive forces as its political and social meaning. In tracing that meaning for Germany's development, the Weimar period is particularly enlightening. The Weimar government by no means lacked *physical* means of coercion. The army, traditional instrument of Germany's rulers against internal challenges (such as those of the socialists or unions), suffered a loss of prestige, 1918–1919, and the terms of peace placed restraints upon its size and its strength. It is also true that precisely those restraints made possible the continued existence of paramilitary organizations in Weimar—which subsequently were to challenge its authority. As Rosenberg wrote:

---

* Prussia's military forces thus assumed police functions beyond their own borders. Between 1829 and 1831, for example, the army's size increased by around 65 percent —mainly to combat civil unrest outside Prussia (Von Reden 1856: II, 521).

The Treaty of Versailles permitted Germany an army of no more than 100,-
000 professional soldiers, allowing for no other militarily trained bodies.
According to the letter of the law, the *Reichswehr* could, therefore, reckon
with no reserves, should an emergency arise. It therefore maintained close
relations with the paramilitary organizations and tended to regard them as
possible reserves for a war, for example, a war against Poland (1961: 114).

Nevertheless, the Reichswehr remained more intact than other traditional organs of government, and proved very able to organize its own
recovery during Weimar—despite the legal restraints referred to earlier.
From the point of view of the Weimar government system as a whole,
indeed, its repressive strength was what was disastrous, because it lacked
legitimation, while the Reichswehr's leadership pursued its own political
aims—steering (as it hoped) toward a mildly right-wing dictatorship.
Bracher writes: "Within the leading circles of *Reichswehr* officers, thinking about the army's possible role in a change of the political system ran
as follows: at first, maintenance of nominal neutrality with behind-the-
scenes manipulation, and then, in the last minute, overt action in favor
of right-wing movements and limited dictatorship" (1955: 267). Accordingly, "where the military's domestic deployment was necessary, it
was quick to mobilize against left-wing trouble and struck with frequently
unjustifiable and draconic harshness; in contrast, disorders by right-wing
elements were treated laxly, and tended to involve 'containing' actions,
rather than the use of weapons" (ibid. 266–267).

The rest of the repressive system displayed similar characteristics. The
legal bureaucracy's disparate treatment of right-wing and left-wing
political criminals is notorious (Bracher 1955: 194).* To some extent
police forces behaved similarly, although, thanks to the weakened army,
they may have generally gained in strength and prestige, as they did in
Berlin (Liang 1970). Even in SPD-controlled cities like Berlin, the
police tended to crack down much more harshly on left-wing than on
right-wing dissidents. SPD leadership even demanded official tolerance
of right-wing demonstrations of force. In 1927 and 1928, for example,
we find the Berlin police expending enormous resources to protect a

---

* Thus, Gumbel's study, *Vier Jahr politischer Mord,* shows 354 political murders
between 1919 and 1922, carried out by right-wing strong men, producing 24 sentences of an average of four months' imprisonment; by contrast, 22 left-wing murders,
produced 38 sentences of an average of fifteen years—and ten death sentences
(cited in Weber 1969: 26, n. 13).

right-wing organization's (the Stahlhelm) right to demonstrate and parade paramilitarily. In anticipation of working-class protest of a Stahlhelm
pro-rearmament demonstration on May 7 and 8, 1927,

The Police President Zörgiebel concentrated the entire Berlin police force
on the protection of *Stahlhelm* . . . He went so far . . . as to release more
than 700 police officers from their regular crime work for duty in IIA Department. All police recruits and officers furloughed for training purposes
were ordered back to duty . . . For weeks the entire police apparatus was
occupied with preparations for the protection of the *Stahlhelm*. In arranging
for the movement of 60 armoured railway cars from Magdeburg to Berlin,
Zörgiebel was in effect displaying his readiness to protect *Stahlhelm* with
civil war-like preparations. As if to complete his image of a man dedicated
to German militarism, Zörgiebel banned (in a letter directed especially to
the KPD and the Red Front Fighters Federation) all outside counter-demonstrations (Laboor 1961: 118–119; see also Liang 1970).

Such tolerance did not extend to antimilitarist demonstrations, as Laboor's
discussion (270–271) of subsequent events in Berlin—in May 1929, for
example—shows.

That official tolerance of naked force breeds little respect for the government's claim to a monopoly of its use seems confirmed by the Weimar
experience. Quite apart from the many instances where violence was obviously initiated by the state, and crowd violence was reaction, this
experience does seem to offer an explanation of why organized masses
should turn to violent, rather than nonviolent, political action, once
mobilized. What it does not explain is why and how political mobilization took place.

The Structure and Personnel of Violent Encounters

Table 19 introduces the problem of mobilization. It summarizes evidence on the participants in popular disorders, 1816–1913, classifying
them into seven categories. The results are striking. First, we see at once
that we are dealing, not with homogeneous masses of angry or desperate
people, but to a large extent with specific groups. Simple crowds not only
decline in importance, but even during the first half of the century are
present at disorders only slightly more often than specific groups. Participants in collective violence, it seems, are far from random samples of the
entire German population.

Table 19. Distribution of formations participating in violent events in Germany, 1816–1913 (percentage)

Type	1816–1847	1848–1849	1850–1881	1882–1913
Simple crowd	26	25	23	12
Religious-ethnic	8	1	3	9
Occupational	15	11	12	24
Organizational	0	9	3	4
Police	13	4	27	38
Civil guard	7	16	1	0
Military	25	31	28	11
Other	6	3	3	2
Total number	642	371	532	440
Formations: Disorders	2.0	1.9	2.3	2.1

Second, the relative decline of simple crowds over time matched almost perfectly the steadily rising participation of occupational groups. The match reflects the replacement of communal issues by associational ones as the basis for collective action. It could be illustrated by comparing the hunger riots of the 1840s with, say, the violent strikes of the 1900s. In the 1840s the local provisions market was still a major and chronic source of exploitation and conflict—and it was communally experienced. By the turn of the century the worker's experience in a specific branch of production dominated conflict; because of the specialization accompanying industrialization, it was no longer a communal experience.*

Third, we note the marked increase in police ability to control disorderly crowds—an important point already discussed.

Fourth, certain ambivalent features are undeniably present. Religious-ethnic formations (Catholics, Jews, Poles, and so on) were a kind of communal-associational mixture, but it is not clear whether the increased importance of such groups in the 1870s and 1880s reflects modern associational ties or traditional communal ones. In general we observe that, though political and economic life becomes organized on a formal and national scale in nineteenth-century Germany, collective violence in-

---

* It is possible that this shift relates to the transition from what C. B. Macpherson has called "simple market society" to "possessive market society," with labor market relations replacing consumption and product market as the major mass experience. In the process, such popular villains as the usurer and corn dealer are replaced by the capitalist employer.

volving such organization does *not* grow apace. Strikes and labor disputes, for example, were rare phenomena in the first half of the nineteenth century, though often accompanied by violence. With the growth of the trade unions in the second period (1850–1913), strikes and labor disputes grew enormously—as did the worker's ability to profit from them—but they only occasionally involved violence. It is also likely that political organizations, such as the Worker's Social Democratic Party, were effective in channeling grievances and conflict into nonviolent forms. This hypothesis has often been raised in connection with the nonmilitance of the German labor movement (Nettl 1965; Roth 1963). Thus, Peter Nettl has interpreted the SPD as an "inheritance party," the political organization which is to take control with socialization of the future. As Nettl argued, Wilhelminian political arrangements offered the SPD absolutely no possibility of meaningful participation in government, so it looked to the future: "This expectation of inheritance is the moral force which makes non-participatory opposition possible, yet prevents violence except as a last resort" (1965: 67).

The matter is complicated to be sure. In a cross-sectional analysis of thirty districts (mainly Prussian) reporting the results of the Reichstag election of 1912, we found the share of SPD votes related to the frequency of violent disturbances, 1882–1913, as yielding a correlation coefficient of 0.42, the share of SPD plus Polish Party votes similarly related yielding $r = 0.59$. However, urbanity, income per head, and some other significant "ecological variables" also relate positively to those electoral results, so further investigation is called for (see R. Tilly and G. Hohorst 1975). Available strike data, on the other hand, seem to tell a less ambiguous story. Between 1864 and 1880 our best inventory counts some 1,200 strikes, 24 of which clearly involved violence. For the 1891–1913 period we have some 31,000 strikes producing 72 violent disturbances. These numbers suggest a decline (from about 5 to 0.25 percent) in strike violence—a decline which inclusion of strike threats would affect still more (see Kaelble and Volkmann 1972; Steglich 1964).

This kind of conformity between collective violence and specific characteristics of national political development is interesting because it suggests close links between the two. In evaluating the last point, that is, the influence of nationwide political mobilization on German collective violence, once again the experience of Weimar is instructive, even if our data are unsystematic. Two major shifts involving mass political mobilization seem to have taken place after 1918. On the one hand, the petite bourgeoisie, especially in the smaller towns, was moving toward the right, its savings eroded by inflation, its fears of proletarianization accordingly intensified. There are some conflicting pieces of evidence in the historical literature on this problem, and a more detailed study is still essential. But the general pattern—particularly the link between the "threatened" petite bourgeoisie and the rise of national socialism—seems indisputable (Bracher 1955; Schonbaum 1966).

On the other hand, certain groups of workers and members of the petite bourgeoisie in the large cities (Munich of 1918–1919 would be a good example, according to Ay 1968; Hamburg another, according to Comfort 1966) moved toward the left. This movement showed itself late in the war, may well have involved large numbers of new entrants to the labor force (especially unskilled workers), supplied most of the dynamism to the revolutionary action of 1918–1923, and led to the founding, in 1920, of the German Communist Party (Kommunistische Partei Deutschlands—hereafter KPD), whose numerical strength in Germany henceforth would serve as a barometer for the fluctuating unhappiness of the industrial working class with middle-of-the-road SPD—union leadership. There is some evidence that employees of large industrial enterprises were particularly prone to radicalism—for example, in the Saxon industrial districts—and that labor-saving technological change in the 1920s also contributed to this result (Ersil 1963; Imig 1958). Fluctuations over time were substantial, however, and some authors have questioned whether the KPD had any really substantial following among the working class (Bracher 1955: 104).* Further detailed study of membership and voting patterns is therefore highly desirable.

What resulted from these major shifts was an array of organizations which became leading actors in the collective violence of the 1920s and early 1930s. First there were the National Socialists, the SPD, the KPD; then, the partly related strong-arm units—the SA, the RFB (around 150,000 members at its peak), the Stahlhelm (at its peak, in 1928, between 500,000 and 1,000,000 members), the *Reichsbanner*

---

* But see Weber 1969: 26–27, on this point. One's answer may depend on the years one examines.

(around 3,500,000 members); finally, the numerous neighborhood militia and labor protective associations (*Arbeiterschutzverbände, Proletarische Hundertschaften,* and so on). For example, police action to protect a Stahlhelm demonstration in Berlin in 1927 produced the following: "On May 7 and 8 a total of 870 persons was arrested. Among these were 12 *Stahlhelm* members and 10 Nazis, whose provocative behavior went so far that not even the police could ignore it [sic!]. Eighty arrestees belonged to the KPD, 12 to the RFB, 9 to the SPD, and 4 to the Reichsbanner. The others were workers without party ties, numbering more than 700" (Laboor 1961: 124).

Typically these formal organizations provided the hard core for street demonstrations—with or without violence—but attracted far larger numbers of politically interested, but not formally organized, working people. Thus, the KPD could summarize the results of Berlin's May Day demonstrations in 1929 as follows:

Between 120,000 and 150,000 more workers gathered at the appointed assembly places than the Party can normally mobilize for legal demonstrations. That shows that tens of thousands of workers who otherwise do not participate in our demonstrations (among them no doubt many SPD voters) were attracted by our message this time, in spite of the dangers involved. The number of persons who took to the streets to demonstrate far exceeded those attending the reformist indoor assemblies (ibid.: 271).

In Weimar, therefore, socioeconomic discontent was likely to find a large-scale organizational focus, even if most individuals remained aloof from organizations. It thus became politicized and, given the approach of Weimar's rulers to popular challenges to its authority, particularly from the left, that often meant violence.

The Objectives of Violent People

The specifically political nature of collective violence must be stressed. We may discuss this further with the help of another taxonomical device, the typology of disorders of Table 20. Although the table's list of specific grievances is far from exhaustive, the variety of issues reflected dispels the notion of collective violence as a homogeneous by-product of large-scale structural change. Violent protest appears to be highly interest-oriented—though large-scale changes such as industrialization shape those interests and strongly influence the timetable according to which they develop. In the 1820s and 1830s, for example, we frequently encounter students violently protesting government intervention in university affairs. We tend to see such conflict in relation to the broader ideological struggle between Metternich's conservatism and university-centered radicalism (Glossy 1912). However, since universities were centers for producing ideology, specific, concrete university interests were often at the heart of such conflict.

Violence produced by religious conflict was another form of politics which generally involved real, concrete grievances. The persistence of this type of collective violence throughout the nineteenth century may be attributed to the close relationships between church and state in Germany. On the one hand, as Marx and Engels wrote (in 1851), the repression of open political opposition in all the German states (before 1848) produced a "religious opposition." Their succinct analysis is worth repeating:

History provides us with many examples of countries—blessed with a state church and effective stifling of all political opposition—where that dangerous profane opposition to the worldy power conceals itself behind a mask of consecrated purpose and selfless struggle against spiritual enslavement. Thus certain governments which normally tolerate no discussion of their acts, will

Table 20. Distribution of German violent events by type, 1816–1913

Grievance	1816–1847	1848–1849	1850–1881	1882–1913
Student-university	18	0	10	1
Religious-ethnic	58	6	42	14
Land forest rights	6	16	10	2
Food	71	8	17	15
Taxation-administration[a]	22	25	6	1
Labor relations	36	18	47	65
Constitutional and electoral[b]	10	54	18	24
Police-military[c]	81	55	67	20
Other	33	15	31	55
Total[d]	335	197	248	203

[a] Including grievances against specific acts and officials.
[b] Related to elections, party organization, and constitutional reform actions.
[c] Directed against police arrests and ordinances and against military presence, brutality, or conscription efforts.
[d] Totals exceed number of disorders since some disorders involved more than one target or grievance.

think very carefully before creating martyrs and mobilizing the religious fanaticism of the masses (Marx and Engels, MELS 1954: II).

On the other hand, religious dispute was not simply a form of vicarious politics. The churches powerfully influenced the educational system, thus regulating both the production of skills and one important avenue of social mobility. Bismarck's Kulturkampf against the Catholic Church's prerogatives in the 1870s is well known as a national manifestation of this duality. But if we examine the numerous local instances of collective violence involving religious parties, we often find at their center concrete grievances concerning education. In 1839, for instance, hundreds of Catholics in the lower Rhenish city of Cleve rioted in protest against the publication and local circulation of an anti-Catholic pamphlet, supposedly authored by the local police commissar, a Protestant. Closer investigation of the incident revealed that control over a local school was one of the principal causes of popular anger (S.A. Koblenz: 403, no. 2523, I). In this case the sending of the military, the harsh sentences handed out (one ringleader was sentenced to twelve and a half years; twenty others to one year each), and the detailed investigation undertaken suggest that sensitive political nerve centers had been touched.* We cite neither this particular example nor the general category of religious disorders because of their political significance per se. What is important is seeing that popular disorders frequently had specific targets related to the communities' regular, nonviolent, collective activities. Collective violence, that is, frequently appears as a rather crude form of politics, a way of righting specific forms of injustice. This point touches on crucial questions concerning the political character and rationality of collective violence.

The concentration of violence in the 1830s and 1840s stemmed not only from the negative effects of industrialization and commercialization, but also from the fact that those effects hurt only, or at least disproportionately, certain groups (mainly poor people), and because they operated by means of local, institutional machinery. Disputes over land reform and land use are a case in point, because not only did "the market" arbitrate, but conscious, political decisions as well. In the Westphalian village

---

* The years 1837 and 1838 were marked by a highly publicized conflict between the Prussian state and the Catholic Church over the appointment of new bishops, and ultimately, about a mixed marriage conflict which led to violence in the Rhineland, Westphalia, and Posen.

of Arensdorf in January 1834 a court decision governing the division of common land—a decision based on the testimony of a wealthy villager —led to a violent street demonstration in which the local mayor and the wealthy witness were singled out as targets. Here, as in many villages and cities at this time, visible, local, perhaps vulnerable, political, administrative, and judicial machinery was one of the chief means by which large-scale changes in economic organization exerted their pressures upon the local poor, all the while shielding the well-to-do (report in S.A. Münster: 350, IV).*

The next point to make about closely observed cases is that the extraordinary action leading to violence very often came as a last resort— after legitimate, nonviolent channels of political pressure had failed to produce redress. The famous revolt of the Silesian cotton weavers in June 1844 was not merely the desperate reaction of starving, exploited workers to a hopeless situation, but ensued after their appeals for relief through normal, administrative channels had gone unheeded. The weavers in Langenbielau requested government intervention in wage-setting in January, those of Peterswaldau in April 1844; neither received a positive response.†

Silesia's history offers another relevant example. Landowning peasants in Upper Silesia engaged in litigation between 1815 and 1848 with local landlords and officials over the division of commons and the amount of compensation to be allowed for the extinction of feudal dues. They formulated petitions to the King, citing earlier decrees and parallels supporting their case. In the 1840s they intensified their efforts. Unsuccessful, in 1843 they resorted to refusal to pay taxes. When tax collectors mobilized police support, they moved to outright revolt. Interestingly, this collective violence involved both landowning and landless peasants. When an 1845 law favorably regulated only some of the disputed claims,

---

* For the Tecklenburg region of Westphalia, A. Gladen 1970 has written: "It was above all the division of commons lands which made the small holders and cottagers conscious of the way the agrarian reforms were reshaping and shifting the balance and structure of social forces in village and peasantry. And the fact that the 'propertied,' simultaneously functioning as 'state' in the formulation and execution of administrative measures, generally acted in their own interest, made the political dimension of the economic and social superiority very clear" (1971: 32–33).

† Nor did the revolt itself (Kuczynski 1960, ch. 3). See also A.A.Z., December 1843, Nr. 166, for an anticipation of the June 1844 revolt.

those whose claims had not been satisfied turned from litigation to participation in the disorders—which continued to take place (Bleiber 1966: 139–160).

Close-up analysis of collective violence reveals a surprising amount of selective, purposeful crowd action. Bleiber's Silesian examples show much class-conscious selectivity. In 1847 Silesian food riots revealed much more than hunger: "Thus, the Silsterwitz weavers in the region of Schweidnitz did not simply march onto *any* peasant farm and demand potatoes, but headed directly to the large estate owner in Striegelmühle . . . In like manner, the two hundred Langenbielau weavers and day laborers out in search of potatoes on November 6, 1847, did not plunder the first excellent field they found, but went into the manorial potato lands at Niederpielau-Schlöbel" (Bleiber 1966: 167–168).

Accounts of the revolt of Hessian peasants in 1830 also recorded many instances of selective violence: the houses of certain officials and clergy were singled out for destruction; enclosing landlords were required to sign "contracts" restoring or compensating for the traditional right of villagers; attacks on the hated tollhouses and government buildings were marked by the destruction of only certain tax rolls and papers—the papers of orphans and wards of the courts, where so marked, were not touched; rebels freed prisoners selectively—only inmates guilty of minor theft, violation of game laws, and trespassing (A.A.Z., October 1830; Franz 1959; 176–177). The behavior of these Hessian peasants had many other German parallels. In that same troubled year, 1830, rioting journeymen in Chemnitz, Saxony, attacked the property of certain employers believed guilty of highly unfair employment practices, and freed from jail only peasants imprisoned for nonpayment of feudal dues (Strauss 1960).

The crude rationality and political character of much collective violence finds expression, finally, in the results frequently achieved. In Leipzig, in 1830, an angry rioting crowd demanded a new police administration; the government immediately acceded. In the same city fifteen years later, the right of the *Deutschkatholiken* to utilize the buildings of the state church and to enjoy other prerogatives was one of the outcomes of the bloody mob massacre related to that very right (A.A.Z., September 1830 and August 1845). The food riots of 1847 in Berlin and elsewhere produced government intervention and the sale of grain and bread at lower prices. And there are many examples of machine-breaking and labor violence which yielded a slowdown in the introduction of machinery and immediate wage increases: Crefeld's silk weavers in 1828, Leipzig's printers in 1830, Pforzheim's (skilled) factory workers in 1838, Iserlohn bronze workers in 1840, among them. If such examples became much rarer in the second half of the century, it is because of the increasing—and increasingly successful—use of the nonviolent strike and/or strike threat.

What Difference Did Violence Make?

These examples call attention to the immediate, short-run effects of collective violence. There were important long-run consequences too, though they are hard to define precisely. The effects of violence in 1848–1849 on the propertied classes and, ultimately, on politics in Germany have already been mentioned. Many instances of violent conflict had the same fear-breeding effects, if on a smaller scale. In Crefeld in 1828 riots of silk workers led to the creation of a bourgeois civil guard (Rosen 1965). The revolt of the Silesian linen weavers in 1844 produced a flurry of political activity throughout the western provinces because it revealed to the well-off a degree of social ferment below which up to then had been easy to ignore. Facts like these were brakes on bourgeois willingness to challenge the old regime. During the Prussian Rhineland's revolutionary days of May 1849, a prominent entrepreneur wrote: "Here on the Rhine, the developments in Elberfeld are very rapidly driving the propertied over to the side of the government. Better absolute monarchy than the Red Republic!" (Gustav Mevissen, cited in Zunkel 1962: 181). And since these revolutions failed to break the power of monarchy and aristocracy, there was subsequently only "unproductive violence" to look back on. The importance of this kind of "nonrevolutionary" tradition for German development is not easily determined; but it is clearly a relevant historical factor.

This view, moreover, considers only the "threatened" propertied classes. Collective violence also contributed to the development of solidarity and class-consciousness among participants—even if it built on and presupposed some degree of such solidarity. Violent protest dissolved smaller barriers and differences among the common people. If brutal repression followed protests, the solidifying effects could be powerful, indeed—as eyewitness accounts of the *Märzrevolution,* or the worried reports of countless Prussian officials between 1815 and 1848 make abundantly clear. Listen to this account of March 18, 1848, in Berlin:

After the magistrate had announced in today's *Bulletin* that His Majesty had granted freedom of the press, a delegation of respectable citizens paid a visit to the palace to express their gratitude and respect. The King appeared on the balcony and spoke, but the noise of the crowd which had gathered drowned out his words. The crowd did not disperse at this point, but, instead, demanded that the citizens' delegation set down in black and white the alleged promises and concessions. The military stationed in the palace apparently ordered the crowd to disperse; the dragoons rained blows on peaceful citizens and fired on the unarmed masses. Even respectable men now voiced doubts about the royal promises. All parts of the city now resounded with the cry: "To arms! We've been betrayed!" (Müller 1954: 316).

Toward the end of the nineteenth century, violent confrontations were still producing this result. At the beginning of this chapter we cited just one of many Berlin examples. It is also interesting, to take another, more celebrated example, that the effective organization of the Ruhr coal miners dates from a violence-ridden strike in 1889—violence in which the massive use of police and military played a prominent role (Köllmann 1969).

The wisdom or "productivity" of collective violence should not be exaggerated. German history offers plenty of examples of purposeless mob violence—much anti-Semitic violence falls into this category—and most violence failed to cure popular ills. The state's immediate and principal response was invariably force, and the balance of force was normally too much in its favor for that response not to be effective. This is reflected in the fact that casualties were almost always overwhelmingly on the side of the rebellious. In any case, we lack a complete record of this history. Until we can systematically distinguish between outcomes and realized aims of rioters (which implies knowing their pre-riot goals), we will have difficulty judging systematically the rationality of collective violence. Yet what we do know about them tells us to reject the older impressions of popular disorders as products of blind anger, of devious manipulation, or as symptoms of large-scale structural sickness ("immiseration" or "anomie"). Our knowledge, though limited, urges us to regard popular disorders as instruments of popular political action, fully deserving the attention historians have focused on more familiar institutions like the ballot box, the political lobby, or the petition.

General Features of Germany's Experience

How, then, may we summarize Germany's experience with collective violence between 1816 and 1933? First, those large-scale transformations of industrialization and urbanization and nationalization of socioeconomic relations produced no direct, uniform effects on the development of collective violence, except in the sense that such violence conformed roughly to the geographical and occupational redistribution of population those transformations implied. Neither faster nor slower economic growth, more nor less economic hardship by themselves, relate closely to collective violence.

Second, if industrialization and urbanization do have some bearing on the overall *quantity* of collective violence, it is probably in a negative sense: rapid economic growth meant high rates of urbanization (and/or population migration) and reflected the rapid movement of people from familiar settings in which protest was easily organized into unfamiliar surroundings in which it was not.

Third, insofar as modernization be viewed as synonymous with commercialization of social relations and the development of a national state, we must attribute to it a significant power to influence collective violence. The growth of social inequalities resulting from the redistribution of access to means of production (such as land, forest, liquid capital) provided grounds for social protest from 1815 to 1845, with the existence of local organizational focal points and the virtual absence of nonviolent channels for redressing grievances insuring that such protest become *violent* protest. The slow development of such channels was, in turn, largely an historical datum—related to the reassertion of the traditional predominance of the aristocracy and military in Prussia during the period. The emerging bourgeoisie challenged this predominance at certain points and times, but the mass violence of 1848–1849 convinced both main contenders of the need for a coalition and for the development of better "contact and control" machinery.

Fourth, Germany's collective violence was highly political. It was political in the sense that it was very much concerned with rights and justice and aimed at specific and (at least temporarily) vulnerable targets. Even food riots usually focused on the unjust behavior of certain food dealers or the injustice of specific food policies. And violence directed against taxes and/or administrative acts was generally grounded in a collective sense of violated rights—as well as in the hope of redressing the violation. Occasionally it fulfilled those hopes.

Fifth, the growth of large-scale, national organization—especially the Social Democratic Party and the "free" trade unions—appears to have weakened the nexus between politics and collective violence from the 1850s or 1860s on.* This happened because these organizations brought masses of working people concrete success—representation in the Reichstag and in municipal governments, recognition of trade unions, and so on—and because they effectively subordinated increasing numbers of people to the explicitly nonviolent strategies (and the rather less explicitly nonmilitant interests) of their leadership. This changed sharply after World War I, however, so that it can hardly be interpreted as a general characteristic of formal, large-scale organizations, or even as a peculiarity of German history.

In conclusion, our three-plus periodization suggests an explanation of collective violence (in Germany, 1815–1933) which has the virtue of being realistically complex but the weakness of being almost tautological. In Phase one, 1815–1850, we observe industrialization accompanied by sharp redistributional tendencies and structural changes, not yet yielding a surplus available for rising living standards, but beginning to create an uprooted, mobile population on a mass scale—and several waves of emigrants (see Hansen 1930; Obermann 1972; Walker 1964). Emigration may have been a significant form of nonviolent protest, but generally protest was violent because, although politically mobilized groups existed, there were no other popular political avenues available for the voicing of dissatisfactions and honoring of demands for change. In Phase two, 1850–1913, industrialization led to rising living standards and more rapid and massive urbanization, while new, national organizations emerged and began to channel the protest potential still being generated. In Phase three, 1919–1933, the predominant economic feature was instability and

---

* This probably explains why the relative and absolute number of disorders unrelated to standard targets or grievances—the category "Other" in Table 20—rises so sharply after 1875.

insecurity, with large-scale organizations channeling protest potential and mounting heavy attacks upon an increasingly discredited state.

Appendix: Chronology of German Industrialization

1800–1830. War (to 1815) reforms, recovery, and gradual improvement with living levels of 1805/6 reattained by around 1830.

1830–1840. Noticeable growth of industry, especially textiles, after founding of Zollverein, 1833.

1840–1850. First burst of heavy industrial growth sparked by railroad building and interrupted by harvest failures of 1846–1847 and Revolutions of 1848–49.

1850–1873. The "Take-off" period with growth particularly marked in the heavy industries: coal and iron and railroads, culminating in the boom following unification, 1870–1873.

1873–1895. A period called the "Great Depression" era, ushered in by a financial crisis in 1873 and characterized by frequent business failures, falling prices, and relatively slow growth (at least until middle 1880s). These features as well as industrialists' political power were reflected in tariff protection for industry in 1879.

1896–1914. Two decades of very rapid growth (with some interruptions) and structural change, led by such new industries as chemicals, steel, and electricity, accompanied by market concentration, cartel-building on a large scale, and an expert drive leading to "Anglo-German Trade Rivalry."

CHAPTER V

Comparisons

What Is There To Compare?

Shortly after recounting his Rhine crossing of 53 B.C., Caesar described the Gauls and the Germans. "In Gaul," he wrote, "there are factions not only in each city-state and each part of the countryside but almost in each household. The chiefs of the factions are the men considered to offer the most authoritative judgments in disputes; the whole range of problems are brought to them for advice and decision. The reason for this ancient institution seems to be to aid the common people against the powerful; a leader does not allow one of his own to be oppressed or cheated; nor would he have any authority among his own people if he did." Yet this principle did not extend very far:

In Gaul as a whole only two groups have any dignity and honor. The common people are almost in the position of slaves; they dare not act for themselves, and the councils do not listen to them. Most of them bind themselves in servitude to the nobles when they are crushed by debt, taxes or abuse of the powerful; the nobles then have the same rights over them as masters have over slaves. One of the two honorable classes consists of the druids, the other of the knights.

But, according to Caesar:

Germans have very different customs. They neither have druids to preside over sacred things nor desire sacrifices. They consider as gods only beings they can see and use: Sun, Fire, and Moon; they have not even heard of the rest. Everyone's life consists of hunting and the military arts; from the time they are small they seek toil and hardship. . . . They do not consider brigandage improper if it is carried on outside one's own city-state. In fact, they recommend it as a way of training youths and checking their sloth (Greenough 1898: 164–171).

Caesar did not describe the Italians in his *Gallic War*. That was not his business; he was, after all, adressing to Romans an account of his colonial exploits. But it is clear that he considered his countrymen superior in wealth, power, technology, and civilization to the barbarians beyond the Alps.

We could, no doubt, fit pieces of those two-thousand-year-old characterizations to the French, Germans, and Italians of recent centuries. The French are still factional. Germans have a reputation for hard work. Italians . . . well, aren't they still cultivated and urbane? To some small degree we have encountered these national characters in our survey of conflicts in France, Germany, and Italy. Each pattern also displayed some more recent national traits: the place of romantic adventurers in Italian rebellions, the exceptional importance of Paris in French conflicts, the eternal nationalistic students in nineteenth-century Germany, and so on. Yes, we recognize contemporary Italians, Frenchmen, and Germans in action. Yet to treat our accounts of the three countries as character sketches would miss the point.

There are three reasons for that. First, the forms and settings of collective violence in the three countries have a lot in common. In the early years, for example, we repeatedly encounter conflicts in which ordinary people temporarily assume the role of the local authorities, carry out the action they, the people, have been demanding, and then disperse. The so-called food riot is the most common example. That pattern is European rather than specifically French or German. In more recent years we find the demonstration in which masses of people identifying themselves with named groups assemble in a public place, hear harangues by leaders of their groups, and stand or march, displaying slogans epitomizing their demands. Although it is by now a worldwide phenomenon, this sort of demonstration is a relative newcomer among the forms of political action, and very likely European in origin. It is certainly the common property of France, Germany, and Italy.

Second, the patterns within each country changed enough, and in sufficiently similar ways, during the rebellious century to make an explanation in terms of national character cumbersome at best. In all three countries the period began with "reactive" forms of collective action (such as the tax rebellion or resistance to conscription) the predominant settings for collective violence. In all three countries the period ended with proactive, demanding forms of collective action—notably strikes and demonstrations —the principal settings in which collective violence occurred. We shall review a number of other standard changes later in this chapter. These changes, too, were European in scale rather than specifically national.

Third, the differences among the three countries were so clearly functions of their distinct political arrangements that it is superfluous to invoke "national character" to explain them. Despite the common forms and standard changes just mentioned, the specific sequences, timing, personnel, and outcomes of collective violence varied significantly. The old, reactive forms of collective action disappeared earlier and more rapidly in Germany and France than in Italy. The bunching of violence into crises was more marked for Germany than for France, less true of Italy than of France. And so on through a number of other traits. In France, Germany, and Italy alike, the century after 1830 contained plenty of violence; it really was a rebellious century. Yet each country, and country-to-be, traced a different pattern. The general course of collective violence in each area followed the particular evolution of power and government in that area.

Violence and power are closely connected. Should anyone be surprised? Not at all. We stress the connection only to emphasize, first, that a great many sociological interpretations of protest, conflict, and violence treat them as occurring outside of normal politics, or even *against* normal politics; and, second, that the equally plausible relationship of collective violence to the pace and scope of economic and demographic change, although frequently alleged in the discussion of these very countries, does not hold up for the modern experiences of Germany, Italy, and France.

In each of these countries violent rebellions played a major part in creating modern states. In none of the three did the pace or timing of urbanization or industrialization govern the tempo of violence. In all, however, the interplay between economic transformation and political reorganization produced a long-run shift in the character and personnel of collective action, and hence of collective violence.

France, of course, had a head start. She was already a great power in 1830, already unified within approximately her present boundaries. The Revolution of 1789 had already weakened the central power's most significant internal rivals; the Revolution had put a strong governmental apparatus under the control of France's vigorous bourgeoisie. It took the Revolution of 1848, nevertheless, to start the serious, continuous struggle of organized peasants and workers for national power, to give special-interest associations their great importance in French political life, and to create the bureaucratic, secular, parliamentary state we know today.

In 1930, fifteen years of involvement with Fascism and war still lay ahead of the three countries. Yet by that time, France, Germany, and Italy had produced governments whose distinctive features are still visible. What is more, they all had undergone decades of industrial expansion, urban growth, population movements, transformation in communications, education, styles of life. All three countries, in short, went through enough change and enough conflict during the century from 1830 to 1930 to make them excellent cases for the examination of ideas linking conflict to structural change. There were also enough differences among them to make a comparison profitable.

In earlier chapters we set out each country's history in its own terms, with no more than passing comparisons with the others. In each case, however, we asked some of the same questions. How much evidence is there that the pace of urbanization or industrialization accounted for the changing levels of collective violence? To what extent did the forms of collective action and of conflict change as the political and economic structures of the country changed? What difference did the approach of the government and of the dominant classes to repression, cooptation, and other strategies for dealing with outsiders make to the extent and character of violent conflict? In general, the answers we have given stress the political context of collective violence and its close connection with nonviolent struggles for power. They have raised doubts about the direct links between hardship and structural change, on the one hand, and conflict or protest, on the other.

"Breakdown" theories of collective violence, the prevailing ideas throughout most of the rebellious century, are still prevalent. We have slowly been shaping a counter-argument to them. This counter-argument emphasizes the importance of solidarity and articulated interests instead of disorganization and hardship. It treats collective violence as a by-product of collective action—a by-product, because the violence grows out of the *inter*action of organized groups which are carrying on sustained collective action. For the most part, the violence occurs when one group resists the claims being made by another.

Agents of governments play an exceptionally large role in such interactions. That is partly because governments often make claims which groups within their jurisdiction resist; we have seen this happening repeatedly in nineteenth-century tax rebellions. But agents of government also play a major role in collective violence as *repressors* of collective action:

—because groups are carrying on a conflict by means over which the government claims a monopoly, as when the Italian Fascists finally checked the vengeance and terrorism of Sicilian mafiosi;

—because a group has no right, under the existing political arrangements, to exist, to act, or to make claims, as when all three of our governments arrested strikers on the ground that they had constituted illegal associations;

—because the claims a group is making are unacceptable to those who hold power over the government, as when all three governments dispersed students occupying university premises in 1968;

—because a conflict threatens to expand and to shake the government's own control over its means of self-perpetuation, as when the French government intervened in the massive demonstrations and counter-demonstrations of communists and rightists in the 1930s.

In Italy, France, and Germany, agents of government almost certainly did the majority of the killing and wounding which occurred in the course of collective violence from 1830 onward.

In more abstract terms, the argument we have been forming has this general shape:

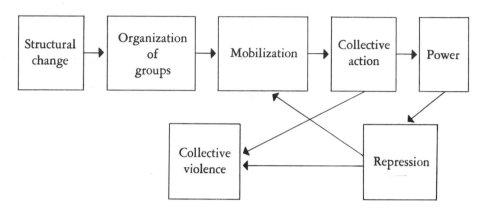

To transform the diagram into a working model, we would have to deal with a number of other connections (for example, the feedback on collective action of the organization of the groups which carry it out) and specify the connections which are already there (for example, a likely curvilinear effect of repression on mobilization: a little repression inciting mobilization, a lot of it depressing mobilization). For our present purposes we need only see that the argument (1) treats structural change as affecting collective violence profoundly but only indirectly, through the creation, transformation, and destruction of groups with common interests and a capacity for mobilization; (2) postulates a sequence running from the existence of such groups to their mobilization (that is, their acquisition of collective control over resources) to their collective action (that is, their application of pooled resources to common ends) to a change in their power (that is, the response they get from other groups for a given amount of effort at moving them) to a change in the extent to which they are subject to repression (that is, actions by other groups which raise their cost of collective action); (3) regards collective violence as an outcome of both collective action and repression.

If these things are true, a number of inferences follow. Rapid mobilization should tend to produce extensive collective violence, all other things being equal. Changes in governmental repressive tactics should strongly affect the level and character of collective violence. Highly mobilized groups and groups rapidly acquiring or losing power should be disproportionately involved in violent conflicts; unorganized groups, casual crowds, and marginal people should not. The general level of discontent, the current pace of change, the extent of "disorganization" (as embodied in such phenomena as crime, family instability, suicide, or mental illness) should have little or no connection with the level of collective violence. At one point or another in our analyses of Italy, France, and Germany we have argued that all of these inferences are correct. If we are right, the whole argument takes on credibility.

Instead of arguing the specific points further, we need to look at the common properties and significant differences of our three cases. Let us begin with the crudest characteristics—how many violent conflicts there were, and how they grouped themselves in time and space—before moving on to the subtle comparisons among the countries.

Frequency and Timing

We are far from having strictly comparable enumerations of collective violence in Germany, France, and Italy. We can make fairly continuous observations for France from 1830 through 1960, for Germany from 1830 through 1913, but for Italy only for the decades beginning in 1850, 1880, and 1890. Given the variation in sources and sampling procedures, furthermore, we cannot treat twenty disturbances in Italy as the equivalent of twenty disturbances in Germany. We can, nevertheless, compare the general configurations of the three countries.

Germany has experienced three main surges of collective violence since 1830: the 1830s themselves; the period around 1848; and the span of Weimar, from the end of World War I to the Nazi seizure of power in 1933. (Let us insist again: Germans produced plenty of other violence which our notion of "collective violence" leaves aside. They had the Austro-Prussian War in the 1860s, the Franco-Prussian War in the 1870s, World War I, the destruction of Jews in the 1930s and 1940s, World War II, to mention only major moments of death. Such instances of governmental violence enter our analysis only when members of the general population take collective action to defend themselves.) In between 1830, 1848, and Weimar, Germany had rather low levels of collective violence.

Italy had many more peaks: 1843–1849, with the Revolutions of 1848 at the center; 1859–1863, the first great period of struggles around Unification; 1868–1870, the completion of Unification; 1893–1894, with the

Sicilian Fasci most prominent; 1897–1898, when the conflicts were more heavily concentrated in the North and Center (Milan's Fatti di Maggio being the most dramatic series of events); 1913–1915, a period of massive strikes, demonstrations, and antiwar actions; 1919–1922, the postwar left/right conflicts which brought the Fascists to power. If our detailed observations reached farther, we would no doubt have new peaks to record for 1946–1947 and around 1968. In between came a lull, a Fascist clampdown which drove all parties and groups, even the Sicilian mafiosi, out of action. Italy probably experienced a higher level of collective violence over the entire period from 1830 to 1960 than Germany did. The striking contrast between Italy and Germany, however, appears in the periodicity of collective violence: a few well-defined peaks around major transitions in Germany; a much larger number of incomplete transitions and a much larger number of violent surges in Italy.

France stands between Germany and Italy in that respect. In terms of numbers of participants in collective violence of any kind, the Revolution of 1848, the labor-management-government conflicts around 1900, and the struggles surrounding the Popular Front in the 1930s were the great moments before 1968. But the Revolution of 1830, the period of the Commune, and the years just after World War II also produced clusters of collective violence comparable in scope to some of the Italian peaks mentioned. More clusters than Germany, fewer than Italy.

Likewise, the transitions were more definitive in France than in Italy: once food riots disappeared around 1848, they did not return; although labor remained at the center of collective action from the 1860s onward, the strike involving direct attacks on machines, mines, and factories came and went rapidly, and so on. The transitions in collective violence correspond to shifts in the pattern of collective action as a whole—which in turn correspond to changes in the structure of power. It is quite possible that from 1830 to 1960 France had a higher average level of collective violence than Germany or Italy. Still, the differences in pattern are more remarkable than the differences in magnitude.

Before examining the differences in pattern, we should reflect on the common properties. Three principal points stand out: (1) time-shapes which represent neither random fluctuations nor a master trend, but the rise and fall of national struggles for power; (2) close connections with fluctuations in routine, nonviolent collective action; (3) a deep long-run alteration in the form and scope of collective actions producing violence.

Time-Shapes

The distribution of collective violence over time is far from random in any of the three countries. Even in Italy there is great bunching around a few crucial years. The timing does not correspond to the pace of urbanization, industrialization, or other structural changes commonly thought to generate "protest" by producing intolerable strains. (We have even encountered some indications of a *negative* relation between level of collective violence and pace of change, and have interpreted the finding as support for our idea that rapid structural change raises the cost of mobilization, thereby reducing the frequency of collective actions which lead to violence.)

The crests of collective violence come at times which are already very familiar to political historians: they are, by and large, periods of national struggles for power. The years 1830 and 1848 stand out in all three countries because the crises in each country at those times interacted with the struggles going on in the other countries; afterward their paths were more diverse, but certainly far from independent. It was, for example, the withdrawal of French troops from Rome during the Franco-Prussian War that made it possible for the other Italians to attack Rome and thereby annex the Papal States to the new Italian kingdom. Again, the left in all three countries responded to the Bolshevik Revolution and to the end of World War I with insurrectionary strikes and calls for revolution. Our neglect of war as well as our choice of working in national contexts tend to obscure the connections between conflicts in one country and conflicts in another.

Despite the definite time-shapes of collective violence in Italy, Germany, and France, there is no noticeable tendency for the general level of violence to rise or fall over the long run. Everything depends on the vantage point. Looking back from the late 1930s, Italians might have been able to congratulate themselves on their escape from past disorders. Not only did the trains run on time, collective action independent of the government was unheard of. But Italians could not have continued the self-congratulation (if order and punctuality still meant so much to them) ten years later. In terms of sheer number of participants in actions producing violence, in all three countries 1968 rivaled the great years of the nineteenth century. Yet 1848 is there to remind us that the twentieth century did not bring a swelling of violence out of a placid past.

There were some secondary trends. The deadliness of collective violence (always excluding war itself) does seem to have declined from the nineteenth to the twentieth century. The substitution of police for troops in crowd control occurred widely in Europe; it seems to have reduced the number of deaths and increased the frequency of light wounding and of arrests. Troops fired; police clubbed. The average number of participants in each violent event rose over time. We have connected that change with the greatly increasing role of associations in collective action. The shift toward cities probably also played its part.

Violent and Nonviolent Collective Action

In beginning our inquiries into European political conflicts we bet on the possibility that violent events would serve as "tracers" of a much wider, but more elusive, set of politically significant encounters. At the start, we failed to see that the central phenomenon we were tracing was collective action, that only some collective action had a significant component of conflict, and that only some of those conflicts would turn violent. Nevertheless, the idea that collective violence was a tracer of something more general led us to look carefully at nonviolent forms of mobilization and of collective action in France, Germany, and Italy. That was easiest to do with organized workers; our information on strikes and on labor organization is far richer and more continuous than our information, say, on student organization and student protests. We were unable to put together anything like a comprehensive record of such everyday twentieth-century forms of collective action as the nonviolent demonstration. The history and sociology of the demonstration as a distinctive modern form of action remain to be written.

Yet enough information about nonviolent collective action came in to make some relations between violent and nonviolent actions clear. First, the great bulk of collective violence in France, Italy, and Germany since 1830 has occurred within the context of well-established forms of collective action which are not intrinsically violent: the demonstration and the strike, to be sure, but also the collective refusal to pay taxes which eventuated in the tax rebellion, the collective refusal to yield a person which gave rise to the anticonscription riot, and so on. Second, the great bulk of such events in a given period did *not* end in violence: for example, our best estimate is that, of the 20,000 strikes which took place in France from 1890 through 1914, only 300 to 400 produced any violence beyond the scale of minor pushing and shoving (Shorter and Tilly 1971). From 1915 through 1935, the figure is 40 or 50 violent strikes out of 17,000. Third, the violent events did not begin much differently from the non-violent ones; for the most part, the presence or absence of resistance by a second party to an action stating a claim by a first party determined whether violence (in our sense of damage or seizure over resistance) resulted. Many of the Italian land occupations of the nineteenth century went on peacefully; the violence typically began when landlords, troops, or mafiosi arrived to expel the occupiers from the land.

In our analysis of France we introduced the distinction among competitive, reactive, and proactive forms of collective action. The *competitive* action: one group which defines another group as an enemy or rival attacks the resources—personnel, property, premises, symbols—of the other; the second group may or may not fight back. We can now distinguish between two types of violent encounters which grow from competitive actions. The distinction depends on the types of groups involved. Where the group is small, informal, or composed of hereditary members, we might call the actions "primitive." At the beginning of the rebellious century, we sometimes find rival groups of artisans and the young people of neighboring villages fighting each other en masse. Later, we occasionally find the bill-posters of competing political parties defacing or destroying each other's work; if we had to have a name for this other sort of violent encounter, we might call it "interest-group" action. Here the groups involved are relatively large, formally organized, and specialized.

Our second broad type is *proactive* collective action: a group lays claim to a resource over which it did not previously exercise control, and another group resists the claim. Normally the group making new claims is relatively large, formally organized, and specialized. In that case, "modern" is a convenient name for the collective violence. Whether there is a counterpart for groups which are small in scale, informal, and so on is an interesting question. There are few or no cases of proactive action involving such groups in the histories of Germany, Italy, and France that we have been analyzing. Nevertheless, it is possible that new religious movements or an occasional action by a linguistic minority fits the type. The main case is certainly the modern one: for example, a group of sitdown strikers temporarily claim to control the premises; then employers, or the government, sometimes challenge the claim by sending in police. More rarely, we have the seizure of the city hall or national capital in the name of a revolutionary committee. In either case, the violence, strictly speaking, begins when the second party or its agents answer back.

Our third type, the *reactive,* is the complement of the second. Here some group, or its agent, lays claim to a resource currently under the control of another particular group, and the members of the second group resist the exercise of the claim. The second group *reacts* to the claim of the first. Again it is convenient to set off two types of violence by means of the groups involved. "Reactionary" violence includes the tax rebellion, the food riot, the movement against conscription. The early nineteenth century produced a high proportion of its collective violence through this reactionary path. (The interesting thing about it is that reactionary movements sometimes had revolutionary, rather than counterrevolutionary, consequences; the French food riots and tax rebellions of 1789 are cases in point; so are Italian land occupations of 1860.) However, twentieth-century forms also qualify: actions of anti-tax associations, or the resistance of Communists whose authorized meetings the Nazis tried to break up. If we need a label to distinguish them from their small-scale predecessors, we might use "defensive."

Our typology now looks like this:

Collective action:	competitive	proactive	reactive
Collective violence:	primitive	?	reactionary
	interest- group	modern	defensive

The question mark indicates the type we have left nameless and dubious; symmetry and the underlying logic of the typology call for violence based on new groups emerging within the traditional framework, but we are unable to supply clear cases from recent European experience.

What is the underlying logic? Essentially that within each type of collective action we distinguish between actions that are small in scale, local in scope, and carried on by communal groups of one variety or another, and actions that are large in scale, regional, national, or international in scope, and carried on by specialized associations, firms, states, and similar complex organizations.

In all three of our countries there were broad tendencies for competitive actions to disappear as contexts for collective violence early in the nineteenth century, for reactive sequences to increase in importance up to some point in the middle or late nineteenth century, and for proactive forms to gain ground in the twentieth century. That means a shift from collective violence centering on challenges to old claims toward collective violence centering on new claims. Later in this chapter we will try to explain why that shift occurred. For the moment, the important thing to see is that all three involve organized groups acting on the basis of controversial conceptions of each other's rights. On the face of it, the nature of the action makes it unlikely that a breakdown of social control or a dissolution of social bonds promotes collective violence; breakdown and dissolution should tend to dampen the collective capacity to make claims, and therefore to reduce collective violence. On the face of it, we have no good reason to expect marginal and desperate populations to mount violence-producing collective actions. Unless breakdown and dissolution lead desperate and marginal populations to *reorganize* themselves around new beliefs and claims, the observed sequence of actions leading to collective violence casts serious doubt on the classic breakdown-dissolution theory.

One popular recent line or argument abandons the old equation of violent movements with rootless masses; as formulated by Norman Cohn, Neil Smelser, and others, it substitutes the mobilization of such masses around beliefs and programs which reject the beliefs and programs prevailing around them. Smelser calls the mobilization "collective behavior." This idea is much more plausible than the old crowd psychology of a Taine or a LeBon. Unfortunately, it is also harder to verify or falsify: to handle it properly we need individual life histories over considerable periods of time. Nevertheless, where our evidence from Germany, France, and Italy does bear on the more sophisticated argument, the evidence looks bad for the argument. Three things in particular fit poorly: (1) the regularity with which the groups engaging in competitive and reactive collective actions were long-established communities, craft groups, and the like defending rights which had long enjoyed public recognition and even legal protection; (2) the considerable amount of time and prior organization it took before a new challenger began mounting proactive claims—or, for that matter, appearing in collective violence at all; (3) the absence of any correlation (except perhaps a negative one) between the pace of structural change in a period, place, or segment of the population and the extent of collective action and collective violence occurring in that period, place, or segment of the population. Where we are able to match the two, the "collective behavior" model fits our observations poorly, as do all the other breakdown models. Our political process model fits the observations much better: instead of being a direct response to hardship, normlessness, or rapid change, collective violence is a by-product of contention for power and of its repression.

Changes in the Scope and Form of Collective Action

The third major common property of the modern experiences of France, Italy, and Germany is a deep long-run alteration in the forms of collective action producing violence. We have already touched on the alteration in discussing the three forms of collective action. Competitive collective actions were once fairly important as contexts for violence. In preindustrial Europe, rival guilds would often disrupt each other's ceremonial processions, and the young men from neighboring villages got into periodic brawls. By the beginning of the nineteenth century, such forms of collective action were on the wane, although they persisted in the United States in competition among fire companies and the wars of ethnic gangs, and on the European rim in vendetta and some forms of banditry.

The reactive forms, in contrast, were very important at the beginning of the nineteenth century; they may even have been gaining in scope and frequency. In Italy, Germany, and France we see the reactive forms most frequently in the tax rebellion and the food riot, with movements against conscription, land occupations, and perhaps machine-breaking following behind. (Machine-breaking is a debatable case; people ordinarily broke machines which threatened their own livelihoods, but whether installing a new labor-saving machine constitutes making a claim on resurces already under the control of another group—and thereby meets our criteria for an incitement to reactive collective atcion—is not obvious; to the extent that the right to work was itself a resource controlled by the members of a particular trade or community, the inclusion of machine-breaking in the reactive category makes sense.)

The proactive forms predominated in the twentieth century. We have encountered them most frequently in the demonstration and the strike. In both, groups make new claims to be heard, and violence usually occurs when some other group resists those claims. The deliberately engineered coup qualifies. So does the deliberate occupation of previously prohibited premises: occupation of a building as lodgings for the poor, seizure of a director's office, and so on. In our own time these have become the principal contexts for collective violence.

At some point in the nineteenth century, the reactive forms peaked and then declined rapidly throughout most of western Europe; the proactive forms rapidly took over. In Germany the reactive forms were relatively rare after the 1860s, although they did recur just after World War I. In France, 1848–1851 brought the last great burst of violence based on reactive collective action. In Italy the process came later; it was also more extended and more variable by region. While the reactive forms had passed their peak in the industrial North by the 1870s, they still prevailed in the far South at the start of the twentieth century.

Comparisons within Italy bring out something which also appears in the contrasts among France, Germany, and Italy. The shift from reactive to proactive collective action occurred where and when the population had moved into extensive involvement in national structures of power, production, distribution, and association. It is clear enough why collective violence might shift from one to the other of the two outgrowths of reactive collective action: from reactionary (small in scale and scope, based on communal groups) to defensive (large in scale and scope, based on complex organizations). But why a shift from reactive to proactive collective actions?

It was not a logical or functional necessity, but an outgrowth of the particular historical process which western Europe was undergoing after 1800. In the earlier phases, agents of national structures—especially the state and the national market—were still working to impose the priority of their organizations over the interests they called "parochial," "traditional," and "retrograde." They demanded conscripts, grain for the market, tax payments, salable land. The resistance of the groups which already had established claims over the labor, grain, money, and land in question took a reactive form. But the merchants and statemakers won. Thereafter the struggle shifted to a national arena in which the majority of groups and the bulk of the population were excluded from direct participation. The next phase of collective action consisted largely of bids for places in the national structures. It was a proactive phase.

The timing of the swing from reactive to proactive occurring in various parts of Europe depended on two main factors: the chronology of the nationalization of production, distribution, and power, and the growth of complex organizations as vehicles of collective action. Both happened relatively early in France; a little later in Germany; later, and in a more prolonged fashion, in Italy. If we were to survey the rest of western Europe, we would find the crucial transition occurring earlier—before the 1840s—in England, later in Spain and Portugal, and so on. In fact, we would discover a considerable connection among nationalization of economics and politics, the rise of complex organizations, industrialization, and urbanization. So urbanization, industrialization, and statemaking are by no means irrelevant to collective violence. It is just that their effects do not work as breakdown theories say they should. Instead of a short-run generation of strain, followed by protest, we find a long-run transformation of the structures of power and of collective action.

National Differences

With the exception of the clustering of violence in time and the timing of the reactive-proactive shift, we have been discussing common properties of the German, Italian, and French experiences with collective action and collective violence. There were differences. Although the broad forms —competitive, reactive, and proactive forms of collective action, primitive, reactionary, and modern forms of collective violence—apply to all three countries, the specific mixes within the categories differ considerably.

In Italy the agricultural labor force proletarianized early and extensively. It proletarianized in the sense that the bulk of the population controlled too little land to support itself and relied on the sale of its labor for survival. Proletarianization proceeded rapidly in the nineteenth century, as noble and bourgeois landlords extended their holdings, took over common lands, and gained the major part of the church lands which the liberal states seized and sold. At first workers in the North and South alike put up a reactive response; the land occupations were the most

dramatic and effective versions of that response. Later, agricultural workers who were a generation or so removed from common rights in the land
organized proactive movements; we have seen them most clearly in the
big agricultural labor unions of the Po Valley and in the ill-fated Fasci of
Sicily.

There were similar movements in the proletarianized rural regions of
Spain. But in France and Germany landless and land-poor agricultural
workers played a much smaller part in both the reactive and the proactive
phases: vineyard workers of southern France resisting proletarianization
in the early 1900s are the largest exception.

On the other hand, France and, especially, Germany differed from
Italy in the extent to which religious groups and religious issues appeared
in collective violence. Group attacks on Jews recurred in both countries
from the mid-nineteenth to the early twentieth century. The great Protestant-Catholic struggles in France had ended by the nineteenth century, but
defenders of the Catholic Church against the secular state entered the
action when church and state separated in the beginning of the twentieth
century. In Germany organized Catholics resisted state intervention in
religious affairs during the 1830s and again during the *Kulturkampf*
of the 1870s.

The contrast with Italy is striking; it does not result from greater re-
ligiosity on the part of Germans and Frenchmen, and surely not from
greater gentleness of Italian officials in religious affairs: after all, the
Italians absorbed the Papal States by force and dispossessed the Church
throughout the peninsula. The great religious homogeneity of Italy (even
as compared with France) no doubt accounts for some of the difference:
Italians lacked the occasions to organize on a religious basis that the be-
leaguered Protestants, Catholics, or Jews sometimes had in Germany or
France. Whatever the more distant reasons for it, the fact that Germans
and Frenchmen had more extensive organization for action on a religious
basis showed up in the differences between their collective violence and
that of Italy.

The extent and character of governmental repression likewise made a
difference. All three of our countries had some periods in which the regime made collective action costly for a major part of the population. In
France, what Howard Payne calls the "police state" of Louis Napoleon
Bonaparte is the outstanding example. From 1848 to 1851 President

Louis Napoleon gradually constructed a lid for the French cauldron, and from 1852 to the early 1860s Emperor Louis Napoleon held the lid on. The press, political associations, and workers' organizations all felt the pressure. The program worked; it produced a massive decline in collective action, a massive diminution in collective violence. Only with the relaxation of controls over association, assembly, and striking in the 1860s did they grow again. The French again felt the weight of repression from 1940 to 1944, under Vichy and the Nazis; again collective action dwindled, and collective violence (the Resistance notwithstanding) practically disappeared. Although the repressiveness of the French government has varied significantly from one regime to another, the French only experienced about fifteen years of comprehensive repression in the period from 1830 to 1960.

The Italian experience was different, and more difficult to summarize. Most of the multiple Italian states which occupied the peninsula before Unification were relatively repressive in policy, and a number of them had foreign troops at their disposal to back up the policy. They kept down collective action and had little collective violence. During and after the Risorgimento, the liberal regimes liberalized their controls over collective action, and violence mounted. The great return to repression came with the Fascists. They fought their way to power, and then clubbed the left and the labor movement into inaction. The period from 1923 to 1943 was one of the longest stretches of cramped collective action, and consequently of low collective violence, that any western European country has undergone since the early nineteenth century. With the end of World War II, Italians reentered the European mainstream: extensive collective action, vigorous contention for power, moderate repression, considerable collective violence.

Not that Italians simply slept through the twenty Fascist years. Agents of the Fascist state did not hesitate to use force, and Mussolini led his people into more than one war. Our analysis means just what it has always meant: that collective violence simultaneously involving substantial numbers of people from the general population was rare under conditions of heavy repression, not because few people were aggrieved or because the state eschewed violence, but because collective action grew too costly for any group which did not already have the state's protection.

The same principle holds for Germany. In our detailed analysis of collective violence in various German states before unification, we stressed the connection between weak repressive apparatus and fairly extensive collective violence. The great decline in German collective violence between 1848 and the end of World War I resulted to an important degree from the concentration of repressive power, first in a smaller number of relatively strong states and then in a single German Reich. The destruction of the Reich in World War I changed the balance completely. The period from 1918 to 1933 brought high levels of collective violence. Then the Nazis took over for a decade; only they and the army retained any significant capacity to damage or seize persons or property. As in Italy, the collapse of the regime at the end of World War II reopened the way to collective action by groups outside of the government; but in Germany, both East and West, the occupying powers stringently controlled that collective action. Only gradually (and more gradually in East than in West) did they relax their repression and pass over the controls to the successor regimes.

Compared with France, Germany's experience with repression fell into larger, better-defined blocs. That helps account for the greater clustering of German collective violence in time: in some periods collective action was next to impossible; in others, the relaxation of repression did not guarantee violence, but it facilitated the collective action which led to violence. Italy's experience was different from that of either one, despite the parallels between the Nazi and Fascist regimes. In Italy, outside of Fascism, the state's capacity to control collective action never reached the French or German levels. In peripheral areas such as Sicily and Sardinia there were other powers, but the national state had little control indeed. The Italian patterns of collective violence reflected in part the uneven distribution of repressive power in space and time.

The Politics of Collective Violence

We have a nice paradox here: high levels of repression produce low levels of collective violence, yet an important part of the actual *violence* occurring in the course of collective action is performed by specialized repressive forces. How can both be true? Both can be true because more than two variables are involved, and not all the relations among the variables are simply linear. At a minimum, we have to consider mobilization and repression as partly independent determinants of the level of violence. All other things being equal, rising repression means declining mobilization.

All other things, however, are rarely equal. Groups mobilize around existing rights which are being infringed, and around rights which they have come to believe are theirs on general principle. The first is the basis of reactive, the second the basis of proactive, collective action. We have seen Silesian weavers, in their revolt of 1844, mobilizing around the right to exercise their craft; we have also seen workers and intellectuals of Munich, in 1918, establishing a socialist government where one had never existed before. Neither the infringement of rights nor the growth of new beliefs about rights depends closely on the prevailing pattern of repression. That is one reason why mobilization and repression do not covary perfectly.

The access that groups have to power affects the kind and degree of collective action they engage in, as well as the readiness of the authorities to put down their actions. The mafiosi of Sicily long enjoyed the protection of the great landlords, who were also typically political magnates. So long as that protection endured, they could intervene freely and en masse in Sicilian elections. (The Fascists deactivated mafia by making that protection less certain, and both less advantageous and more costly to the landlords; see Blok 1974; Romano 1963.) The organized workers of northern Italy found themselves alternatively tolerated and attacked in the 1880s and 1890s, as their coalitions with bourgeois politicians waxed and waned. Remember the electoral "reform" of 1894, in which over 2 million of the 7.5 million previously eligible Italian voters lost the franchise. The capacity of workers for collective action decreased, but the propensity of the authorities to intervene violently when workers *did* carry on collective action increased. In this regard, too, the negative relation between repression and collective violence is imperfect.

Nor is the pattern peculiarly Italian. In Saxony fear of the Social Democratic Party led to the introduction, in 1896, of the three-class electoral system. Although by no means as restrictive as its Prussian model, it eliminated the SPD from local Saxon politics—at least until 1909, when the law was again liberalized (Huber 1957–69: IV, 405–407). In Hamburg, similar fears caused a tightening of residential and tax requirements for voting in 1906. Here, too, a reduction in the SPD's parliamentary representation ensued (Comfort 1966: 18). The repression worked, and without much violent resistance. In this regard also the negative relationship between repression and collective violence is imperfect.

We keep rediscovering the political basis of collective violence. The factors which account for the changes in collective violence within France, Italy, and Germany, taken individually, and the factors which account for the differences among them are the standard items of political analysis: the organization of contenders for power, the character of repression, the extent and form of political participation, rights in conflict. The German, Italian, and French states are in the middle of the action.

States are not heavily involved in collective violence merely because they have a responsibility for keeping the peace. It takes sleight of hand to make a general association between states and peace plausible, for states have grown up as warmaking organizations through the use of violence, have "kept the peace" by means of violence, and have generated violence on every side as they have grown (see C. Tilly 1974). We have already pointed out the considerable share of all the killing and wounding in collective violence performed by professional agents of the state. That is not the issue here. We want to point out how much of the change and conflict we have been reviewing belongs to the very processes a recent, optimistic literature has called "state- and nation-building."

Suppose we resist the temptation to call any government or any great concentration of power a state. Instead we restrict our attention to a particular type of organization: it controls the principal concentrated means of coercion in a well-defined, contiguous territory; it is relatively distinct and independent from other organizations, relatively centralized, internally differentiated, and internally coordinated. To the extent that an organization meets those standards, we recognize it as a state. Now, if that is what we mean by a state, states have only been the dominant organizations in the world for a short time—perhaps two centuries. The work of mapping the entire world into self-contained states is still not quite finished. The massive decolonization following World War II accomplished a significant part of the task, but it left plenty of client states, quasi-colonies, disputed territories, and bitterly dissident minorities.

Even in Europe, where the present world state-system originated, the dominance of states was still in doubt only five centuries ago. In the fifteenth century there was still a chance that churches, federations of cities, empires, or networks of power-wielding landlords would become dominant in Europe as a whole, as they were in different parts of the continent. In fact, the managers of European states were still combatting major challenges to their survival as states as late as the eighteenth century. The challenges came from both outside and inside: from rivals elsewhere, from rebels at home. Although the Treaty of Westphalia (1648), which ended the Thirty Years' War, played an important part in locking a European state-system in place, a number of the states which then existed or then came into existence failed to survive. The substantial powers in Europe at that time included the Ottoman Empire, the Kingdom of Naples, the Electorates of Saxony and of Bavaria, the Spanish Netherlands, the Kingdom of Hungary, the vast Kingdom of Poland, a Denmark which included what we now call Norway, and a Sweden which included what we now call Finland. In the next three centuries each either shrank enormously or disappeared into some other state.

As the managers of states sought to routinize their power to tax, to conscript, to control the use of land, and to limit the use of force by other organizations and by individuals, they met massive resistance from magnates and common people alike. The great rebellions of the seventeenth century marked the highest point of the struggle. The English Revolution, the Fronde, the revolts of Portugal and Catalonia, and a whole string of other major seventeenth-century conflicts began with the efforts of kings to impose new and larger tax burdens on an indignant populace. Tax rebellions declined in frequency and importance in the eighteenth century, but they did not disappear until the nineteenth. We have observed their last moments in Italy, France, and Germany during the rebellious century; they still mattered then. Until people stopped challenging with force of arms the right of states to extract incomes from their citizens and subjects, the states' dominance over other organizations was unsure.

Conscription had a similar history: a long span of dogged resistance exactly covering the period of statemaking, an irregular decline in the nineteenth century. Movements against conscription usually remained smaller and shorter-lived than tax rebellions. The great insurrection of the Vendée, which broke out in western France at the nationwide call for 300,000 conscripts in March 1793, however, brought something like 100,000 men into armed rebellion against the revolutionary government (Petitfrère 1973; Tilly 1964). In the Vendée, as in other large anti-draft movements, opposition to military service was real but was only part of a more general challenge to the claims of the existing regime. No nineteenth-century movement against conscription was that important. The conflicts observed in nineteenth-century Germany, France, and Italy consisted mainly of local opposition to the forced departure of particular individuals. Group opposition to military service as a form of resistance to specific wars, on the other hand, grew more significant in the twentieth century. Socialist and anarchist opposition to Italian warmaking, for instance, tore Italy apart between 1913 and 1915. But, in the twentieth-century conflicts, the general right of the government to require military service was not ordinarily at issue. States had won that argument by the nineteenth century.

Conflicts around taxation and conscription illustrate the importance of statemaking to collective violence clearly because state demands for cash contributions and for military service cut directly into everyday life. It is a bit harder to see that other reactive collective actions, such as the food riot and the land occupation, also occurred in part as a consequence of the concentration of power in national states. With varying degrees of efficiency and enthusiasm, all European states promoted the delivery of food to their cities, armies, and civilian staffs. They all helped create national markets. That meant reducing, and even attacking, the claims of particular communities on the food supply. Although the immediate participants in food riots were ordinarily local merchants and/or officials and members of the local population, the state lay behind the conflict as a promoter of the demand from outside and as the supporter of the legitimacy of the demand. State officials recognized their responsibility by sending in troops and police to "restore order" and to make sure that the market would not be "disturbed" again (see L. Tilly 1971).

Land occupations fall into the same general category. The immediate targets of those who smashed the fences or seized the land were the substantial men who had taken over fields or forests in which whole communities had common rights. But the substantial men acquired exclusive control over the land with the approval, and often with the assistance, of the state. We have seen the process work itself out in southern Italy: there the sale of church lands during the Risorgimento excluded all but the wealthiest strata of the peasantry, gave the bourgeois the chance to become big landlords, and led to the abridgment of common rights in the land. In 1848, in 1860, and at few other moments when the local power of the national state diminished temporarily, the dispossessed peasants of the South recaptured lost land with dispatch and enthusiasm. But each time the state and the landlords returned with a vengeance.

European states, then, were heavily involved in all the major reactive forms of collective action which commonly led to violence. The collective violence was to an important extent a consequence of statemaking. States were not involved in quite the same way in the *proactive* collective action which commonly led to violence. That does not mean they were less involved. The violent strike is a mixed case: many strikes were directed exclusively against individual firms, and turned violent either when workers smashed property of the firm, or when strikebreakers or hired toughs fought with the strikers. In an intermediate class of violent strikes, the main business still went on between employees and individual firms, but state-employed troops and police intervened when employers or local officials thought the workers had stepped out of line. There is a third category of violent strike—in the European experience, by far the largest in scale and in degree of violence—which directed demands to the state itself. The great insurrectionary strikes of 1918 and 1919 in all three of our countries comprise our type case.

In the other frequent proactive form of collective action, the demonstration, the state itself is a usual participant. Demonstrators are commonly making claims for some sort of response from a government. That government may be a local government. It may be a quasi-government, such as the authorities of a prison, a school, or a military installation. Most often it is the national state. The slogans people shout deal with national politics and national policies: "Vive la République!" "A basso la guerra!" "Rote Front!" If by statemaking we mean the creation of governmental organizations which are autonomous, differentiated, centralized, and so on, and the assurance of their priority over the organizations, then the demonstrations we have encountered are not generally consequences of statemaking. They involve struggles to influence a state which is already constituted and powerful. The shift from reactive to proactive forms of collective action records the victory of the national state.

Let us not overdo the equation of reactive forms of collective violence with statemaking and of proactive forms with the victorious state. Two things are wrong with those equations. First, we are talking about a net shift, not an absolute one. The great period of statemaking saw competitive collective actions continue, and also produced some proactive collective action at a national level and at a smaller scale. Although the string of events called the French Revolution contained plenty of reactive movements (including tax rebellions and food riots of the classic types, the participants now allying themselves with major national contenders for power), the actions which made it revolutionary articulated claims for rights never before recognized. After the German, French, and Italian states were irremovably entrenched, on the other hand, competitive and reactive actions still occurred from time to time: in Germany, Italian and German laborers fought each other for jobs in the 1900s; in the Italy of 1943, Italians resisted the efforts of the retreating Germans to destroy or remove valuable machinery. Within the reactive category, the considerable transformation of the organization of the action—from communal groups acting on a small, local scale to associational groups acting on a large, national scale—has led us to distinguish between "reactionary" and "defensive" types of collective violence. The *defensive* types belong mainly to the recent period. So we are dealing with a net movement along two dimensions: toward a large scale, and so on; from reactive toward proactive.

There is a second reason for avoiding the complete identification of proactive collective action with the victorious state. The European national state grew up with capitalism. The growing structures of capitalism—the national markets, the mercantile and industrial firms, the cash-crop farm—also shaped collective action. Statemaking and the development of capitalism intertwined so thoroughly that it is hard to distinguish their effects. Still, some of the forms of collective action we have been surveying focus directly on agents of the state, while others focus on agents of firms or markets. We have already mentioned the strike: the growth of large firms promoted the formation of parallel labor organizations, which in turn promoted the shift to the strike as a major form of collective action. Likewise, producers' associations—especially in agriculture—formed to press the claim of one interest against the market. In the early 1960s, organized French farmers blocked highways and dumped potatoes in the main squares of market towns. The farmers, like the strikers, had at least one eye on the state, but the immediate target of their action was not the state itself.

Collective Violence and the Timing of Industrial Growth

Does the reintroduction of capitalism to our analysis open the way for some form of the argument, earlier rejected, that industrial growth generates protest? Let us review the returns from our countries. In the very long period stretching from the beginning of the nineteenth century to around 1930 all three experienced substantial industrial growth. France showed the way, already achieving between 1815 and 1850 a rate of industrial growth of 3.25 percent per annum (Lévy-Leboyer 1964). Germany followed at first, its industrial "take-off" coming in the 1840s; from that point on, it quickly overtook France. Italy trailed throughout the century, but began to grow very rapidly from the 1890s to World War I; during that period, according to Gerschenkron's estimates, it grew more rapidly than France or Germany. We can observe increasing similarities among the three countries in the phasing of industrial growth. Both France and Germany achieved fairly rapid progress from the early 1830s to the late 1840s, even more rapid growth from 1850 to the 1870s, relative stagnation from then into the 1890s, and relatively rapid growth from the middle 1890s to World War I. The Italian economy begins to share these rhythms from the 1870s. Its difficulties from that point to the 1890s, and its upsurge thereafter, match the French and German performances.

Still, there were differences. France began industrializing first; by World War I she was clearly one of the world's great industrial nations. Nevertheless, historical discussion of French industrialization has been much concerned with explaining the stagnation of France as compared with England and, especially, with Germany (Cameron 1961). In our period, the growth of income, of population, and of industrial production, the shift of population and labor force out of rural areas and out of agriculture into urban industry were less substantial in France than in a number of other countries. Slow French industrialization, historians explain, resulted both from the initial advantages in world trade seized by Great Britain between 1780 and 1815 (which made French growth more dependent upon its domestic market), and from the Revolutionary land settlement, which confirmed hundreds of thousands of French peasants in their rights—thus making them unlikely recruits for the industrial labor force and a drag on the labor supply (Cameron 1958; Crouzet 1958, 1964, 1970; Lévy-Leboyer 1964).

This did not mean that ordinary Frenchmen were losing much ground to Englishmen or to Germans, because in per-capita-income terms the relative change was much smaller. By the second half of the century France was receiving income from past foreign investments (not reflected in current production data). Besides, noncash income was reportedly higher there than in other countries. A relatively large, far-from-impoverished rural population not only hampered industrial growth but may have had direct political importance. The base for a chronic or recurring swell of agrarian populism remained incomparably larger and stronger in France than in countries like Germany, where a conservative, more thoroughly capitalist land settlement had prevailed and where land ownership became more highly concentrated (Hobsbawm 1962; but see Weis 1970).

Germany's land settlement was hardly ideal—either for industrial growth or for political stability; it was certainly not the only important factor distinguishing German from French development. In the long run it did much more to cut labor loose from agriculture and to encourage population growth than its French counterpart did (Habakkuk 1953). It gave Germany an advantage over France in the industrial growth race. But a more plentiful supply of labor was not its only advantage. German industry also possessed an increasing ability to attract the systematic support of the state for the promotion of industrial interests. The fruits of this ability can be seen in the state-subsidized railroad building in Prussia in the 1840s (when France was falling behind in this respect), and in the government's systematic manipulation of the railroads to encourage industrial users in the 1860s (with the lowering of freight rates) and 1870s (with nationalization on terms favorable to private owners). As the educational system becomes increasingly relevant for industrial needs in the 1860s, the German governments step in and build up the necessary capacity.

David Landes (1969) has told a good part of the relevant story with regard to Germany's industrial superiority over Great Britain; it applies to France as well. Much more work needs to be done on this issue, but it seems probable that government policies—not the least of all local government policies—benefited industry much more in Germany than in France. In a comparative sense it is tempting to speculate on the extent to which French political centralization turned out to be an industrial disadvantage. The relatively close relations between the state and large-scale industry in Germany, however, also have their roots in the undemocratic character of the country's political system, and are thus a clue to the relative weakness of disorderly challenges thrown down to it before 1914.

The observer of nineteenth-century development tends to single out Italy's extreme backwardness vis-à-vis France and Germany rather than the parallels among their growth patterns. Italian backwardness manifested itself in several noteworthy respects. Italy's notorious regional disparities are significant indicators of backwardness. For northern Italy (Piedmont and Lombardy), scholars have reported early industrial progress—for example, from 1830 to 1840 and again during the 1840s (Cameron 1961; Tremelloni 1947: 110, 179–180, 256–263). Nevertheless, at Unification there were extreme differences unlike anything known at the time in France or Germany. Thereafter, one finds few signs of their diminution (Clough and Livi 1956). Given the economic and political dominance of the North, the problem of domestic colonialism thus presents itself. Perhaps southern bandit attacks on northern-owned railroads building into the South reflected popular resentment of northern domination.

Huge regional differences do not establish Italian backwardness as strictly an internal, regional problem. According to one reputable estimate, "the private per capita wealth of the richest and most advanced areas in northern Italy in the second half of the eighties was still very much below one half of the contemporaneous figure for France as a whole" (Pantaleoni, cited in Gerschenkron 1962: 72). This backwardness and the concerted attempt to modernize the country's infrastructure since the 1850s explain Italy's marked dependence upon foreign capital and technical help. That foreign involvement was especially French at first; later, Germans played an important part (Cameron 1971; Cohen 1967; Gerschenkron 1962). To the extent that foreign capital stimulated investment in Italy more than it added to the country's savings or imports, it increased pressure on popular living standards; it may thereby have had important political consequences.

One schema which immediately suggests itself to this kind of attempt to apply comparative analysis to the nexus between industrialization and collective violence is Gerschenkron's typology of backwardness. Drawing on Gerschenkron's own writings and on an explicit, comparative application of his concept of backwardness by Stephen Barsby (1969), we can reenact the following drama: ever since England industrialized, there have been "backward" countries which have had to cross the threshold of industrialization abruptly, through achievement of an initial "big spurt" (analogous to Rostow's "take-off"). The more backward the country, relative to England, the leader, the more abrupt the transitional spurt, the higher the rate of industrial growth. The higher the industrial growth rate, the greater the associated social changes and tensions—above all, because extreme backwardness means growth through increase in producer goods and curtailment of consumption. We thus have the ingredients of a model positively linking rapid growth and political tensions through increased deprivation. Unlike the standard "breakdown" arguments, moreover, this model helps specify the mechanisms which connect protest with rapid growth.

In most European countries considerable violence did occur during the early stages of industrialization: in England from 1780 to the 1840s, in France from 1830 to 1851, in Germany from 1830 to 1850, in Italy from 1860 to 1914, and so on. If we follow Gerschenkron and Barsby closely, however, we run into some difficulties. Table 21 supplies the relevant "spurt dates" and "big spurt" growth figures for our countries.

Barsby shows that Italy "suffered" most of all countries experiencing their big spurt because her rate of industrial growth during the first ten- and twenty-year spurt period (1) was highest, (2) was most strongly concentrated in the producers' good sector of the economy, and (3) was high-

Table 21. Growth in output for France, Germany, and Italy (percentage)

Country	Year spurt began	After 10 years		After 20 years	
		Agriculture	Manufacturing	Agriculture	Manufacturing
France	1829	15	41	27	80
Germany	1850	13	43	25	89
Italy	1896	9	85	20	156

SOURCE: Stephen Barsby, "Economic Backwardness and the Characteristics of Development," *Journal of Economic History*, 29: 449–473.

est relative to agricultural productivity change. It is also true that Italy experienced a great deal of violence during her initial spurt; the troubles of 1897–1898, especially the great violence in Milan in 1898, have already caught our attention.

Seen comparatively, however, three qualifying observations are essential. First, France saw *more* violence during her initial spurt of industrialization, 1830–1850, than did Italy between 1896 and 1914 or, for that matter, Germany at any time. But France suffered least of the countries in the sense that agricultural productivity rose more relative to industrial production and especially in relation to producer goods production than in Italy or Germany during *their* big spurts. Second, Italy herself experienced a good deal of violence between 1848 and 1896; that was before the first spurt of industrial growth. According to our evidence, some of that violence reflected pressure on the agricultural sector and on consumption standards; the pressure built up in the largely unsuccessful attempt to force agricultural resources into industrial growth channels. Third, Germany experienced far less violence during the initial growth spurt attributed to her (1850–1870) than earlier (1830–1850).

The comparison of timetables of industrialization tells something about the ways that economic change shaped, and even generated, collective violence. The particular grievances around which people organized in Germany, Italy, and France grew to an important degree out of the particular relations among classes created in each country by industrialization. The shift toward proactive, large-scale, collective action involving associations resulted to a significant extent from the organizational changes wreaked by industrialization. Organized proletarians became more and more prominent in collective violence as industrialization proceeded. So there are many connections between industrialization and collective violence. The one that is missing is a direct connection between the sheer pace of change and the acuteness of violence, protest, or collective action.

It would waste space to raise the same questions again for urbanization. Since 1800 the timetables and geographies of urbanization and industrialization have corresponded closely. In their recent forms, they depend on each other. So the broad relationships with collective violence are the same. Where we have been able to look at the detail, industrialization appears to have had a larger effect on the whole character of collective action, hence on collective violence, than urbanization. So far as we can detect, for example, there is no tendency for recent migrants to Italian, German, and French cities to become exceptionally involved in movements of protest or in collective violence; on the contrary, we have some small indications of their *under*involvement. New members of established industries, however, quite rapidly seem to take on the basic modes of collective action within their industries. Communication, organization, and leadership take a long time to build up; once they are built up, new recruits respond to them rapidly. Since the early nineteenth century, communications, organization, and leadership have tended to build up within firms, industries, and social classes, but not within territorial communities. In this sense, industrialization has affected collective action more profoundly than urbanization has.

The major qualification to that conclusion is a negative case. At the beginning of our period, communities as such appeared in collective violence with fair frequency; the movements against taxation, conscription, and removal of food ordinarily recruited from individual communities; they activated communal claims over the money, labor, or commodities in question. As cities became more dominant in Germany, Italy, and France, both the bases of those claims and the capacity of members of communities to act together on them declined.

Communities did not disappear completely from the action. In 1871 a number of French cities besides Paris declared themselves autonomous, revolutionary communes. In 1971 Reggio in Calabria was up in arms over the assignment of the regional capital to its rival Catanzaro. Nineteenth-century labor organizations frequently brought their forces together into citywide organizations which coordinated political demands and strike movements: *camere di lavoro, bourses de travail, Fachvereine.* Nevertheless, over the long run associations have taken up the bulk of collective action in all three countries—and associations only form exceptionally on a territorial basis.

The conclusion we have to draw for urbanization, then, parallels our conclusion for industrialization: although the impact of urbanization on collective action was weaker and more indirect than that of industrialization, in both cases the essential process was the creation of new solidarities and new structures of power. If we must choose flatly between breakdown and solidarity theories, we have to take solidarity. If we have a chance to revise existing theories, we must build in representations of mobilization, contention for power, and repression. Instead of a direct line from "change" to "protest" through "strain" or "hardship," we discover multiple lines. The rearrangement of everyday life transforms the organization of collective action.

CHAPTER VI

Conclusions

Marx and Collective Action

Karl Marx knew the importance of solidarity to collective action. His own acerbic commentaries on nineteenth-century European conflicts stated many of the themes in our treatments of France, Germany, and Italy. Although our emphasis on the state and on contention for political power will make some Marxists uncomfortable, our chief theoretical choices are choices that Marx made a century ago.

One apparent difference may occur to Marxophiles. Occasionally Marx slipped into volcanic language: revolutions and rebellions are sometimes eruptions, explosions, outbursts. At one point he characterized the immediate background of the French Revolution of 1848 as "the eruption of general discontent," declared that the agricultural crises of 1845 and 1846 "increased the general ferment among the people," and concluded that the food shortage of 1847 "called forth bloody conflicts" in France and elsewhere (Marx 1958: 143). We might preserve our Marxist orthodoxy by pointing out that in these passages Marx did not specifically commit himself to a direct causal chain from hardship to anger to action, or by recalling that in other analyses of artisanal movements, local struggles over the land, and other small-scale, short-run protests Marx usually took care to emphasize the coherence and durability of the claims and grievances involved.

The point, however, is not to establish orthodoxy or unorthodoxy. To the extent that Marx *did* propound a view of small-scale protests as eruptions of discontent, our view differs in stressing local organization and durable grievances. There we are at least consistent with other parts of the Marxist view of collective action. In general, Marx and Marxists argue against breakdown and hardship theories of collective action, in favor of different versions of a solidarity thesis.

In the same analysis of 1848 (some details of which are included in Chapter II), Marx described the French working class. "The industrial bourgeoisie," he wrote, "can only rule where modern industry shapes all property relations to suit itself, and industry can win this power only where it has conquered the world market, for national bounds are inadequate for its development."

But French industry, to a great extent, maintains its command even of the national market only through a more or less modified system of prohibitive duties. While, therefore, the French proletariat, at the moment of a revolution, possesses in Paris actual power and influence which spur it on to a drive beyond its means, in the rest of France it is crowded into separate, scattered industrial centres, being almost lost in the superior numbers of peasants and petty bourgeois . . . Nothing is more understandable, then, than that the Paris proletariat sought to secure the advancement of its own interests *side by side* with those of the bourgeoisie, instead of enforcing them as the revolutionary interests of society itself, that it let the *red* flag be lowered to the *tricolour* (Marx 1958: 148–149).

Although Marx never molded this line of argument into a general analysis of collective action, his political writings are full of similar observations. There is the emphasis on industrialization as the shaper of organizational forms and hence of the forms of collective action. There is the treatment of class coalitions as crucial in the making of revolutions—not to mention the observation that the proletariat (as it was organized in midcentury France) was destined to be the dupe of its bourgeois coalition partners. In short, Marx suggested a number of the extensions and revisions of simple-solidarity notions adopted earlier in this book.

For all its plausible application to the experiences we have been examining, the Marxian line is not self-evident. It is not even widely accepted. In the sociological analysis of collective action, it has been a minority view. Of the three fundamental sociological theorists—Marx, Weber, and Durkheim—only Marx propounded an analysis of collective action in which the making of claims by solidary groups organized around articulated interests played the central part.

Each of the others had some interesting ideas concerning collective action. Weber's theory of the recurrent emergence and routinization of charisma, for example, effectively links the specific beliefs, personnel, actions, and organizational evolution of radical movements. Durkheim's analysis of the disorganizing effects of increasing division of labor was, in our view, a great impediment to the proper understanding of connections between collective action and large-scale structural change. Nevertheless, in *The Elementary Forms of the Religious Life,* Durkheim presented a functional analysis of public ceremonies, assemblies, and rituals which still deserves attention. Weber's and Durkheim's conceptions of collective action—as innovative movements oriented to deviant definitions of reality, as irrational responses to the strain and hardship brought by extensive social change—have dominated modern sociological thinking on the subject. Our argument has genuine competitors.

When we turn to recent *historical* work on collective action, however, we do not discover the same predominance of Weber and Durkheim. There, Marxian ideas and Marxist scholars have had an enormous influence. The movement for "history from below" calls for the concrete study of the actual, ordinary participants in major political events, of their organization, origins, aspirations, and day-to-day actions. The movement first took hold in studies of the French Revolution; there Albert Soboul, Richard Cobb, and many others made their trademark the person-by-person, place-by-place reconstruction of revolutionary classes and organizations. Many people became aware of this painstaking work through syntheses such as George Rudé's *The Crowd in History* and Eric Hobsbawm's *Primitive Rebels.*

Soon other scholars were making the same approach to revolutions, rebellions, protests, and (more rarely) other collective actions throughout the world; ancient Rome, the American Revolution, and Chinese rebellions all inspired history from below. The Marxism of many such studies is attenuated, to say the least. But at a minimum they share the assumption that the social base, the organizational form, the prior claims and grievances, the present mobilization of the ordinary actors in political conflicts provide a major part of the explanation of their actions. In that weak sense they fall into the tradition of Marx rather than into the tradition of Weber or Durkheim.

This preference of historians of collective action for Marx might result not from the superior general power of Marx's scheme, but from the fact that Marx wrote specifically and historically about collective action in our own era, about the impact of industrialization, urbanization, the expansion of capitalism, and (to a small extent) the rise of national states on the experiences, grievances, and strivings of ordinary people. Marx said a great deal about the struggle over the enclosures, about proletarian insurrections, about peasant politics, and about a host of related topics on the agenda of history from below. Weber said much less about such matters, and Durkheim almost nothing at all. That may account for some of the attractiveness of ideas in the Marxian tradition to scholars who hold no particular brief for today's Marxist parties and programs. But we are inclined to believe that as a general theory of collective action, the broadly Marxist formulation we have been following also holds up better than its main competitors.

Collective Action Elsewhere

Does our analysis apply outside of Germany, Italy, and France? Only sustained studies of other parts of the world over large spans of time will tell for sure. We have not made the necessary studies. Nor has anyone else. However, a preliminary look at the experiences of other countries in western Europe reveals some familiar features.

Spain displays some interesting parallels with Italy. In Spain the transition from the classic reactive forms of collective violence—the food riot, the tax rebellion, and so on—came late and on a schedule which varied markedly with the modernity of the region. In Spain agricultural proletarians (especially the *braceros* of the south) played a major part in nineteenth- and twentieth-century political conflicts. In Spain there were many crises, each surrounded by its own array of collective violence. In Spain long periods of widespread repression—the dictatorships of Primo de Rivera and Francisco Franco—practically eliminated collective action on the part of the general population, and thus eliminated most types of collective violence as well. Furthermore, the differences observed make political sense: in Spain, unlike Italy, we find military units acting autonomously, making their own bids for power instead of simply executing the commands of the governmental authorities. In chaotic Spain, as well as in Germany, Italy, and France, the texture of collective violence is essentially the texture of politics.

The same is true for orderly Britain. Great Britain actually saw more violence during the nineteenth and twentieth centuries than her reputation for peaceful resolution of political problems would lead us to believe. For example, 1830 was a turbulent year in Britain as well as on the continent. The famous Swing movement appeared that year. (In the "Swing Riots" rural people throughout much of south-central England burned hayricks, smashed threshing machines, destroyed rural property, and demanded tribute of substantial citizens, sometimes after circulating threatening notices in the name of the mythical avenger Captain Swing.) The Swing Riots brought on vigorous repression: 2,000 persons charged, 250 condemned to death (of whom 19 were eventually executed), nearly 500 transported to Australia, over 600 imprisoned (Hobsbawm and Rudé 1969).

That was not all. The year 1830 was also one of widespread strikes, some leading to violence. It was a year of Protestant-Catholic conflicts, of meetings in support of the French Revolution, of agitation for parliamentary reform, of tax protests. In 1830, 8,000 ironworkers of Glamorgan are reported to have attended nightly readings from the radical works of William Cobbett (Rudé 1967: 101). In 1830, 50,000 or 60,000 people commemorated the Peterloo Massacre of 1819 at the massacre's site near Manchester by listening to an address by the Radical Henry Hunt. ("Mr. Hunt also adverted to the recent transactions in France," reported the *Manchester Mercury* for August 17, "which he characterized as of the most glorious description," and then compared the English working classes unfavorably with the French.) The years from 1830 to 1832 in Great Britain resembled the time of the French and German revolutions of 1848 in two important respects. First, they brought a great swelling of both proactive and reactive collective action on the part of many different segments of the population, often in some sort of alliance with middle-class reformers. Second, they marked the transition from predominantly reactive to predominantly proactive popular movements; after that point, the food riot, the tax rebellion, machine-breaking, and kindred actions faded fast away. From the 1830s on, petitions, demonstrations, strikes, mass meetings, special-purpose associations predominated in British collective action. Essentially the same transition occurred in France and Germany two or three decades later.

The British comparison adds something to our analysis. In discussing the changing forms of collective action in Italy, Germany, and France, we have stressed two factors: the growth of complex organizations as vehicles of collective action; and the nationalization of production, distribution, and power. The British experience suggests that the growth of electoral politics at the national level supplied a major link between these two big clusters of changes and the shifts in collective action. Derek Fraser sees the Reform agitators of 1830 to 1832 as building their unprecedented organizations on the model of O'Connell's successful Catholic Association in Ireland:

Like some latter-day influential American campaign manager, O'Connell could deliver the block vote of the Irish Catholics and they would jump when and where he commanded. Attwood quite consciously modelled his Political Union on the Catholic Association, whose success legitimised the lobbying of this sort of pressure group. Many realised this point: "We never were the advocates of self-constituted political clubs until our present ministers confessed they had succumbed to the Catholic Association and by the enactment of the Relief Bill, sanctioned the means by which it was obtained" (1970: 34–35, citing *Birmingham Journal,* 23 January 1830).

That sharp observation brings to mind the great importance of electoral campaigns in the mobilization of workers and peasants during the German and French revolutions of 1848. It recalls the later interplay, in Italy, of proletarian mobilization, collective action, and electoral participation through such organizations as the Partito Operaio. Even tightly controlled elections give some legitimacy to assembly, association, and public discussion of the issues. To the extent that they are open contests, national elections give a peculiar advantage to interests organized in centralized associations. As Robert Michels put it, "The principle of organization is an absolutely essential condition for the political struggle of the masses" (1915: 26).

That the development of national electoral systems promotes the formation of durable political parties is well known (see Duverger 1963). The confrontation of British, French, Italian, and German experiences, however, suggests a much wider effect of elections: they legitimized and promoted the growth of associations as vehicles for collective action. Religious associations, trade associations, friendly societies, and even social clubs whose everyday activities were drinking and talk flowered in the age of elections. They became the means by which ordinary people carried out their collective business.

Association and Collective Action

We oversimplify. Some, perhaps many, of these associations formed in the legal shadows before ordinary people had the vote or the right to strike, before they had extensive freedom to assemble or to associate. In France we have seen political associations and mutual-aid societies forming underground as early as the 1830s. We have seen people "overloading" legal forms of assembly and association: protesting government policy at the theater, gathering in cafes to talk and organize political action, getting together under the auspices of ostensibly religious fraternities, organizing strikes beneath the shield of legally tolerated mutual benefit societies.

In his rich analysis of nineteenth-century local life in Provence, Maurice Agulhon points out that the *chambrée populaire* took on extraordinary importance as an opinion-maker and as a vehicle for collective action. The *chambrée* resembled the bourgeois *cercle:* it was essentially a homogeneous private club for men, at which the members passed the time reading newspapers, playing cards, drinking, and talking. Many went further; they had both a treasury and a program for mutual aid. Although most were quite secular, a few took the form of religious societies sponsored by a particular parish. Furthermore, the predominance of the chambrée in nineteenth-century Provence undoubtedly owed a good deal to the importance of local religious confraternities there before the Revolution. According to Agulhon's analysis, they flourished most in the concentrated winegrowing villages of western Provence. Indeed, the government became interested in bringing them to light in the 1820s because a great deal of the wine drunk in these private clubs was escaping the excise tax.

Members of chambrées did more than drink and talk. In the 1830s, Agulhon sees the chambrées as being much involved in local conflicts, but little tied into national politics. During the forest conflicts of 1830 in Ampus, for example, we see "two chambrées, flags and drum before them, shout against the mayor, 'destroyer of the commune,' and against the curé, who seems to have been of his party" (1970: 243). By the 1840s, however, Agulhon sees the chambrées politicizing and spreading democratic ideas. During the Revolution of 1848, in his analysis, they formed the nuclei of many popular associations, and the immediate predecessors of many of the secret societies which Louis Napoleon sought to stamp out in 1851.

The irony is that the earlier regimes' selective tolerance of this form of association encouraged its growth: "These monarchical regimes which were so suspicious of any form of association encouraged *mutualism* . . . They feared the subversive forms of association into which hardship might push the workers; but the mutual society was a panacea both against hardship (by thrift and mutual aid) and against rebellion (by educating people to a sense of responsibility)" (Agulhon 1970: 212). So the permitted form of association eventually became the means of rebellion.

In the case of England, E. P. Thompson has argued that the working class formed its whole armature of collective action underground. When Luddism began in Lancashire, he says, "There were already, in Manchester and the larger centres, artisan unions, secret committees of the weavers, and some old and new groups of Painite Radicals, with an ebullient Irish fring" (1966: 595). The evidence concerning these groups is thin—some would say because the groups were tiny, ephemeral, or even nonexistent. Thompson says it is because the groups deliberately hid themselves from the authorities, and thus from the historians who later consulted the papers of the authorities.

By the time of Luddism, underground unions had unquestionably been around for some time. As Aspinall points out, "The fact that, at the end of the eighteenth century there were more than forty Acts of Parliament to prevent workmen from combining, is suggestive both of the widespread existence of trade unions over a long period of years, and of the willingness of the Legislature to support the labour policy of the employers" (1949: ix).

A good deal of local organization showed up in Luddism. At Ashover, according to a report of December 1811:

Two men came to this place who called themselves inspectors from the committee; they went to every stockinger's house and discharged them from working under such prices as they gave them a list of, and said they should come again in a few days, and in case any of them were found working without having a ticket from their master saying that he was willing to give the prices stated in their list, they should break their frames. They summoned all the stockingers, about 12 or 14 in number of master men to a public house with as much consequence as if they had had a mandate from the Prince Regent. When they got them hither, all I can learn at present, was for the purpose of collecting money from them for the support of those families who were deprived of getting their bread by having their frames broken. Where they found a frame worked by a person who had not served a regular apprenticeship, or by a woman, they discharged them from working, and if they promised to do so, they stuck a paper upon the frame with these words written upon it—"Let this frame stand, the colts removed"—colt is the name given to all those who have not served a regular apprenticeship (H. O. 42/118, as quoted by Aspinall 1949: 118).

Anyone who still thinks of Luddism as enraged assaults on machines should read this report, and the many like it, carefully; there is outrage, all right, but nothing like blind fury. The whole sequence bespeaks premeditation and prior organization.

As in France, the British government had been tolerant of mutual benefit societies while the Combination Acts forbade trade unions. As in France, "the Unions could easily shelter under the title of Friendly Societies Acts. There was, too, reason to believe that even when a trade union was not disguised as a Benefit Club, it obtained financial assistance from this source during a turn-out" (Aspinall 1949: xxiv-xxv). The dense organizational background makes it less surprising that the 1824 repeal of the Combination Acts brought an immediate flowering of trade unions: "Now that they were no longer under the ban of the law, trade unions sprang up everywhere, thus confounding [Francis] Place's confident prediction that repeal would lead to their disappearance. There was an epidemic of strikes which quickly alarmed not only the masters but the Government" (ibid.: xxviii). E. P. Thompson has traced the transformation of trade unions and kindred associations into major instruments of the Reform campaign which led to the expansion of the electorate in 1832, and then into constituent parts of the mass Chartist movement (1966, esp. Ch. 16). In England, it seems, widespread working-class organization both helped assure and benefited from the expansion of the electorate and the consequent toleration of groups and gatherings organized around electoral affairs.

England of the 1820s and 1830s happens to be an exceptionally well analyzed case. Elsewhere, we know less of the detail. In general, all we can be sure of is that (1) organizational nuclei existed before the great bursts of working-class association—England in the 1830s, France and Germany in 1848, and so on—and played significant parts in them; (2) the extension of the vote tended to accompany and encourage the legalization of working-class associations; (3) legalization gave a great boost to the strength and prevalence of associations. Organization gave working people the strength to demand their rights. The acquisition of those rights brought expanded use of them in formulating new demands or pursuing old ones. The sequence is not peculiar to elections and parties. It is not peculiar to workers. It is a general rule for collective action.

The Effectiveness of Violence

In the history we have been examining, holders of power never granted rights without pressure. Newcomers (and, for that matter, old groups which were losing power) fought for their rights; they often broke the law, and often engaged in violence. The fact that violent conflicts occurred routinely in the struggle for power, however, does not establish that they had to happen, that the violent strategy was the best strategy, or that the violence itself made any difference to the political outcome. We have often heard, after all, that Britain accomplished peacefully, lawfully, and effectively what other people attempted through disruptive conflict.

Some of Britain's orderly reputation results simply from her survival without revolution since 1688. We tend to forget the challenges which fail and to pacify retroactively those which succeed short of revolution. In the Britain of the nineteenth and twentieth centuries, Luddism, Temperance, feminism, pacifism, and the organization of labor all had their violent moments. Because a number of the events we have studied in Germany, Italy, and France would not have been violent if troops and police had not attacked, it is likely that some of the apparent difference between Great Britain and other countries results from greater British constraints on military and police violence.

Even the claim to nonrevolutionary continuity fades away if we are so ungenerous as to include Ireland or North America in our scheme. Nevertheless, since 1800 Great Britain probably *has* experienced lower overall levels of collective violence and of extralegal action than most other western countries. Britain probably *has* experienced greater transfers of power without revolution. If so, the British experience raises the possibility that the collective violence we have been analyzing was ultimately unimportant and unnecessary.

We must divide the question in two: With respect to the goals of the participants, how effective was the resort to illegal and/or violent means of action? Whether or not they accomplished the goals of the participants, how much difference did violent events make to the course of history? In this book we have neglected both questions. We have neglected them in favor of an effort to explain why, how, and when violent encounters occurred and a companion effort to see how the pattern of collective action—effective or ineffective, violent or nonviolent—changed under the influence of urbanization, industrialization, and the nationalization of power.

To judge the effectiveness of violent means, we must not only identify the goals of the actors but also compare the violent means with the nonviolent means available to the group. Our inquiry has produced no cost-effectiveness formulas, nor anything like them. It has, however, made some small contributions toward evaluating the effectiveness of collective violence.

First, we have discovered that by and large the participants in European collective violence knew what they were doing. They said so, too. We have made no effort to peer into their minds and discern individual motives for being on the scene. We have, nevertheless, found a fairly good fit between the actions people took, the demands and complaints they made, their prior collective action, and the social situation they currently found themselves in. The fit is far too good to justify thinking of participation in collective violence as impulsive, unreflective, spur-of-the-moment. Strikers who battled troops or occupied factories almost always made well-defined demands. The demands were ordinarily ones the same people had been making for some time. People who attacked tollbooths and tax collectors usually accompanied their violence with specific complaints against the taxes in question. If so, we can reasonably take the goals articulated in the course of collective action as standards for judging its effectiveness. We need not search for the "real" goals behind the "pretexts" for action, or condescendingly substitute our own versions of what a group should have been attempting for what it said it was attempting.

Second, we have not found a sharp division between violent and non-violent collective action. Instead, we have found a close connection. We have learned that the very distinction is misleading. Forms of collective action do vary in the probability that they will lead to the damage or seizure of persons or objects, but (1) practically no common forms of collective action which we have encountered are intrinsically violent; (2) for most common forms of collective action the probability of violence is far closer to zero than to one; (3) the great bulk of collective violence emerges from much larger streams of essentially nonviolent collective action; (4) a substantial part of the violence we observe consists of the forcible *reaction* of a second group—often of specialized repressive forces in the employ of governments—to the nonviolent collective action of the first. Violent demonstrations, for example, do not form a separate class of events; for the most part, they occur amid much larger numbers of otherwise similar nonviolent demonstrations. They are simply the ones in which the demonstrators carry through their threat to occupy the city hall, or in which counter-demonstrators attack, or in which the police arrive with instructions to clear the streets, by force if necessary. Even machine-breaking ordinarily occurs in the midst of an extended nonviolent (although rarely amiable) effort to keep employers from substituting machines for men.

If all this is true, the fundamental strategic choice is not between violent and nonviolent means. It is between different forms of collective action which vary in the probability that they will lead to violence. They also vary in legality, in cost, and in effectiveness.

Are the forms with a high probability of violence more or less likely to be effective? Although we have no reliable evidence on the point, several strands of our earlier analyses suggest the following conclusions:

(1) *Illegal forms of collective action have a higher probability of violence,* largely because the people behind the laws and professional law-enforcement agencies are likely to respond to them with violence; because they are illegal, they are also more costly in other regards. If there is no legal means available to the particular end in question, of course, the comparison loses its sense.

(2) *The short-run and long-run effectiveness of violence-prone forms differ.* In the short run, if means of collective action with high and low probabilities of violence are equally available—a very large if—the low-

probability means are more effective, if only because they attract more adherents.

(3) *It depends on the power positions of the groups involved.* For a powerful group, almost by definition, it will rarely make sense to choose a means of collective action which currently has a high probability of producing violence; the main exception is when the violence is likely to cripple a significant opponent. For a powerless group, on the other hand, courting violence, or even deliberately initiating violence, will sometimes pay. That is true for various reasons. First, a powerless group whose grievances have some claim on the sympathies of significant powerholders, but are not being heard, can sometimes acquire the support of the powerholders through the dramatic use of protest and by becoming the victims of official repression. The powerholders form a tacit, temporary coalition with the powerless and against the government or against other powerholders. The Sicilian Fasci, in temporary alliance with the island's liberal bourgeois, illustrate the short-run success—and the long-run failure—of this tactic.

Second, the range of collective actions open to a relatively powerless group is normally very small. Its program, its forms of action, its very existence are likely to be illegal, hence subject to violent repression. As a consequence, such a group chooses between taking actions which have a high probability of bringing on a violent response (but which have some chance of reaching the group's goals) and taking no action at all (thereby assuring the defeat of the group's goals).

Third, where governmental repression is weak or inefficient, focused and violent terrorism magnifies the power of a small group by discrediting the government; it also threatens the small group's enemies with retaliation. Our European survey has turned up little nongovernmental terrorism. The main cases are groups enjoying tacit government support, as did the Nazis and the Fascists before they came to power. However, The French Resistance during the Second World War and the mild terrorism of the Luddites or of the Demoiselles (who trampled the fences and laid waste the crops of enclosing landlords in the Ariège during the 1830s and 1840s) illustrate the possibilities. For these various reasons, we should be surprised to discover very many initially powerless groups which accomplished any significant part of their objectives without some involvement in violence.

(4) *It depends on the type of collective action.* Remember the distinctions among competitive, reactive, and proactive pursuit of common goals. The competitive action typically aims for, and typically produces, a test of strength and a minor readjustment of group positions within a local system of power. The European inter-village fight, for example, commonly sprang from the attempt of a lad in village A to court a young woman from village B, commonly pitted the eligible bachelors of both villages against each other, and commonly led either to the abandonment of the suit or to the payment of some form of compensation from B to A. The action is effective in its own terms, but those terms are far removed from national politics.

The reactive form typically aims for the retention of established rights in the face of a challenge. As we examine the tax rebellion, the anti-conscription movement, machine-breaking, food riots, and the like, we uncover many short-run successes: tax payments suspended, young men kept from the draft, and so on. But the record of short-run success needs two important qualifications: first, that the events occurred at all tells us that the rights in question were decaying; second, that they were violent tells us that the routine ways of reminding the powerful of their obligations—through petition, ritual satire, intervention via a patron—were not working. These are signs of a losing battle.

Over the long run, the most we claim for the reactive types of collective action is that they delayed the disappearance of some kinds of popular rights, that they gave some groups a unity and a tactical experience which carried over into other sorts of collective action, and that once in a while —notably in the national revolutions of the nineteenth century—they produced temporary but effective coalitions between large numbers of ordinary people, who were intent on retaining their rights, and small numbers of elites, who were intent on establishing new rights.

The proactive forms also have a mixed record. This time, though, the pattern is more like short-run failure and long-run success. Most individual bids to claim new rights by directly exercising them disintegrated in the face of governmental repression or opposition by other groups. Yet in the countries we have been studying no major political rights came into being without readiness of some portions of those groups to overcome the resistance of the government and of other groups, consequently, without considerable involvement of those groups in collective violence. Coalitions of challengers with holders of power, to be sure, played an important part in the extension of the franchise, the establishment of the right to strike, and so on. They were the work of coalitions, not unilateral gifts. The apparent exceptions—the right to public education, the right to social security, and so on—are generally claims on public services and resources which do not imply any control over public decisions; in any case, they ordinarily come into being as consequences of important transfers of power.

(5) *Repression works.* The business of governments is to maximize their positions with respect to rivals and to maintain the structures of power prevailing within their own domains. Agents of government therefore face a different set of calculations from challengers. They have access to concentrated repressive forces. Despite hopeful liberal mythology to the contrary, furthermore, violent repression works. It works in the short run. It works even better in the long run: so far as we can tell, it is not true that a population beset by consistent tyranny eventually becomes so frustrated that it will do anything to throw off the yoke; in fact, repressed populations demobilize, work through the approved channels of collective action, and seek noncollective means of accomplishing their ends. Repression works in the sense that the imposition of violent penalties—damage or seizure of persons or objects—to collective action diminishes its frequency and intensity. In general, then, the choice of the violent path is much more effective for governments than for challengers.

With all these qualifications, we finally come to the conclusion that in nineteenth- and twentieth century Europe, collective violence often worked. The actions which generated violence, that is, often accomplished some of the stated objectives of the participants. That is especially true of limited, concrete objectives: seizing this shipment of grain, getting rid of this obnoxious official, pushing through this particular wage demand. As the ends become broader, more abstract, and longer-run, the group's capacity to organize, accumulate resources, and form alliances begins to tell more than the willingness of its average number to inflict and endure harm.

The Political Setting

Does the truth of these generalizations vary from one political system to another? We have the impression, though not the proof, that it does.

The most important variable is probably the regime's repressiveness: how expensive it makes collective action for the average nongovernmental contender. Highly repressive regimes increase the likelihood that the group which takes the risk of violence will be wiped out. Under heavy repression, collective action subsides, collective violence subsides, and the effectiveness of those collective actions which do occur, and do generate violence, declines. Under the Nazis it was more effective to pull strings than to organize illegal protests. Highly tolerant regimes also diminish the effectiveness of those collective actions which have considerable probabilities of violence. They do so by multiplying the available paths to any particular objective, thus making the violence-strewn path less attractive. The maximum relative effectiveness of the high-violence path probably falls between the extremes of repression and nonrepression, toward the repressive end of the range. Under relatively repressive regimes few alternative paths to power are open, mobilization is expensive, coalitions with powerful groups are especially valuable. Thus, there is little possibility of a nonviolent success. But there is some hope that the violent alternative will either succeed directly or attract allies who will help assure success.

Other features of a political system besides its repressiveness affect the relative effectiveness of collective violence within the system. In general, reliance on popular elections as a means of determining succession to power is negatively related to repressiveness. Yet equally repressive regimes vary in their reliance on elections. Where elections are both available and effective, they probably tip the balance toward low-violence means. (Remember, we are not saying that binding elections reduce the level of violence in a political system; we are saying they reduce the cost-effectiveness of violence.) Most likely the extent to which the government has monopolized the means of violence likewise reduces the effectiveness of a violent strategy; where many different groups have their own stores of weapons, for example, an approach to power via collective violence is likely to be not only more prevalent but also more effective.

Other variables include the regime's choice of means of repression, the extent to which control over valued resources is concentrated, and the degree to which patronage and coalition-formation are built into the political system. The general formula goes something like this: the relative effectiveness of collective action with a high risk of violence declines as the political system approaches a situation in which any segment of the population involved in that system which articulates a claim has a recognized right to a share of all resources in the system, a share proportionate to the group's size.

On general grounds, we ought also to expect the actual prevalence of collective violence to be low in these circumstances. Whether it is in any particular case, however, will depend on whether there are dissenting minorities which reject the entire system, whether some groups currently have control over extensive means of violence, whether violence gives some kinds of people direct satisfaction, and so on. We conclude with hesitations and qualifications, but we conclude that an approach to democracy diminishes both the effectiveness and the prevalence of collective violence. Since no large political system in the modern world comes very close to the democratic ideal, collective violence remains prevalent and, for some purposes, strategically sound.

Violence and History

We began this discussion with two questions: With respect to the goals of the participants, how effective was the resort to illegal and/or violent means of action? Whether or not they accomplished the goals of the participants, how much difference did violent events make to the course of history? If violence-producing collective action works under some conditions, it is still possible that it makes little difference to the drift of history. In singling out collective violence, have we been dealing with superstructure, epiphenomena, ripples on the surface?

If the answer is yes, it will not affect the main purposes of this book. We are concerned chiefly with learning how large social changes affect collective action. We have simply chosen to use violence as a tracer of collective action. Nevertheless, whether collective violence is an epiphenomenon matters to the users of our results. It matters, first, because it bears on the profound old problem of the cost of revolution. The less impact attributable to the violent actions, presumably the less justification for choosing the violent way. It matters, second, because historians and others who have analyzed the same European experience which this book has surveyed have customarily treated most of the events in question as inconsequential: perhaps symptoms of the big changes, but neither components nor causes of them.

Our own analysis produces a divided verdict: the presence or absence of violence itself makes little difference to the historical outcome, but the collective action which leads to violence is the very stuff of history. The process is like the smelting of iron: iron emerges, but so does slag. All smelting produces some slag, although the quantity and quality depend on both the raw materials and the procedures used. What kind of slag emerges, and how much, does not matter very much to people who are not on the scene; what kind of iron emerges matters a great deal. The connections between iron-smelting and slag are reliable enough for us to trace the smelting process by examining the slag it leaves behind. He who chooses to produce iron also chooses, willy-nilly, to produce slag. That is what we mean by calling collective violence a by-product of the political process. Yet the by-product is so intimately connected with the political process that we can use it to detect what sort of politics is going on.

Concretely, we conclude that it made little historical difference whether a given food riot or demonstration actually resulted in damage to persons or objects. At most, the presence of physical harm polarized the parties a bit more and provided a justification for the next use of force. But over the nineteenth and twentieth centuries the forms of collective action which characteristically led to violence were also the principal means ordinary people had of making known their wants and grievances. Nor is that simple coincidence. To an important degree the damage to objects and, especially, to persons *consisted* of elite reactions to the claims made by ordinary people: troops, police, and thugs acting under instructions from owners and officials attacked demonstrators, strikers, and squatters.

Whether those collective actions—violent or not—occurred did make an historical difference. Groups which did not develop the capacity to strike, to demonstrate, to turn away the tax collector lost power—or never gained it. The cumulative effect of tax rebellions, food riots, or unruly demonstrations helped discredit governments, topple regimes, and bring new coalitions to power. It goes without saying that the new coalitions did not always turn out as the rebels, rioters, and demonstrators desired. Think of the rural rebels who helped Garibaldi take over Sicily in 1860, only to find themselves outflanked by the island's landowners, and in rebellion against the new, unified Italian government. That is why we must distinguish between the effectiveness of collective action from the actors' point of view and its historical significance from the whole population's point of view.

In "history from below" as written by E. J. Hobsbawm, George Rudé, and their followers, we often encounter the idea that the sorts of collective action this book has treated—especially the competitive and reactive forms —were "pre-political," stating grievances and aspirations which the people involved could not form into a coherent analysis, program, and organization. In his *Primitive Rebels*, for example, Hobsbawm takes up social bandits, mafia, rural and urban millenarianism, the city mob, and labor sects. The participants are for the most part ordinary people unknown outside their own immediate circles. "Moreover," he writes, "they are *pre-political* people who have not yet found, or only begun to find, a specific language in which to express their aspirations about the world. Though their movements are thus in many respects blind and groping, by the standards of modern ones, they are neither unimportant nor marginal" (1959: 2).

We have to cavil with this argument. The term "pre-political" is misleading in two regards. First, it implies that the collective actions in question were only tangentially related to the struggle for power. On the contrary, we have found the competitive and reactive forms of collective action to be part and parcel of struggles for power. Second, it suggests that the participants did not know what they were doing, or at least were less aware than are twentieth-century revolutionaries. By contrast, we have uncovered considerable evidence that by their own lights the so-called rioters (not to mention the troops who put them down) were often following a sensible, established procedure. When Hobsbawm speaks of "collective bargaining by riot," he makes exactly that point.

In order to call most competitive and reactive collective action "pre-political," we have to adopt a stringent definition of politics. Politics, in this definition, refers to the pursuit of explicit, long-range programs concerning the distribution and exercise of power at the national or international scale. It probably requires a coherent analysis of the origins of current ills, a vision of the good society, and durable organizations committed to the analysis and the program. In this stringent sense, most of the world's collective action up to our own time has been pre-political, and the proportion of the population involved in politics has risen pro-

digiously since 1800. We concede the need for special labels to call attention to that change. We also insist on the need for terms to remind us of
the struggles for power underlying Hobsbawm's "primitive" rebellions
and our "competitive" and "reactive" ways of acting together.

In short, we emerge more confident of our initial premise. Although
the study of violence itself is not a particularly important pursuit, it leads
easily and profitably to an understanding of collective action. That *is* an
important pursuit. The homely forms of collective action this book has
traced were the principal means by which aggrieved and inspired groups
of ordinary people shaped the European structure of power.

Contemporary Parallels

Our analysis has often carried us close to the present day, but we have
not tried to integrate our conclusions with detailed analyses of today's
conflicts—other people's analyses, or our own. We have tried instead to
use a systematic analysis of European historical experience in criticizing
general ideas which are commonly used in explanations of today's collective violence. In doing so, however, we have reshaped the general ideas
into an argument which could apply elsewhere. Does it?

Surely the most general conclusions apply outside of modern western
European experience. Breakdown theories of collective action and collective violence, so far as we can tell, suffer from irreparable logical and
empirical difficulties. Some sort of solidarity theory should work better
everywhere. No matter where we look, we should rarely find uprooted,
marginal, disorganized people heavily involved in collective violence. All
over the world we should expect collective violence to flow out of routine
collective action and continuing struggles for power. In the present as
well as in the past, we ought to discover the forms of collective action
(hence the forms of collective violence) to be intimately dependent on
the structure of everyday life instead of having a logic, or illogic, all their
own. As a further consequence, we should expect changes in the structure
of everyday life and changes in the structure of power to transform the
character of collective violence. Since breakdown theories of all these
relationships are still being proposed throughout the world, it is some
contribution to have looked critically at their applicability to one significant part of recent experience.

When it comes to our detailed analyses, we have to recognize real limits on their applicability. Take the sequence competitive/reactive/proactive, for example. Treating it as a sequence at all assumes the displacement or absorption of one structure of power by another. It also assumes a middle period in which the two coexist. It may only make sense when the second structure of power is much larger in scale than the first. It assumes a starting point in which the main groups which hold power and contend for power are sets of people in frequent, direct contact with each other; that would be hard to apply to systems in which patron-client networks or dispersed kin groups are major holders of power. All these are plausible assumptions for a Europe in which states, international markets, and sprawling organizations are winning out over villages, guilds, and localized kin groups. Since the same sort of displacement has been going on in other parts of the world, the sequence should not be unique to Europe. But would the disintegration of an empire produce the opposite sequence: proactive/reactive/competitive? If a system of power crystallizes after a period of drastic change, does the sequence run competitive/reactive/proactive/competitive? These searching questions require evidence we do not have.

Furthermore, our analyses assume a limited number of well-defined governments having considerable resources and coercive powers. That is why we can speak of "repressive forces" without great confusion. In a condition of anarchy, perhaps even in a condition of small-scale tribalism, the term—and therefore the analyses attached to the term—would begin to lose its meaning. Our analyses would be hard to apply in the absence of national states. The mapping of the world into mutually exclusive national states is an extraordinary recent experience. Our arguments are not obviously applicable outside our own extraordinary era. In our era, however, most of the world lives in the shadow of well-defined governments and relatively strong states. So there is room for extension of our arguments outside of western Europe.

Within the contemporary world of states, markets, and big organizations, arguments like ours appear to apply quite widely. That includes the contemporary United States. During the frequent episodes of collective violence in the black ghettos of American cities during the 1960s, breakdown theories showered upon us from every direction. One famous example is the report of the Governor's Commission (the "McCone Commission") on the riot in the Watts district of Los Angeles during August 1964. Part of the summary runs:

Yet the riot did happen here, and there are special circumstances here which explain in part why it did. Perhaps the people of Los Angeles should have seen trouble gather under the surface calm. In the last quarter century, the Negro population here has exploded. While the County's population has trebled, the Negro population has increased almost tenfold from 75,000 in 1940 to 650,000 in 1965. Much of the increase came through migration from Southern states and many arrived with the anticipation that this dynamic city would somehow spell the end of life's endless problems. To those who have come with high hopes and great expectations and see the success of others so close at hand, failure brings a special measure of frustration and disillusionment (Governor's Commission 1965: 3–4).

"When the rioting came to Los Angeles," the commissioners concluded, "it was not a race riot in the usual sense. What happened was an explosion—a formless, quite senseless, all but hopeless violent protest—engaged in by a few but bringing great distress to all" (ibid.: 4–5). Pure breakdown theory.

Three years and many ghetto conflicts later, a president's commission on civil disorders (the "Kerner Commission") edged away from the simplest version of breakdown theory. It still described the "basic causes" of the 1967 conflicts as (1) pervasive discrimination and segregation; (2) black migration and white exodus; (3) black ghettos; (4) frustrated hopes; (5) legitimation of violence and erosion of respect for authority; (6) powerlessness; (7) incitement and encouragement of violence by extremists; (8) bad police-civilian relations in the ghetto. These were, to the commissioners' minds, the prime components of an "explosive mixture" which led to a "chain reaction of racial violence" (National Advisory Commission 1968: 206).

As the rest of the report makes clear, the main points the commission wanted to make were that the United States was becoming increasingly and dangerously divided along racial lines, and that blacks really had something to protest about. Nevertheless, the essential *explanation* of ghetto violence they offered was that grievances accumulated, organized protest movements sharpened those grievances, then small incidents were enough to touch off an "explosion."

As the dust settled and evidence accumulated, people began to see the discrepancies between what happened in Watts, Detroit, or elsewhere and theories which emphasized the explosion of accumulated discontent—however the discontent was supposed to have accumulated, and however justified it might be. By 1973 one of the most thoughtful and comprehensive reviews of the literature and the evidence concerning the ghetto conflicts of the 1960s ran like this:

Viewing ghetto riots as politically disruptive acts in a continuing politically motivated struggle between competing vested interest groups on the urban scene . . . seems the most promising and suggestive framework for a comprehensive understanding of recent shifts in the direction of collective violence . . . Violence did not result primarily from the failure of ghetto residents to adjust satisfactorily or normally to the tensions or strains imposed on them in an urban context to which they were unaccustomed. Rather, in the main, collective violence was occasioned by the failure of the existing urban political system to respond adequately to their desires and aspirations, to allow them a proportionate role in the urban structure of power. Ghetto rioting, therefore, reflected an attempted reclamation of political authority over ghetto areas and a type of political recall, not necessarily of specific public officeholders, but of the entire political apparatus that had failed to grant a reasonable share of the political pie to ghetto residents (Feagin and Hahn 1973: 53).

The authors then lay out a rich, broad array of evidence for their strongly political interpretation. Among other things they point out that the great majority of the events began with either police actions (typically white police arresting a black man) which led immediately to reactions from the blacks on the scene, or black "protest activities" which produced some sort of confrontation with authorities and/or the police.

Although they find no typical rioter and suggest that the kinds of people involved change to some extent as the violence proceeds, Feagin and Hahn dispel the idea that participants in collective ghetto violence came disproportionately from the ghetto's marginal, depressed, disorganized populations. They bring out the selectivity of attacks on stores and other property. They conclude that the police and the National Guard did almost all the killing. Finally, they emphasize the extent to which injustice and discrimination (rather than, say, absolute or relative material hardship) dominated the complaints of people in the areas which experienced major conflicts.

The character and extent of group organization among participants in the collective violence remains unclear. It seems as though the people involved resemble our food rioters or tax rebels more than our militant demonstrators: drawn in clusters from well-defined local populations, but not called into action by specific formal associations. In other regards the evidence concerning violent conflicts in American ghettos during the 1960s are consistent with out treatment of collective violence as a political by-product. The pronouncements of the American authorities sound a good deal like the pronouncements of nineteenth-century European authorities who had to interpret the protests of workers and villagers. And the role of the repressive forces is familiar, all too familiar.

The observations apply beyond the ghetto. Many recent studies of American urban conflicts have converged on a treatment of "protest" as a form of bargaining. Michael Lipsky has summed up the idea in the phrase "protest as a political resource." In his study of New York City rent strikes during the 1960s, Lipsky makes a strong case that the strike movement owed what success it had (which was not enormous) to the fact that dramatic protests activated powerful third parties who then put pressure on the responsible authorities to respond to the grievances of the protestors.

Peter Eisinger followed up Lipsky's line of thought by examining all "protests" reported in forty-three American cities during six months of 1968. "Protests" were "marches, sit-ins, demonstrations, pickets, protest meetings or rallies, and any other incidents which might possibly be construed as collective protest" (1973: 16) Eisinger found 120 reports of such incidents with enough information to analyze. From an analysis of the relation between frequency and intensity of protest to characteristics of the forty-three cities, he concludes that "the incidence of protest is mildly related to the nature of a city's political opportunity structure, which I have conceived as a function of the degree to which groups are likely to be able to gain access to power and to manipulate the political system" (ibid.: 25). Studies of this sort are still scattered and primitive. For now, the evidence accumulating from them minimizes the importance of breakdown and maximizes the importance of struggles for power.

The same goes for the few systematic, longitudinal studies we have of American conflicts. The most comprehensive investigation so far is one conducted by William Gamson. Instead of following events, as we have,

Gamson has followed American "challenging groups" which made bids for power of one kind or another between 1800 and 1945. He argues that the American political system is a relatively (but not completely) closed one, in which only groups which are able to make a considerable show of strength and/or to establish strong coalitions with existing powerholders can themselves accomplish their ends.

Gamson's preliminary findings support and refine that view. By "success" he means public acceptance of the group's existence and/or the group's acquisition of new advantages; the two are closely related. Successful challengers, according to Gamson's analysis, tended to have goals which did *not* require displacing other groups from power and which were concentrated on a single issue; they tended to be large, bureaucratic, and centralized; they tended to offer selective incentives to their members instead of relying on diffuse solidarity. Most interesting from our point of view, groups which were passive recipients of violence had a high rate of failure, but those which engaged actively in deliberate physical injury to persons or property had a high rate of success. For reasons we have already explored, the simple comparison does not prove that violence breeds success. Yet it is certainly consistent with our observations concerning France, Germany, and Italy.

Finally, recent quantitative international studies of collective violence have cast a few glimmers on our problem. The comparison of many countries over a narrow period of time has some serious disadvantages. It tends to group together evidence of highly variable quality and origin, emanating from rather different reporting procedures in the various countries. It is vulnerable to the peculiarities of the time period; within our single countries, at least, we have seen the geographic pattern of collective violence changing radically and rapidly as the issues changed and the national struggle for power shifted. If we are to make inferences concerning the effects of structural change, we must either draw them from changes over short periods or assume that the countries represent different points in the same progression—for example, that poor countries are now where rich countries used to be. Within these limits, the big cross-national studies have begun to yield intriguing results.

For example, Douglas Hibbs's analysis of data from 108 countries from 1948 through 1967 distinguishes *collective protest* (riots, antigovernment demonstrations, and political strikes) from *internal war* (deaths from political violence, armed attacks, assassinations). In his summary model for 1958–1967, the standardized partial regression coefficients run:

collective protest

+.516   negative sanctions by government in same decade
—.126   energy consumed per capita, 1955–1965
+.169   Communist Party membership
+.190   group discrimination as of 1960
—.378   presence or absence of a Communist regime;

internal war

+.824   negative sanctions by government in same decade
—.491   negative sanctions by government in previous decade
+.163   political separatism as of 1960
—.279   presence or absence of a Communist regime.

There are other variables in the statistical background. The remarkable thing about the central variables in the whole analysis is their essentially political character. The only variable in this list which is not immediately and obviously related to struggles for political power is energy consumption. After much worrying of the data, Hibbs finds a weak tendency for countries consuming more energy (which are generally richer countries) to have lower levels of protest. Despite Hibbs's inclusion of such items as rates of population growth, changes in GNP, and welfare indexes in his statistical analyses, the sturdy survivors of his analyses refer to the political structures of the regimes and the operation of repression.

At least as interesting is the broadly similar sort of analysis carried out by Ted Gurr. As recently as 1970, Gurr published a much-discussed book whose main argument emphasized "relative deprivation" as the fundamental cause of collective violence. On the whole, the book gave special credit to breakdown explanations of relative deprivation. This passage conveys the book's tone:

Exposure to a new way of life or to ideologies depicting a golden millennium seldom themselves generate either dissatisfaction or new expectations. But to the extent that men are already discontented and see opportunities open to them to attain those goals . . . they are strongly susceptible to ideological conversion. An especially violent, often revolutionary response is likely when men who have been persistently deprived of valued goods and conditions of life are led to believe that their government is about to remedy that deprivation, but then find the hopes false . . . Once socioeconomic change is underway within any segment of a society, other processes become operative. If a number of groups experience value gains, the most rapidly gaining groups are most likely to be chosen as the reference groups by which other men set their expectations (1970: 121).

The analysis attributes individual anger to discontinuities and disappointed expectations, then leaps easily from individual anger to group action.

We disagree with both steps of the argument, especially the second. But our concern here is with the results of the analysis. In his most detailed and comprehensive quantitative investigation (Gurr and Duval 1973), Gurr studies "conflict events" in eighty-six countries from 1961 through 1965. Conflict events include riots, political demonstrations, general strikes, political clashes, localized uprisings, plots, coups, terrorism, civil war, and some other related forms of collective action. The list of variables which, in various compounds, carry the main explanatory weight in his statistical analyses is as follows:

—proportion of population subject to economic discrimination
—proportion of population subject to political discrimination
—number of major religious bodies
—proportion of population politically separatist
—intensity of political separatism
   negative net factor payments abroad as percentage of gross domestic
      product
—short-term trend in export value, 1950 to 1961–1965
—declines from short-term trends in export value, 1961–1965
—defense expenditures as percentage of gross national product
—number of negative government sanctions, 1958–1960
—durability of regime as of 1960
—relative scope and success of internal wars, 1850–1960
—frequency and success of coups, 1900–1960
—recency of last military intervention in civil politics as of 1960
—union opposition status, 1955–1965.

There is no need to discuss the details of these variables or the ingenious ways that Gurr and Duval put them together. The main point is the nature of the list. As compared with Hibbs's list, Gurr's puts more stress on economic performance and, especially, exploitation. Nonetheless, the variables are overwhelmingly power variables. Political conflict turns out to require explanations based solidly on the structure and change of political power.

We do not claim for a moment that the work of Hibbs and Gurr supports the specific arguments we have advanced in this book. We have not stated the arguments in a way that *could* be tested directly through cross-national analyses of the Hibbs-Gurr variety. We do claim that the international comparisons, as well as the studies of American violence, are reducing the credibility of most breakdown theories as they increase the credibility of some solidarity and political-process theories. That is happening in two main ways: through increasing doubt that the sum of individual changes in attitude produced by structural change accounts directly for much of the ebb and flow of protest, conflict, collective violence, or collective action, as compared with increasing confidence that the people whose behavior has to be accounted for are organized contenders for power; and through accumulating evidence that the structure and dynamics of political power themselves account for patterns and fluctuations of protest, conflict, collective violence, and collective action. The next step, we believe, is to introduce explicit models of the structure of power, and explicit statements of the rights and obligations of the participants, into the analysis.

Back to Political Theory

Something interesting has happened in this discussion. It happens every time we start to analyze "protest" and "violence." Despite the ostensibly unpolitical, disorderly character of protest and violence, their careful study drives us back to the analysis of rights and political organization. It drives us back to standard questions of political theory. What difference to the satisfaction of collective aspirations do the form and extent of representation make? What sorts of political arrangements provide the best defense against tyranny? What are inalienable rights, and how do they come into being?

No need to misunderstand. We do not mean that the analysis of protest and violence *answers* the standard questions. We mean that analysis of protest and violence eventually drives us back to considering the same

phenomena that concern political philosophy, and then to seeing something fundamental: ordinary people engaged in apparently trivial, ineffectual, or self-serving actions such as the tax riot are actually participating in the great debates over political right and obligation.

Through the earlier part of the period we have been analyzing, most
ordinary people grouped and acted around the theory that small social
units such as households and communities had a prior collective right to
the resources they accumulated and produced. That included land, labor,
capital, food, and symbolic objects as well. They struggled with others
who grouped and acted around the theory that the welfare of a state and/
or of its population should take priority over the welfare of any segment
of it, but who typically also held that the general welfare would be served
by the individual pursuit of self-interest. Among these nationalists—conservatives, liberals, and socialists alike—great divisions developed over
how to articulate the national interest, about who should decide what the
national interest was. Over the longer run, some branch of the nationalists
generally won.

In this day, when bigness and nationalism are such evident curses, it is
easy to side with the localists. We easily fancy ourselves clenching fists
and lining up against the merchant, the tax collector, the recruiting
sergeant. Wouldn't it be a better world if they had all lost decisively?
Better still if they had never come?

Of that, we are not confident. Like Marx, we think a parochial world
is a stifling world. Like Marx, we think that the logic of some form of
world economy organized around industrial production and large capital
accumulations was already in motion well before the nineteenth century.
Like Marx, we think that the world knit together in the wrong way, but
that it had to knit together. Our problem today is to transform a single
world of war and injustice into a single world of peace and justice. The
corresponding historical problem is to explain how our world of war and
injustice came into being, and perhaps to decide what other paths were
open.

Measured by that huge historical challenge, this book is tiny. It has,
we think, given some documented reasons for doubting that the stresses
and strains of industrialization directly impelled Europeans to protest
and destroy. It has questioned whether the breakdown of social control
and the dissolution of interpersonal bonds, however they happen, en-

gender mass violence. It has given some documented reasons for thinking that European collective violence was a by-product of struggles for power, that the extent and character of the violence depended strongly on the reactions of governments to the claims being made by different contenders for power, and that the active contenders—hence the active participants in collective violence—stood out from the rest of the population by virtue of their degree of organization, their orientation to shared standards of right and obligation, their collective control of politically significant resources. It has indicated how urbanization, industrialization, and the concentration of power in states shaped the contenders and set the conditions for power struggles. It has sketched how the major forms of collective action changed in Italy, Germany, and France as the rebellious century moved on. It has offered tentative explanations of the changes.

We have left, for others and for ourselves, the really large tasks: to trace how the particular structures of power and of government which Europeans fashioned for themselves affected the collective action of ordinary people; to say how else it could have happened; to draw conclusions for the political course which is still before us.

APPENDIX A

A Rough Chronology of Collective Violence in France, 1830–1960

1830   After few, small, and scattered disturbances during the first half of the year, the July Revolution in Paris, with immediate repercussions in Nantes, Bordeaux, Toulouse, Nimes, and a few other places; later tax rebellions, food riots, workers' protests, and violent demonstrations in many parts of France.

1831   Continuation of smaller disturbances, many attacks on machines (e.g., St. Etienne, Bordeaux, Toulouse), multiple violent demonstrations in Paris and a few other big cities, silk workers' insurrection in Lyon.

1832   Major rebellions in Paris; minor ones in a number of other cities; food riots in the East and Southwest, large Legitimist protests at several points in the South, and an even larger Legitimist insurrection through important parts of the West.

1834   Silk workers' rebellion in Lyon, with significant responses in St. Etienne and Paris.

1839–   Frequent food riots, invasions of forests, several large conflicts in
1840   Paris, notably the abortive Insurrection of the Seasons (May 1839).

1841   Tax rebellions and closely related resistance to the census, concentrated in the Southwest.

1846–   Widespread food riots and similar conflicts in a semicircle around
1847   Paris.

1848   February Revolution (especially Paris, but with a much wider response elsewhere than in 1830), continued rioting and agitation up to the June Days; attacks on machines and railroads, resistance to tax collectors, anti-Semitic violence, attacks on convents and chateaux throughout many parts of France.

1849–   Tax rebellions (the Forty-Five-Centime Revolt), forest disorders,
1850   and similar small-scale events; recurrent fighting between government forces and demonstrators, including one serious attempt at a coup, in Paris and a few other cities.

1851   Armed resistance to Louis Napoleon's coup in almost a third of France's departments.

1869–   Major strikes, leading to battles with police and troops, worst at
1870   St. Etienne and Aubin.

1870–   Insurrection in Alsace, revolution after the French defeat at Sedan
1871   beginning in Paris, with strong responses in Lyon and Marseille; further disturbances during and after the seige of Paris, followed by the Commune; similar but smaller rebellions in Marseille, Lyon, Toulouse, Limoges, Le Creusot, St. Etienne.

1880   Numerous violent strikes.

1891–   Many violent strikes and much terrorism attributed to Anarchists,
1894   including the assassination of President Carnot in Lyon, 1894.

1900–   Turbulent, insurrectionary strikes in Belfort, Montceau-les-Mines,
1901   Marseille, and elsewhere.

1906–   Many violent strikes, involving struggles with troops or retaliation
1907   against nonstrikers and bosses; winegrowers' protests in the South.

1911   More violent confrontations of strikers, nonstrikers, owners, troops.

1919– Attempted general strikes and national workers' demonstrations lead-
1920   ing to fights with troops, police, other workers.

1934– Large demonstrations of both right and left leading to frequent
1935   clashes among demonstrators, counterdemonstrators and forces of
       order; attempted general strikes, violent meetings of peasant organ-
       izations.

1936– Great sit-down strikes, clashes between adherents of political ex-
1937   tremes, particularly Communists and extreme right-wing organiza-
       tions.

1944   Extensive Resistance activity, including a few large demonstrations
       and strikes.

1947– Violent resistance to fiscal controls; frequent rioting and conflicts
1948   with police based on protest demonstrations and on meetings of
       political extremes; insurrectionary strikes, including the occupation
       of railroad stations and public buildings, throughout France.

1950– Numerous clashes beginning with strikes, demonstrations, or political
1952   meetings, focusing on French and American foreign policies (e.g.,
       violent demonstrations against Eisenhower in 1951), coupled with
       bombings and other terrorism directed mainly against Communists.

1955– Turbulent meetings, demonstrations, and street battles, featuring
1956   Poujadists and partisans of various policies in Algeria.

1958   Coups in Algeria and Corsica, attempted coups elsewhere followed
       by street battles in Paris and other cities, eventuating in De Gaulle's
       coming to power.

APPENDIX B

A Rough Chronology of Collective Violence in Italy, 1830–1960

1831   Parma, Modena, Bologna and elsewhere in Papal States: revolt.

1837   Naples (Cosenza, Salerno, Avellino, Abruzzi) and Sicily (Syracuse, Catania, Messina). Cholera epidemic disorders led to attempted takeover by liberals.

1843   Romagna: attempted insurrection in Savigno.

1844   Cosenza (Calabria): liberal plotters and invasion.

Bandiera expedition, inspired by news of the Cosenza uprising.

1845   Romagna: Rimini revolt.

1846   Lombardy: protest over bread prices.

1847   Sicily: attempted mutiny (Messina). Demonstrations and riots Palermo and elsewhere.

1848–   Sicily: January 12–13 revolution in Palermo, followed by
1849   other Sicilian cities.

Naples: constitution granted; counterrevolution in May.

Milan: March "Cinque Giorni."

Venice: March 1848 Revolution.

Rome: Republic set up in February 1849.

Besides these events in the capitals, the period is studded with strikes, land invasions, demonstrations concerned with food.

1851   Palermo: bakers' "mutiny" against lowering of wages.

1853   Milan: Mazzinian plot and attempted insurrection. "I Barabba."

        Lombardy, Piedmont, Papal States: protest over bread prices, grain shipments.

1855   Belfiore (Venice): attempted insurrection.

1856   Corleone (Sicily), Genoa, Livorno: insurrectionary attempts.

1859   Tuscany, Modena, Parma: "peaceful revolutions" during Piedmontese Austrian war; countermoves by reactionary popular groups.

        Papal States: popular demonstrations.

1860   Carrara: food protest.

        Palermo: urban revolt followed by peasant protest.

        Sicily: land occupations, attacks on landlords.

        Apulia: popular resistance to attempted anti-Bourbon revolt.

        Basilicata: peasant protest, mostly in support of Bourbon regime.

        Napoletana: peasant demonstrations against annexation.

1861– South, especially Basilicata, but in other mountainous areas,
1863   also: brigandage and counterrevolution.

        Sicily: continued occasional land seizures.

1862   Sicily: demonstrations, riots.

1863   Naples: government workers "mutiny" against wage cuts.

Turin: violent demonstrations on occasion of removal of capital to Florence.

1864   Sicily: tax protests.

1865   Sicily (Palermo): riot over selling of confiscated church property.

Arpino (Lazio): machine-breaking by unemployed wool workers.

1866   Sicily (Palermo): "Seven and a half Revolt."

1866–   Lunigiana: series of demonstrations and land invasions protesting
1868   the sale of common land.

1868–   Macinato Revolt: urban demonstrations in early 1868 in Turin,
1869   Pavia, Leghorn, Milan, Pistoia, Bologna.

Rural disorders near Verona, in Lombardy, Piedmont, Veneto, Emilia, Marches, Abruzzi, Calabria in December. Attacks on municipal buildings, mills, demonstrations, and riots continued into 1869.

1870   Pavia, Piacenza, Bologna, Volterra, Genoa, Lucca, Reggio, Carrara, Milan: Republican insurrections or attempts.

1871   Lombardy: agricultural strikes with violence.

1872   Lombardy, Emilia: violent strikes of rice workers.

1873   Pisa: violent textile strike.

1874   Tuscany, Emilia-Romagna: bread riots and price-setting.

Bologna-Taranto: Bakunin-inspired insurrection.

1875   Lombardy (Milan, Pavia): agricultural strikes.

1876   Apulia, Sicily, Lombardy: scattered protest against taxes.

1877   Benevento-San Lupo: another Bakunin-inspired insurrection.

1878   Monte Labro (Tuscany) : Lazzarettist insurrection.

Naples, Florence, Pisa: anarchist violence.

Rome: anticlerical riots.

1879   Carrara: violence over economic crisis.

1880–   Po Valley: violent agricultural strikes and demonstrations in
1885   Cremona and Parma regions, 1882; Verona region, 1883; the
Polesine, 1884; Mantovano, 1885 ("La Boje" Revolt).

1889   Rome: large strike of masons.

Lombardy (Upper Milanese, Como, and Varese) : Strikes of textile
workers and agricultural workers with violence.

1890   Ravenna area: large violent strike among day laborers in rice.

1891   Rome, Florence, Milan, Bologna: anti-French violent demonstrations.

1893–   Sicily: Sicilian Fasci demonstrations and repression.
1894

1894   Massa-Carrara: insurrectionary attempt.

1896   Milan and elsewhere: violent demonstrations protesting war.

1898   Ancona, Sicily: protest against high bread prices and taxes.

Naples and central Italy: spread of protest.

Milan, Pavia, Florence: April–May, protest demonstrations and
violence.

1901–   Apulia, Sardinia: agricultural strikes, violence.
1906

1906–   Violent strikes in northern industrial areas.
1907

1910–   Po Valley: agricultural strikes, occasionally violent.
1913

Northern industrial area: violent strikes.

1914   Marches and Romagna: June 7–14, Red Week.

Demonstrations at the news of the death of Jaurès.

Agricultural strikes and battles of strikers and strikebreakers.

1915   Radiant Days of May. Prowar demonstrations.

1917   Turin: "Fatti di Agosto" general strike and insurrection.

1919   Milan: Fascist-socialist clashes.

Emilia, Romagna, Tuscany, Marches, also South: food price protest.

1919–   Lazio and South: land occupations; also in Cremona area.
1920

1920   Milan, Sienna, Romagna: anarchist, Fascist, socialist violence.

Naples: sit-down strike.

Ancona: mutiny.

Bari: agricultural strike with violence.

Turin, Milan, elsewhere: factory occupations.

1921   North and center: Fascist violence.

1922   North and center: March–July, Fascist assassinations, attacks.

July–August. Alleanza del Lavoro attempt at general strike, further wave of Fascist violence.

1924–   Fascist government installed; Fascist violence continued.
1926

1943–   North: CLN movement.
1945

1947   Sicily: Labor strife.

1948   Rome, Genoa, Turin, Milan: attempted assassination of Togliatti
       led to strike and street fighting.

1949– Calabria and Po Valley: labor strife in cities, land
1950   occupations in South.

1959   Florence: factory occupation.

1960   Genoa: socialist-communist, and neo-fascist MSI fights. Nationwide
       demonstrations, violence, general strike.

APPENDIX C

A Rough Chronology of Political Protest and Collective Violence in Germany, 1815–1933

1817   Wartburg Festival: student-dominated demonstration.

1818–   Student rioting in several universities.
1819

1819   Anti-Semitic riots in Hamburg, Frankfurt am Main, Würzburg, Karlsruhe, and smaller places.

1830   Rioting, revolts, and rebellion in many parts of Germany, August–November. Anti-tax, anti-administration, food, and workers' riots, especially in Saxony, Hessen, Braunschweig, and Hannover.

1831   Anti-tax and anti-police riots throughout the year, especially in Saxony, Hessen, and Hannover (Insurrection in Göttingen).

1832   Considerable unrest, especially in Hessen and the Palatinate. Hambacher Festival: huge anti-aristocratic, nationalistic demonstration in Palatinate.

1835   "Fireworks Revolt" of Berlin journeymen spurs enactment of riot laws for Prussia.

1837– Catholics riot against government intervention in "church affairs"
1839   in Rhineland, Westphalia, and Posen.

1844   Outbreak of labor unrest. Weavers' Revolt in Silesia.

1845– Escalation of violence throughout Germany. Labor unrest and
1847   religious riots eclipsed in 1847 by exceptionally bitter and widespread food riots.

1848– March Revolution, especially in Berlin and Munich, but spreading
1849   throughout Germany with much unrest. Near-civil war situation in Posen and Baden in 1848, and in Baden, the Palatinate, and Rhineland-Westphalia in May 1849.

1850– Much violence in territories occupied by Prussian, Austrian, and
1851   Bavarian troops. Wave of arrests of radicals, especially in Prussia.

1866   Rioting against conscription in Prussia, and subsequently against military presence in other parts of Germany.

1869   Outburst of labor violence in many parts of Germany.

1873   Massive bloody riots protesting beer prices, especially in Frankfurt am Main.

1874   Flurry of Catholic riots against Prussian *Kulturkampf*.
1875

1881   Anti-Semitic riots in eastern Prussia, especially Pomerania.

1889   Violent miners' strikes in Ruhr and Silesia.

1890   Large clashes between socialist workers and police in Berlin.

1901   Polish riots against Prussian school policies in Posen.

1909– Increased number of violent strikes, high points bloody strikes in
1913   Berlin, 1910, in Ruhr, 1912.

1913   Anti-Prussian riots in Zabern, Alsace (November).

1914   July. Massive socialist antiwar demonstrations in many cities.

1915   Bread and Peace demonstrations in Essen and Berlin.

1917   Late-summer bread riots in Bavaria, Silesia, Stettin, and Düsseldorf; mutiny in North Sea Fleet.

1918   Spring and Summer riots hindering troop movements to front, especially in Bavaria.

1918   November. Mutiny of Fleet at Kiel leading to successful revolution in Kiel and spreading to Lübeck, Hamburg, and throughout Germany. Socialist revolution in Munich. Provisional government puts down right-wing military putsch attempt in Berlin.

1919   January. Spartacus Revolt in Berlin (lynching of Rosa Luxembourg and Karl Liebknecht); communist revolts in many German cities; general strike and street fighting against military putsch in Berlin and Ruhr. Reich troops crush revolutionary government in Munich.

1920   Kapp putsch in Berlin; "Ruhr Army" revolt.

1921   Strikes and communist revolts, especially in Saxony, Hamburg, and the Ruhr.

1922   Nazi disturbances in Bavaria; riots and political demonstrations all over Germany.

1923   Separatist riots in Rhineland; Nazi Beer Hall putsch in Munich; Communist putsch attempts in Hamburg and Saxony.

1929   May Day riots in Berlin.

1930   Violent strikes in Mansfeld mining area.

1931–   Period of great violence with much street fighting all over Germany
1933   and especially in Berlin; related to political demonstrations and to strikes.

APPENDIX D

Sources and Procedures

In general, our analyses have three elements: a series of collective actions; a set of social structures within which the actions take place; a political process linking the one to the other. We try to verify or falsify the analyses through reliable evidence collected independently for each of the three elements. The evidence and the use we make of it usually fall short of decisive proof, but that is the aim. In this book the chief collective actions for which we use continuous observations over considerable blocks of time and space are violent, with less extensive treatments of strike activity and fragmentary discussions of other forms of nonviolent collective action such as meetings and demonstrations. Elsewhere (e.g. Shorter and Tilly 1974) nonviolent actions are often the main focus of our studies. The violent events analyzed systematically in this book exclude military actions in which civilians played no direct part; actions outside of France, Germany, and Italy (even if Frenchmen, Germans, or Italians took part); and conflicts taking place entirely within total institutions such as prisons or garrisons. They include actions in which at least one formation (a group acting together) above a certain size—twenty or more in Germany, fifty or more in Italy and France—took part, and in which at least one group seized or damaged persons or objects not belonging to itself. Our general approach was to search for sources which mentioned such events in a fairly uniform manner over substantial areas and time spans, to attempt to identify the sampling bias of each source, to abstract the accounts of all such events from the sources, to seek supplementary information concerning the same events elsewhere, and then to code the resulting dossier into a standard machine-readable form.

Although the chapters on Germany, Italy, and France contain a wide variety of observations on social structure, the largest bodies of data we assembled in this category were aggregate observations of population characteristics for major political divisions: most often *Länder* in Germany, *compartimenti* in Italy, *départements* in France. These we frequently found in census reports and similar publications, and likewise transcribed in machine-readable form. A number of the quantitative analyses behind the three single-country chapters consist of relating the collective actions taking place in a given set of areas during a particular period to the social characteristics of those same areas at that time—that is, of meshing parts of the two sets of evidence.

For our third element, the political process, our observations are less comprehensive and reliable. Although we have used some national-level time series on political activity and have done some close studies of the organization and mobilization of particular groups and events, through most of this book our characterizations of political processes depend on scholarly consensus or our own interpretation of the sources. Which is to say, they contain a larger share of judgment than the observations of collective action and social structure.

Other detailed discussions of our sources and methods appear in Rule and Tilly 1965; Shorter and Tilly 1974; Snyder 1974; Snyder and Tilly 1972, 1973, 1974; C. Tilly 1969b, 1972c, 1974d; L. Tilly 1972; R. Tilly 1970.

France

Our systematic observations of France cover the years from 1830 through 1960. For the years from 1830 to 1860 and 1930 to 1960 we enumerated the events to be studied by scanning two daily national newspapers completely for every day of publication. In the earlier period, the four newspapers most commonly used were *Le Constitutionnel, Le Moniteur, Le Siècle,* and *Le Droit.* In the later period, they were *Le Temps, Le Monde,* the *Journal des Débats,* and *Combat.* For the period from 1861 through 1929, we read two daily national newspapers for each day of three randomly drawn months per year, including all events reported in those issues regardless of whether they occurred during the month in question, and multiplying the results obtained by four to represent the missing months.

Once we had identified the reported events which met our criteria, we searched elsewhere for further information concerning the events in the sample. That is least true for 1861–1929; there we consulted some secondary sources, but relied heavily on the newspaper accounts. In the earlier and later periods, we often found supplementary information in a third newspaper or a specialized periodical such as the *Gazette des Tribunaux*. We searched historical publications—books and articles—for details of all events from 1830 to 1860 and from 1930 to 1960. For the first three decades we also did an extensive search of French archives: examining the documents for every one of our events mentioned in the inventories of Archives Nationales series BB[18] and BB[30], making an extensive search of Archives Nationales F[7] and less complete studies of other series in departmental and national archives. For the period after 1929 we did some exploring of documents in departmental archives, but none of the relevant and available series were sufficiently rich for a systematic study.

In this further search, when we encountered appropriate events we had not identified in the newspapers (either because we missed them or because the newspapers did not report them), we prepared reports, but did *not* add them to our samples. Sometimes, however, we discovered that according to our rules two events we had originally enumerated separately were actually the same event, or an event we had recorded consisted of two or more separate events; in that case we changed the enumeration. In fact, we rarely encountered clearly qualifying events involving one hundred people or more which were not already in our samples. Such comparisons as we have made with the main archival series and with existing studies of French regions lead us to two conclusions: first, that our samples are biased toward events involving more than one hundred people, events occurring in Paris and other large cities, and events of manifest significance to national politics; second, that the newspaper scanning provides a more comprehensive and uniform sample of events than any alternative source available to us.

Using the evidence thus assembled, we prepared a machine-readable record for each event in the sample. For events from 1830 to 1860 and from 1930 to 1960 we actually produced two sets of records: (1) a detailed coding of each event, which typically filled eight or ten eighty-column punched cards with numerical data, plus another ten with alphabetic commentary; (2) an even more detailed coding of each event we estimated to involve a thousand or more person-days of participation plus a systematic tenth of the remaining events, which typically filled ten to twenty numerical cards and a somewhat large number of alphabetic cards. From 1861 through 1929 we settled for summary coding of all events in a format which typically produced a half-dozen cards for an event. Most of the actual analysis of these files was done on large, high-speed electronic computers with greatly condensed tape or disk versions of the files. The basic machine-readable files are being made available to scholars through the Historical Archive of the Inter-University Consortium for Political Research. We are preparing documentation containing details on coding procedures, reliabilities, and sources.

In tabulations on France in this volume which refer to the full set of events (for example the over-time correlations with number of participants in collective violence), we have estimated missing data at the decade mean for that item. That is not so serious as it sounds, since in most decades we had enough information to make an estimate of the number of participants in more than nine-tenths of all events.

We have assembled and analyzed a great deal of other information concerning France in machine-readable form. The largest files include demographic, economic, and political descriptions of cities, arrondissements, and departments at multiple points in the nineteenth and twentieth centuries; reports of charges and convictions for criminal activity by department for a number of points in the nineteenth century; information on every strike for which we could find an individual record from 1830 through 1967; standard descriptions of 11,616 persons arrested for participating in the June Days of 1848; departmental summaries of the 26,000-odd arrests in the insurrection of 1851; and a time-series file containing observations of a wide variety of characteristics for France as whole in single years from 1830 through 1968. Only a small portion of this information comes directly into view in Chapter II.

Italy

The basic nineteenth-century data for the chapter on Italy were a series of more or less uniform reports on violent events meeting essentially the same criteria as those used in enumerating the sample of French conflicts. The format of these reports called for recording date, place, participants, type of event, and whatever additional material could be gathered. The reports were drawn mainly from Alfredo Comandini, *L'Italia nel cento anni del secolo XIX* (1918). This book, full of helter-skelter detail, has entries for each month of the century. It was compiled in the early twentieth century from contemporary newspapers, official gazettes, and miscellaneous other publications. A wide variety of information is gathered together in it, but political events and the lives of important people predominate. Only occasionally is the original source mentioned. Leonetti's *Mouvements ouvriers et socialistes* (1952), Candeloro's multivolume *Storia dell'Italia moderna* (1966–1970), and Del Carria, *Proletari senza rivoluzione* (1966) were used to cover the twentieth century.

These sources are much more heterogeneous than the comprehensive newspaper coverage used for the other chapters, so the monographic literature was used not only to complete and fill out descriptions but to make the list of events itself more complete. The Italian reports were not coded and analyzed by computer. Our reports are adequate to spell out main lines of the chronology of collective action in Italy. Small-scale disturbances and disturbances in small towns were surely undercounted, however, and questions about trends in scale are simply unanswerable. Any claims to complete coverage or attempts at fine analysis will have to wait for a more broadly based chronology.

Amassing the evidence for Italy presented some different problems than for France. Distinctions among war, revolution, and routine political conflict, relatively easy to maintain in the case of modern France, swam before our eyes as we examined Italy since 1830. In France we had to worry about the periods of the Franco-Prussian War and World War II, but not much more. But in Italy, how to treat a Piedmontese invasion of Lombardy? Mazzini's repeated stabs at insurrection? Garibaldi's invasion of Sicily? What we did was to be generous in our definitions of conflicts worth examining.

The regional fragmentation of Italian politics—both before and after the theoretical Unification—fragmented the evidence as well. Where the student of France can dig into national archives, national newspapers, and the residues of national bureaucracies, his Italian counterpart must deal with a multiplicity of governmental remains, newspapers, archives. Furthermore, Italian scholars have not gone far in providing the solid documentation on social change, region by region, needed to address serious basic questions about conflict and structural change. A high proportion of Italian scholarship has gone into thinly documented debate over such questions as Gramsci's *rivoluzione mancata:* did the nineteenth-century statemakers stifle a social revolution aborning? As a consequence, even the monographic evidence we had to call on was scattered and incomplete.

Our strategy, therefore, was to focus on periods and events which left more than the usual amount of evidence behind them: the period of national unification, especially the 1850s and 1860s; the 1880s and 1890s with the coming of industrialization; and the years after World War I, when the Fascist movement formed and eventually came to power. In each of these periods, geographic and temporal comparisons of political disturbances were emphasized. Our purpose was not to construct convincing descriptions and explanations of these crises, but to ask what they tell us about the supposed relation between collective violence and large-scale structural change.

Germany

The quantitative evidence discussed in Chapter IV derives largely from an inventory of reports on disturbances of the peace involving twenty or more persons taken from two daily newspapers: for 1816–1871 the *Augs-burger Allgemeine Zeitung,* and for 1871–1913 the *Kölnische Zeitung.* For technical reasons the coverage of the years 1897–1899 is very poor. For many years, moreover, events have been reconstructed out of other sources, even if not reported in the newspapers, as long as sufficient information enabling comparison with the rest of our sample was available. Our sample, that is, is not purely a newspaper sample. Both newspapers offer for their periods fairly comprehensive national coverage. A comparison with other sources—news-papers, archives, and monographs—for certain regions, years, and types of events revealed a number of gaps. In particular, our newspapers showed a tendency to overlook and underreport small-scale, rural disturbances. They also tended to report briefly and somewhat superficially. Nevertheless, for the purpose of gathering a comprehensive, systematic, and quantifiable sample, the newspapers were probably the best over-all source. Other sources—government archival materials, for example—have deficiencies of their own* and a more comprehensive sample than ours would doubtless cost considerably more in time, money, and effort. Two things are clear, how-ever: first, that further research can enlarge the present sample (which con-tains at the moment nearly one thousand events for the 1815–1913 period); and second, that local and central government archival materials will remain indispensable for detailed, fine analysis.

Our quantitative sample defines collective violence as a disturbance of the peace within an autonomous political system (German states excluding Austria) involving physical violence or damage to persons or property by at least twenty persons.

The twenty-person threshold is empirically derived. Our hunch as we began researching this question in Germany was that twenty persons divided small-scale nonpolitical violence of the barroom brawl type from collective political challenges often enough to warrant its use as a general criterion. In the course of further observation it became difficult to change; moreover, the discovery was made that the number twenty had legal significance. Not only was the twenty the standard maximum for public gatherings allowed by the siege laws, but under Rhenish penal law at least members of crowds of twenty persons or more could be prosecuted for "revolt," rather than for mere disturbance of the peace (Dowe 1970; Venedey 1831). In fact, how-

---

* See R. Tilly 1970 for some examples—which could be multiplied.

ever, our sample contains only a small number of events involving twenty, thirty, or forty members, so that the difference between our lower threshold and that used for the French evidence (fifty) should not be overweighted.

In determining whether an event reported in newspapers "belonged" to our sample or not, direct quantitative estimates pertaining to the crowd, or to the repressive forces sent against it, as well as more qualitative or indirect evidence (the words "huge mob," the area involved, duration, kinds of government reactions reported, and so on) were employed. Estimating long-term trends in crowd size is problematical, however. In the first place, crowd estimates by contemporary observers tended to vary with the political persuasion, the physical location, and the experience of the observer as well as with the time of day or stage of development being observed. Dieter Dowe's investigations of an important demonstration in Cologne in 1848 turned up no less than eight estimates of crowd size.* A good deal of historical detective work would be essential to justify taking any one of them or, indeed, for taking an arithmetical average of them all. Second, there is the problem of estimating numbers from qualitative statements (such as "a great sea of people"), or other nonexact evidence. And third, there is the matter of extrapolating size, estimates for individual events to the entire sample. For Table 16 we extrapolated the following information to the entire inventory.

	1816–1849		1850–1913	
	Number	Average	Number	Average
Crowd size	50	3,198	66	923
Duration	497	1.27	446	1.13

It is only fair to underline the provisional and approximate nature of such figures. For example, a quick check of our files using qualitative and direct evidence revealed lowered crowd size estimates for both periods through the same downward trend. On the other hand, adding just two large electoral law demonstrations from the year 1910—events excluded because the evidence on violence related thereto was too vague—would be sufficient to reverse the trend.† But that, in turn, results from the use of arithmetic means as trend indicator—a not wholly unobjectionable technique. As a possible way out of these difficulties a scalar index classifying events as very large, large medium

* They ran from 200 to 10,000 persons (Dowe 1970: 187).

† In Königsberg and Berlin demonstrations involved 100,000 and 150,000 persons, respectively, but violence was peripheral to their outcome and importance (see Groh 1972, 60: 141–146).

and small has merits. The following table sums up these problems by comparing our inventory with a list of all events known to us (including those excluded from our sample on the grounds of insufficient evidence); and by presenting the results of a scalar index for the four periods covered and based on the events we did include.*

Period	Our number	Total known	Scalar index points
1816–1847	330	375	1325
1848–1849	195	261	930
1850–1881	244	286	868
1882–1913	264	303	788

A further problem in determining the number of events derives from the interdependence of some collective violence. It would have been desirable to fall back on some "hard" rule of thumb such as calling two or more events part of the same event where 10 percent of the personnel involved overlapped. That we did in the case of France. Unfortunately, the German data were almost never good enough to play such a rule. Instead, where the evidence of overlapping seemed overwhelming, for example, in reports on Hecker's army in Baden or the Polish "Sensenmänner" in Posen in April 1848, or on Ruhr miners in 1889—we treated separate reports of collective violence as parts of one large event; otherwise as independent.

Our inventory of systematic data also permitted some summary estimates of crowd characteristics. Table 19 is the main single example. It contains eight categories, three of which are repressive. It is an attempt to discover broad patterns of change in the kinds of groups participating in collective violence. A formation is simply a distinct group of people acting collectively, and can range from the undifferentiated mass of people labeled "crowd" to specific occupational groups. Any event will have at least one formation, usually two (including the repressive forces), and can have more. Due to a coding error discovered too late, the machine-readable file could not be utilized for this purpose, necessitating use of an older hand-tabulated version employing a periodization somewhat different from that used in other tables. Of course, these data are not adequate substitutes for comprehensive and detailed lists of individual participants classified by age, occupation, religion, and so on.

* This index is the sum of frequency of events, frequency of reports on events, and values 1–4 on crowd size.

That type of information will have to come from more detailed archival research. One may doubt whether it will ever become available on a comprehensive and national scale, additional grounds for not regretting the rather broad approach adopted here (though not for giving up the search for more detailed data).

At a more general level, let us report a supplementary analysis of urbanization and collective violence in Germany. (We are grateful to Gerd Hohorst for assistance in this inquiry.) The following table reports correlations between the numbers of disturbances and both (a) the urbanity and (b) the rate of recent urbanization of German regions for various periods between 1816 and 1913. The correlations run from +.24 to +.65—from weakly to strongly positive.

Relationship[a]	Period	N	r
Urbanity I and number of violent events	1816–1847	37	+.37
	1816–1848	37	+.39
	1850–1881	36	+.37
	1882–1913	53	+.65
Urbanity II and number of violent events	1816–1847	22	+.34
	1816–1848	22	+.42
	1850–1881	26	+.60
	1882–1913	43	+.50
Urbanization I and number of violent events	1816–1847	36	+.35
	1816–1848	36	+.37
	1850–1881	53	+.34
	1882–1913	53	+.24
Urbanization II and number of violent events	1816–1847	22	+.37
	1816–1848	22	+.40
	1850–1881	40	+.27
	1882–1913	51	+.39
Urbanity II and number of convicted rioters	1882–1913	30	+.41
Urbanization II and number of convicted rioters	1882–1913	29	+.45

a Urbanity refers to the percent of the total population living in communities with at least 5,000 inhabitants (Urbanity I), or at least 20,000 inhabitants (Urbanity II); urbanization refers to the rate of growth of the urban population in the one category or the other.

Further analyses of the same data show (1) that the connection between collective violence and urbanity or urbanization becomes significant in the period from 1850 to 1913; (2) that urbanity is in virtually all tests the stronger independent variable; and (3) that statistical tests indicate that urbanization exerts a positive influence only when urbanity exceeds a certain threshold. This is especially true of the period from 1882 to 1913. We interpret these results to mean that after regions have reached a certain size or population density, further migration ceases to exert a significant disintegrating influence upon their social and political structures. A receiving network has been built up.

A further correlational analysis of violent events as a function of the growth rates of individual cities indicates that, whatever the impact of urbanization on violent conflict, the current pace of the city's expansion was not the essential factor. The condensed table following tells the story.

Period	r	Number of cities	Number of events
1816–1847	−.07	69	96
1848[a]	−.03	69	43
1849[a]	−.02	69	15
1850–1881	−.03	73	99
1882–1913	−.10	83	125

[a] The population growth rate is the same as for the 1816–1847 test period.

BIBLIOGRAPHY

NOTE ON ARCHIVAL SOURCES

Material from European archives enters our analyses in four different ways. First, and most conventionally, we use documentary evidence to prepare our own descriptions of important times, places, and conflicts: the political situation of Milan in 1898, for example, or the revolution of 1848 in Limoges. Second, having used newspapers or other published sources to enumerate a set of events for systematic study, we then search major archival series for additional information concerning each event on the list. Third, we sometimes do an independent enumeration of such events from a relevant archival source—typically a series of reports concerning political surveillance and control—and compare the list thus generated with the lists derived from published sources. Fourth, we occasionally compile our own indicators of change and variation in social characteristics of areas and periods directly from archival material. Although we have done that sort of compilation extensively in other work, the fourth use of the archives is rare in this book; we have generally compiled our evidence concerning the background characteristics of the areas and periods under study from published reports.

In the case of England, we have examined the correspondence of the Home Secretary (Public Record Office, Home Office Papers) for selected years from 1800 to 1850.

In France, the largest body of documentary evidence has come from the Archives Nationales (Paris). The major series analyzed there were BB^{18}, BB^{30}, and F^7, but we have also drawn significant blocks of information from C, CC, and other subseries in BB and F. For major insurrections of the nineteenth century, we have drawn documentation from the Archives Historiques de l'Armée at Vincennes (especially series B, E, F, and G) and from the Archives de la Préfecture de Police in Paris (notably series AA). Our work in departmental archives has consisted mainly of going through the principal series of reports on political surveillance and control, especially in series M, for two purposes: to locate additional information concerning events already in our samples; and, where possible, to prepare independent enumerations of events meeting our criteria for comparison with the newspaper samples. We have done such surveys in the departmental archives of Bouches-du-Rhône, Cher, Côte d'Or, Eure-et-Loir, Maine-et-Loire, Morbihan, Indre-et-Loire, Isère, Seine, Somme, and Haute-Vienne.

In Italy, archival sources were consulted for matters touching the city of Milan only. The chief series reviewed were the police records (Fondo Questura) in the Archivio di Stato di Milano for the decades between 1880 and 1900; these included strike reports, surveillance reports, and reports on violent incidents.

For Germany, only the Prussian government records for the provinces of Rhineland and Westphalia were used extensively; these provided additional enumeration of instances of collective violence. The police reports (*Zeitungsberichte*) of the various districts as collected in the State Archives in Koblenz and Münster proved especially valuable. These regional records also produced detailed information on specific instances unavailable in the published sources (for instance on the violence of Iserlohn's bronze workers in 1840). Useful though these sources were, we realize that we have only scratched the surface of a highly heterogeneous and regionally differentiated material. A comprehensive history of protest and collective violence in Germany during the Rebellious Century based on archival materials presently available could—and remains—to be written.

SECONDARY SOURCES

Abrate, Mario. 1967. *La lotta sindacale nella industrializzazione in Italia, 1906–1926.* Milan: Franco Angeli.

Acerbo, Giacomo. 1961. "L'agricoltura italiana dal 1861 ad oggi," in *L'Economia italiana dal 1861 al 1961.* Milan: Giuffrè.

Afanassiev, Georges. 1894. *Le commerce des céréales en France au dix-huitème siècle.* Paris: Picard.

Aguet, Jean-Pierre. 1954. *Les grèves sous la Monarchie de Juillet (1830–1847).* Geneva: Droz.

Agulhon, Maurice. 1966. *La sociabilité méridionale.* 2 vols. Aix-en-Provence: Penseé Universitaire.

——— 1970. *La République au village.* Paris: Plon.

Alatri, Paolo. 1956. *Le origini del Fascismo.* Rome: Editori Riuniti.

Alberoni, Francesco. 1968. *Statu nascenti: Studi sui processi collettivi*. Bologna: Mulino.

Almond, Gabriel, and Sidney Verba. 1963. *The Civic Culture*. Princeton University Press.

Amiot, Michel, and others. 1968. *La violence dans le monde actuel*. Paris: Desclée de Brouwer for Centre d'Etudes de la Civilisation Contemporaine.

Anderson, Eugene N., and Pauline R. Anderson. 1967. *Political Institutions and Social Change in Continental Europe in the Nineteenth Century*. Berkeley and Los Angeles: University of California Press.

Anderson, Robert T., and Barbara Gallatin Anderson. 1965. *Bus Stop for Paris*. Garden City, N.Y.: Doubleday.

Ardant, Gabriel. 1965. *Théorie sociologique de l'impôt*. 2 vols. Paris: SEVPEN.

Armengaud, Andre. 1961. *Les populations de l'Est-Aquitain au début de l'époque moderne*. Paris: Mouton.

Aron, Raymond. 1959. *Immuable et Changeante: De la IVe à la Ve République*. Paris: Calmann-Levy.

———— 1968. *La révolution introuvable*. Paris: Arthème Fayard.

Aspinall, A. 1949. *The Early English Trade Unions*. London: Batchworth.

Associazion per lo Sviluppo dell'Industria nel Mezzogiorno (SVIMEZ). 1961. *Un secolo di statistiche italiane, nord e sud*. Rome: SVIMEZ.

Ay, Karl-Ludwig. 1968. *Die Entstehung einer Revolution*. Berlin: Duncker und Humblot.

Baechler, Jean. 1970. *Les phénomènes révolutionnaires*. Paris: Presses Universitaires de France, series SUP.

Balser, Frolinde. 1962. *Sozial-Demokratie 1848/49–63: Die erste deutsche Arbeiterorganisation: Allgemeine Arbeiterverbrüderung nach der Revolution*. Stuttgart: E. Klett.

Balzac, Honoré de. 1947. "Ce qui disparaît de Paris" *Les Parisiens comme ils sont*. Geneva: La Palatine.

Banfield, Edward C. 1959. *The Moral Basis of a Backward Society*. Glencoe, Ill.: Free Press.

Barberi, Benedetto. 1961. "Aspetti dinamici e strutturali di un secolo di sviluppo economico dell'Italia," in *L'Economia italiana dal 1861 al 1961*. Milan: Giuffrè.

Barsby, Stephen. 1969. "Economic Backwardness and the Characteristics of Development," *Journal of Economic History*, 29: 449–473.

Basile, Antonio. 1958. "Moti contadini in Calabria dal 1848 al 1870," *Archivio storico per la Calabria e Lucania*, 27:67–108.

Becker, Walter. 1960. "Die Bedeutung der nicht-agrarischen Wanderungen für die Herausbildung des industriellen Proletariats in Deutschland," in F. Mottek, ed., *Studien zur Geschichte der industriellen Revolution in Deutschland*. Berlin: Akademie.

Bendix, Reinhard. 1964. *Nation-Building and Citizenship*. New York: Wiley.

326   BIBLIOGRAPHY

Bergmann, Dieter. 1971. "Die Berliner Arbeiterschaft in Vormärz und Revolution, 1830–50," in Otto Büsch, ed., *Untersuchungen zur Geschichte der frühen industrialisierung, vornehmlich im Wirtschaftsraum Berlin-Brandenburg.* Publikation zur Geschichte der Industrialisierung, vol. 6. Berlin: de Gruyter.

Bernardello, Adolfo. 1970. "La paura del communismo e dei tumulti popolari a Venezia nel 1848–49," *Nuova rivista storica,* 54: 50–113.

Bernieri, Antonio. 1961. *Cento anni di storia sociale a Carrara.* Milan: Feltrinelli.

Bernstein, Eduard. 1907–1910. *Die Geschichte der Berliner Arbeiterbewegung.* 3 vols. Berlin: Buchhandlung Vorwärts (H. Weber).

Bienen, Henry. 1968. *Violence and Social Change: A Review of Current Literature.* Chicago: University of Chicago Press.

Birnbaum, Norman. 1969. *The Crisis of Industrial Society.* New York: Oxford University Press.

Blanqui, Auguste. 1955. *Textes choisis.* Paris: Editions Sociales.

Bleiber, Helmut. 1955. "Die Moabiter Unruhen, 1910," *Zeitschrift für Geschichtswissenschaft* 3: 173–212.

——— 1966. *Zwischen Reform und Revolution.* Berlin: Akademie.

——— 1969. "Bauern und Landarbeiter in der bürgerlich demokratischen Revolution von 1848/49 in Deutschland," *Zeitschrift für Geschichtswissenschaft,* 17: 289–310.

Blok, Anton. 1974. *The Mafia of a Sicilian Village, 1860–1960.* New York: Harper and Row.

Boehme, Helmut. 1966. *Deutschlands Weg zur Großmacht: Studien zum Verhältnis von Wirtschaft und Staat während der Reichsgründungszeit 1848–1881.* Cologne and Berlin: Kiepenheuer and Witsch.

Boldrini, Marcello. 1961. "Un secolo di sviluppo della popolazione italiana," in *L'Economia italiana dal 1861 al 1961.* Milan: Giuffrè.

Boscolo, Alberto. 1954. "Lo sciopero di Buggerù del 1904," *Movimento Operaio,* n.s., 6: 459–463.

Bouju, Paul M., and others. 1966. *Atlas historique de la France contemporaine.* Paris: Armand Colin; Collection U.

Bracher, Karl D. 1955. *Die Auflösung der Weimarer Republik: Eine Studie zum Problem des Machtverfalls in der Demokratie.* Düsseldorf: Ring.

Breese, Gerald. 1966. *Urbanization in Newly Developing Countries.* Englewood Cliffs, N.J.: Prentiss-Hall.

Brinton, Crane. 1968. *The Anatomy of Revolution.* New York: Norton.

Bry, Gerhard. 1960. *Real Wages in Germany, 1871–1945.* Princeton: Princeton University Press.

Cameron, Rondo. 1958. "Economic Growth and Stagnation in France, 1815–1914," *Journal of Modern History,* 30: 1–14.

——— 1961. *France and the Economic Development of Europe, 1800–1914.* Princeton: Princeton University Press.

——— ed. 1970. *Essays in French Economic History.* Homewood, Ill.: Irwin.

Cameron, Rondo, Olga Crisp, Hugh T. Patrick, and Richard Tilly. 1967. *Banking in the Early Stages of Industrialization. A Study in Comparative Economic History.* New York: Oxford University Press.

Candeloro, Giorgio. 1966–1970. *Storia dell'Italia moderna.* 6 vols. Milan: Feltrinelli.

Cantor, Norman F. 1970. *The Age of Protest. Dissent and Rebellion in the Twentieth Century.* London: George Allen and Unwin.

Caracciolo, Alberto. 1952. *Il Movimento contadino nel Lazio.* Rome: Rinascità.

Cassese, Leopoldo. 1954. "Una lega di resistenza di contadini nel 1860 e la questione demaniale in un comune del Salernitano," *Movimento Operaio,* n.s., 6: 684–723.

Castagnoli, Clara. 1954. "Il Movimento contadina nel Mantovano dal 1866 al movimento de 'La Bojc,'" *Movimento Operaio, Origini e prime linee di sviluppo del movimento contadino in Italia,* n.s., 7: 406–419.

Cavour, Camillo. 1884. *Lettere edite ed inedite,* vol. II. Turin: Roux e Favale.

Chapman, Brian. 1970. *Police State.* London: Pall Mall.

Chevalier, Louis. 1958. *Classes Laborieuses et classes dangereuses.* Paris: Plon.

Ciasca, Raffaele. 1923. "L'Evoluzione economica della Lombardia dagli inizi del secolo XIX al 1860," *La Cassa di Risparmio delle Provincie lombarde nella evoluzione economica della regione.* Milan: Alfieri and Lacroix, 1923.

Cipolla, Carlo M. 1952. "The Decline of Italy: The Case of a Fully Matured Economy," *Economic History Review,* 2nd. ser., 2: 178–187.

Clark, Colin. 1957. *The Conditions of Economic Progress.* 3rd ed. New York: St. Martin's.

Clough, Shepard B., and Carlo Livi. 1956. "Economic Growth in Italy: An Analysis of the Uneven Development of North and South," *Journal of Economic History,* 16: 334–349.

Cohen, Jon. 1967. "Financing Industrialization in Italy, 1894–1914: The Partial Transformation of a Latecomer," *Journal of Economic History,* 27: 363–382.

Cohn, Norman. 1957. *The Pursuit of the Millennium.* Fairlawn, N.J.: Essential Books.

Colajanni, Napoleone. 1895. *Gli Avvenimenti in Sicilia e le loro cause.* Palermo: Sandon.

——— 1898. *L'Italia nel 1898 (Tumulti e reazione).* Milan: Società editrice lombarda.

Cole, W. A., and Phyllis Deane. 1965. "The Growth of National Incomes," in *The Cambridge Economic History of Europe.* Cambridge: Cambridge University Press, VI, 1–55.

Coletti, Francesco. 1911. "Dell'Emigrazione italiana," in *Cinquanta Anni di Storia italiana,* vol. III. Milan: Hoepli.

Comandini, Alfredo. 1918. *L'Italia nel cento anni del secolo XIX giorno per giorno illustrata,* vol. III, 1850–1860. Milan: Vallardi.

Comfort, Richard. 1966. *Revolutionary Hamburg: Labor Politics in the Early Weimar Republic*. Stanford: Stanford University Press.

Conant, Ralph W., and Molly Apple Levin, eds. 1969. *Problems in Research on Community Violence*. New York: Praeger.

Conze, Werner. 1954. "Vom Pöbel zum Proletariat. Sozialgeschichtliche Veraussetzungen für den Sozialismus in Deutschland," *Vierteljahrschrift für Sozial-und Wirtschaftsgeschichte*, 41: 333–364. Wiesbaden: Franz Steiner.

——— 1962. "Das Spannungsfeld von Staat und Gesellschaft im Vormárz," in Conze, ed., *Staat und Gesellschaft im deutschen Vormärz, 1815–48*. Stuttgart: Klett.

Cornelius, Wayne, Jr. 1971. "The Political Sociology of Cityward Migration in Latin America," in Francine F. Rabinowitz aad Felicity M. Trueblood, eds., *Latin American Urban Research*, vol. I. Beverly Hills, Calif.: Sage.

Crouzet, François. 1958. *L'Economie britannique et le blocus continental (1806–1813)*. Paris: Presses universitaires de France, 1958.

——— 1964. "Wars, Blockade, and Economic Change in Europe, 1792–1815," *Journal of Economic History*, 24: 567–588.

——— 1970. "Essai de construction d'un indice annuel de la production industrielle française au XIXe siècle," *Annales; Economies, Sociétés, Civilisations*, 24: 24–60.

Crozier, Michel. 1964. *The Bureaucratic Phenomenon*. Chicago: University of Chicago Press.

Dahrendorf, Ralf D. 1959. *Class and Class Conflict in an Industrial Society*. Stanford: Stanford University Press.

d'Anna, F. Coppola. 1956. *Poplazione, reddito e finanze pubbliche dell'Italia dal 1860 ad oggi*. Rome: Partenia.

Davies, Ioan. 1970. *Social Mobility and Political Change*. London: Pall Mall.

De Felice, Renzo. 1963. "Ordine pubblico e orientamenti delle masse popolari italiane nella prima metà del '17," *Rivista storica del socialismo*, 20: 467–504.

——— 1965. *Aspetti e momenti della vita economica di Roma e dal Lazio nei secoli XVIII e XIX*. Rome: Edizioni di Storia e Letteratura.

——— 1966. *Il Fascismo e i partiti politici italiani: Testimonianze del 1921–1923*. Bologna: Cappelli.

——— 1969. *Le interpretazioni del Fascismo*. Bari: Laterza.

DeMaddalena, Aldo. 1961. "Rilievi sull' esperienza demografica ed economica milanese dal 1861 al 1915," in *L'Economia italiana dal 1861 al 1961*. Milan: Giuffrè.

De Marco, Domenico. 1950. "Le Rivoluzione italiane del 1848," offprint from *Studi in Onore di Gino Luzzatto*. Milan: Giuffrè.

——— 1956. "L'Economie italienne du nord et du sud avant l'Unité: Aux sources de la 'Question meridionale,'" *Revue d'historie économique et sociale*, 34: 368–391.

———— 1957. "L'Economia degli stati italiani prima dell'Unità," *Rassegna storica del Risorgimento,* 54: 191–258.

———— 1960. "Il crollo del regno delle Due Sicilie. I. La struttura sociale," in Università degli studi di Napoli, Istituto di storia economica e sociale, *Annali,* I: 83–274.

Del Carria, Renzo. 1966. *Proletari senza rivoluzione: Storia delle classe subalterne italiane dal 1860 al 1954.* 2 vols. Milan: Oriente.

Della Peruta, Franco. 1953. "I contadini nella rivoluzione lombarda del 1848," *Movimento Operaio,* n.s., 5: 525–575.

———— 1954. "La Banda del Matese e il fallimento della teoria anarchica della moderna 'Jacquerie' in Italia," *Movimento Operaio,* n.s., 7: 337–384.

Dieterici, C. F. W. 1846. *Der Volkswohlstand im preußischen Staate.* Berlin: Mittler.

Dolléans, Edouard, and Michel Crozier. 1950. *Mouvements ouvrier et socialiste: chronologie et bibliographie. Angleterre, France, Allemagne, Etats-Unis (1750–1918).* Paris: Editions Ouvrieres.

Dowe, Dieter. 1970. *Aktion und Organisation (Arbeiterbewegung, sozialistiche und Kommunistiche Bewegung in der preußischen Rheinprovinz, 1820–52).* Hannover: Verlag für Literatur und Zeitgeschehen.

Dronke, Ernst. 1846. *Berlin.* 2 vols. Frankfurt/am Main: Rutter.

Dupeux, Georges. 1964. *La société francaise, 1789–1960.* Paris: Armand Colin; Collection U.

Durkheim, Emile. 1960. *Les formes élementaires de la vie religieuse.* 4th ed. Paris: Presses Universitaires de France.

Duverger, Maurice. 1963. *Political Parties.* New York: Wiley.

———— 1962. *Les institutions françaises.* Paris: Presses Universitaircs de France.

Egret, Jean. 1970. *Louis XV et l'opposition parlementaire.* Paris: Armand Colin.

Ehrmann, Henry. 1968. *Politics in France.* Boston: Little, Brown.

Eichholtz, Dieter. 1962. "Bewegungen unter den preussischen Eisenbahnarbeitern im Vormärz," *Beiträge zur deutschen Wirtschafts und Sozialgeschichte des 18, und 19. Jahrhunderts.* Berlin: Akademie.

Eisinger, Peter K. 1971. "Protest Behavior and the Integration of Urban Political Systems," *Journal of Politics,* 33: 980–1007.

———— 1973. "The Conditions of Protest Behavior in American Cities," *American Political Science Review,* 67: 11–68.

Eliasberg, George. 1970. "Der Ruhrkrieg 1920, Zum Problem von Organisation und Spontaneität in einem Massenaufstand und zur Dimension der weimarer Krise," *Archiv für Sozialgeschichte,* 10: 291–379.

Engels, Friedrich. "Die preußische Verfassung," in MELS, *Zur deutschen Geschichte,* 2: 145.

Engelsing, Rolf. 1968. "Zur politischen Bildung der deutschen Unterschichten, 1789–1863," *Historische Zeitschrift,* 206: 337–369.

Ersil, Wilhelm. 1963. *Aktionseinheit stürzt Cuno. (Zur Geschichte des Massen-*

kampfes gegen die Cuno-Regierung in Mitteldeutschland). Berlin: Dietz.

Falzone, Gaetano. 1960. "La Sicilia alla vigilia del '60," *Nuova Antologia,* 480: 493–508.

Fasel, George W. 1968. "The French Election of April 23, 1848: Suggestions for a Revision," *French Historical Studies,* 5: 285–298.

Feagin, Joe R. 1974. "Community Disorganization: Some Critical Notes," *Sociological Inquiry.*

Feagin, Joe R., and Harlan Hahn. 1973. *Ghetto Revolts.* New York: Macmillan.

Fenoaltea, Stefano. 1973. "Riflessioni sull'esperianza industriale italiana dal Risorgimento alla Prima Guerra mondiale," in G. Toniolo, ed., *Lo sviluppo economico italiano, 1861–1940.* Bari: Laterza.

Fischer, Wolfram. 1966. "Social Tensions at Early Stages of Industrialization," *Comparative Studies in Society and History,* 9: 64–83.

Förster, Alfred. 1970. *Die Gewerkschaftspolitik der deutschen Sozialdemokratic während des Sozialistengesetzes.* E. Berlin: Tribün.

Franklin, S. H. 1969. *The European Peasantry: The Final Phase.* London: Methuen.

Fraser, Derek. 1970. "The Agitation for Parliamentary Reform," in J. T. Ward, ed., *Popular Movements, c. 1830–1850.* London: Macmillan.

Fricke, Dieter. 1962. *Bismarcks Praetorianer (Die Berliner politische Polizei im Kampf gegen die deutsche Arbeiterbewegung (1871–1918).* E. Berlin: Rütter and Loening.

Fried, Robert. 1963. *The Italian Prefects: A Study in Administrative Politics.* New Haven: Yale University Press.

Gamson, William A. 1968. *Power and Discontent.* Homewood, Ill.: Dorsey.

——— 1968. "Stable Unrepresentation in American Society," *American Behavioral Scientist,* 12: 15–21.

——— 1973. "The Strategy of Social Protest." (Unpublished working paper, University of Michigan.

Gandini, Francesco. 1833. *Viaggi in Italia: Ovvero descrizione geografica, storica, pittorica, statistica, postale e commerciale dell'Italia.* 8 vols., 2nd ed. Cremona.

Genoino, Andrea. 1948. "I moti comunisti del 1848 nel Regno di Napoli," Istituto per la storia del Risorgimento italiano, Comitato di Milano, *Atti e memorie del XXVII Congresso Nazionale:* 251–261.

Gerschenkron, Alexander. 1962. "The Rate of Industrial Growth in Italy, 1881–1913," in *Economic Backwardness in Historical Perspective.* Cambridge, Mass.: Harvard University Press.

Girard, Louis. 1964. *La Garde Nationale.* Paris: Plon.

Girard, Louis, Antoine Prost, and Remi Gossez. 1967. *Les conseillers généraux en 1870.* Paris: Presses Universitaires des France; Publications de la Faculté des Letters et Sciences Humaines, Paris, "Recherches" 34.

Giusti, Ugo. 1936. "Lo sviluppo demografico dei maggiori centri urbani italiani dalla fondazione del regno ad oggi," *Giornale degli economisti,* 76: 153–174.

——— 1945. *Dai Plebisciti alla Costituente.* Rome: Faro.

——— 1951. "I tre grandi rami di attività professionale (agricoltura, industria, servizi) come altrettanti stadi di progresso economico," *Rivista di Economia agricola,* 6: 180–208.

Gladen, Albert. 1970. "Der Kreis Tecklenburg an der Schwelle des Zeitalters der Industrialisierung." Unpublished dissertation, University of Bochum.

Glossy, Karl. 1912. "Literarische Geheimberichte aus dem Vormärz," *Jahrbuch der Grillparzer-Gesellschaft,* 21.

Goetz-Girey, Robert. 1965. *Le Mouvement des grèves en France, 1919–1962.* Paris: Sirey; "l'Economique," 3.

Governor's Commission on the Los Angeles Riots. 1965. *Violence in the City—An End or a Beginning?* Los Angeles: The Commission.

Graham, Hugh Davis, and Ted Robert Gurr, eds. 1969. *Violence in America: Historical and Comparative Perspectives.* Washington: U.S. Government Printing Office.

Gramsci, Antonio. 1952. *La questione meridionale.* Rome: Rinascità.

——— 1955. *L'Ordine Nuovo, 1919–1920.* Turin: Einaudi.

Greenough, Benjamin L., Benjamin L. D'Ooge, and M. Grant Daniell, eds. 1898. *Caesar's Gallic War.* Boston: Ginn.

Groh, Dieter. 1973. *Negative Integration und revolutionärer Attentismus.* Frankfurt: Ullstein.

Gurr, Ted Robert. 1970. *Why Men Rebel.* Princeton: Princeton University Press.

——— and Raymond Duvall. 1973. "Civil Conflict in the 1960s: A Reciprocal System with Parameter Estimates." Paper presented at the annual meeting of the International Studies Association.

Haalck, T. 1959/1960. "Die Staatspolizeiliche Koordinierungsmaßnahmen innerhalb des Deutschen Bundes zwischen 1851 und 1866," in *Wissenschaftliche Zeitschrift der Universität Rostock,* 9: Rostock.

Habakkuk, H. J. 1955. "Family Structure and Economic Change in Nineteenth-Century Europe," *Journal of Economic History,* 15: 1 12.

Halbwachs, Maurice. 1930. *Les causes du suicide.* Paris: Alcan.

Hamerow, T. S. 1958. *Restoration, Revolution, Reaction, Economics and Politics in Germany, 1815–71.* Princeton: Princeton University Press.

Hansen, Joseph. 1967. *Rheinische Briefe und Akten zur Geschichte der politischen Bewegung 1830–1850,* 2 vols. Osnabrück: Biblio. (Gesellschaft für rheinische geschichtskunde Publikationen XXXVI; originally published 1919–1942).

Hartwich, Hans-Hermann. 1967. *Arbeitsmarkt, Verbände und Staat, 1918–33.* Vol. 23, Historische Kommission zu Berlin. Berlin: de Gruyter.

Hennicke, Otto. 1956. *Die Rote Ruhrarmee.* Berlin: Ministerium für nationale Verteidigung.

Hibbs, Douglas A., Jr. 1973. *Mass Political Violence: A Cross-National Causal Analysis.* New York: Wiley.

Hippeau, C. 1864. *Le Gouvernement de Normandie au XVIIe et au XVIIIe siecle.* Caen: Goussiaume de Laporte.

Hirsch, Herbert, and David Perry, eds. 1973. *Violence as Politics.* New York: Harper and Row.

Hobsbawm, E. J. 1959. *Primitive Rebels.* Manchester: Manchester University Press.

———— 1962. *The Age of Revolution: Europe 1789–1848.* London: Weidenfeld and Nicholson.

Hobsbawn, E. J., and George Rudé. 1969. *Captain Swing.* London: Lawrence and Wishart.

Hoffmann, Stanley, and others. 1963. *In Search of France.* Cambridge: Harvard University Press.

Hoffmann, Walter. 1963. "The Take-off in Germany," in W. W. Rostow, ed., *The Economics of the Take-off into Sustained Growth.* London: Macmillan; New York: St. Martin's.

———— Franz Grumbach, and Helmut Hesse. 1965. *Das Wachstum der deutschen Wirtschaft seit der Mitte des 19. Jahrhunderts.* Berlin, Heidelberg, New York: Springer.

Hofstadter, Richard, and Michael Wallace, eds. 1970. *American Violence: A Documentary History.* New York: Knopf.

Hüber, E. R. 1957–1969. *Deutsche Verfassungs-Geschichte seit 1789.* 4 vols., 2d ed. Stuttgart, Berlin, Cologne, Mainz: Kohlhammer.

Hübner, Hans. 1963. "Die ostpreußischen Landarbeiter im Kampf gegen junkerliche Ausbeutung und Willkür (1848–1914)," *Zeitschrift für Geschichtswissenschaft,* II, 552–570.

Huntington, Samuel P. 1968. *Political Order in Changing Societies.* New Haven: Yale University Press.

Imberciadori, Ildebrando. 1961. *L'Economia toscana nel primo '800 dalla Restaurazione al Regno, 1815–1861.* Florence: Valsecchi.

Imig, Werner. 1958. *Streik bei Mansfeld, 1930.* Berlin: Tribün.

Istituto Centrale di Statistica (ISTAT). 1958. *Sommario di statistiche storiche italiane.* Rome: ISTAT.

Jacobs, A., and H. Richter. 1935. "Die Grosshandelspreise in Deutschland von 1792 bis 1934," *Sonderhoffe des Instituts für Konjunkturforschung, XXXVII.*

Jantke, Carl. 1955. *Der vierte Stand: Die gestaltenden Kräfte der deutschen Arbeiterbewegung im XIX. Jahrhundert.* Freiburg: Herder.

Johnson, Chalmers. 1966. *Revolutionary Change.* Boston: Little, Brown.

Kaelble, Hartmut, and Heinrich Volkmann. 1972. "Konjunktur und Streik in Deutschland während des Ubergangs zum organisierten Kapitalismus," *Zeitschrift für Wirtschafts- und Sozialwissenschaften* (formerly *Schmollers Jahrbuch*), 92: 513–44.

Kan, S. B. 1948. *Dva vosstania slyeskich Tkachyei (1793–1844).* Moscow.

Kerr, Clark. 1960. "Changing Social Structures," in Wilbert E. Moore and Arnold S. Feldman, eds., *Labor Commitment and Social Change in Developing Areas.* New York: Social Science Research Council.

Klein, Peter. 1961. *Separatisten an Rhein und Ruhr: Die Konterrevolutionäre separatistische Bewegung der deutschen Bourgeoisie in der Rheinprovinz und in Westfalen, Nov. 1918–Juli 1919.* Berlin: Rütter and Loening.

Kocka, Jürgen, 1969. *Unternehmensverwaltung und Angestelltenschaft am Beispiel Siemens, 1847–1914.* Stuttgart: Klett.

———— 1973. *Klassengesellschaft im Krieg, Deutsche Sozialgeschichte, 1914–18.* Gottingen: Vandenhoeck and Ruprecht.

Köllmann, Wolfgang. 1959. "Industrialisierung, Binnenwanderung und 'Soziale Frage': Zur Entstehungsgeschichte der deutschen Industriegroßstadt im 19. Jahrhundert," *Vierteljahrschrift für Sozial- und Wirtschaftsgeschichte,* 46: 45–70. Wiesbaden: Franz Steiner.

———— 1968. "Die Bevölkerung und Arbeitskräftepotential in Deutschland, 1815–1865: Ein Beitrag zür Analyse des Pauperismus," in *Jahrbuch: Landesamt für Forschung, Nordrhein-Westfalen.*

———— ed. 1969. "Der Bergarbeiterstreik von 1889 und die Gründung des 'Alten Verbandes,' " in *Ausgewählte Dokumente der Zeit.* Bochum: Berg.

Kosselleck, Reinhart. 1967. *Preussen zwischen Reform und Revolution.* Stuttgart: Klett.

Krusch, Hans-Joachim. 1963. "Zur Bewegung der revolutionären Betriebsträte in den Jahren 1922/23," *Zeitschrift für Geschichtswissenschaft,* I, 360–378. Berlin: Rutten and Loening.

Kuczynski, Jürgen. 1948. *Die Bewegungen der deutschen Wirtschaft von 1800 bis 1946.* 2d ed. Meisenheim: Westkultur.

———— 1960. *Die Geschichte der Lage der Arbeiter unter dem Kapitalismus,* vol. X. Berlin: Akademie.

———— 1966. *Die Geschichte der Lage der Arbeiter unter dem Kapitalismus,* vol. V. Berlin: Akademie.

———— 1967. *Darstellung der Lage der Arbeiter in Frankreich seit 1848.* Berlin: Akademie.

———— 1967. *The Rise of the Working Class.* New York: McGraw-Hill.

———— and Ruth Hoppe. 1964. "Eine Beruf- bzw. auch Klassen- und Schichtenanalyse der Märzgefallenen 1848 in Berlin," in *Jahrbuch für Wirstschaftsgeschichte,* 4: 200–277.

Kuznets, Simon. 1966. *Modern Economic Growth: Rate, Structure and Spread.* New Haven: Yale University Press.

Laboor, Ernst. 1961. *Der Kampf der deutschen Arbeiterklasse gegen Militarismus und Kriegsgefahr 1927–1929.* Berlin: Dietz.

Labriola, Arturo. 1910. *Storia di dieci anni, 1899–1909.* Milan.

Labrousse, Ernest, and others. 1970. *Histoire économique et sociale de la France. T. II: Des derniers temps de l'âge seigneurial aux préludes de l'âge industriel* (1660–1789). Paris: Presses Universitaires de France.

Lampedusa, Giuseppe Tomasi di. 1963. *Il Gattopardo.* Milan: Feltrinelli.

Landes, David. 1968. *The Unbound Prometheus: Technological Change and In-*

dustrial Development in Western Europe from 1750 to the Present. Cambridge: Cambridge University Press.

Lange, Annamarie. 1967. *Das Wilhelminische Berlin: Zwischen Jahrhundertwende und Novemberrevolution.* Berlin: Dietz.

Langer, William L. 1969. *Political and Social Upheaval, 1832–1852.* New York: Harper and Row.

Le Bon, Gustave. 1913. *The Psychology of Revolution,* trans. Bernard Miall. London: Unwin.

Lees, Lynn, and Charles Tilly. 1973. "Le peuple de juin 1848," *Annales; Economies, Sociétés, Civilisations;* forthcoming in 1975.

Lenin, V. I. 1954. "Der preußische und der amerikanische Weg fur kapitalistischen Entwicklung in der Landwirtschaft," in MELS, *Zur deutschen Geschichte,* II. Berlin: Dietz.

Leonetti, Alfonso. 1952. *Mouvements ouvriers et socialistes (chronologie et bibliographie). L'Italie (Des origines à 1922).* Paris: Ouvrières.

Lerner, Franz. 1965. *Wirtschafts- und Sozialgeschichte des Nassauer Raumes, 1816–1964.* Wiesbaden: Nassauer Sparkasse.

Levasseur, Emile. 1889–1893. *La population française.* 3 vols. Paris: Rousseau.

Lévy-Leboyer, Maurice. 1964. *Les banques européennes et l'industrialisation internationale au XIXe siècle.* Paris: Presses Universitaires de France; Publications de la Faculté des Letters et Sciences Humaines, Paris, "Recherches," 16.

——— 1968. "La croissance économique en France au XIXe siècle: résultats préliminaires," *Annales: Economies, Sociétés, Civilisations,* 23: 788–807.

Lhomme, Jean. 1960. *La grande bourgeoisie au pouvoir (1830–1880).* Paris: Presses Universitaires de France.

Lidtke, Vernon. 1966. *The Outlawed Party: Social Democracy in Germany, 1878–90.* Princeton: Princeton University Press.

Lindau, G. 1960. *Revolution, 1918–19.* Berlin: Dietz.

Lipsky, Michael. 1968. "Protest as a Political Resource," *American Political Science Review,* 62: 1144–1158.

——— 1970. *Protest in City Politics: Rent Strikes, Housing and the Power of the Poor.* Chicago: Rand McNally.

——— and David J. Olson. 1969. "Riot Commission Politics," *Trans-Action* (July/August), pp. 9–13.

Livi, Livio. 1961. "La prolificità in rapporto alla produzione agricola in Italia dal 1861 al 1960," in *L'Economia italiana dal 1861 al 1961.* Milan: Giuffrè.

Livi Bacci, Massimo. 1965. *I fattori demografici dello sviluppo economico italiano.* Rome: Istituto di statistica economica dell'Università di Roma.

Lodhi, A. Q., and Charles Tilly. 1973. "Urbanization, Criminality and Collective Violence in Nineteenth-Century France," *American Journal of Sociology,* 79: 296–318.

Lorwin, Val. 1958. "Working Class Politics and Economic Development in Western Europe," *American Historical Review,* 63: 338–351.

Lowi, Theodore. 1971. *The Politics of Disorder.* New York: Basic Books.

Luethy, Herbert. 1955. *France Against Herself.* New York: Meridian.

Luraghi, Raimondo. 1961. *Pensiero e azione economica del Conte di Cavour.* Turin: Museo Nazionale del Risorgimento.

Lyttelton, Adrian. 1973. *The Seizure of Power: Fascism in Italy, 1919–1929.* London: Weidenfeld and Nicolson.

MacDonald, John S. 1963. "Agricultural Organization, Migration and Labour Militancy in Rural Italy," *Economic History Review,* n.s., 16: 61–75.

—————— and Leatrice MacDonald. 1964. "Institutional Economics and Rural Development: Two Italian Types," *Human Organization,* 23: 113–118.

Mack Smith, Denis. 1950. "The Peasants' Revolt of Sicily in 1860," in *Studi in Onore di Gino Luzzatto,* vol. III. Milan: Giuffrè.

—————— 1966. "The Latifundia in Modern Sicilian History," *Proceedings of the British Academy,* 6: 85–124.

—————— 1967. "Italy," in J. P. T. Bury, ed., *The New Cambridge Modern History,* vol. X. *The Zenith of European Power.* Cambridge: Cambridge University Press.

—————— 1968. *A History of Sicily: Modern Sicily after 1713.* London: Chatto and Windus.

—————— 1969. *Italy, a Modern History,* rev. ed. Ann Arbor, University of Michigan Press.

MacRae, Duncan, Jr. 1967. *Parliament, Parties and Society in France, 1946–1958.* New York: St. Martin's.

Marchetti, Leopoldo. n.d. "I moti di Milano e la fusione col Piemonte" in Ettore Rota, ed., *Il 1848,* vol. II. Milan: Vallardi.

—————— 1960. "Il decennio di resistenza, 1849–1859," in *Storia di Milano,* vol. XIV. Milan: Fondazione Treccani degli Alfieri.

Marczewski, Jean. 1966. *Introduction à l'histoire quantitative française de 1789 à 1964.* Paris: Institut de Science Economique Appliquée; Cahiers de l'I.S.E.A., AF7.

Markow, Alexis. 1889. *Das Wachstum der Bevölkerung und die Entwicklung der Aus- und Einwanderungen, Ab- und Zuzüge in Preußen und Preußens einzelnen Provinzen, Bezirken und Kreisgruppen von 1824 bis 1885.* Tübingen: Laupp.

Marraro, Howard, ed. 1952. *Diplomatic Relations between the United States and the Kingdom of the Two Sicilies.* 2 vols. New York: Vanni.

Marx, Karl. 1935. *The Civil Wars in France.* New York: International Publishers.

—————— 1958. "The Class Struggles in France," in Karl Marx and Frederick Engels, *Selected Works.* Moscow: Foreign Languages, I, 139–242.

—————— 1964. *Pre-Capitalist Economic Formations,* Eric Hobsbawm, ed. London: Lawrence and Wishart.

Masnovo, Omero. 1932. "Carattere nazionale dei moti parmensi del 1831," *Rassegna storica del Risorgimento,* 19: 81–109.

Mayer, Arno J. 1971. *Dynamics of Counterrevolution in Europe, 1870–1956: An Analytic Framework*. New York: Harper and Row.

McCone Commission. 1965. *Governor's Commission on the Los Angeles Riots, Violence in the City—An End or a Beginning?* Los Angeles: The Commission.

McManners, John. 1969. *European History, 1789–1914*. New York: Harper and Row.

von der Mehden, Fred. 1973. *Comparative Political Violence*. Englewood Cliffs, N.J.: Prentice-Hall.

MELS. 1954. *Marx-Engels-Lenin-Stalin. Zur deutschen. Geschichte*. Berlin: Dietz.

Michels, Robert. 1915. *Political Parties*. Glencoe: Free Press. (1958 reprint.)

Milone, Ferdinando. 1950. "Le industrie del Mezzogriorno all'unificazione dell'Italia," in *Studi in Onore di Gino Luzzato*, vol. III. Milan: Giuffrè.

——— 1955. *L'Italia nell'economia delle sue regioni*. Turin: Einaudi.

Monnerot, Jules. 1969. *Sociologie de la révolution*. Paris: Arthème Fayard.

Moore, Barrington, Jr. 1966. *Social Origins of Dictatorship and Democracy*. Boston: Beacon.

——— 1973. *Reflections on the Causes of Human Misery and upon Certain Proposals to Eliminate Them*. Boston: Beacon.

Mori, Renato. 1958. *La Lotta Sociale in Lunigiana (1859–1904)*. Florence: Le Monnier.

Moss, Leonard W., and Stephen C. Capponnari. 1960. "Patterns of Kinship, Comparaggio and Community in a South Italian Village," *Anthropological Quarterly*, 33: 24–32.

Muller, R. H. Walter. 1954. "Briefe eines Augenzeugen der Berliner Märztage 1848," *Zeitschrift für Geschichtswissenschaft*, vol. II.

Nardin, Terry. 1972. "Conflicting Conceptions of Political Violence," in Cornelius P. Cotter, ed., *Political Science Annual*, vol. IV. Indianapolis: Bobbs-Merrill.

National Advisory Commission on Civil Disorders. 1968. *Report of the National Advisory Commission on Civil Disorders*. Washington: U.S. Government Printing Office.

Nelson, Joan. 1970. "The Urban Poor: Disruption or Political Integration in Third World Cities?" *World Politics*, 22: 393–414.

Nettl, J. P. 1965. "The German Social Democratic Party, 1890–1914, as a Political Model," *Past and Present*, 30: 65–96.

——— 1967. *Political Mobilization*. London: Faber and Faber.

Nieburg, H. L. 1969. *Political Violence*. New York: St. Martin's.

Noyes, P. 1966. *Organization and Revolution. Working-Class Associations in the German Revolutions of 1848–49*. Princeton: Princeton University Press.

Obermann, K. 1953. *Die deutsche Arbeiter in der Revolution von 1848*. Berlin: Dietz.

——— 1970. "Die soziale Zusammensetzung der Bürgerwehr in Köln (1848)," *Jahrbuch für Wirtschaftsgeschichte* 10: 129–141. Berlin: Akademie.

———— 1972. "Die Arbeitermigrationen in Deutschland im Prozess der Industrialisierung," *Jahrbuch für Wirtschaftsgeschichte,* 12: 133–157.

Oberschall, Anthony. 1973. *Social Conflict and Social Movements.* Englewood Cliffs, N.J.: Prentice-Hall.

Öertzen, Peter Von. 1958. "Die grossen Streiks der Ruhrarbeiterschaft im Frühjahr 1919," *Vierteljahrschrift fur Zeitgeschichte,* 6.

Omodeo, Adolfo. n.d. *L'Opera politica del Conte di Cavour: Parte I: 1848–1857.* Florence: Nuova Italia.

Orsagh, Thomas. 1968. "The Probable Geographical Distribution of German Income, 1882–1963," in *Zeitschrift für die gesamte Staatswissenschaft* (May 1968), pp. 280–311. Tübingen: J. C. B. Mohr.

Passigli, Stefano. 1969. *Emigrazione e comportamento politico.* Bologna: Mulino.

Payne, Howard C. 1966. *The Police State of Louis Napoleon Bonaparte.* Seattle: University of Washington Press.

Pedio, Tommaso. 1960. "La borghesia lucana nei moti insurrezionali del 1860," *Archivio storico per le provincie napoletane,* n.s., 40: 185–233.

Pelger, Hans. 1965. "Zur sozial demokratischen Bewegung in der Rheinprovinz vor dem Sozialistengesetz," *Archiv für Sozialgeschichte* 5: 377–407. Hannover: Verlag für Literatur und Zeitgeschehen.

———— 1968. "Zur demokratischen und Sozialen Bewegung in Norddeutschland im Anschluss an die Revolution von 1848," *Archiv für Sozialgeschichte,* 8: 161 229. Hannover: Verlag für Literatur und Zeitgeschehen.

Petitfrère, C. 1973. "Les grandes composantes sociales des armees vendéennes d'Anjou," *Annales historiques de la Révolution française,* 45: 1–20.

Pierrard, Pierre. 1965. *La vie ouvrière à Lille sous le Second Empire.* Paris: Bloud and Gay.

Pinzani, Carlo. 1963. *La crisi politica di fine secolo in Toscana.* Florence: Barbèra.

Pitt-Rivers, Julian, ed. 1963. *Mediterranean Countrymen.* The Hague: Mouton.

Pollini, Leo. 1953. *Mazzini e la rivolta milanese del 6 febbraio 1853.* Milan: Ceschina.

Ponteil, Felix. 1966. *Les institutions de la France de 1814 à 1870.* Paris: Presses Universitaires de France.

Price, Jacob M., and Val Lorwin. *The Dimensions of the Past.* New Haven: Yale University Press.

Procacci, Giuliano. 1964. "Geografia e struttura del movemento contadino della valle padana nel suo periodo formative (1901–1906)," *Studi storici,* 5: 41–120.

Quazza, Guido. 1951. *La lotta sociale nel Risorgimento: Classe e governi della Restaurazione all'Unità (1815–1861).* Turin.

———— 1961. *L'Industria laniera e cotoniera in Piemonte dal 1831 al 1860.* Turin: Museo Nazionale del Risorgimento.

Racioppi, Giacomo. 1867. *Storia dei moti di Basilicata.* Naples: Morelli.

Raseri, E. 1907. "L'Aumento di popolazione delle grandi agglomerazioni urbane in Italia durante il secolo XIX," *Giornale degli economisti,* 34: 532–549.

Reden, Friedrich Von. 1856. *Allgemeine vergleichende Finanz-Statistik,* vol. II. Darmstadt: L. Jonghaus.

Reis, K. 1910. *Agrarfrage und Agrarbewegung in Schlesien im Jahre 1848.* Breslau: F. Hirt.

Rémond, René. 1965. *La vie politique en France.* Paris: Armand Colin; Collection U.

Reynaud, Jean-Daniel. 1966. *Les syndicats en France.* Paris: Armand Colin; Collection U.

Richardson, Lewis F. 1960. *Statistics of Deadly Quarrels.* Pittsburgh: Boxwood.

Rimlinger, Gaston V. 1960. "The Legitimation of Protest: A Comparative Study in Labor History," *Comparative Studies in Society and History,* 2: 329–343.

Ringer, Fritz. 1969. *The German Inflation of 1923.* London: Oxford University Press.

Ritter, Gerhard Albert. 1959. *Die Arbeiterbewegung im wilhelminischen Reich 1890–1900.* Berlin: Colloquim.

——— 1967. *Historisches Lesebuch 2, 1871–1914.* Frankfurt am Main and Hamburg: Fischer Bücherei.

Rokkan, Stein. 1970. *Citizens, Elections, Parties: Approaches to the Comparative Study of the Processes of Development.* Oslo: Universitetsforlaget.

Romano, Salvatore Francesco. 1952. *Momenti del Risorgimento in Sicilia.* Messina-Florence: d'Anna.

——— 1959. *Storia dei Fasci siciliani.* Bari: Laterza.

——— 1963. *Storia della Mafia.* Milan: Sugar.

——— 1965. *Le Classi sociali in Italia dal Medioevo all'età contemporanea.* Turin: Piccola Biblioteca Einaudi.

Rösen, Heinrich. 1965. "Der Aufstand der Krefelder 'Seidenfabrikarbeiter' 1828 und die Bildung einer 'Sicherheitswache,' " in *Die Heimat, Zeitschrift für Niederrheinische Heimatpflege,* 36: 32–61.

Rosenberg, Arthur. 1961. *Geschichte der Weimarer Republik.* Europäische Verlagsanstalt.

Rosenberg, Hans. 1958. *Bureaucracy, Aristocracy, and Autocracy: The Prussian Experience, 1660–1815.* Cambridge, Mass.: Harvard University Press.

——— 1967. *Grosse Depression und Bismarckzeit.* Berlin: de Gruyter.

Ross, Arthur M., and George W. Hartman. 1960. *Changing Patterns of Industrial Conflict.* New York: Wiley.

Rossi Doria, Manlio. 1958. "The Land Tenure System and Class in Southern Italy," *American Historical Review,* 68: 46–53.

Rostow, W. W. 1960. *The Stages of Economic Growth: A Non-Communist Manifesto.* Cambridge: Cambridge University Press.

Roth, Gunter. 1963. *The Social Democrats in Imperial Germany.* Totowa, N.J.: Badminster.

Rothman, Stanley. 1970. *European Society and Politics.* Indianapolis and New York: Bobbs-Merrill.

Rubenstein, Richard E. 1970. *Rebels in Eden: Mass Political Violence in the United States.* Boston: Little, Brown.

Rudé, George. 1959. *The Crowd in the French Revolution.* Oxford: Oxford University Press.

—— 1964. *The Crowd in History.* New York: Wiley.

—— 1967. "English Rural and Urban Disturbances on the Eve of the First Reform Bill, 1830–1831," *Past and Present,* 37: 87–102.

Ruge, Wolfgang. 1968. "Vom Herbst 1917 bis 1933," in *Deutsche Geschichte,* vol. III. ed. Collective, J. Streisand et al. Berlin: VEB Verlag der Wissenschaft.

Rule, James, and Charles Tilly. 1965. *Measuring Political Upheaval.* Princeton: Center of International Studies.

—— 1972. "1830 and the Unnatural History of Revolution," *Journal of Social Issues,* 28: 49–76.

Salvatorelli, Luigi, and Giovanni Mira. 1964. *Storia d'Italia nel periodo fascista.* Turin: Einaudi.

Santarelli, Enzo. 1954. "L'Azione di Errico Malatesta e i moti del 1898 ad Ancona," *Movimento operaio,* n.s., 6: 248–274.

Sauvy, Alfred. 1965. *Histoire économique de la France entre les deux guerres.* 2 vols. Paris: Artheme Fayard.

Schoenbaum, David. 1967. *Hitler's Social Revolution.* New York: Anchor Books.

Schumann, Wolfgang. 1961. *Oberschlesien 1918–19.* Berlin: Rütter and Loening.

Schumpeter, Joseph. 1939. *Business Cycles: A Theoretical, Historical and Statistical Analysis of the Capitalist Process.* 2 vols. New York: Macmillan.

Sereni, Emilio. 1948. *Il capitalismo nelle campagne (1860–1900).* Turin: Einaudi.

Shorter, Edward, and Charles Tilly. 1970. "The Shape of Strikes in France," *Comparative Studies in Society and History,* 13: 60–86.

—— 1971. "Le déclin de la grève violente en France de 1890 à 1935," *Le mouvement social,* 79: 95–118.

—— 1973. "Les vagues de grèves en France," *Annales: Economies, Sociétés, Civilisations,* 28: 857–887.

—— 1974. *Strikes in France, 1830 to 1968.* New York: Cambridge University Press.

Silver, Allan. 1967. "The Demand for Order in Civil Society: A Review of Some Themes in the History of Urban Crime, Police and Riots," in David J. Bordua, ed., *The Police.* New York: Wiley.

Simiand, François. 1932. *Le salaire, l'evolution sociale et la monnaie.* 3 vols. Paris: Alcan.

Skolnick, Jerome H. 1969. *The Politics of Protest.* New York: Simon and Schuster.

Smelser, Neil J. 1963. *Theory of Collective Behavior.* New York: Free Press.

—— 1966. "Mechanisms of Change and Adjustment to Change," in Bert F.

Hoselitz and Wilbert E. Moore, eds., *Industrialization and Society*. Paris: Mouton.

Snyder, David. 1974. "Determinants of Industrial Conflict: Historical Models of Strikes in France, Italy and the United States." Unpublished doctoral dissertation, University of Michigan.

Snyder, David, and Charles Tilly. 1972. "Hardship and Collective Violence in France, 1830–1960," *American Sociological Review*, 37: 520–532.

———— 1973. "How to Get from Here to There," *American Sociological Review*, 38: 501–504.

———— 1974. "On Debating and Falsifying Theories of Collective Violence," *American Sociological Review*, forthcoming.

Soboul, Albert. 1958. *Les sans-culottes parisiens en l'an II*. La Roche-sur-Yon: Potier.

Società Umanitaria. 1904. *Scioperi, serrate e vertenze fra capitale e lavoro in Milano nel 1903*. Milan: Società Umanitaria.

———— 1909. *Origini, vicende e conquiste delle organizzazioni operaie aderenti alla Camera del Lavoro in Milano*. Milan: Società Umanitaria.

Soldani, Simonetta. 1973. "Contadini, operai e 'popolo' nella Rivoluzione del 1848–49 in Italia," *Studi storici*, 14 (July–September), 557–613.

Sorlin, Pierre. 1969. *La société française: T.I. 1840–1914*. Paris: Arthaud.

Spiethoff, Arthur. 1955. *Die wirtschaftlichen Wechsellagen*. 2 vols. Tübingen: Mohr.

Spreafico, Alberto, and Joseph LaPalombara, eds. 1963. *Elezioni e comportamento politico in Italia*. Milan: Edizioni di Communità.

Spriano, Paolo. 1964. *L'Occupazione delle fabbriche, Settembre 1920*. Turin: Piccola Biblioteca Einaudi.

Stearns, Peter N. 1965. "Patterns of Industrial Strike Activity in France during the July Monarchy," *American Historical Review*, 70: 371–394.

Stendhal, (Henri Beyle). 1964. "Vanina Vanini" in *Chroniques italiennes*. Paris: Julliard.

Strauss, Rudolf. 1960. *Die Lage und die Bewegung der Chemnitzer Arbeiter in der ersten Hälfte des 19. Jahrhunderts*. Berlin: Akademie.

Sturzo, Luigi. 1926. *Italy and Fascism*. New York: Harcourt, Brace.

SVIMEZ. See Associazione per lo Sviluppo dell'Industria nel Mezzogiorno.

Szymanski, Albert. 1973. "Fascism, Industrialism and Socialism: The Case of Italy," *Comparative Studies in Society and History*, 15 (October 1973), 395–404.

Taine, Hippolyte. 1888–1894. *Les origins de la France contemporaine*. 6 vols. Paris: Hachette.

———— 1965. *Voyage en Italie*. 2 vols. Paris: Julliard. (First published in 1866.)

Tarrow, Sidney. 1967. *Peasant Communism in Southern Italy*. New Haven: Yale University Press.

———— 1971. "The Urban-Rural Cleavage in Political Involvement: The Case of France," *American Political Science Review*, 65: 341–357.

Tasca, Angelo. 1963. *Nascita e avvento del Fascismo: L'Italia dal 1918 al 1922.* Rev. ed. Florence: Nuova Italia.

Thompson, E. P. 1964. *The Making of the English Working Class.* London: Gollancz.

———— 1966. *The Making of the English Working Class.* Rev. ed. New York: Vintage.

Thümmler, Heinz Peter. 1971. "Zur sozialen Struktur der Ausgewiesen unter dem Sozialistengesetz (1878 bis 1890)," *Jahrbuch für Wirtschaftsgeschichte,* 3: 131–141.

Thun, Alphons. 1879. "Die Industrie am Niederrhein und ihre Arbeiter" in *Staats- und Sozialwissenschaftliche Forschungen.* Leipzig.

Tilly, Charles. 1964. *The Vendée.* Cambridge, Mass.: Harvard University Press.

———— 1969a. "Collective Violence in European Perspective," in Graham and Gurr.

———— 1969b. "Methods for the Study of Collective Violence" in Conant and Levin.

———— 1972a. "The Modernization of Political Conflict in France," in Edward B. Harvey, ed., *Perspectives on Modernization: Essays in Memory of Ian Weinberg.* Toronto: University of Toronto Press.

———— 1972b. "How Protest Modernized in France," in William Aydelotte, Allan Bogue, and Robert Fogel, eds., *The Dimensions of Quantative Research in History.* Princeton: Princeton University Press.

———— 1972c. "Quantification in History, as Seen from France," in Price and Lorwin.

———— 1974a. "The Chaos of the Living City," in Charles Tilly, ed., *An Urban World.* Boston: Little, Brown.

———— 1974b. "Reflections on the History of European Statemaking," in Charles Tilly, ed., *The Formation of National States in Western Europe.* Princeton: Princeton University Press; forthcoming.

———— 1974c. "Revolutions and Collective Violence," in Fred I. Greenstein and Nelson Polsby, eds., *Handbook of Political Science.* Reading, Mass.: Addison-Wesley.

———— 1974d. "Computers in Historical Analysis," *Computers and the Humanities.*

Tilly, Louise. 1972a. "I Fatti di Maggio: The Working Class of Milan and the Rebellion of 1898," in Robert J. Bezucha, ed., *Modern European Social History.* Lexington, Mass.: D. C. Heath.

———— 1972b. "La révolte frumentaire, forme de conflit politique en France," *Annales; Economies, Sociétés, Civilisations,* 27: 731–757.

———— 1972c. "Materials for the Quantitative History of France since 1789," in Price and Lorwin.

Tilly, Richard. 1966a. *Financial Institutions and Industrialization in the Rhineland, 1815–1870.* Madison: University of Wisconsin Press.

———— 1966b. "The Political Economy of Public Finance and the Industrialization of Prussia, 1820–1866," *Journal of Economic History,* 26: 484–498.

———— 1970. "Popular Disorders in Germany in the Nineteenth Century: A Preliminary Survey," *Journal of Social History,* 4: 1–41.

Tilly, Richard, and Charles Tilly. 1971. "An Agenda for European Economic History in the 1970s," *Journal of Economic History,* 31: 184–197.

Tocqueville, Alexis de. 1876. *Democracy in America.* Boston: John Allyn.

———— 1955. *The Old Regime and the French Revolution.* Garden City, N.Y.: Doubleday.

Todt, Elisabeth. 1950. *Die gewerkschaftliche Betätigung in Deutschland, 1850– 1859.* Berlin: Freie Gewerkschafts Verlagsgesellschaft.

Touraine, Alain. 1968. *Le mouvement de mai ou le communisme utopique.* Paris: Seuil.

Toutain, J.-C. 1963. *La population de la France de 1700 à 1959.* Paris: Institut de Science Economique Appliquée; Cahiers de l'I.S.E.A., AF3.

Tremelloni, R. 1947. *Storia dell'industria italiana contemporancea.* Turin: G. Einaudi.

———— 1961. "Cent'anni dell'industria italiana," *L'Economia italiana dal 1861 al 1961.* Milan: Giuffrè.

Tudesq, André-Jean. 1964. *Les grands notables en France.* Paris: Presses Universitaires de France; Publications de la Faculté des Lettres et Sciences Humaines, Paris, "Recherches," 21.

———— 1967. *Les conseillers généraux en France au temps de Guizot.* Paris: Armand Colin; Cahiers de la Fondation Nationale des Sciences Politiques, 157.

Tugault, Yves. 1973. *La Mesure de la mobilité. Cinq études sur les migrations internes.* Paris: Presses Universitaires de France, 1973; INED Travaux et Documents, Cahier No. 67.

Uhen, Leo. 1964. *Gruppenbewusstein und informelle Grupenbildungen bei deutschen Arbeitern im Jahrhundert der Industrialisierung.* Berlin: Duncker and Humblot.

Valente, Gustavo. 1951. "Le Condizioni ed i moti dei contadini in Sila nel 1848," *Rassegna storica del Risorgimento,* 38: 679–690.

Valenti, Gino. 1911. "L'Italia agricola dal 1861 al 1911," in *Cinquanta anni di storia italiana,* vol. II. Milan: Hoepli.

Valentin, Veit. 1930–1931. *Geschichte der deutschen Revolution, 1848–49.* 2 vols. Berlin: Ullstein.

Vannutelli, Cesare. 1961. "Occupazione e salari del 1861 al 1961," in *L'Economia italiana dal 1861 al 1961.* Milan: Giuffrè.

Varain, Heinz-Josef. 1956. *Freie Gewerkschaften Sozialdemokratie und Staat: Die Politik der Generalkommission unter der Führung Carl Legiens, 1890–1920.* Düsseldorf: Droste.

Venedey, J. 1831. *Darstellung der Verhandlungen vor den Assisen zu Köln über die Teilnehmer des am 30. August 1830 in Aachen stattgehabten Aufruhrs.* Cologne: von G. Pappers.

Verba, Sidney, and Gabriel Almond. 1964. "National Revolutions and Political Commitment," in Harry Eckstein, ed., *Internal War.* New York: Free Press.

Vicentini, Raffaele A. n.d. *Il movimento fascista veneto attraverso il diario di un squadrista.* Venice: Zanetti.

Villani, Pasquale. 1968. "Il capitalismo agrario in Italia (secoli XVII–XIX)," in *Feudalità, riforme, capitalismo agrario.* Bari: Laterza.

Vincelli, Guido. 1958. *Una communità meridionale (Montorio nei Frentani) Preliminari ad un' indagine sociologico culturale.* Turin: Taylor Torino.

Visconti Venosta, Giovanni. 1966. *Ricordi di gioventù: Cose vedute o sapute, 1847–1860.* 3rd ed. Milan: Cogliati.

Vivarelli, Roberto. 1967. *Il Dopoguerra in Italia e l'avvento del Fascismo (1918–1922).* Vol. I, *Dalla fine della Guerra all'Impresa di Fiume.* Naples: Istituto italiano per gli studi storici.

Volkmann, Heinrich. 1972. "Wirtschaflicher Sru' Konflict in der Frühindustrialisierung: Eine Fall studie zum Aachener Aufruhr von 1830," in P. C. Ludz, ed. *Soziologie und Sozialgeschichte,* Sonderheft 16 of *Kölner Zeitschrift für Soziologie und Sozialpsychologie.* Opladen: Westdeutscher.

Wagner, Woldemar. 1953. "Zu einigen Fragen des Crimmitschauer Textilarbeiterstreiks von 1903/04," *Zeitschrift für Geschichtswissenschaft,* 1: heft 4, pp. 566–592.

Walter, E. V. 1969. *Terror and Resistance: A Study of Political Violence.* New York: Oxford University Press.

Weber, Adna F. 1963. *The Growth of Cities in the Nineteenth Century.* Ithaca: Cornell University Press.

Weber, Hermann. 1969. *Die Wandlung des deutschen Kommunismus: Die Stalinisierung der KPD in der Weimarer Republik.* Frankfurt am M.: Europäische Verlagsanstalt.

Weber, Rolf. 1970. *Die Revolution in Sachsen, 1848–49.* Berlin: Akademie.

Weber, Max. 1930. *The Protestant Ethic and the Spirit of Capitalism.* London: George Allen and Unwin.

Wehler, Hans-Ulrich. 1969. *Bismarck und der deutsche Imperialismus.* Cologne: Opladen: Kiepenheuer and Witsch.

Weis, Eberhard. 1970. "Ergebnisse eines Vergleichs der grundherrschaftlichen Strukturen Deutschlands und Frankreichs vom 13. bis zum Ausgang der 18. Jahrhunderts," *Vierteljahrschrift für Sozial- und Wirtschaftsgeschichte,* 57: 1–14.

Wilkinson, Paul. 1971. *Social Movement.* London: Pall Mall.

Williams, Philip. 1958. *Politics in Post-War France.* 2nd ed. London: Longmans.

Wolf, Eric. 1969. *Peasant Wars of the Twentieth Century.* New York: Harper and Row.

Wolff, Adolf. 1898. *Berliner Revolutionschronik.* Berlin: Dummlers.

Wright, Gordon. 1964. *Rural Revolution in France.* Stanford: Stanford University Press.

Wrigley, E. A. 1969. *Population and History.* New York: McGraw-Hill.

Wylie, Laurence, and others. 1966. *Chanzeaux.* Cambridge, Mass.: Harvard University Press.

Young, Arthur. 1915. *Travels in France and Italy During the Years 1787, 1788, and 1789.* New York: Dutton.

Zorn, Wolfgang. 1962. "Gesellschaft und Staat im Bayern des Vormärz," in Conze, ed., *Staat und Gesellschaft im deutschen Vormärz, 1815–48.* Stuttgart: Klett.

Zunkel, Friedrich. 1962. *Der Rheinisch-Westfälische Unternehmer, 1834–1879.* Cologne, Opladen: Westdeutscher.

Zwing, Karl. 1926. *Geschichte der deutschen Freien Gewerkschaften.* Jena: Zwing.

INDEX